Developments in Foundation Law in Europe

IUS GENTIUM

COMPARATIVE PERSPECTIVES ON LAW AND JUSTICE

VOLUME 39

For further volumes:
http://www.springer.com/series/7888

Chiara Prele
Editor

Developments in Foundation Law in Europe

Springer

Compagnia di San Paolo

This work was possible thanks to Compagnia di San Paolo's support.

Editor
Chiara Prele
Independent legal scholar
and consultant on foundation
and non-profit organization
Turin, Italy

ISSN 1534-6781 ISSN 2214-9902 (electronic)
ISBN 978-94-017-7861-9 ISBN 978-94-017-9069-7 (eBook)
DOI 10.1007/978-94-017-9069-7
Springer Dordrecht Heidelberg New York London

Softcover reprint of the hardcover 1st edition 2014

Printed on acid-free paper

Springer is part of Springer Science+Business Media (www.springer.com)

Preface

The idea for this book arose during a conference of American Professors of Charity Law in Chicago, in late 2009. I was the only European scholar attending the conference. I became involved, and took up the challenge.

My idea started to take shape: getting together a collection of contributions by renowned authors on Foundation or Charity Law from different European countries. They would follow common guidelines, yet take a critical approach, depending on the extant situation in their own country. I asked the authors to describe Foundation Law as it exists today in their country, and to include remarks about the current situation, together with suggestions for changes, if needed.

Foundation Law is developing in several ways, for reasons that may differ per country. In Europe, for instance, in February 2012, the European Commission presented a proposal for a European Foundation Statute, in order to facilitate the cross-border activities of public benefit foundations.

The book considers countries whose territory is located entirely in Europe, with these countries being either member States, or non-member States of the EU. It includes three countries that suffered from totalitarian regimes until a few decades ago. For some countries, the lack of freedom did not allow the creation of foundations, and in these countries Foundation Law is still in its initial stages.

The book contains contributions related to the five European countries with the largest population, including one very small European state. The sum of the contributions covers territories with 400 million inhabitants.

As a whole, the book offers an intriguing description of the developments that Foundation Law has undergone in recent years and it offers several suggestions for the future.

Almost all authors finished their contributions by the end of 2011; a few asked to revise them afterwards.

I thank all the authors for their collaboration.

I am very grateful to Piero Gastaldo, General Secretary at Compagnia di San Paolo, for making this book possible.

Turin, Italy

Chiara Prele

Contents

List of Contributors

Oonagh B. Breen Sutherland School of Law, University College Dublin, Belfield, Dublin 4, Ireland

Isabelle Combes Expert Conseil Juridique et Fiscal, Fondation de France, Paris, France

Zoltán CSEHI Chair of Department of Civil and Commercial Law, Pázmány Péter Catholic University, Budapest, Hungary

Alison Dunn Newcastle Law School, Newcastle University, Newcastle upon Tyne, UK

Rui Hermenegildo Gonçales Calouste Gulbenkian Foundation, Lisbon, Portugal

Dominique Jakob Center for Foundation Law, University of Zurich, Zurich, Switzerland;

Niederer Kraft & Frey Ltd., Zurich, Switzerland

C. Helen C. Overes Faculty of Law, Vrije Universiteit, Amsterdam, The Netherlands

Isabel Peñalosa Esteban Spanish Association of Foundations, Madrid, Spain

Chiara Prele Independent legal scholar and consultant on foundation and non-profit organization, Turin, Italy

Kateřina Ronovská Department of Civil Law, Faculty of Law, Masaryk University, Brno, Czech Republic

Francesco A. Schurr Institut für Finanzdienstleistungen, Universität Liechtenstein, Vaduz, Liechtenstein

Goran Studen Civil Law and Civil Procedure Law, Zurich, Switzerland;

Niederer Kraft & Frey Ltd., Zurich, Switzerland

Tymen J. van der Ploeg Faculty of Law, Vrije Universiteit, Amsterdam, The Netherlands

Ralitsa Velichkova Bulgarian Center for Not-for-Profit Law, Sofia, Bulgaria

Birgit Weitemeyer Lehrstuhl für Steuerrecht, Institut für Stiftungsrecht und das Recht der Non-Profit-Organisationen, Bucerius Law School, Hochschule für Rechtswissenschaft, Hamburg, Germany

Johannes Zollner Institut für Österreichisches und Internationales Unternehmens- und Wirtschaftsrecht, Karl-Franzens-Universität Graz, Graz, Austria

Chapter 1
Foundations in Austria: The Law of Public and Private Foundations

Johannes Zollner

1.1 Foundations in Austria: Facts and Figures

Since the mid-1970s, there have been two possible ways of setting up foundations in Austria. Foundations established for the public-benefit (*Gemeinnützig*) or charitable purposes (*Mildtätig*), which are founded according to the Federal Foundations and Funds Act/*Bundesstiftungs- und Fondsgesetz* (BSFG) or according to additional provincial legislation.[1] Since 1993, it has been possible to establish foundations as a private foundation according to the Private Foundation Act/*Privatstiftungsgesetz* (PSG). The benefactor of a public welfare foundation can decide whether to set up a foundation according to federal or provincial legislation or to establish such a foundation according to the Private Foundation Act.

Today, the private foundation is more common than the foundation according to federal or provincial law. On December 30, 2010, the Austrian Federal Ministry for Internal Affairs reported the existence of 200 foundations according to federal law[2] compared to 3,284 private foundations (Zollner 2011: 1).

During the past few years, the initial fast growth of establishing private foundations has slowed down.[3] In 1994, there were only 110 private foundations; in 1998, the number had already risen to 969; at the end of 2002, there were 2,336; and at the end of 2010, there were 3,284 private ones. One possible reason for this development was the modification of the tax law regarding private foundations.

---

[1] The rules concerning foundations laid down in the ABGB have been abandoned; see Welser in Rummel, ABGB, § 646 Rz 6 ff.

[2] On the reporting date 30/11/2008, 228 public-benefit foundations existed (Kalss et al. 2009).

[3] Statistics provided by the Bundesrechenzentrum.

J. Zollner (✉)
Institute für Austrian and International Corporate Law and Commercial Law, Karl-Franzens-Universität Graz, Universitätsstraße 15 C4, A-8010 Graz, Austria

Alpen-Adria University of Klagefurt, Klagefurt, Austria
e-mail: j.zollner@uni-graz.at

C. Prele (ed.), *Developments in Foundation Law in Europe*, Ius Gentium: Comparative Perspectives on Law and Justice 39, DOI 10.1007/978-94-017-9069-7_1,

Establishing a private foundation exclusively for tax-saving purposes is not that attractive anymore.

1.2 The Two Types of Foundations in Austria

As already indicated, there are two main categories of foundations in Austria: those according to the BSFG and those according to provincial law. The latter category is available exclusively for public-benefit or for charity purposes. Foundations according to the Private Foundation Act, by contrast, can be established for any legal purpose: for their own or the public benefit or even for a combination of both.

1.2.1 Foundation According to Federal or Provincial Law

Whether a foundation is subject to federal or provincial law depends on the impact of the foundation. If the impact of the foundation is nationwide, it is set up in accordance with the BSFG; should the impact be restricted to a province of Austria, the respective provincial law is applicable. The practical importance of such foundations is marginal. New foundations in accordance with these laws have been the exception since the foundation of private foundations became legal in 1993.

A federal foundation has its own legal personality and has to use its revenues solely for public-benefit purpose or charity purposes. In line with German foundation law, federal foundations in Austria must maintain their initial capital, with spending the initial capital not permitted even for the foundation's very purpose. In such cases, the benefactor can resort to the legal form either of a private foundation or of a federal or provincial trust (Kalss et al. 2009). In contrast to the private foundations, federal foundations are publicly supervised. Supervision is permanent and not only restricted to the establishment of the foundation. If all requirements for the establishment of a federal foundation are fulfilled, the foundation is approved by the appropriate authority without any discretionary power (Kalss et al. 2009). The continuous supervision of the foundation consists of monitoring the foundation's bodies as well as the authority's approval required for certain aspects. This supervisory authority may even dissolve an existing foundation under special circumstances (Kalss et al. 2009).

1.2.2 Private Foundations

Private foundations are legal persons with their own legal personality that have received assets dedicated to the pursuit of purposes specified by the founder.

They may pursue any private or public-benefit purposes as long as these are not prohibited by law. As is common in most legal systems, private foundations have to have an outward-directed purpose. A foundation with maintenance of its capital as its only purpose is not possible. It is hard to distinguish between the two different purposes mentioned above.[4] The purpose has to be strictly delineated from the activities the foundation pursues in order to fulfill its purpose (Kalss et al. 2009). According to § 1 para 2 PSG, any commercial activities exceeding ancillary activities are prohibited. Likewise, the foundation is not allowed to take over the management of a partnership or to become a personally liable partner in a partnership.

With regard to private foundations, there is nearly no supervision of authorities. The establishment of a private foundation follows a so-called Normative system. Foundations fulfilling the legal requirements have to be registered in the company register at the Commercial Court. This registration means the "birth" of the private foundation. The entry in the company register constitutes a certain publicity (Kalss et al. 2009). Any continuous supervision by authorities is not intended. Legal monitoring by court is provided for in certain situations. This is necessary as no supervision is performed by owners or persons with the interests of an owner.[5]

Private foundations are characterized by their freedom of legal arrangement since there are few mandatory rules in the PSG. The PSG consists of only 42 sections, which provide a large freedom of legal arrangement. The founder has the opportunity to arrange the private foundation according to his own needs. As a result of the small number of rules laid down by the Private Foundation Act, many questions remain unsolved which often have to be answered by the Supreme Court.

1.3 The Formation of a Private Foundation

The private foundation begins to be a legal entity with the entry in the company register at the Commercial Court. The private foundation is established when filing the statutes of foundation in the company register. The legal personality of a private foundation starts with the entry in the company register. The period between registration and filing the statutes (special form of a notarial deed) is called *foundation prior to registration*. This foundation prior to registration is similar to the company prior to registration. The foundation prior to registration is a specific legal form already capable of holding rights. Once the registration is accomplished, the foundation prior to registration is automatically subsumed in the private foundation registered in the company register (Kalss et al. 2009).

---

[4] Recently seen in the German opinion *Rawert/Hüttemann* in Staudinger, BGB (Neubearbeitung 2011) BGB Vorbem zu §§ 80 f. Rz 150 ff.

[5] Compare in detail below Sect. 1.6.1.

Irrespective of the number of benefactors, the private foundation is established as soon as the statutes are filed and always remains a unilateral legal transaction since there is only one party, viz., that of the benefactor; it is only the number of persons constituting the party of the benefactor that may vary.

A private foundation can be established *mortis causa* or if the benefactor is still alive (*inter vivos*) (Zollner 2011). A foundation *mortis causa* has only one benefactor. A private foundation *inter vivos*, by contrast, can be established by one or more persons. The status as benefactor is independent of any capital which he has dedicated to the private foundation. According to the statutes of the foundation, the benefactor can be obliged to dedicate only a low sum of capital or none at all. The legal consequence of the status as benefactor is a joint guarantee for the provision of the minimum capital. Obtaining the status of a benefactor on the basis of dedication of capital to the private foundation after its establishment is explicitly precluded.

The statutes of a foundation must be certified by a notary and have to fulfill certain minimum requirements. A formation of a private foundation *mortis causa* additionally has to fulfill all formal requirements of the testamentary disposition (Kalss et al. 2009). The general term for declaration for the foundation deed plus the addendum (ancillary document) is the declaration of foundation. The main difference between those documents lies in the fact that the foundation deed has to be filed with the company register at the Commercial Court and is publicly accessible. The addendum, however, is not publicly accessible; it need not be disclosed to the Commercial Registration Court. Only the date of the formation of an addendum and the dates of any amendments have to be entered in the company register. Nonetheless, the addendum has to be filed with the fiscal authorities responsible. Any further amendments to the addendum have to be disclosed to the fiscal authorities.

The declaration of foundation has to contain at least the following: the capital (minimum €70,000); the purpose of the foundation; the name and location of the private foundation; the name and the address of the benefactor; and the duration of the foundation. The beneficiaries have to be disclosed according to § 9 para 1 no 3 PSG in the foundation deed; it is, however, possible to delegate the disclosure of the beneficiaries to an additional board. Beyond that, additional information may be included in the foundation deed or the addendum, whereas specific contents can only be included effectively in the foundation deed and not in the addendum (see § 10 PSG).

Besides the traditional formation of a private foundation described above, a private foundation can also be established according to special regulations. Thus, a federal public-benefit foundation can be transformed into a private foundation according to § 38 para 1 PSG; saving banks as well as mutual insurance companies can be transformed into private foundations under specific circumstances.

1.4 The Founder and His Rights and Duties

1.4.1 Definition

The founder is defined as the natural or legal person who had the wish to establish the private foundation. The founder files the declaration of the foundation in his own name and declares the purpose of the private foundation. Involvement in the formation of the private foundation is essential in order to gain the status of a founder (Zollner 2011). Even underaged persons may be founders of a private foundation, as long as this is approved by the relevant authority.[6] This legally unregulated definition leads to the conclusion that gaining the status of a founder after the establishment of private foundation is impossible. Natural or legal persons who dedicate capital to an already existing private foundation will never become founders as explicitly provided for in § 3 para 4 PSG. It is not possible to revoke the status as founder after having established the private foundation.[7] Nonetheless, a founder is allowed to renounce rights (e.g., right of amendment or revocation) reserved by him beforehand. This is often used to establish a clear distinction between foundation and founder.[8]

1.4.2 The Founder's Duties

The dedication of the minimum capital is not a genuine founder's duty. The minimum capital – which has to be at least € 70,000 – can also be dedicated by a third party. The decisive legal issue is that the private foundation has the minimum capital available when the application for the entry into the company register is filed at the latest. The status as founder, however, implies the joint guarantee for the provision of the minimum capital. If there is more than one founder, all the founders are all jointly responsible for the provision of the capital (Zollner 2011: 17). Another founder's duty is the creation of the foundation statutes with the minimum requirements according to § 9 para 1 PSG. In addition, the founder has to appoint the first board of directors according to § 15 para 4 PSG. If he fails to do so, the curator of the foundation appoints the board.

The ideal legal form would require a clear division between the founder and the private foundation after its formation. This would result in a situation where the

[6] OGH 25.2.1999, 6 Ob 332/98m, RdW 1999, 409 = wbl 1999/227 = EFSlg 89.745 = RZ 1999/69.

[7] OGH 24.05.2006, 6 Ob 78/06y, HS 37.173 = ecolex 2006, 910 = ecolex 2007/2 = JEV 2007/9 = Jus-Extra OGH-Z 4183; NZ 2007, 28 = RdW 2006, 541 = RdW 2006, 631 = wbl 2006/228 = ZfS 2006, 118; gleich lautend OGH 25.05.2007, 6 Ob 18/07a, GesRZ 2007, 346 (*Arnold*) = ZfS 2007, 75 = RdW 2007, 730 = Jus-Extra OGH-Z 4384 = ecolex 2007, 867 = wbl 2008/17 = NZ 2008, 25 = SZ 2007/84 = HS 38.163 = HS 38.170.

[8] As for the reasons, compare Zollner (2011): 175.

founder has duties vis-à-vis the private foundation after its establishment only in very exceptional cases. Such duties, however, may result from the declaration of foundation. One such duty would be the founder assuming of a certain board function. In such capacity, the founder would then be obliged vis-à-vis the private foundation to take, or refrain from, certain actions. Such duties and rights, however, would result from that functional responsibility and would have to be strictly distinguished from the rights and duties as a founder.

A founder may have fiduciary duties toward other founders. The fiduciary duty depends on the situation: It can oblige the founder to agree to some specific action and can also limit the use of the founder's rights (Zollner 2011 for details). The Austrian Supreme Court has, for example, approved the duty to agree to a modification of the foundation's statutes if the original declaration of foundation has provided the establishment of an additional board which could not be implemented effectively because of an unclear legal situation at that time.[9]

1.4.3 The Founder's Rights

The Exercise of Reserved Founder's Rights

A private foundation *inter vivos* may have one or more founders. According to § 3 para 2 PSG, if there is more than one founder, they must exercise their rights jointly. Therefore, the approval of each founder is needed in order to exercise the specific founder's right (Zollner 2011: 146; Kalss et al. 2009). In accordance with a Supreme Court ruling, the founder's rights cease to exist upon death of a founder in the absence of a deviating provision in the declaration of foundation. Following a Supreme Court decision, such deviating provisions in the declaration of the foundation have to be interpreted objectively; the wishes of the founder are taken into consideration only if explicitly stated in the declaration of foundation (Kalss and Zollner 2006: 227; Kalss et al. 2009). In reality, the exercise of the founder's rights is hierarchized: Specific founders (so-called main founders) may exercise their rights on their own, whereas the other founders may only exercise these after the death of the main founder and that only jointly with the other founders. This provision, on the one hand, guarantees the exercise of the founder's rights over several generations of founders; on the other hand, it enables the main founder to exercise the rights by himself while alive. In the declaration of the foundation, the founders may stipulate joint exercise with majority decision-making. In this decision-making process, the founders do not have to be treated equally; thus,

---

[9] OGH 09.03.2006, 6 Ob 166/05p, HS 37.171 = AnwBl 2008, 10 = ecolex 2006, 1009 = FJ 2006, 465 = GesRZ 2006, 203 = JBl 2006, 521 = JEV 2007/6 = NZ 2006, 347 = RdW 2006, 438 = ZfS 2006, 76.

some founders may have more voting rights than others (Kalss and Zollner 2006: 227; Kalss et al. 2009).

The Founder's Rights by Act of Law

The Private Foundation Act only provides for a few founder's rights. This is due to the law's underlying assessment which does not qualify founders as an essential part of the *Foundation Governance*. According to § 15 para 4 PSG, the founder is allowed to appoint the first board of directors. According to § 35 para 3, the founder can additionally fight wrong resolutions of the board of directors concerning the dissolution of the foundation. If the founder is not a beneficiary, he is not allowed to ask for information concerning the private foundation. The right to information laid down by law should be expanded for a founder who has reserved a right to revoke the private foundation and who at the same time is the ultimate beneficiary (Zollner 2011: 207 ff.).

Optional Founder's Rights

Due to the far-ranging freedom of legal arrangement, the founder may reserve expansive rights when forming the declaration of the foundation. Dependent on these optional rights, the private foundation may resemble a corporation; in this context, the right to amendments and the right to revoke the private foundation have to be mentioned. The right to amendments permits the founder to amend the declaration of foundation in any way and at any time. This encloses the amendment of the private foundation's purpose as well as the exchange of the beneficiaries. This right can be limited by the rights of co-founders as well as already existing claims of beneficiaries in specific constellations (Zollner 2011: 145). The right to amendments also permits the founder to appoint himself beneficiary and consequently to order payouts to himself.

The right to amendments can only be exercised if the founder has reserved this right in the declaration of foundation when establishing the private foundation; an ex post establishment of this right is impossible.

The right to revoke the private foundation allows the founder to dissolve the private foundation at his absolute discretion. This enables him to reverse his decision to establish a private foundation. As with the right to amendments, the right to revoke the private foundation has to be reserved when establishing the private foundation. According to the prevailing opinion, the right to revoke the private foundation and the right to amend are asset rights and therefore can be realized by a creditor in an execution (Zollner 2011: 148). Consequently, both rights avoid *asset protection* because an effective division of the founder's assets and the private foundation's assets does not exist at the moment of establishment. The founder can relinquish or limit both rights later, which would lead to a final division between the assets. The missing division of the assets may cause problems regarding the right to a compulsory portion in the law of succession. Assets dedicated to the private foundation *inter vivos* are still assigned fictitiously to the assets of the founder and must be taken into account for the calculation of the legal portion. The missing division of assets may also cause problems regarding insolvency law or any challenge by a creditor (Zollner 2010: 116).

The right to amend and the right to revoke the private foundation are sometimes called "genuine founder's rights" (Zollner 2011: 7 ff.). The meaning of this term implies that these rights cannot be assigned to a third party, neither *inter vivos* nor *mortis causa*. The right to amend can be reserved by every founder, while the right to revoke can only, according to § 34 PSG, be reserved by a founder who is not a legal person. The reason for this measure is to avoid any circumvention, because the members of a legal person may vary and the revocation of the private foundation would no longer depend on the will of the original founder. The fact that this prohibition is only provided for the right to revoke the private foundation and not for the right to amend causes a discrepancy which is hard to justify (Zollner 2011: 126 ff.). Even though both rights are not transferable, the Supreme Court permits the exercise of these rights through a procurator (Zollner 2011: 130 f.[10]). Creditors of the founder and liquidators may execute these rights in case of insolvency (Zollner 2011: 131 ff.).

In the statutes of the foundation, the founder may reserve the right to monitor the management of the foundation and other rights. Some of those rights worth mentioning include the right to appoint the board of directors and to recall the board under special circumstances; moreover, the right to information and right to inspection – both ensure the effective monitoring of the management of the private foundation. Additionally, an authority can be established to give directives, at least to a limited extent. But the Supreme Court has not yet drawn a borderline between permitted and prohibited directives. In contrast to the right to revoke the private foundation and the right to amend, an assignment of these rights is possible.

A founder or relatives of his may be part of the board of directors throughout their lifetime as long as neither he nor his relatives are beneficiaries.[11]

Founders can be members also of all other bodies, as long as they or their closest relatives are not beneficiaries at the same time. In particular, founders can be members of the advisory board, in which case their status as beneficiary is of no relevance.

---

[10] Compare OGH 11.09.2003, 6 Ob 106/03m, NZ 2005, Ps 5 = ÖJZ 2004/59 (EvBl) = GeS 2003, 483 = RdW 2004/65.

[11] For more details, see Sect. 1.5.4.

1.5 The Beneficiaries and Their Rights

1.5.1 Types of Beneficiaries

§ 5 PSG may suggest to some that there is only one type of beneficiary. But this is not true as there are several rather different types of beneficiaries depending on the declaration of the foundation. The Supreme Court has developed a differentiated beneficiary concept according to the prevailing opinion (compare Arnold 2007: § 5 Rz 26; Kalss and Zollner 2008: 126; Kalss et al. 2009: Rz. 7/68; Zollner 2011: 240 f.). Similar to the private foundation law of Liechtenstein (compare Lorenz in Schauer 2009: Art. 552 § 52 Rz 1 ff.), this concept distinguishes between a beneficiary with an enforceable title, a so-called effective beneficiary (*aktuell Begünstigter*) and a potential beneficiary.[12] The distinction is not only academic – the classification is tied to legal consequences: first, as to whether a beneficiary has any enforceable claim for donation and, second, whether a beneficiary is entitled to the rights laid down by law.

Beneficiaries must be strictly differentiated from ultimate beneficiaries. Whereas the beneficiaries can be considered addressees of the purpose of the private foundation (Zollner 2011: 232), the ultimate beneficiaries are those natural and legal persons who benefit from the proceeds in case of the dissolution of the private foundation. The ultimate beneficiaries may or may not be the same as the beneficiaries – what is decisive is the provisions made in the declaration of the foundation. The foundation deed or the addendum has to indicate the names of the ultimate beneficiaries; otherwise any profit after liquidation becomes the property of the Austrian Republic (see § 36 para 3 PSG).

Beneficiaries with an enforceable title possess a right enforceable by law to the benefits of the private foundation. The board of directors has no discretionary power as to whether they allocate the benefits to the beneficiary of this type or not. Depending on what is laid down in the statutes of foundation, the board of directors may have discretionary power regarding the extent of the benefits. In such a case, the beneficiaries may defend themselves against any unreasonable execution of discretionary power (Kodek and Zollner 2009: 9 f.; Zollner 2011: 392 f.). Beneficiaries with an enforceable title enjoy every legal beneficiary right. Within the different types of beneficiaries, the beneficiaries with an enforceable title have the most powerful position.

Effective beneficiaries do not have any enforceable title to the benefits from the private foundation. The board of directors has the discretionary power of distributing the benefits to this type of beneficiaries; the discretionary power can be limited by the provisions of the statutes of the foundation.

[12] OGH 15.12.2004, 6 Ob 180/04w, SZ 2004/177 = GesRZ 2005, 140 = wbl 2005, 332 = ecolex 2005/210 = RdW 2005, 295 = GeS 2005/154 (*Arnold*) = AnwBl 2006, 369; OGH 2.7.2009, 6 Ob 101/09k, PSR 2009, 46 (*Hofmann*) = ecolex 2009, 874 = PSR 2009, 64 (*Resch/Schimka/Schörghofer*) = ZfS 2010, 12 (*Leitner*) = NZ 2010, 29 = AnwBl 2010, 213 = RdW 2009, 717.

Potential beneficiaries can best be described as follows: They are addressees of the purpose of the foundation but are neither beneficiaries with an enforceable title nor *effective beneficiaries* (Zollner 2011: 250). Benefits for this kind of beneficiaries are subject to a twofold condition which may vary according to the declaration of the foundation. If the beneficiaries have been sufficiently individualized, they can be qualified as *potential beneficiaries* as long as the donation depends not only on some positive decision of the board of directors but also on some other additional condition. As soon as the second condition is met, a *potential beneficiary* turns into an *effective beneficiary*. Before that moment, the board of directors is not allowed to distribute the benefits to the *potential beneficiaries* (Zollner 2011: 250 f.).

If the beneficiaries have not yet been sufficiently individualized, the board of directors, in a first theoretical step, has to appoint certain persons (beneficiaries) and, in a second theoretical step, has to decide on the distribution of benefits. Persons who have not been sufficiently individualized must always be qualified as *potential beneficiaries* (Zollner 2011: 251). The Supreme Court has, in a current ruling, laid down the differentiation between already individualized and not individualized *potential beneficiaries*.[13] Persons who have not been sufficiently individualized in the statutes of the foundation (or in a decision of the relevant body) are – according to the accurate opinion of the Supreme Court – not entitled to legal beneficiary rights.[14]

1.5.2 The Beneficiaries' Rights

The different types of beneficiaries involve different legal consequences: first, as to whether a beneficiary has any enforceable claim to the donation and, second, as to whether a beneficiary is the addressee of the beneficiaries' rights stipulated by law. There are only few rights laid down by the Private Foundation Act: the right to information (see § 30 PSG), the right to monitor the resolutions concerning the dissolution of the private foundation (see § 35 para 3 and para 4), and the right to demand the recall of the members of the board of directors by court (see § 27). Additional rights are not explicitly mentioned in the PSG, but may derive from general legal principles (compare, e.g., for the right of information, Zollner 2008: 78).

According to § 30 para 1 PSG, the beneficiary is entitled to request information from the board of directors concerning the achievement of the purpose of the private foundation. He may also ask for access to the annual balance sheet, the annual report, the audit report, the accounts, and the foundation deed and

[13] OGH 17.12.2010, 6 Ob 244/10s, GesRZ 2011, 170 = PSR 2011, 35 = ZfS 2011, 24 = RdW 2011, 65 = AnwBl 2011, 257 (*Saurer*) = RdW 2011, 143 = ecolex 2011, 239 = NZ 2011, 221 = wbl 2011, 272.

[14] OGH 17.12.2010, 6 Ob 244/10s, GesRZ 2011, 170; compare Zollner 2011: 251.

addendum. This right implies the right to copy those documents at his own expense (Zollner 2011: 335 f.). If the right to information or the right to access is refused by the board of directors, the court may enforce this right (see § 30 para 2 PSG). The right to information is the most important right of a beneficiary since it permits the beneficiary to monitor the administration of the private foundation and so to initiate further steps if necessary. Many details concerning the right to information need a final review by the Supreme Court: Whereas there are many rulings concerning the addressees of the rights of a beneficiary,[15] the content of these rights has not yet been conclusively discussed. In this context, the question arises in particular as to the extent to which beneficiaries may ask for information or access to the documents concerning the subsidiaries of a private foundation. One gap here, for example, is the unresolved issue of whether beneficiaries may request information which concerns the time before they became beneficiaries (Zollner 2011: 454 ff.).

If a beneficiary has found misconduct of the board of directors after exercising his right to information, he may, depending on the form of his status as beneficiary, demand at court the dismissal of the members of the board of directors according to § 27 para 2 PSG (Zollner 2011: 439 ff.). The right to dismissal of a member of a body is not possible for every type of beneficiary.[16] This right does, however, entitle the beneficiary to recourse should the court's decision be negative.[17] Other beneficiaries who have the right neither by act of law nor because of the form of the statutes of the foundation may only initiate such a demand. The possibility to initiate the demand does not imply the legal right to appeal a negative decision, which means that there is no secured legal position for the beneficiaries.

Beneficiaries, independent of their type, are not allowed to claim damages of the private foundation from the board of directors. The enforcement of damages from (former) directors or other members of bodies of the foundation may only be claimed by the board of directors.[18] Prior to the enforcement of damages against an incumbent director, the director concerned has to be recalled by court, as can be seen in § 27 para 2 PSG.

According to § 35 para 4 PSG, the beneficiaries have the right to claim the removal of dissolution resolutions of the board of directors at court if those were passed wrongly. On the other hand, the beneficiaries may, according to § 35 para 3 PSG, even request a dissolution resolution at court in lieu of a resolution by the board of directors because they failed to pass such a resolution.

However, the right to request the conduct of a special audit cannot be exercised by the beneficiaries; this request may only be filed by the members of the bodies.

In constant case law, in the meantime, the Supreme Court decided that the *potential beneficiaries* cannot be seen as beneficiaries according to § 5 PSG. *Potential beneficiaries* are therefore not addressees of the legal beneficiaries'

[15] Compare in detail Sect. 1.5.2.

[16] Compare in detail below.

[17] As to the personal scope of this right, compare Zollner 2011: 428 f.

[18] As to the question of competence in existence of a supervisory board, compare Zollner 2011: 428 f.

rights.[19] By act of law, the beneficiaries do not have the right to information, neither the empowerment to request the recall of members of the board according to § 27 para 2 PSG nor the right to monitor resolutions according to § 35 para 3 and para 4. Concerning the right to fight dissolution resolutions, the Supreme Court differentiates between *potential beneficiaries* who have been individualized sufficiently in the declaration of foundation and those who have not, with those individualized sufficiently having such right. According to the Supreme Court, the *potential beneficiaries* have no right to information according to § 30 para 1 PSG, although it has not yet made any differentiation between sufficiently individualized and not sufficiently individualized *potential beneficiaries*. Even a possible monitoring vacuum because of the nonexistence of beneficiaries with a monitoring power does not, according to the Supreme Court, justify an extension of the right to information to the *potential beneficiaries* (Zollner 2011: 452). Even the right to recall a director through a court's decision (see § 27 para 2 PSG) may not be exercised by every type of beneficiary. Only beneficiaries with an enforceable title as well as *effective beneficiaries* may file a petition to recall a director according to § 27 para 2 PSG and fight a negative decision of the court via repeal.

The law does not grant any further rights. However, the founder may, based on the freedom of legal arrangement, grant further rights to the beneficiaries. In practice, the following rights in particular have been granted: the right to recall the board of directors directly, if there are significant reasons to do so, and furthermore, the right to appoint the board of directors, the right to approval, and the right to veto certain business transactions; and finally the authority to give directives in special matters.

1.5.3 Excursus: The Beneficiaries' Advisory Board

In private foundations, beneficiaries' advisory boards are very often established (Arnold 2009: 348). These advisory boards are assigned to fulfill duties and responsibilities of the *Foundation Governance* instead of leaving these assignments to the individual beneficiary. In the advisory board, as current practice shows, the different types of beneficiaries are represented, and even external persons are sometimes members of the advisory board. Since the PSG was amended in 2010,[20] the legitimacy of advisory boards with a majority of beneficiaries has been clarified. The legitimacy of such advisory boards had been dubious at best ever since the Supreme Court ruling of 5/8/2009.[21] Following the said amendment,

[19] OGH 15.12.2004, 6 Ob 180/04w, SZ 2004/177 = GesRZ 2005, 140 = wbl 2005, 332 = ecolex 2005/210 = RdW 2005, 295 = GeS 2005/154 = AnwBl 2006, 369; OGH 2.7.2009, 6 Ob 101/09k, AnwBl 2010, 213 = ecolex 2009/337 = RdW 2009/726 = NZ 2010/9.

[20] BGBl I 2010/111.

[21] The Supreme Court identified advisory boards with a majority of beneficiaries which have specific competences similar to supervisory boards. The consequence of this similarity was the prohibition that these kinds of advisory boards were not allowed to have a majority of

advisory boards with a majority of beneficiaries are now legally admissible, and extensive responsibilities and duties of the *Foundation Governance* can be transferred to such an advisory board. The 2010 PSG amendment introduced some specific provisions concerning the recall of the board of directors. If the board of directors should be recalled by the beneficiaries' advisory board for an important reason (see § 27 para 2 no 1–3), there has to be a majority of at least three quarters of the votes cast. In an advisory board with only four members, all members have to agree to the resolution. These special majority requirements are intended to provide a guarantee for the correctness of the resolution. If the founder has provided reasons other than those under § 27 para 3 no 1–3 PSG for a recall of the board of directors in the declaration of foundation, the beneficiaries (or their eligible relatives) cannot represent the majority of the votes in these matters. It is advisable to provide explicit provisions in the declaration of foundation for such cases.

1.5.4 Incompatibilities

The differentiated concept of beneficiaries is important not only for the beneficiaries' rights but also for the scope of application of the incompatibilities according to § 15 para 2, para 3, and para 3a PSG. According to § 15 para 2, beneficiaries and their eligible relatives are not allowed to be members of the board of directors, with eligible relatives defined as husband and wife, common-law spouses, registered partners, as well as persons up to the third degree of relationship. If the beneficiary is a legal person, natural persons who are in control of the legal person according to § 244 para 3 Commercial Code[22] (UGB) are not allowed to become a member of the board of directors (see 15 para 3 PSG). Likewise, persons who have been instructed by the beneficiaries or their relatives to represent their interests in the board of directors (see § 15 para 3a PSG) are precluded from becoming members of the board of directors. The crucial criterion is the existence of the authority of the beneficiary to give directives to the board of directors (Zollner 2011: 339; 981. BlgNR 24. GP 68).

If one of the provisions concerning the incompatibility is fulfilled, the person cannot be appointed to be a member of the board of directors, and any such appointment would be noneffective (Zollner 2011: 350). If the incompatibility

beneficiaries. OGH 05.08.2009, 6 Ob 42/09h, wbl 2009/243 = GeS 2009, 300 (*Mager*) = GesRZ 2009, 348 (*Arnold*) = GesRZ 2009, 372 (*Hochedlinger*) = ZfS 2009, 152 (*Eiselsberg*) = ZfS 2009, 164 (*Oberndorfer*) = ZfS 2009, 189 = PSR 2009, 108 (*Kalss*) = NZ 2009, 348 = ecolex 2009, 959 (*Rizzi*) = ecolex 2010, 56 (*Feltl/Rizzi*) = ZFR 2010, 33 = PSR 2010, 4 (*Csoklich*) = PSR 2010, 19 (Limberg) = GesRZ 2010, 155 = PSR 2010, 56 (*Briem*) = ZfS 2010, 73 (*Leitner*) = RdW 2009, 717.

[22] Included are persons who have the majority of votes; the right to appoint or recall the majority of administrative, leading, or supervisory bodies; or who have other control rights.

commences after the appointment, the member of the board drops out automatically. Such compatibility provisions are a specialty in comparison with other countries' private foundation laws (for details, see Zollner 2011: 337 ff., 350). The reason for these incompatibility provisions is, according to the historical legislator, the intention to guarantee the objectivity of the enforcement of the beneficiaries' rules through the board of directors and to avoid any conflicting interests (Zollner 2011: 339). Generally speaking, the enforcement of the founder's will is to be safeguarded (Zollner 2011: 339 ff.).

1.6 Principles of the *Foundation Governance*

1.6.1 Overview

Like every foundation, the Austrian private foundation is characterized by a "foundation-typical structural monitoring deficit," which results from the absence of owners and members who would be a natural monitoring authority (Thymm 2006: 7 ff.; Zollner 2011: 329). The board of directors acts on somebody else's behalf and might be tempted to pursue its own interests, which might put the execution of the private foundation's actual purpose at risk (Zollner 2011: 329 ff.). The Austrian private foundation law assumes a combined system of private foundation monitoring. This means that supervision is effected primarily through its own bodies. Founders and/or beneficiaries by themselves have few monitoring possibilities under the law. Founders and beneficiaries have no central role in the *Foundation Governance* of the Austrian private foundation. The supervisory authority is generally not involved, with court review intended only in select cases.

1.6.2 Judicial Review

Court involvement in the Austrian private foundation law is based on two different levels. On the one hand, courts are involved in the course of entry in the company register. The court examines the entries on their formal and, to some extent, on their substantive correctness. In addition to such examination, the court is involved in certain issues such as a change in the declaration of the foundation by the board of directors (Kodek and Zollner 2009: 4 f.; Zollner 2011: 333 f.).

Judicial review focuses on the stage of formation, where the Commercial Registration Court has to examine if the private foundation complies with the legal requirements (Zollner 2011: 333 f.). Continuous reporting and accountability duties are nonexistent in the Austrian Private Foundation Act; the courts are involved only at certain stages. The Commercial Registration Court has to examine entries of private foundations in the company register with regard to the form, to the correctness of the content, and to the completeness (Kodek and Zollner 2009: 4 f.; Zollner 2011: 333 f.). That way, for example, amendments of the declaration of foundation can be reviewed as to whether there are any conflicts with legal regulations.[23]

The court (*Außerstreitgericht*) does not usually get active *ex officio* – even though it would have the authority to do so – but usually on suggestion or upon request (Zollner 2011: 333 f.). Put simply, one might speak of external control because of internal inducement. Examples of this would be the recall of directors by the court on claim (see § 27 para 2 PSG), the review by the court concerning dissolution resolutions (§ 35 para 3 and para 4 PSG), and the involvement of the court in the process of an amendment of the declaration of foundation by the board of directors because of changes of the situation of the private foundation according to § 33 para 2 PSG. Such amendment by the board is possible only if the founders fail to come to an agreement or no founders are left. The involvement of the court in absence of a supervisory board in case of a business transaction between the private foundation and a director is absolutely necessary. If there is no court approval, the business transaction is invalid. The economic success of the unapproved business transaction can thus not result in an enrichment claim of the director because of his services already rendered.[24] Likewise, the involvement of the court is needed in evaluating the level of the payment in the absence of a provision in the declaration of foundation. In the absence of a supervisory board, the appointment of the auditor is made by the court according to § 20 para 1 PSG.

1.6.3 Internal Monitoring and Structure of Organization

The key aspect of the *Foundation Governance* is the system of internal monitoring (Zollner 2011: 333 f.). The monitoring system of the private foundation is based on reciprocal supervision of the different bodies of the foundation. The output of such a system of internal monitoring is the so-called six-eyes principle; according to this system, the board of directors has to have at least three natural persons as its members. As described above, each director has to be independent of the beneficiaries to fulfill the founder's will objectively (Zollner 2011: 339 f.). Case law requests a minimum appointment period of the board to ensure the independence of

[23] Such a constellation was existent in the important ruling of the Supreme Court OGH 16.10.2009, 6 Ob 145/09f, GesRZ 2009, 348 = ZfS 2009, 152 = ZfS 2009, 164 = ZfS 2009, 192 = PSR 2009, 99 = GeS 2009, 336 = ecolex 2010, 59 = GesRZ 2010, 63 = wbl 2010/17 = PSR 2010, 19 = GesRZ 2010, 155.

[24] For further information, see *Zollner*, Eigennützige Privatstiftung (2011) 333 ff. OGH 24.02.2011, 6Ob195/10k, JBl 2011, 321 (*Karollus*) = ecolex 2011, 429 (*Rizzi*) = GesRZ 2011, 161 (*Kalss*) = ZfS 2011, 68 (*Kalss*) = PSR 2011, 52 (*Hochedlinger*) = PSR 2011, 86.

the board of directors. A deviation from the minimum period is allowed only under specific circumstances.[25]

It is mandatory for every private foundation to appoint an auditor. The duties of a private foundation's auditor exceed those of a company's auditor. He is part of the private foundation's bodies and is therefore authorized, even obligated, to demand a special audit (see § 31 PSG) if necessary to request the appointment of missing directors or to demand the recall of directors who have acted in violation of their duties. All in all, the foundation's auditor is obliged to examine the lawful performance of the private foundation and to review the foundation's activities regarding any infringement of the duty of care.

The establishment of any other bodies is not provided for by the Private Foundation Act. That is why an establishment of a supervisory board is only necessary if the private foundation exceeds certain key figures. Such key figures are the number of employees employed by the private foundation or by companies which are under control of the foundation. The founder may establish a supervisory board on a voluntary basis, but this is quite rare in reality. Statistics show that only very few private foundations have established a voluntary or mandatory supervisory board, that is, about one percent (Arnold 2007: § 22 Rz 1). The duties of a supervisory board include the representation of the private foundations in terms of business transactions with directors according to § 17 para 5 PSG as well as the monitoring of the management and the performance of the private foundation. Additionally, the private foundation's supervisory board has approval rights similar to those of the supervisory board of a public limited company. Also the appointment of the auditor is the responsibility of the supervisory board by act of law. The appointment and the recall of directors are, however, not part of the responsibilities of the supervisory board. This falls within the responsibility of the supervisory board only if the declaration of foundation provides an explicit provision to this effect.

The beneficiaries' rights by law may also be seen as part of an internal *Foundation Governance* (Zollner 2011: 336 ff.). One such right worth mentioning specifically is the beneficiaries' right to information and access according to § 30 PSG (Zollner 2011: 335 ff.). Also the right to demand at court the recall of members of the bodies for important reasons can be seen as part of internal monitoring (see § 27 para 2 PSG). The same can be said for monitoring resolutions according to § 35 para 3 and para 4 PSG, but this right can be claimed by ultimate beneficiaries and beneficiaries of a private foundation as well.

---

[25] OGH 24.02.2011, 6Ob195/10k, JBl 2011, 321 (*Karollus*) = ecolex 2011, 429 (*Rizzi*) = GesRZ 2011, 161 (*Kalss*) = ZfS 2011, 68 (*Kalss*) = PSR 2011, 52 (*Hochedlinger*) = PSR 2011, 86.

1.7 Dissolution

1.7.1 Reasons for Dissolution

The law (see § 35 para 1 and para 2 PSG) provides for different reasons why a private foundation may be dissolved. The dissolution of a private foundation when the period of time for which it has been set up has expired is one reason for dissolution. The initiation of insolvency proceedings and the decision not to initiate such proceedings for a lack of cost-covering assets are also reasons for dissolution. The board of directors has to pass a dissolution resolution if the private foundation's purpose is achieved or cannot be achieved any more, for instance, if the assets are insufficient for the achievement of the purpose (Kalss et al. 2009). If the founder has reserved the right to revoke the foundation, the board of directors has to dissolve the foundation when the founder has issued a valid revocation declaration. A noncharitable private foundation whose predominant purpose is to provide for natural persons has to be dissolved after 100 years. In this case, ultimate beneficiaries are allowed to extend the existence of the private foundation for a further 100 years. This provision shows similarities to the "rule against perpetuities" under trust law (Zollner 2011: 12). Furthermore, the founder is allowed to introduce other reasons for the dissolution in the declaration of foundation according to § 35 para 1–4.

1.7.2 The Consequences of Dissolution

After the dissolution resolution of the board of directors or after the automatic dissolution without any resolution, the next step is liquidation. The board of directors has to point out to the creditors of the private foundation that they have to lodge their claims within 1 month after the announcement of the dissolution. The residual assets have to be transferred to the ultimate beneficiaries, which have a claim on the liquidation profit. The ultimate beneficiaries have to be mentioned in the declaration of foundation (an addendum is sufficient). If there is no ultimate beneficiary or the mentioned beneficiary no longer exists, or the ultimate beneficiary does not want the residual assets, the assets become the property of the Austrian Republic. If the private foundation has been dissolved because of a revocation of the founder, the founder is deemed to be the ultimate beneficiary if there are doubts as to who the ultimate beneficiary is (see § 36 para 4 PSG). Hence, the Austrian Republic does not become the owner of the assets in such case. After completion of the liquidation, the private foundation has to be deleted.

1.8 Summary

Private foundations are an essential part of Austrian economic life. Especially the wide scope for design compared to federal and provincial foundations is an advantage of this relatively new form of organization. The most important persons under the private foundation law are the beneficiaries and the founders. The will to establish a private foundation emanates from the latter, while the beneficiaries are the addressees of the private foundation's purpose. Whereas the legislator perceives the role of the founder as limited to the establishment of the foundation – this can be seen, for instance, in the fact that no supervisory rights for the day-to-day private foundation are provided for – beneficiaries may supervise the administration of the private foundation, even if only to a limited extent. The private foundation's bodies, however, constitute the central element of the "Foundation Governance." The compulsory six-eyes principle of the board of directors is intended to ensure mutual monitoring of the directors. This monitoring is secured by the compulsory appointment of a foundation auditor, whose duties and responsibilities are broader than those of an annual auditor. This internal audit of the administration is additionally secured by partial supervision from the outside, viz., by the court. In this context, review by the Commercial Register Court has to be distinguished from review by the *Außerstreitgericht*. The latter acts especially at the request of the private foundation's participants. Broad and continuous monitoring of the activities of a private foundation is not provided for. It will be very interesting to see how the Austrian system of *Foundation Governance* will hold up especially once the founder's generation is gone.

Bibliography

Arnold, N. 2007. *Kommentar zum Privatstiftungsgesetz*. Wien: LexisNexis/ARD ORAC.

Arnold, N. 2009. E Bespr zu OGH 5.8.2009, 6 Ob 42/09h. *GesRZ* 1–872.

Kalss, S., and J. Zollner. 2006. Ausübung und Änderung von Stifterrechten. *GesRZ* 227–238.

Kalss, S., and J. Zollner. 2008. Die gesetzlichen Rechte der Begünstigten. *GesRZ* 125.

Kalss, S., C. Nowotny, and M. Schauer. 2009. *Österreichisches Gesellschaftsrecht*. Wien: Manz.

Kodek, G., and J. Zollner. 2009. Rechtsschutz der Begünstigten – Die verfahrensrechtliche Absicherung der Rechte der Begünstigten. *PSR* 4–16.

Rummel, P. (ed.). 2000. *Kommentar zum Allgemeinen Bürgerlichen Gesetzbuch*. Wien: Manz.

Schauer, M. (ed.). 2009. *Kurzkommentar zum liechtensteinischen Stiftungsrecht*. Basel: Helbing Lichtenhahn Press.

Staudinger, J. 2011, Neubearbeitung. *Kommentar zum Bürgerlichen Gesetzbuch mit Einführungsgesetz und Nebengesetzen*, 1. Buch.

Thymm, N. 2006. *Das Kontrollproblem in der Stiftung und die Rechtsstellung der Destinatäre*. Köln/Berlin/München/Heymann: Nomos.

Zollner, J. 2008. Das Österreichische Privatstiftungsrecht als Schauplatz der Verwirklichung und Weiterentwicklung allgemein privatrechtlicher Prinzipien. *Jahrbuch Junger Zivilrechtswissenschaftler* 2009:67–84.

Zollner, J. 2010. Der Stifter in der Krise – Anfechtung von Vermögenswidmungen an eine Privatstiftung durch Masseverwalter und Gläubiger. *PSR* 116.

Zollner, J. 2011. *Die eigennützige Privatstiftung aus dem Blickwinkel der Stiftungsbeteiligten*. Wien: Manz.

Chapter 2
Foundation Law in Bulgaria

Ralitsa Velichkova

2.1 Legal Definition and Main Characteristic of the Foundation

2.1.1 Overview

A legal definition of the foundation first appeared in the Legal Entities Act in 1933. A foundation is defined as a separate property, whose purpose is to accomplish a certain goal. The funds and foundations which were active at the time Bulgaria was a monarchy contributed to a large extent to the development of charity and the formation of a charity culture.

This tradition was put to an end when the state system in Bulgaria was changed in 1944. In the next 45 years, foundations existed legally and were regulated by the existing legislation, but their regime was marked by greater state control both in the process of their formation and in their subsequent activity. Their activity was regulated by the Persons and Family Act (PFA).

A third stage in the legal regulation and the activity of foundations began when the current Not-for-Profit Legal Entities Act (NPLEA) was enacted (2001).

This piece of legislation is the primary law which regulates the activity of not-for-profit legal entities (NPLE) and their legal forms of existence as foundations and associations. This law regulates the establishment, registration, structure and the prerequisites for the termination of not-for-profit legal entities. It is also the first one to introduce the public benefit status of organisations and the distinction between public and private benefit organisations.

According to statistical data, 5,238 foundations were registered in Bulgaria at end 2010, of which about 1,260 had public benefit status. Not-for-profit legal entities in Bulgaria total about 33,000 (both associations and foundations), which

R. Velichkova (✉)
Bulgarian Center for Not-for-Profit Law, 6 Dobrudja str., 1000 Sofia, Bulgaria
e-mail: ralitsa@bcnl.org

C. Prele (ed.), *Developments in Foundation Law in Europe*, Ius Gentium: Comparative Perspectives on Law and Justice 39, DOI 10.1007/978-94-017-9069-7_2,

means that foundations account for 16 % of all not-for-profit legal entities in the country. Twenty-four percent of them are public benefit foundations.

2.1.2 *Main Characteristics of the Foundation*

The current Not-for-Profit Legal Entities Act does not provide a legal definition of foundations. They can be defined by interpreting the statutory provisions concerning foundation regulation:

Thus, the foundation:

- Is a legal entity which is established as such after being entered at the Register of the District Court based on the foundation's headquarters
- Is established by a unilateral constituent act during one's lifetime or in case of death
- Has its separate property at the time of establishment for achieving certain not-for-profit goals
- Requires no membership but does have a one- or two-tier organisational and management structure

The provided description outlines the following characteristics of a foundation:

1. Property: the type and size which will differentiate the foundation is determined by its founder. The property of the foundation may include all types of measurable rights. The law does not prescribe any requirements for a minimum amount of the constituting property. Thus, a foundation in Bulgaria can be established by a significantly small constitutive donation or a will as the law does not prescribe any minimum of it.
2. The establishment takes place by means of a unilateral constituent act which is in the form of a constitutive donation or will.
3. The foundation is a *non-corporate legal entity* – it does not have any members and no legal membership relations exist.
4. The foundation has its own *management structure* (one- or two-tier system) depending on the foundation's status of public or private benefit.
5. Goals: the foundation is established to achieve certain not-for-profit goals.

2.2 Types of Foundations

The law recognises two types of foundations – public benefit or private (mutual) benefit foundations.

A sovereign right of the founder(s) is to determine the scope and type of activity which the newly established foundation will be carrying out as well as to determine whether these activities will be performed in public or mutual benefit.

Defining a foundation as being one registered in public benefit means that it has to comply with certain legal requirements from the moment of its creation and subsequently in its operation. For instance, for a public benefit foundation to be registered, its goals have to firstly fall under the exemplary list of socially significant activities recognised by the law such as 'development and strengthening of spiritual values, civil society, healthcare, education, science, culture, physical education, assistance to socially vulnerable people, protection of human rights or the environment'. At the time of registration, the court decides whether the specified goals can be considered as socially significant or in public benefit.

Secondly, foundations carrying out public benefit activities are obliged to have a two-tier management system which consists of a collective supreme body and a governing body. The supreme body takes all important decisions about the existence of the foundation, such as the following:

- Amending and supplementing the Statute of the foundation
- Selecting and dismissing the members of the governing body
- Taking decisions on the reorganisation or dissolution of the foundation

Practice shows that the naming of the supreme body varies among different foundations. The most widely used title is Board of Trustees or Foundation Board. The supreme body may consist of either founders of the foundation and/or other individuals. The common practice is to set criteria in the foundation's Statute, which will have to be met by the people who sit on the supreme body of the foundation. The law does not provide for an explicit number of members or terms of offices the supreme body's members may have.

The governing body of the foundation may be either individual or collective. It manages and represents the foundation in accordance with the founder's will and the goals of the foundation as well as the decisions of the supreme body, the Statute of the foundation and the country's legislation.

Unlike public benefit foundations, those registered in private benefit may have a one-tier management system including a governing body which may be individual or collective. In practice, there are many private benefit foundations in Bulgaria which are managed only by one Director/Manager.

Along with the compulsory bodies, foundations can create facultative ones, whose structure and legal powers are regulated in the foundation's Statute. Practical examples for such include the Foundation's Friends Board, the Supervisory Board, etc., whose primary functions are to assist the activities of the foundation's compulsory bodies.

Apart from the aims and organisational structure, there are also other differences between public and private benefit foundations, and they can be noticed in respect to the rules for gratuitous expenditure of property of public benefit foundations, in the way of dissoluting public benefit foundations compared to private ones and, lastly, in respect to tax incentives available only to public benefit foundations.

The legislator's idea when legally introducing the statute for public benefit organisations was to have higher requirements for their establishment, the spending of their funds, holding them accountable and terminating their existence. In return, the general rule of Art. 3 of the NPLEA stipulates that the state may support these organisations through tax, customs, financial and other economic incentives.

Public benefit organisations and public benefit foundations in particular are required to have additional registration at an administrative body – the Central Register (CR) of Not-for-Profit Legal Entities at the Ministry of Justice of the Republic of Bulgaria.

The registration at this authority makes it legally possible for registered organisations to enjoy some tax and other types of concessions prescribed by the law. These incentives relate to the public benefit status of the organisation, but the prerequisite for its usage is the registration at the administrative body. The legal powers and functions of the CR regarding public benefit organisations will be further addressed in this chapter.

Finally, as already highlighted above, public benefit foundations registered at the CR are the only ones that may use existing tax concessions as opposed to private benefit foundations that do not enjoy a preferential tax regime.

2.3 Establishment of the Foundation: Founder, Founder's Rights, Property

The substantive and legal actions for the establishment of a foundation aim to differentiate between a certain property which will be used to achieve the not-for-profit goals of the foundation in accordance with the will and desire of the founder(s).

The foundation is established by means of a unilateral act which allows the founder to gratuitously provide certain property for achieving the aims of the foundation. The foundation may be established by a unilateral donation act by the founder(s) while they are still alive. The law states that a foundation may also be established in case of death, that is, after disclosing a will, in which the testator has expressed his/her will that the testamentary property will be used to set up a foundation with a specific goal.

In both cases, the minimum and necessary content of the Constituting Act, whether it is a donation act or a will, includes specifying the aims of the future foundation and determining the constituting property which will be used for its operation.

For a foundation to be entered in the court's register, it is also necessary that its name, headquarters, authorities/structure, representation and type of activity (private or public) be specified. In case these additional but essential specifying legal characteristics are not determined in the Constituting Act and cannot be added later on by the founders, they may be added by the court if demanded by the interested parties. In practice, this hypothesis can occur when the foundation is set up by a will which specifies only the goals and property provided to the future foundation. To ensure greater certainty and guarantee that the will of the founder/testator will not be changed, the right to supplement the establishing statute with the missing statutory essential elements is vested with the registration court.

When the foundation is created during one's lifetime, its founders usually list all the legally specifying characteristics in the Constituting Act. Otherwise, at the time of registration, the court will require them to supplement the Constituting Act.

The law makes a provision for a form of validity of the Constituting Act – a written one with a certificate of acknowledgement. When the Constituting Act is in the form of a will, the legal requirements have to be taken into account depending on the form of the will – whether it is a holographic will or it is notarially attested.

The property of the foundation is the total amount of measurable rights which, by virtue of the constitutive effect of the court decision, are transferred from the patrimony of the founder to the foundation's patrimony. The subjects of constituting property can be real and movable property including money, as well as all types of measurable rights. In all cases, the specific requirements for the form of validity at the time of transfer of the particular property must be met (e.g. when transferring real estate, the Constituting Act must be notarially attested).

The founders of the foundation may be legally capable physical persons and legal entities of Bulgarian or foreign/non-Bulgarian origin.

Directly related to the founders is the question with their reserved rights. NPLEA is the first law to introduce the institute of founder's reserved rights. To a large extent, this is determined by the fact that when regulating the foundation under the Persons and Family Act's regime, the state represented by the respective minister supervised the activities of the foundation and could therefore take the main decisions in relation to the amendments to the Constituting Act or to its governing body. If such regulation exists, the idea of having some form of control exercised by the founder is incompatible as the state control was predominant and did not correspond to any opportunity for the founders to influence the important decisions related to the future of the foundation.

Essentially, the institute of reserved rights legally allows the founder not to stay away from the activity of the foundation but to participate in the important decision-making process, without him/her being part of its governing authorities. Such (a) reserved right(s) is an additional warranty that the foundation's governing bodies will not deviate from the will and the original goals of the founder at the time of its establishment. The practice shows that most founders reserve the rights for themselves; without their consent, no decisions may be made on the dissolution of the foundation, amending its Statute, electing new members of the board or modifying the activities and aims of the foundation.

The founder can reserve certain rights for himself/herself or for (a) person (s) specified by him/her. Reserving rights for a third party will be appropriate especially if the foundation is set up by a will. In this way, the founder will ensure that the nominee will be able to monitor if the establishing will of the foundation will be followed. Often when foundations are established during one's lifetime, the founders reserve certain rights for themselves. Reserving these rights does not prevent them from being included as part/members of the foundation's authorities. If the founder is a legal entity, it can also reserve certain rights for itself. These rights will be exercised by its legal representative.

In case of death or termination of the founder or the person(s) with reserved rights specified by him/her, the law stipulates that the rights are transferred to 'the relevant body of the foundation'. Furthermore, the legislator has taken into account that if the parties with reserved rights are not exercising them with the necessary care or are permanently unable to do so, the registering court may, when demanded by the governing body, rule that their legal powers have to be transferred to the specific authority of the foundation for a certain period of time or permanently.

2.4 Registration

The factual establishment of a foundation ends when it is entered in the court register of not-for-profit legal entities. The registration is a secure court proceeding and is carried out by the District Court in the legal district where the registered office of the foundation will be located. NPLEA regulates the circumstances which are subject to entry in the court register. The court decision is constitutive and leads to the establishment of a new legal entity in the legal world. In case the court denies entry, an appeal can be brought forward to the higher court.

This court registration aims to exercise judicial control over the lawful establishment of not-for-profit corporate bodies (legal entities). Over the last couple of years, the idea of registering foundations and associations out of court arose. Such a reform has been recently introduced for companies which are now registered at the Trade Register at the Registry Agency. However, until now the registration of the not-for-profit legal entities has been done by the courts.

In relation to the public benefit organisations, in this case public benefit foundations, there is an additional requirement for registration at the Central Register at the Ministry of Justice. This additional registration at an administrative body was introduced by the current law vis-à-vis the existing distinction between public and private benefit organisations. The main functions of the Central Register are to maintain a public online register of public benefit organisations and carry out ongoing and annual control over their activities.

The registration at the CR is not difficult and is associated with the presentation of a certain number of documents, such as a transcript of the court decision on the registration of the foundation, a copy of the registration BULSTAT[1] card and a certificate of good standing, which should not be required at all if there was better communication between the different registers in the country. All mentioned documents may be officially delivered to the CR by the respective authorities issuing them in case the registers kept by different institutions are connected.

[1] Identification code for tax and insurance purposes.

This is still a problem in Bulgaria and part of the future development of e-reform and the establishments of the connection among different registers.

The time limit provided for registration at the Central Register totals 2 months and starts as soon as the court has released its decision on the registration of the foundation. As the time limit is only instructive, exceeding it does not prevent the organisation from having the right to be entered in the register.

The review of the register's work over the last 10 years has lead to the following observations and findings.

In the first place, entry in the register done by administrative officials is followed by a second verification for conformity with the law of the foundation's establishment, in case such has already been carried out by the court. The reason for that, to a certain extent, is the ambiguous legal texts which do not clarify the scope of the verification done by the CR when registering public benefit organisations. Thus, particularly over the last years, an unlawful practice of CR has been observed. An example for such a practice in the past year is the refusal by CR to register the organisations which plan to have economic activities and have stated so in their Statutes. Carrying out economic activities is permissible for foundations in Bulgaria, provided they abide by certain legal requirements for complementarity and consistency of their not-for-profit activity with the goals of the organisation. What happens in practice is that the CR acts as a second instance court which verifies the decision of the registry court. Concentration of almost all CR resources on this activity leads to poor or partial fulfilment of its other functions – to maintain a current database of registered organisations and to monitor their activities.

The CR must oversee the activities of registered organisations. Registered organisations are obliged by law to submit to the CR annual information about their activities and financial statements. The information is provided in the form of annual accounting and financial reports which should be made available for public usage to the users of the database. In addition, the Minister of Justice has the right to make periodical checks on foundations' activities by asking them to submit updated information about their activities. If any violations are found or suspected in the activities of registered organisations, the Minister of Justice shall inform the appropriate authorities such as the Prosecutor's Office, tax authorities, etc. The consequences for the organisations consistently failing to submit the required current information or annual financial and narrative reports on their activities include deregistration from the register. One year after the grounds for deletion have expired, the deregistered organisation can apply for a re-entry in the Central Register.

The position and role of the CR need to be subject to future legislative amendments. In any case, clarification of the verification scope which the register will carry out, simplifying the procedure by officially sending some of the documents to the register, is among the most urgent and important changes which have to be embraced by any future amendments to the law.

2.5 Governance and Activities of the Foundation

2.5.1 Governance of the Foundation

The NPLEA is short-spoken in regulating the organisational structure and governance of foundations as compared to the regulation of associations.

In respect to the governance of private benefit organisations, as already mentioned above, they may have only one governing body which can be either collective or individual. Practice shows that most private benefit foundations are managed by one director and do not have any other bodies.

When the foundation is incorporated as a public benefit organisation, the law requires a two-tier system of management that consists of a high (supreme) and a governing body. For foundations with a dual form of governance, the law stipulates that the rules for the General Assembly and governing body of the association will be appropriately applicable to the supreme and governing bodies of the foundation. The common practical issue which lies here is to what extent these rules are applicable to foundations.

As to the legal powers of the General Assembly of the association, as well as the supreme body of the foundation, there is an understanding that they can both decide on the most important issues which affect the activity and dissolution of the organisation. For example, amending the Constituting Act, deciding on the dissolution or reorganisation of the organisation, selection and dismissal of its governing body's members are all legal powers which are within the competence of the General Assembly of the association, and the law prescribes that they may not be transferred to other bodies. Accordingly, the supreme body of the foundation with a two-tier system of management should also have these powers in case they are not part of the founder's reserved rights, and therefore, it can lead to him/her exercising them individually.

Respectively, the rules affecting the legal powers of the Governing Board of the association should be also appropriately applied to the Governing Board of the foundation.

When the foundation is registered in public benefit and it has chosen to have a collective governing body, the latter should consist of at least three persons, physical or legal.

The NPLEA provision that the rules for the association's bodies are to be accordingly applied means that only the provisions corresponding to its non-corporative nature of a legal entity can be applied to foundations. Thus, an example can be the legal prohibition for a member of the General Assembly of an association to vote on matters relating to him/her, his/her spouse or relative, which cannot find application in any family foundation in which the members of the family constitute the supreme and executive bodies of the foundation.

This illustrates some possible issues that might arise from practice but are not explicitly regulated in the law and the court has no experience with. In any case, the scarce legal regulation of foundations, compared to associations, to some extent allows for greater freedom of interpretation and gives rise to interesting cases which can have different interpretations.

2.5.2 *Activities of the Foundation*

The activities that the foundation engages in are linked to its mission and goals.

In relation to public benefit foundations, there is a requirement that they adopt rules for exercising their public benefit activity, including rules which will regulate the cases of gratuitous spending of their funds. These rules have to be presented to the Central Register at the Ministry of Justice which verifies their legality and accordance with the law.

The law stipulates certain safeguards to prevent the unlawful spending of the foundation's money gratuitously. On one hand, this is the requirement for adoption of rules which will specify how to determine the beneficiaries that the foundation will support. The rules are submitted to the Central Register where they are published in the publicly available online database. Secondly, the law requires that the decision for the gratuitous spending of the funds in the Director's or other bodies' benefit, as well as in their spouses' or relatives' benefit up to a certain degree of kinship, must be made by a qualified majority of 2/3 of all supreme body members. The law also prescribes the same qualified majority in case of gratuitous spending of the foundation's property to some other categories of people.

The law also provides that a public benefit foundation may not make business deals with members of its governing body or their spouses and relatives, unless these deals are in obvious benefit to the foundation or they are concluded in accordance with general terms which are publicly announced.

An achievement of the NPLEA is that it introduces the possibility for not-for-profit legal entities to carry out economic activities regardless of their legal form (a foundation or an association) and irrespective of whether they are public or private. For the economic activity of a foundation to be exercised legally, it has to meet certain requirements:

1. To be legally permissible
2. To be regulated in the Statute of the organisation
3. To be relevant to the main activity of the foundation
4. To be complementary to the main activity of the foundation

The purpose of the economic activity is to support the main activity of the foundation. Its tax treatment will be discussed below.

2.6 Accountancy and Transparency

The requirements for accountancy of foundations will be discussed in terms of the requirements for internal accountancy and the requirements for accountancy to the state bodies and public institutions.

Notwithstanding it was already mentioned several times, the regulation of foundations is more fragmented than that of association and that explains why some texts concerning associations have to be applicable to foundations. For example, when the foundation acts as a public benefit organisation, that is, it has a two-tier management system, the governing body is obliged to be accountable to the supreme body for its actions. Practice shows that most of these accountancy reports occur once a year, at the end of the calendar year.

In respect to private benefit foundations, which are allowed to have only a single-tier management system, it is very likely that they will not have an internal form of accountancy. Frequently, the founder is also the director of a private benefit foundation and at the same time there is no other internal body which he/she will be accountable to.

The public and legal requirements for accountancy of foundations are associated with their annual accounts/reports and tax forms of their received income submitted to the National Revenue Agency. The requirement to submit an income tax form applies to both private and public benefit foundations. According to the current tax law, not-for-profit legal entities (foundations in this case) are exempt from submitting tax forms if they have not carried out any economic activity or rented out their property.

It is a general principle that NPLE are only taxed based on their income, which is a result of their economic activity. The income from donations and grants is an income from non-economic activity, and it is tax exempt. Therefore, when a foundation has not done any economic activity within the reporting year, it must submit only a simplified model of a tax declaration.

Annually, foundations fill in and submit a statistical form for their activities to the National Statistical Institute. The purpose of this accountancy to the NSI is to gather statistical data on the different types of corporate bodies.

In relation to public benefit foundations, there is an additional requirement for annual reporting to the Central Register at the Ministry of Justice. By 31 May of the year following the reporting year, public benefit foundations submit an annual descriptive report of their activities, as well as a financial report. These reports are available to the public and are published on the website of the CR.

Private benefit organisations are required to publish, online or in an economic edition, their financial statement for the past year by 30 June of the year following the reporting year. They are not required to publish a descriptive report of their past year activities. The situation raises reasonable criticism and allegations for non-transparency of private benefit foundations. In addition to the fact that the information on the CR of public benefit organisations is outdated, even technically inaccessible until recently, the allegations for non-transparency of foundations and associations are justified.

The requirement for an audit of foundations is regulated and contained in the *Accountancy Act*.

The conditions for a compulsory audit are different depending on the status of the organisation – whether it is incorporated in public or private benefit. In any case, the preconditions for a statutory audit involve very high values of some of the financial criteria which makes the audit applicable to only a few number of organisations. At the same time, any organisation can do a voluntary audit.

For the sake of thoroughness of the content, it is worth mentioning that over the years attempts have been made to self-regulate the civil sector and to introduce rules and standards for good management of not-for-profit legal entities. An integral part of these standards is the criteria for publicity of organisations' activities, the financing and the parties behind it. Practice shows that in most cases the attempts to self-regulate the sector are sporadic and do not reach the majority of organisations in the sector.

2.7 Transformation and Dissolution of the Foundation

Dissolution of foundations can be divided into voluntary and involuntary, into dissolution with or without liquidation.

The NPLEA general provisions stipulate that the decision for dissolution of a not-for-profit legal entity has to be taken by its supreme body. When a foundation is incorporated in the public benefit and has a two-tier system of governance, it is logical that this legal power will belong to its supreme body. Moreover, Art. 35, Par. 2 of the NPLEA stipulates that if the foundation has a two-tier management system, the rules for the General Assembly of an association will be applicable to the supreme body of the foundation. The law prescribes that part of the legal authority of the General Assembly of the association is to decide on the dissolution of the organisation and also that this power cannot be transferred to other authorities of the association. Therefore, even though there is no express regulation in the Constituting Act of the foundation and the decision to dissolve is not a reserved right of the founder, this decision should be made by the supreme body of the foundation according to the general rule of Art. 35, Par. 2 of the NPLEA. More interesting is the issue with the private foundations which may have only one existing authority – a governing one. Some authors are of the opinion that the cited general legal provision cannot be applied to foundations in case the Constituting Act does not determine the way of dissolution of the foundation. 'The Governing body derives from the founder and without any express authorization, i.e. if the Constituting Act does not specify the way of dissolution, respectively that this to be done by its authorities, the possibility to dissolve the foundation goes beyond the powers granted'.[2] The institute of the reserved rights also finds application to private benefit foundations, that is, the hypothetical founder of a private benefit foundation can reserve the right to decide on the dissolution of a foundation. In case the founder did not reserve this right, it remains an open question whether the Director of a private benefit foundation can decide on its dissolution. According to the author of the material, especially if the foundation is established in case of death, the parties concerned, in this case the Director of the foundation, can ask the court to complement the Constituting Act in relation to the ways of dissolution. Thus, it will be ensured that the court, as an independent authority, would comply with the will of the founder when deciding on the provisions in the Constituting Act, which will affect the future dissolution of the foundation.

In any case, as it was repeatedly mentioned, the regulation of foundation law and particularly of private benefit foundations is scarce and leads to different interpretations and practical applications.

The involuntary dissolution of a foundation is done by a court proceeding and is based on a court decision, when the relevant circumstances provided by law are present. The legal proceeding is instituted when demanded by the interested party or the prosecutor in case the foundation:

1. Is not established in accordance with the law.
2. Its activity is contrary to the Constitution, laws and the good morality.
3. Is declared bankrupt.

Depending on the ground for dissolution, the court may give a time for correction or removal of the fact leading to dissolution. For example, if the Constituting Act for setting up the foundation was void, this circumstance cannot be corrected and the court must terminate the foundation. However, the court decision will have effect ex nunc. Another case would be if the foundation carried out any economic activity without this being regulated in its Statute. If this circumstance provided grounds for a court referral demanding dissolution of the foundation, a specific period could be determined, in which the foundation can appropriately regulate its economic activity and can thus avoid the dissolution.

Dissolution of a foundation without liquidation happens when the legal entity is transformed through one of the following accepted methods: mergers and acquisitions, division and separation.

Subject to various comments in the literature is the provision of Art. 12 of the NPLEA which states that: 'NPLEs can be transformed into another type of not-for-profit corporate bodies...' This rule must also be interpreted in accordance with Art. 42 of the NPLEA, which provides that public benefit organisations may not transform into private benefit ones.

The interpretation of legal provisions leads to the conclusion that a public benefit foundation may not transform into a private benefit one. (The reverse is possible.) It is possible, however, that a public benefit foundation is transformed into a public

[2] Margarita Zlatareva "Non-profit Legal Entities" 2002 Sofia.

benefit association and vice versa. There is a view that: 'replacing the will in the Constituting Act and transforming the foundation into an association by the recruitment of members and creating articles of association despite having the same purpose as stated in the Constituting Act, sounds contrary to good morals'.[3]

Except for the hypothesis for the transformation of foundations without liquidation, liquidation proceedings are initiated both for voluntary and involuntary dissolution of the foundation. Liquidation proceedings are an institute of commercial law, and their main principles are regulated in the Commerce Act (CA). The NPLEA refers to the Commerce Act and stipulates that the rules regarding the procedures for liquidation and the powers of the liquidator which are regulated in the CA are to be respectively applied to the dissolution of an NPLE. Because of the detailed regulation in the CA, the liquation of an NPLE does not give rise to any practical issues.

There is a legal prohibition for public benefit foundations to distribute the property which remains after satisfying the creditors among the founders, the parties that constitute the foundation's authorities or their spouses and relatives. To contra argue, it is hypothetically possible that the founder of the private benefit foundation receives the whole or a part of the undistributed after liquidation property.

As to public benefit foundations, there is a requirement that if some undistributed property is left after liquidation, it must be given to another NPLE: 'which carries out the same or a similar non-profit activity'. The decision where the remaining property of the foundation will go after it has ceased to operate can be made at the time of establishment, it can be subject to a reserved right of the founder and it can also be part of the legal powers of the authority, which decides on the dissolution of the foundation, for example, the supreme body. In case the procedure for distributing the remaining property is not established in the Constituting Act or the Statute of the foundation, this decision is made by the court, which is to be approached with proceedings for the dissolution of the foundation. If the court in these proceedings does not decide that the remaining property must be allocated to another NPLE, then the property is allocated to the relevant municipality hosting the headquarters of the dissolved foundation. The municipality will be required to deal with the property in a way that best conforms to the goals of the dissolved foundation.

2.8 Tax Regime

The income from not-for-profit activities of a foundation is tax exempt, whereas the income from additional economic activity is taxed with a 10 % corporate tax. This is considered to be one of the lowest tax rates in the European Union. The taxed profit generated by economic activity may not be distributed as a dividend to the

[3] Margarita Zlatareva "Non-profit Legal Entities" 2002 Sofia.

founder or to the parties that constitute the foundation's authorities (the ban on the distribution of profit is one of the substantial differences between not-for-profit legal entities and trade companies). The profit from economic activity can be considered also as a tool for achieving the non-profit goals of the foundation.

Foundations also pay an annual local tax for the real estate they own. Foundations are subject to a VAT registration if the legal prerequisites are present, regardless if they are registered in public or private benefit. The VAT registration can be voluntary or mandatory. For example, mandatory registration is necessary when the foundation has reached a taxable turnover of BGN 50,000 (approx. 25,000 Euro) within 12 consecutive months. The exempt supplies are not included in the taxable turnover, as well as the revenue from donations, grants or state funding for the provision of social services. The VAT rate for services and goods received by foundations is the same as for other entities – 20 %.

2.8.1 Tax Benefits

Taxation of donations and grants: the income from donations and grants is considered to be part of the income from not-for-profit activity; therefore, it is tax exempt for both public benefit and private benefit foundations. However, only public benefit foundations are exempt from paying a local tax on donations, whereas private benefit foundations are not (it is a special tax paid to the municipality where the foundation has its seat).

Tax benefits for donors: there are exemptions only for donors of PBOs (not for private benefit organisations). Public benefit organisations registered at the Central Register at the Ministry of Justice are among the organisations to which the donators enjoy tax concessions after making a donation. Individuals can deduct from their annual income up to 5 % of the donations made to public benefit foundations, whereas corporate donors can deduct up to 10 % of their profit for donations made to such foundations.

Tax benefits for donations apply also to donations made to not-for-profit organisations established in an EU member state.

Tax benefits on passive investments: the income of a foundation formed by bank account interests is exempt from taxes, if the interest arose from the revenues from not-for profit activity of the foundation. The income accumulated from sales of shares or securities on the regulated Bulgarian securities' market is exempt as well.

Exemptions from VAT: there are some exemptions from VAT for NGOs (respectively foundations) that are already registered under VAT law, for example, when they organise fundraising activities related to their non-profit purposes. This means that the NGO must not calculate VAT for the goods and services provided by it if they are related to an organised fundraising event (e.g. organising a charitable auction for fundraising money for renovation of the local school).

The tax treatment of foundations is also related to the issue of legal regulation and the option to create endowments by foundations in Bulgaria.

Firstly, we should mention that there is no legal provision for the creation of endowment by foundations. At the same time, there is no explicit prohibition for the establishment and investment of certain property of foundations, the incomes from which are to be used for achieving the purposes of the foundation. According to a study conducted in 2007, which included analysis of the environment for the development of endowment in Bulgaria, the following conclusion was outlined[4]: 'A general conclusion may be drawn that the legal frame in which foundations exist and function is free and dispositive enough and enables the development of endowment. If the main elements of the definition of endowment are reviewed in sequence, it could be found that, with the lack of legal provisions and the prohibitive rules, there is no obstacle for similar mechanisms to be created under the autonomous will of each foundation provided this does not prejudice imperative norms of the legislation or the moral rules.'

An illustration of this conclusion is the existence of several foundations in Bulgaria which have created an endowment. However, there are a number of obstacles which impede the wider development of the creation of endowment by foundations functioning in Bulgaria.

Existing obstacles may be specified as follows: first, the lack of 'charity culture' is a serious obstacle on the way of the establishment of a critical mass of donators 'for whom donation is to become a conscious necessity and they are to start looking for a worthy cause in the name of which they can donate their wealth[5]'.

Secondly, it is important to think about the adoption of various concessions aiming to create a more stimulating environment in the tax treatment of investments from endowment.

Last but not least, it is important to take into consideration the existing economic environment.

In conclusion, the following trends in the development of the legal regime of foundations over the recent years can be summarised:

1. In Bulgaria, since 2001, there has been a statutory law which provides for the main principles of the creation, functioning, structure and termination of not-for-profit legal entities. One of the legal organisational forms under which a not-for-profit legal entity may exist in Bulgaria is the foundation. The provisions referring to a foundation in the law are more fragmented compared to the ones referring to an association. In many cases, there is even no explicit provision and the rules for association should be applied by analogy. It is recommended that future legal changes on the part of the law treating foundations be developed in more details in view of its future supplementation with provisions referring to their organisational structure, the formation of its bodies and their authority.
2. To summarise the possible amendments to the law, the position and role of the CR (where public benefit foundations are registered) should be also mentioned.

---

[4] The study was conducted by the Bulgarian Centre for Not-for-Profit Law, the Center for Economic Development and the Association of Public Foundations, Sofia, 2007.

[5] See the above study.

In any case, clarification of the verification scope which the register will carry out, simplifying the procedure by officially sending some of the documents to the register, is among the most urgent and important changes which have to be embraced by any future amendments to the law.

3. Regarding the tax regime for treatment of foundations, the treatment is not different than the one for associations which are also considered not-for-profit legal entities. The condition which the legislator sets for providing a more favourable tax regime is not the legal organisational form (foundation or association) but the aims of the organisation – whether they are public or private.

Bibliography

BCNL. 2011. *The law on non for profit legal entities – Questions and answers*. Sofia: Bulgarian Center for not for Profit Law.

Goleva, P., Tz. Kamenova, and K. Stojchev. 2003. *The non for profit legal entities*. BCNL and Institute for Legal Studies of the Bulgarian Academy of Sciences. Sofia.

Stoykov, M., and S. Krystanov. 2011. *Taxation of non for profit legal entities*. Sofia: Bulgarian Center for not for Profit Law.

Zlatareva, M. 2002. *The non for profit legal entities*. Sofia: Ciela.

Chapter 3
Foundations in the Czech Republic: Yesterday, Today and Tomorrow

Kateřina Ronovská

3.1 Introduction

It seems that the tradition – almost a thousand years old – of *permanent donation of private property for the purpose of public benefit* has been enjoying a renaissance also in the Czech Republic over the past years. The understanding of the social importance foundations is – slowly but surely – growing, and it has increasingly led to discussions on the position, significance and function of foundations in the society as well as their delimitation within the applicable law.

The Czech situation somewhat differs, however, from the situation in Western Europe. While the development of philanthropy in the west is related mainly to the accumulation of property in the private sphere and the growing realisation of one's responsibility for the sustainable development of the *world*, the current development in the Czech Republic is affected primarily by efforts aimed at least partial liberalisation of the legal regulation of foundations and a return to the original roots in continental Europe.

K. Ronovská (✉)
Department of Civil Law, Faculty of Law, Masaryk University, Veveri 70, 611 80 Brno, Czech Republic
e-mail: katerinaronovska@gmail.com; katerina.ronovska@law.muni.cz

C. Prele (ed.), *Developments in Foundation Law in Europe*, Ius Gentium: Comparative Perspectives on Law and Justice 39, DOI 10.1007/978-94-017-9069-7_3,

3.2 Historical Background

3.2.1 Constitution of the Foundation Sector in Czechoslovakia After 1918

Until the formation of the independent Czechoslovak state in 1918, what is now the Czech Republic, used to be a part of the Austro-Hungarian Empire. The Austrian Civil Code (ABGB) of 1911 entirely did not contain any legal regulation of foundations (mentioning it only in passing in the provisions of Section 646 of the ABGB) and referred it to a special regulation under public law (see Ronovská 2013, 463).

As late as the first half of the nineteenth century, there were no uniform rules applicable within the territory of the Austrian Empire for the establishment and administration of foundations, and all was left up to the individual lands that constituted the empire. This situation changed, however, in 1841, when a royal decree was issued,[1] which institutionalised the state supervision of foundations (both centrally and on the level of the individual lands). The central bodies of supervision had jurisdiction as long as the purpose of a given foundation extended the interests of individual lands; in other cases, the relevant land authorities served as supervisory bodies. What was needed for the establishment of a foundation was the manifestation of the founder's will to donate his or her property to particular permanent purpose and the approval of the state with such an establishment.[2]

After the formation of independent Czechoslovakia, the Austrian legal system was – in order to ensure continuity of law – taken over by means of the so-called reception norm (the Act No. 11/1918 Coll.). As a result, the regulation of legal persons and foundations in its undeveloped form was likewise taken over (Hurdík and Telec 1998, XXVI). Foundations were affected by the *Saint-Germain Peace Treaty* of September 1919, primarily Article 266 thereof, which was subsequently implemented by the *Agreement related to the implementation of Article 266, last paragraph, and Article 273 of the Saint-Germain Peace Treaty*, under No. 4/1929 Coll.[3]

---

[1] Das Hofkanzleidekret vom 21. Mai 1841, politische Gesetzssammlung, Band 69, nr. 60. This decree was in effect in Austria until the adoption of the Bundesgesetz über Stiftungen und Fonds in 1974, with effect from 1.1. 1975.

[2] For more details, see Stammer (1975, 280).

[3] Article I of this agreement read as follows: '*The Austrian Republic shall surrender to the Czechoslovak Republic as a whole all designated references, donations, stipends and foundations of all kinds, including family foundations, founded or established in the former Austro-Hungarian empire, (hereinafter referred to generally as designated foundations), as long as they are located within the territory of the Austrian Republic, where they are intended exclusively for persons who are currently Czechoslovak citizens and if they were founded or established before 28 July 1914, and in their state as of 28 July 1914. During the process, regard shall be paid to payments properly made for the purpose of foundations*'.

This final arrangement ultimately led to the constitution of an independent foundation sector within the territory of the then Czechoslovakia. However, due to the economic crisis and the onset of fascism, there was little chance for the drafting of new legislation on foundations, even though just before the beginning of the Second World War, a draft proposal for a legal regulation of foundation law was ready.[4] Due to the subsequent historical development, it was never passed.

After the Second World War, the situation in the field of foundation law was negatively affected by the communist coup in 1948 and the subsequent events that culminated in the cancellation of the legal form of foundations as well as the existing foundations themselves (1953).[5]

3.2.2 Reconstruction of Legal Framework for Foundations After 1990

The fall of the 'iron curtain' undoubtedly meant a turning point in the development of the foundation sector. The foundation institute came to be rediscovered in all countries of the former Eastern bloc, initially thanks to the financial and institutional support of large US foundations,[6] which set as their priority the reinstitution of the legal framework for the public society in central and eastern European countries.

At the beginning of the 1990s, however, those countries had to deal with a number of difficult tasks, such as the establishment of the constitutional basis, the first reforms of private and public law, the formation of suitable environment for the operation of market economy, etc. It thus comes as no surprise that foundation law was not on the top of their list of priorities[7]; the need for suitable and prompt regulation in this field was sometimes even trivialised. At the same time, there was also the practical need to immediately deal with the entirely new situation: various foreign humanitarian foundations started to operate spontaneously in the individual post-communist countries, even though there was no legislative basis for their operation. The situation was different only in Poland and Hungary,[8] where the legal systems had already made provisions for the legal position of foundations.[9]

[4] A certain tendency in this respect can be detected, see, e.g. Hermann-Otavský (1938).

[5] The only foundation that managed to survive, albeit deprived of the major part of its foundation property, was the Hlávka Foundation (i.e. Nadání Josefa, Marie a Zdenky Hlávkových, also known as Hlávkova nadace). Established in 1904 by the architect Josef Hlávka, it is still active in supporting the education of Czech citizens.

[6] For more details, see Hondius (2001, 581).

[7] There was interest to introduce the foundation institute into the then Czechoslovak legal system as early as the beginning of the 1990s.

[8] While Poland adopted the foundation act in 1991, Hungary regulated foundations under Section 74A and subsequent sections of the (former) Civil Code of 1987. However, even these legal regulations had to be modified to the new situation in the society.

[9] For more details, see Drobing (2001, 542).

While there was no legal framework for foundations in the Czechoslovak Socialist Republic,[10] it became necessary in the tumultuous situation of the early 1990s to instantly address the non-existence of legislation concerning foundations and associations. As a result of the fictional conception of legal persons and the peremptory regulation of the individual types of legal persons, the absence of any regulation of foundations caused many problems that were hoped to be at least generally addressed by means of the amendment No. 103/1990 Coll. of the then Economical Code,[11] with effect from May 1, 1990. The foundation institute was reintroduced into the legal system by means of a single provision (Section 389b), under which foundation entities were assigned the legal position of an independent kind of legal person.

The foundation was perceived as a purpose-oriented fund with a legal personality that could be established 'for the purpose of developing spiritual values, protecting human rights or other humanitarian goals, protecting the environment and preserving natural values'. This regulation was crucial in forming the legal framework for a reborn legal person and 'legalising' the existence of foundations. On the other hand, it was only very partial, thus deforming the real legal life of the foundation sector. Another problem consisted in the systematic inconsistency when placing the legal regulation of foundations into the Economic Code and ignoring the significant differences between foundations, corporations and other entities.

The unsatisfactory legal regulation was hoped to be improved by the so-called 'major' amendment of the Civil Code.[12] This attempt was partly successful; for instance, it expressly provided for the possibility of establishing a foundation by a person's last will and specified the basic elements of foundation statutes. The provision of Section 20e (2) of the Civil Code also contained a reference to a more detailed regulation that was to be contained in a separate act. In fact, such special regulation was adopted - for several reasons - as late as 6 years after,[13] i.e. in 1998. While the working group which drafted the new act on foundation (in the spirit of the Central European tradition) submitted it to the government in 1992, the regulation was never actually passed due to the break-up of the then Czech-Slovak Federation Republic.

---

[10] The legal regulation of foundations was cancelled during the 1950s.

[11] The Act No. 109/1964 Coll., Economical Code (*hospodářský zákoník*), as subsequently amended, was repealed as of 1.1. 1992, by the Act No. 513/1991 Coll., Commercial Code (*obchodní zákoník*), as subsequently amended.

[12] Namely, the provisions of Sections 18, 20b to 20e and 477 (2) in the Act No. 509/1991 Coll., amended the Act No. 40/1964 Coll., Civil Code (*občanský zákoník*), in effect from 1.1. 1992.

[13] It is true that during the interim period, the Act No. 248/1995 Coll., on Public Benefit Institutions (*o obecně prospěšných společnostech*), was adopted, setting the legal framework for a special type of legal persons of the foundation (germ. *Anstalt*) type – public benefit institutions, whose conception approximates, from a comparative European perspective, foundations that offer services of public benefit (so-called operating foundations). The law, however, led to the fragmentation of the understanding of the foundation institute and the confounding of terms rather than stabilising the foundation sector.

Despite criticism from foundations and legal experts, foundation law with all its shortcomings existed in the Czech Republic without a more detailed regulation until the end of 1997, which saw the adoption of the Act No. 227/1997 Coll. on Foundations and Endowment Funds (*o nadacích a nadačních fondech*), amending also some related legislation (referred to as 'ZNNF'). The causes for this unwelcome situation were mostly legal but also political since there was also a lack of political will to adopt the necessary legal regulation. Even though several draft proposals for legal regulation of foundations were prepared, reflecting the ideas of legal theory and practice, the situation in the field of foundation law changed only upon the adoption of the act on foundations and endowment funds in 1997, while the previous situation had to be understood as temporary and provisional.

Nevertheless, because it was so long, the provisional legal situation had broad negative consequences. The excessive liberalism of the previous regulation meant that the institute of foundation was frequently abused. As a result, the public lost its trust in the honesty of foundations and their intentions to meet their proclaimed goals of working for the public wellbeing. It must be mentioned that such a sceptical attitude is held often by the public until today, as well as the lacking interest by many politicians to change the strict legal regime in any way whatever.

3.3 Foundation Law in Czech Republic under the Act on Foundations and Endowment Funds (till 31.12.2013)

Till the end of 2013, foundation law in the Czech Republic was regulated by the Act No. 227/1997 Coll. on Foundations and Endowment Funds (ZNNF).[14] As the title indicates, the act regulates the legal regime of two specific types of legal persons of private law – foundations and endowment funds[15]; though the differences between these legal forms were not very significant. Other legal regulations important for foundation law were included the Civil Code and also Commercial Code,[16] which provided for the general regulation of the liquidation of foundation entities, Rules of Civil Procedure[17] (for registration purposes) and the Labour Code.[18] As regards public law regulations, special provisions for foundations and endowment funds

[14] Apart from foundations regulation provided by civil law, there are also foundations regulated under canon law.

[15] Since the present article focuses mostly on foundations, the specific nature of endowment funds will be backgrounded. The latter are discussed here only where absolutely necessary or suitable for clarifying the broader implications. The differences between foundations and endowment funds are treated in Ronovská (2009, 64–65) and Hurdík and Telec (1998, 36–38).

[16] Act No. 513/1991 Coll., Commercial Code.

[17] Act No. 99/1963 Coll., Civil Procedure Act (Rules of Civil Procedure).

[18] Act No. 262/2006 Coll., Labour Code.

were contained in former tax regulations[19] and the Accounting Act,[20] as well in some special laws delimiting the scope of activity for individual foundation entities.

The ZNNF was quite extensive and rigid, limited foundations only for public benefit purposes. It was a reaction to the above-mentioned liberal regulation of foundations contained in the Civil Code.[21] Another reason for the extensive scope of the regulation was also the brevity of the general regulation of legal persons in the Civil Code, as well as foreign legal regulations that served as an inspiration for Czech law-makers – mostly the Austrian act on foundations and funds of 1974.

Foundations could generate income from their property and have long-term (permanent) existence. A foundation's property was made up of the foundation endowment, the amount of which is entered into the foundation registry, in the minimal amount of 500,000 CZK (about 20,000 Euro), and other property. In order to attain the purpose for which it was founded, a foundation had to use only its incomes from the foundation endowment and other property.

By contrast, an endowment fund was able operate also for a short period of time, e.g. as an institutionalized public collection. Endowment funds did not typically create foundation endowments and used all of their property for attaining their purposes – the property could be used up, consumed and even indebted. Where such a situation was permanent, it could constitute a reason for an authoritative cancellation of an endowment fund. On the one hand, there was an absolute ban on entering into any indirect commercial activities but, on the other, endowment funds had a looser regime as regards their obligation to have their accounting audited. The difference between the legal forms of the foundation and the endowment fund was increased as a result of the latest amendment No. 158/2010 Coll. An endowment fund was possible to cancel on the basis of a decision of termination adopted by its administrative board, which was not possible in the case of foundations.[22]

The government's original 1996 draft of the act on foundation did not actually consider the legal form of an endowment fund at all.[23] The regulation of endowment funds was inserted in the law only during the debate over the government's draft proposal in the Chamber of Deputies of the Parliament of the Czech Republic.

[19] Act No. 337/1992 Coll. on the Administration of Taxes and Fees, sec. 6 (*zákon o správě daní a poplatků*), Act No. 586/1997 Coll., on income tax (income tax law) (*zákon o dani z příjmů*), Act No. 357/1992 Coll., on Gifts, Inheritance and Real property Tax (*zákon o dani darovací, dědické a dani z převodu nemovitosti*), Act No. 253/2004 Coll., on VAT (*o dani z přidné hodnoty*), Act No. 16/1993 Coll., on Road Tax (*o dani silniční*).

[20] Act No. 563/1991 Coll., on accounting (*zákon o účetnictví*).

[21] Act No. 40/1964 Coll., Civil Code, before revision No. 227/1997 Coll., cancelled by the New CC(/inforce 1.1.2014).

[22] For more details, see Ronovská (2010, 409).

[23] However, the bill of the Foundation Act of 1991, drafted on the model of the Austrian Foundation Act of 1974, originally included this two-layer approach, cf. Hurdík (1994, 42).

3.3.1 *The Main Differences from the* European Standard

When the previous Czech foundation law was compared with the regulation of foundation law in other European countries (and some other comparative projects which had been done in this field), several significant differences can be pointed out.

The Meaning of the Term *Foundation*: Terminological Problem

The former legal framework for foundations in the Czech Republic was favourable to the creation and operation of foundations, endowment funds and public benefit institutions, which are the counterpart to the English term 'foundations'. But, because of historical reasons, it was not possible to state that 'public benefit institutions' make up a third type of foundations, existing alongside foundations and endowment funds.

The main difference between foundations and endowment funds on the one hand and public benefit institutions on the other consists mainly in the following: foundations and endowment funds are characterised by the accumulation of financial means which are then, by means of foundation contributions, provided to third parties for the performance of services beneficial to the public. Public benefit institution,[24] by contrast, may use own property for the direct performance of public benefit services (similar to operating foundations). In the European context, the legal form of a foundation is used in all of these cases.

To conclude, an institution is a foundation-like type of legal person.[25] Because of historical reasons, it is not possible to claim that 'institution' is a third type of 'foundations', existing alongside foundations and endowment funds. For this reason, this particular type of legal persons is set aside and mentioned only where absolutely necessary for understanding the broader consequences.

Asset Management

Under the regulation based on ZNNF assets of the foundation/endowment fund had to be used in general, be used only in harmony with the purposes and conditions set forth in its foundation charter or statutes – mostly in the form of grants given to third

---

[24] The *public benefit institution*, defined under the *Act No. 248/1995 Coll. on Public Benefit Institution*, was a special legal person obliged to provide public benefit services under conditions which have been set in advance and were the same for everybody. It could be involved in economic (commercial) activities (such activity may only be ancillary, i.e. the economic activities may not constitute the prevailing activity). However, its profit, if any (the generation of profits is not explicitly prohibited), was not distributed among founders, members of its bodies or its employees but is used for the financing of public benefit services (non-distributing constrain).

[25] For more details, see Ronovská (2012, 18).

persons. After the revision of foundation law in 2010, it was also possible to use the assets for other activities (e.g. education, cultural events, etc.).[26]

Further on, the registered foundation's endowment was inalienable if this was determined by the founder or the donor; in other cases, it could be disposed of, including the change of the composition of the assets, but only in line with the purpose of the foundation and with all due care. The law provided a detailed regulation of the manner in which a foundation may invest its means[27]; everything was aimed at maximum protection of foundation property for the publicly beneficial purpose.

The statutes of foundation had to also contain an explicit maximum limit for administration costs. Only a restricted portion of the assets available could be used to cover the administrative (operational) costs of the entity. The foundation charter or statutes had to establish rules, fixed for 5 years and limiting the use of their assets for administrative purposes as well as for all salaries, remunerations and other management-related expenditures. The assets of the foundation/endowment fund had to be neither used as collateral nor become subject to any other way of securing liabilities. The costs pertaining[28] to the administration of the organisation had to be kept separate from the foundation contributions.

Limits for Economic Activities

The essential difference between the former *Czech* conception of foundation law and most regulations in Europe consists in the acceptability (or unacceptability) of possible economic activities and limitations concerning the use of the assets of foundation. As a rule, the Czech legal regulation prohibited foundations from any direct trading, while permitting only a few economic activities in the context of fundraising (leasing real estate and organising lotteries, raffles, public collections as well as cultural, social, sports and educational events).

A foundation (but not an endowment fund) could be also be the founder of a public benefit institution. This possibility is often used by foundations; a foundation may establish a public benefit institution, which can be supported by this foundation.

As regards the possibility of foundations in the Czech Republic to engage in indirect trading, this option were also very limited. Assets of the foundation/endowment fund was not possible to be used for the participation in the property of any other persons, unless the law provided for an exception to this rule. Such an exception was the property participation of foundations (but not endowment funds).

---

[26] However, this possibility was still quite limited.

[27] § 23 Act on Foundations and Endowment funds.

[28] Costs pertaining to the administration of the foundation/endowment fund include, above all, the costs to achieve and valorise assets of the foundation/endowment fund; costs to promote the purpose of the foundation/endowment fund; and operating costs of the foundation/endowment fund, including emoluments for the board of directors, the supervisory board or the controller.

A foundation (but not an endowment fund) may participate in the business of joint-stock companies only. The entire involvement of assets by the foundation couldn't exceed 20 % of the foundation's property after deducting the value of the foundation equity. Publicly negotiable securities issued by joint-stock companies had to be purchased and sold by the foundation only in regulated markets. The foundation's stake in a joint-stock company's assets may not exceed 20 %. By contrast, the law strictly provided that foundations and endowment funds may not become members of an unlimited liability company, general partners in a limited partnership company, silent partners or members of a cooperative whose members are obliged to cover the losses of the cooperative over their membership contributions, or members of other legal persons if such members are liable for the obligations of such persons.

The main reason for the restriction under Czech law was the protection of the foundation from losses incurred through economic activities rather than the protection of the potential creditors of a foundation involved in such economic activities. This conception, however, caused many problems in real life. This is why the concept was changed in the new Civil Code.

3.4 The Tendencies of Development of Foundation Law in the Czech Republic

3.4.1 Trends Towards Liberalisation

The former Czech foundation law ranked among those regulations that tend to be conservative and limiting. Such a narrow understanding, however, did not provide a sufficient space either for the application of an autonomous will of the founders or the actual activities of foundations itself. Due to its historical circumstances, however, the strictness of the legal regulation was hardly surprising.

The social relations have, however, changed so much since the mid-1990s that a new discussion started some years ago about the possible liberalisation of foundation law and the ways in which it could be achieved. At least partial liberalisation in the area of foundation law and the strengthening of the role of the founder appeared to be a suitable and acceptable trend. Experience from abroad indicated that a loosening of the legal framework could have a positive effect and lead to the development of philanthropy and greater involvement of citizens in the public sphere. The conception of limiting the foundation activities to mere administration of its own property and distribution of endowment contributions turned out to be hardly tenable.

The first legislative move that reflected this tendency has been the amendment of ZNNF by the Act No. 158/2010 Coll. (came into force on July 1, 2010) which has enabled foundations and funds to implement their own programmes. Another important change was the emphasis on the differences between the legal forms of foundations and endowment funds. The latter have come to enjoy a looser legal regime (at least in some respects). The changes included the possibility of cancelling an endowment fund more easily, the possibility of its merger with another foundation entity and the transformation of an endowment fund into a foundation. The previous legal regulation did not allow for such a transformation. However, practice showed that when endowment funds became financially strong, there could be the need to allow the possibility to continue existence in a new legal form.[29]

3.4.2 Foundation Law in the New Czech Civil Code from 1.1.2014

Conceptual Delimitation

The trends towards a (partial) loosening of the strict conceptual framework of foundation law may also be identified in the new Czech Civil Code[30] which clearly shows the attempt to return to the traditional conception of private law in the continental European tradition. The new code includes the legal form of the foundation (and the endowment fund (Ronovská and Havel 2014, 18)) among special types of legal persons that are regulated as a systematic part of the new CC.

The new CC seeks for inspiration in foreign legal systems,[31] primarily Austrian, German, Swiss, Quebec and Dutch legal regulations. In addition, its proclaimed effort is to take into consideration modern trends in the area of foundation law by extending the possible purpose of foundations from strictly public benefit also to any lawful purpose and enable the establishment of family foundations. Further is allowing foundations to engage in business as ancillary activities and extending the possible activities of foundations necessary to implement their own programmes.

The very first draft of the general part of the Civil Code (which was published in autumn of 2002)[32] contained many shortcomings concerning foundations. They stemmed mostly from the fact that the drafting did not take into consideration the specific nature of the foundation and funds, i.e. the fact that foundations perform an entirely different role in the society from business companies. In the final phase of the preparation of the new CC have been finally many problematic points removed and improved; some still remain.

The regulation in the new Czech CC uses the Czech expression *fundace* as a superordinate term to foundations and endowment funds that will be used as a general designation of the foundation (fund) type of legal persons. For the purposes

---

[29] See Section 9a of ZNNF.

[30] Act No. 89/2012 Coll., Civil Code, which came into force from 1st January 2014.

[31] See explanatory memorandum to NOZ, pp. 17 and also 93, available online at http://obcanskyzakonik.justice.cz/tinymce-storage/files/DZ_NOZ_89_%202012_Sb.pdf. Accessed on 23.5.2012.

[32] See Eliáš (2002, 35 et al.).

of performing public beneficial activities and services that are typically served by foundation entities in other European countries should be preserved again a special legal form of 'institution' (*ústav* in Czech),[33] replacing the legal regulation of the currently existing public benefit institutions.[34] Unfortunately, the institution remains outside the legal category of foundations, though it is a special fund-type form of legal persons.

A characteristic feature of the regulation of foundation law in the new CC is its broad extent.[35] On the one hand, one may see the attempt to remove some detailed regulations, e.g. as regards the procedure when investing the foundation property, but, on the other, some detailed provisions are being newly introduced. What remains is the duality of foundations and endowment funds. Such conceptual approach may be guided by an attempt to achieve as complex a regulation as possible, but – together with the extensive regulation of the general part of legal persons – it makes the proposed regulation of foundation law difficult for a lay person to grasp.

Some Notes on the Content of the New Civil Code

As regards its content, the new CC foundation law is based on the previous regulation in ZNNF (Act No. 227/1997 Coll). One of the crucial changes is the (partial) loosening of the foundations' purpose. Till 31.12.2013, the purpose could be only public benefit. Although the new CC expressly states that foundations *pro futuro* may not serve any for-profit purposes, it allows them to engage in commercial activities, provided that the income from such activities is used only for the support of their purpose and as long as this is specified in the foundations' statutes in harmony with the foundation deed. Such commercial activities may solely be ancillary.[36]

Some other changes should affect also the establishment of foundations. The new code abandons the former law which distinguishes between unilateral foundation deeds and contractual deeds. It unifies the regulation, providing that foundation deeds (for establishing foundations inter vivos) as well as last wills (in case of mortis causa) are the founders' unilateral legal acts. This can be considered as suitable, particularly with view to the impersonal nature of foundations. As regards the establishment of a foundation as a legal entity upon its entry into the foundation registry, the new CC recycles – with some minor specifications – the existing legal regulation.

[33] Section 402 and subsequent sections of the New Civil Code.

[34] The Act No. 248/1995 Coll. should be repealed.

[35] Foundation law is covered in almost 90 provisions, while the general regulation of legal persons is covered in almost 100 provisions.

[36] See Section 307 of the New Civil Code.

Another innovation is the provision concerning the change of a foundation's purpose. The absence of any such provision in the previous law causes many problems in practical applications.

The new code also introduces the possibility that third persons may entrust their own property to foundations for asset administration, while its ownership is retained by the donor – this is the so-called dependent fund (*přidružený fond* in Czech).[37]

A rather sensitive and specific issue is the cancellation of foundations. Foundations are distinct from corporations, among others, by their inability to cancel themselves on the basis of a decision of their own internal bodies. It may therefore be considered as suitable that the New Civil Code authorises the court to dissolve a foundation – as long as some of the circumstances specified in law occur[38] – either upon a motion or ex officio. The only exception is when the purpose is achieved: in such a case a foundation becomes cancelled directly *ex lege*.[39]

As regards the decision-making on the dissolution of a foundation, the court should always prefer to maintain the existence of a foundation entity. For this reason, it is suitable that the general part of the new CC contains the possibility of remedying the situation voluntarily.[40] However, what is missing is the court's authorisation to attempt to save a foundation by changing its legal form to an endowment fund or by a 'forced' merger with some other foundation. It is certainly good that the code does not allow – as is the case under current law – a foundation to split into two as one of the ways of transforming foundation entities; such a practice would actually be in conflict with the basic conceptual understanding of foundations.

However, the new CC aims to allow foundations to change their legal status to endowment funds[41] on the basis of a decision adopted by the administrative board, which will result in the loosening of the legal form that is 'stricter' in the case of foundations, and this might even lead to 'asset-stripping' of foundation property. This option is therefore possible only if it is allowed expressly in the foundation deed by the founders and only in exceptional cases.

Svěřenský Fond: The New Czech *Trust-Like* Institute

The relatively narrow and limiting formal conception of foundations under existing law fails to exploit the significant potential that the foundation institute offers in the broader (functional) sense. The limitation of the foundation purpose solely to matters of public (or general) benefit narrows down its applicability for mixed or

[37] Section 349 of the New Civil Code.
[38] Section 377 of the New Civil Code.
[39] Section 376 of the New Civil Code.
[40] Section 172 (2) of the New Civil Code.
[41] Section 391 of the New Civil Code.

private purposes (e.g. administration of family property, maintenance of continuity of family businesses or as an alternative to hereditary succession). That deficit, however, is slowly starting to show in the society, which may have been the reason why the New Civil Code aims to introduce the institute of *svěřenský fond* (*trust fund*),[42] which can be considered (with some exaggeration) as a continental-Europeanised version of trusts.

The Czech Republic will thus be next country in continental Europe (in addition to Lichtenstein Frame etc.) that will most likely introduce this *trust-like* institute. The New Civil Code did not look for its inspiration to the legal regulation in Liechtenstein (perhaps surprisingly); instead, it takes over – with some modifications – the legal regulation valid in the Canadian province of Quebec.

3.4.3 Conclusion

The situation as regards the foundation sector in most Central and Eastern European countries[43] became essentially stabilised during the second half of the 1990s as a result of the adoption of foundation laws (independent in almost all cases) that bear certain common characteristics. It is then not surprising that a *more narrow* conception prevailed[44] that tends to limit the purpose of foundations exclusively to public benefit.[45] Another common feature of these legal regulations is the overall backgrounding of the position of the founders and the possibility of founders to assert their will, as well as the insufficient distinction of the legal form of foundations from corporations. This approach mirrors, in a sense, the *charity concept* (of publicly beneficial trusts and non-profit organisations) from the Anglo-Saxon law that penetrated into the area of Central Europe in connection with the above-mentioned operation of American foundations in Central and Eastern European countries.[46]

---

[42] Section 1448 and subsequent sections of the New Civil Code.

[43] However, Slovakia saw the adoption of the new foundation law as late as in 2002, when the Act No. 34/2002 Z. z. on foundations, as subsequently amended, was passed.

[44] For a discussion of the problematic nature of the differing approaches and divergent understandings of the foundation institute, see also Feasibility Study on European Statute, p. 13, available online at http://ec.europa.eu/internal_market/company/docs/eufoundation/feasibilitystudy_en.pdf. [Accessed on 23.5.2012]. See also Jakob (2006, 44–45).

[45] Foundations in Poland, Romania, Slovakia, Slovenia and Latvia may be established only for publicly beneficial purposes. By contrast, foundations in Bulgaria, Estonia and Lithuania may exist for any propose that does not conflict with law (any lawful purpose); for more details, see the illustrative table in Feasibility Study on European Foundation Statute, pp. 52 and 53.

[46] As a result, the traditional continental European understanding of legal persons was supplemented with a new element. With the passage of time, the resulting mix appears to be problematic. The Anglo-Saxon influence became evident mainly in connection with the preparation of the Act on public benefit institutions (Act No. 248/1995 Coll). The law regulates the position of special foundation-type of legal persons that provide services for public good, which replaces foundations in this area. Similar experience can be identified also in the case of the Slovak

However, this influence was not, by far, so strong in the Czech Republic as in other countries in the region, particularly because of the relatively reserved attitude of the political representation of the first half of the 1990s towards any attempts aimed at constituting the civic society. The strict and mandatory nature of the regulation seems to be related to the underlying goal of discrediting foundations, which resulted from the liberal regulation of the first half of the 1990s. In any case, there was a deviation from the traditional conception of foundations established in Savigny's work and subsequently elaborated mainly in German jurisprudence.[47]

The previous legal regulation contained in the Act No. 227/1997 Coll., on Foundations and Endowment Funds, was one of the strictest in Europe, mainly due to historical reasons. The main differences from what is common in other European countries are, above all, the limitation of the foundation purpose exclusively to public benefit, the prohibition of (both direct and indirect) commercial activities of foundations and the mandatory nature of the regulation concerning asset management and the internal organisational structure.

However, the situation in the society has changed so much since the mid-1990s that a partial liberalisation of the foundation institute in the Czech Republic appears as suitable and socially acceptable. The new Czech Civil Code can be considered – as regards its provisions concerning foundation law – a step in the right direction since it could contribute towards the emancipation of the institute of foundations, a greater flexibility and perhaps even an increase of the number of foundations in the Czech Republic.

Bibliography

Drobing, U. 2001. Grundzüge des Stiftungsrechts in Mittel- und Osteuropa. In *Stiftungsrecht in Europa*, ed. J.K. Hopt and D. Reuter, 542. Köln: Karl Heymanns Verlag KG.

Eliáš, K. 2002. *Věcný záměr nového občanského zákoníku* (The legislative intent to the new regulation of the Civil Code). Justiční praxe No. 9, 35 et al.

Feasibility study on European Foundation Statute. Available online at: http://ec.europa.eu/internal_market/company/eufoundation/index_en.htm. Accessed 5 Oct 2012.

Hermann-Otavský, E. 1938. Návrh na zákonnou úpravu nadačního práva. Otisk veřejné správy, no. 7–8.

Hondius, F. 2001. Trends and Developments of Foundation Law in Europe. In *Stiftungsrecht in Europa*, ed. J.K. Hopt and D. Reuter, 581. Köln: Carl Heymanns Verlag KG.

Hurdík, J. 1994. *Problémy nadačního práva* (Problems of Law on Foundations), 42. Brno: Masarykova univerzita.

Act No. 213/1997 Coll. on Organizations Providing Services of Public Benefit and the Hungarian Act on Public Benefit Organizations of 1997 (now repealed). The legal forms that came into existence in this way are difficult to grasp from the point of view of the *classic*, i.e. European continental conception of legal persons. This problem became also evident during the work on the draft of the New Civil Code.

[47] Further Schulze (2001, 64).

Hurdík, J., and I. Telec. 1998. *Zákon o nadacích a nadačních fondech* (Act on Foundations and Endowment Funds), Komentář, XXVI. Praha: C.H. Beck.

Jakob, D. 2006. Schutz der Stiftung, Die Stiftung und ihre Rechtsverhältnisse im Wiederstreit der Interssen, 44–45. Tübingen: Mohr Siebeck.

New Czech Civil Code no. 89/21012 Coll. Available online at: http://obcanskyzakonik.justice.cz/tinymce-storage/files/sb0033-2012.pdf. Accessed 5 Oct 2012.

Ronovská, K. 2009. *Tendence vývoje českého nadačního práva v rámci sjednocené Evropy* (Tendencies of Development of Czech Foundation Law in European Context), 64–65. Brno: Masarykova University.

Ronovská, K. 2010. *Novinky na poli nadačního práva: krok správným směrem*. Právní forum VII./2010. Wolters Kluwer, no. 8, 409.

Ronovská, K. 2012. *Nové české nadační právo v evropském srovnání* (New Czech Law on Foundations in a comparative European perspective), 18. Praha: Wolter Kluwer.

Ronovská, K. 2013. Proměny nadačního práva [Metamorphosis of foundation law in Europe]. *ČPVP* (4): 461 ef.

Ronovská, K., and B. Havel. 2014. Nadační fond v realitě nového občanského zákoníku. *Právní rozhledy* (3), 17 ef.

Schulze, R. 2001. Die Gegenwart des Vegangen – Zu Stand und Aufgaben der Stiftungsrechtsgeschichte. In *Stiftungsrecht in Europa*, ed. J.K. Hopt and D. Reuter, 64. Köln: Karl Heymanns Verlag KG.

Stammer, O. 1975. *Das österreichisches Bundes- Stiftungs und Fondgesetz, Gesetztext mit ausfürlichen Erlauterungen*, 280. Eisenstadt: Prugg Verlag.

Chapter 4
Regulation Absent: The Chimera of Charitable Foundation Law in England and Wales

Alison Dunn

4.1 Introduction and Context

Charitable foundations play an important part in the voluntary sector of England and Wales, particularly as enablers of creative and innovative voluntary action.[1] As independent grant-making bodies, they offer a vital alternative to state funding and are often able to take a long-term, flexible and broader approach to the causes they support (Anheier and Leat 2002, 13). Given this ability, it is unsurprising that such grant-making organisations have a key role in encouraging philanthropy and active citizenship, as well as facilitating capacity building within the voluntary sector.

Charitable foundations, as grant-givers, have purposes which are distinct from the more traditional charitable activity of service delivery. This distinctiveness means that charitable foundations often face different legal challenges to the majority of organisations within the voluntary sector. In addition, those with sufficient funds to create a foundation often need to be encouraged to do so through a non-burdensome regulatory regime. Despite this, the legal framework for charities in England and Wales does not make separate regulatory provision for charitable foundations, whether at the point of creation, operation, supervision or

This chapter was written in 2011, an earlier version was delivered at the International Society for Third-Sector Research's 9th International Conference at Kadir Has University, Istanbul, in July 2010. I am grateful to Chiara Prele for organising the conference panel, to Ann Sinclair for her research assistance and to Oonagh Breen, Francesco Schurr, Anthony Zito and the panel audience for their comments and suggestions.

[1] For a broad ranging historical account of foundations, see Smith and Borgmann (2001, 2–34) and Leat (2001, 268–281).

A. Dunn (✉)
Newcastle Law School, Newcastle University, 21-24 Windsor Terrace, Newcastle upon Tyne NE1 7RU, UK
e-mail: Alison.Dunn@ncl.ac.uk

C. Prele (ed.), *Developments in Foundation Law in Europe*, Ius Gentium: Comparative Perspectives on Law and Justice 39, DOI 10.1007/978-94-017-9069-7_4,

dissolution. There is no separate foundation law.[2] Rather, the legal regime in England and Wales treats all charitable organisations as a unified group, and charitable foundations are placed under the all-encompassing general charity regulation of the Charities Acts of 1993 and 2006, consolidated in a 2011 Act. This is despite extensive lobbying by the charity foundation sub-sector in the lead up to the reform in the 2006 Act and despite a recommendation by the Joint Committee on the Draft Charities Bill for lighter regulation of charitable foundations (Joint Committee on the Draft Charities Bill 2004a). Whilst allowing for sector cohesion, it is arguable that the approach within English and Welsh charity law fails to adequately meet the legal and societal challenges facing charitable foundations.

Before turning to a discussion of the legal regime, it is worth saying a little by way of background and context to charitable foundations in England and Wales. Charitable organisations which exist as foundations are often considered just to be grant-making, that is, set up to distribute funds to charities and other organisations according to a defined charitable purpose. Foundations, however, also may be set up to carry out their own charitable projects rather than exist as grant-making entities. Foundations can be funded by a permanent endowment (usual for foundations created by wealthy individuals), by covenant providing annual allocation (usual for corporate foundations created by companies) or by a mixture of endowment and fundraising (predominantly for community foundations but also used by other foundation types (Wiggins 2009)). Whilst grant-making foundations have a long heritage in England and Wales, community foundations are in their infancy (just 57 exist) having been established in the last 30 years and gained prominence in the last decade. These foundations allow individual donors to distribute funds collectively through one body to projects and charities in a particular locality or geographical community.[3] Donors can have as much or as little control as they wish on which projects or charities their funds are distributed to by the foundation. In terms of individual giving, community foundations are proving popular as an alternative to setting up one's own foundation, giving the advantage to the donor of anonymity as well as freedom from the bureaucracy attached to creating and operating a charity.[4] Community foundations have also acted as a vehicle for the distribution of government grants, for example, distribution of Local Network Funds for the Department of Education and Skills.

Across the UK as a whole, it is estimated that there are some 900,000 organisations that make up the voluntary sector and broader civil society, with combined assets of £244 billion (€291.6bn, US$361.3bn), comprising *inter alia* charities,

[2] Foundations with non-charitable purposes can also exist but are unable to take the advantages of charitable status such as taxation relief. Such foundations similarly fall under the general law.

[3] Calls have been made to extend these types of foundations from geographical communities to communities of interest similar to the situation in the USA, see Driscoll and Grant (2009, 17–19). For a discussion on community foundations in the UK and their role in both philanthropy and community development, see Daly (2008).

[4] The Community Foundation Network (2010) reports a doubling of donations to community foundations in 2008/2009.

faith groups, housing associations, friendly and benevolent societies, trade associations and unions, industrial and provident societies, cooperatives, universities and informal community organisations (Clark et al. 2010).[5] Almost one-fifth of these organisations are charities (171,000). In terms of charitable foundations as an informal sub-sector of general charities, there is very little comprehensive data for England and Wales, but on current figures, there are some 11,687 grant-making foundations in the UK as a whole, with a collective income of £3.4 billion (€4.5bn, US$5.5bn), expenditure of £2.6 billion (€3.8bn, US$4.75bn) and total assets of £28.3 billion (€34bn, US$41.8bn) (Clark et al. 2010). In 2007–2008, the last year for which figures are currently available, the top 400 grant-making trusts in the UK distributed some £2.53 billion to organisations, up from £2.3 billion on the previous year (Traynor and Chronnell 2010, iv).[6] Whilst these figures show a relatively slight increase in distributed funds, they come at a time when the collective assets of the same organisations have fallen by some £4 billion in the recent economic recession (Traynor and Chronnell 2010, iv). Poor performing investments account for a proportion of the decrease, but a real decrease in income has been seen by some corporate foundations as a result of the economic instability in the company which created them and which provides covenanted annual allocation to the charitable foundation.[7]

As already noted, the legal regime in England and Wales does not provide a separate legal category, organisational vehicle or supervisory framework specifically for charitable foundations. Because foundations are not legally separate organisations, they fall within the general law of charities and must comply with common organisational, governance and accounting requirements. UK charity regulation is a devolved matter and so created and administered according to three jurisdictions, viz. England and Wales, Scotland and Northern Ireland. This chapter focuses upon the jurisdiction of England and Wales alone. The Charities and Trustee Investment (Scotland) Act 2005 (amended by the Public Services Reform (Scotland) Act 2010) lays down the regulatory regime for Scottish charities which are subject to their own independent regulator, the Office of the Scottish Charity Regulator, which has parallel statutory objectives to its English counterpart. A similar position exists for charities in Northern Ireland, coming under the jurisdiction of the Charity Commission for Northern Ireland, in operation from 2009 (Charities (Northern Ireland) Order 2007 and the Charities Act (Northern Ireland) 2008). Other regulations that are non-charity specific but which nevertheless may affect charities, such as taxation regimes, employment laws and

[5] Figures are for the year 2007–2008.

[6] It should be noted that these figures need to be put in context of the fact that most the grants were given by a small handful of very large foundations such as the Welcome Trust.

[7] The Northern Rock Foundation is a prime example. The foundation's funding from Northern Rock bank was cut in the wake of the financial crisis affecting the bank, leading to the Foundation having to cut its own programmes.

requirements under the European Convention of Human Rights, often apply across all jurisdictions.

English and Welsh charities are subject to the Charities Act 1993 as amended by the Charities Act 2006, consolidated in the Charities Act 2011.[8] Under these provisions, organisations, which comply with a statutory meaning of 'charitable purpose' and a public benefit requirement, as well as acting exclusively for charitable purposes, are deemed to be charities (Section 2(1) Charities Act 2011). A broad range of charitable purposes are set out in Section 3 of the Charities Act 2011. Section 3 of the Act lays down the requirement, though not a definition, of public benefit, which falls to be determined by the principles set out in the pre-2006 Act case law as applied by the regulator. Charities in England and Wales must register with and be regulated by an independent regulator, the Charity Commission for England and Wales, though registration of itself does not confer status (Section 6(1) Charities Act 2006, Section 13 Charities Act 2011).[9] The Charity Commission as regulator has a number of statutory objectives and functions.[10] Its statutory objectives are to increase public trust and confidence in charities, to promote awareness and understanding of the public benefit requirement, to promote compliance by trustees with legal obligations, to promote the effective use of charitable resources and to enhance accountability of charities to donors, beneficiaries and the general public (Section 7 Charities Act 2006, Section 14 Charities Act 2011). These objectives are accountability led and give precedence to an external regulatory focus upon charities over an internal encouragement mechanism, though the latter remains important. The Charity Commission's functions are both internally and externally directed, with a regulatory eye as well as an advisory approach. They include determining if organisations are charities, encouraging better administration of charities, investigating misconduct and taking protective action, determining the need for public collection certificates, disseminating information on the performance or its functions and advising the government on the same (Section 7 Charities Act 2006, Section 15 Charities Act 2011).

Given that there is no separate legal distinction which applies to foundations in England and Wales; that the term 'foundation' does not confer, designate or determine status; and that general charity law applies to creation, registration, legal form, supervision and dissolution of charitable foundations, this chapter will briefly outline the general law as it applies to all charities in the jurisdiction. After this brief summary, this chapter will turn to an examination of the recent reform of

---

[8] The Charities Act 2006 amended provisions in the Charities Act 1993. The provisions of both Acts are now consolidated in the Charities Act 2011. References in this chapter are to the 2006 and 2011 Acts.

[9] However, note that not all charities need to register with the Charity Commission (there is a £5,000 threshold) and former exempt charities that have another principal regulator do not need to register, for example, universities which are principally regulated by the Higher Education and Funding Council for England.

[10] It also has general duties and incidental powers to facilitate performance of its functions and duties set out in (Section 7 Charities Act 2006, Sections 16, 20 Charities Act 2011).

charity law in England and Wales, placing a focus upon the (ultimately unsuccessful) arguments raised by and on behalf of charitable foundations for separate treatment under the law. These reform debates highlighted the stifling effect of a regulatory framework that treats all charities as one and the unforeseen consequences that arise from the absence of specific foundation law.

4.2 Distinct but Not Separate: The Regulation of Charitable Foundations in England and Wales

An organisation seeking to become a charitable foundation in England and Wales will need to comply with general charity law with regard to all aspects of its creation, governance, accounting and administration, officers and beneficiaries, supervision, taxation and dissolution. In this context, regulatory parity exists between all organisations that fall within the charity sector: no separate distinctions are made between different types of charities, different types of charitable purposes or different types of charitable activities. As a consequence, this also means that charitable foundations are able to take advantage of the same legal and fiscal privileges as all other charities, such as the ability to exist in perpetuity and to receive relief or exemption from various taxation requirements. In addition to the general charity law as set out in the Charities Acts of 1993, 2006 and 2011, all charities in England and Wales (including foundations) fall under the general law regarding such matters as criminal and tortious liability and public law.[11]

4.2.1 Creation and Registration

An organisation will become a charity in England and Wales if (1) it falls within one of the thirteen statutory purposes set out in Section 2 of the Charities Act 2006[12]; (2) it has public benefit in accordance with Section 3 of the Charities Act

[11] For an in-depth examination of the regulation of charities in England and Wales, see Luxton (2001).

[12] Section 2(2) Charities Act 2006 replaces the previous four 'heads' of charitable purposes from Commissioners for Special Purposes of Income Tax v Pemsel [1891] AC 531 with a new list of 13 purposes: prevention or relief of poverty; advancement of education; advancement of religion; advancement of health or the saving of lives; advancement of citizenship or community development; advancement of the arts, culture, heritage or science; advancement of amateur sport; advancement of human rights, conflict resolution or reconciliation or the promotion of religious or racial harmony or equality and diversity; advancement of environmental protection or improvement; relief of those in need by reason of youth, age, ill-health, disability, financial hardship or other disadvantage; advancement of animal welfare; promotion of the efficiency of the armed forces of the crown; and other purposes already recognised as charitable under existing law or analogous/within the spirit section of the purposes listed in Section 2(2).

2006, that is, if it provides a benefit that arises directly from the charitable purpose and which is afforded to either the public as a whole or a sufficient cross section of it (*Verge v Somerville [1924]* AC 496, *In Re Compton* [1945] Ch. 123, 128 per Lord Greene MR); (3) its purpose is wholly and exclusively charitable, that is, admitting of no political, private or other non-charitable purpose; and (4) it is non-profit distributing. These purpose, benefit and distribution constraints justify the general taxation benefits and privileges that are afforded to charitable organisations. Unless excepted or exempt, charities with a gross annual income over £5,000 are required to register with the sector regulator, the Charity Commission for England and Wales (Section 9 Charities Act 2006, Section 30 Charities Act 2011).[13] This regulatory body determines the charitable status of organisations and maintains the charities register open to public inspection (Section 6(1) Charities Act 2006, Section 13 Charities Act 2011). Since foundations do not fall within the exempt category and only rarely in the excepted category, if they satisfy the four criteria above and have a gross income over £5,000, they will be required to register with the Commission.

4.2.2 *Organisational Structure and Governance*

In terms of organisational structure, charities including charitable foundations can choose from a number of different unincorporated or incorporated legal forms, including the trust, the unincorporated association and the company limited by guarantee (model documents for which are available from the regulator).[14] Unincorporated forms are flexible, but the charity's assets are held in the names of the trustees and provide little protection from liability for the trustees of the charity.[15] Incorporated legal forms provide a greater measure of protection for the trustees, with the charity's assets held by the company. An analysis of the Charity

[13] See also Schedule 5 of the 2006 Act. Excepted charities (which include churches chapels and associated funds of certain Christian denominations, charitable service funds of the armed forces, scout and guide groups) are not required to register with the Charity Commission but will still remain within the Commission's supervisory remit. This is subject to the provision that from 2012 excepted charities with an annual income over £100,000 will be required to register with the Commission. Exempt charities are not required to register with the Charity Commission and generally have a separate 'principal' regulator that ensures their compliance with charity law. Universities are exempt charities but are regulated by the Higher Education Funding Council for England. See Schedule 3 Charities Act 2011.

[14] Some older foundations have been established by Royal Charter or Act of Parliament. For model documents, see http://www.charitycommission.gov.uk/start_up_a_charity/guidance_on_registering/mgds.aspx

[15] Under (Section 38 Charities Act 2006, Section 191 Charities Act 2011), the Charity Commission has power to relieve a trustee from personal liability where the trustee has acted honestly and reasonably and ought fairly to be excused.

Commission's register of charities reveals that the majority of charitable foundations in England and Wales have taken the corporate legal form.

The Charities Act 2006 introduced for the first time a specific legal form for charities, the Charitable Incorporated Organisation, with the purpose of providing a bespoke incorporated legal vehicle designed specifically for the particular needs of charities but which stands outside of the complex framework of company law (Schedule 7 Charities Act 2006 consolidated in Part 11 Charities Act 2011).[16] This new organisational structure offers protection for trustees outwith the company form. Yet to be implemented, this new legal form provides the benefits of an asset lock and a requirement of a social mission through the charitable purpose. By contrast with corporate forms, such as the company limited by guarantee, the charitable incorporated organisation has the added advantage of placing the charitable organisation solely within the registration requirements and regulatory supervision of the Charity Commission as sector regulator. This will remove the need for incorporated charities to register with and account to both the charity regulator and the registrar for companies, Companies House. The fact that the specific asset lock is derived from the new organisational form (rather than needed to be applied through the memorandum and articles of association of the charity as with the company limited by guarantee) and the removal of duplication of accounting to separate regulators will be two significant benefits of this new legal form once it comes into force.

The organisational structure chosen by a charity in England and Wales will determine how that charity is governed through its governing document, be it a trust deed (trust), the rules of the association (unincorporated association), memorandum and articles of association (company limited by guarantee) or its constitution (unincorporated association and charitable incorporated organisation). Those officers of the charity who have control and management of its administration are known as 'charity trustees' (schedule 8, Section 175 Charities Act 2006, Section 177 Charities Act 2011). Such trustees are required to comply with the express duties and powers set out in the charity's governing document as well as with the statutory duties imposed by the Charities Acts of 1993 and 2006 and general trust law, where it applies, in relation to matters such as fiduciary duties, duties and powers on protection of assets and investment and attendant standards of care and skill. In addition to statutory requirements, a voluntary sector-wide Code of Practice setting out principles of good governance has been created by sector organisations (Governance Code Steering Group 2010).[17] This code is voluntary but

[16] Separate legislation also introduced a further specific organisational form, the 'community interest company', for non-charitable social enterprises. This organisational form similarly includes an asset lock, a requirement of a social mission, and has its own regulator: see Companies (Audit, Investigations and Community Enterprise) Act 2004, Part 2. For discussion of the corporate forms, see Dunn and Riley (2004).

[17] The code has been promulgated, among others, by the National Council for Voluntary Organisations, the Association of Chief Executives of Voluntary Organisations as well as the Charity Commission. For discussion, see Dawson and Dunn (2006).

provides an essential guide to meeting standards of care and skill in carrying out charitable purposes and protecting charitable assets. Nonetheless, neither the code nor the governance rules specifically address particular needs of charitable foundations.

4.2.3 Economic Activity and Taxation Reliefs

Although less relevant to foundations than other charities, a charity may undertake trading activities where to do so is ancillary to and in pursuit of its charitable purposes.[18] More extensive trading activities will be a non-charitable activity, and, even where ancillary, the trading activities must not put at risk the assets of the charity. In both these circumstances, it is common to create a separately administered trading subsidiary so as to not endanger the charity's primary charitable purpose as well as to protect the charity's assets. The trading subsidiary will generate income for the parent charity, but it too must operate in accordance with the charity's charitable purposes. Although profits made by the trading subsidiary are taxable, any profits paid to the charity from the trading subsidiary or applied solely for charitable purposes will not be subject to taxation (Section 505(1)(e) Income and Corporation Taxes Act 1988, amended by Part 10 and Schedule 1 Income Tax Act 2007).

To take advantage of the taxation privileges, organisations must be formally recognised by Her Majesty's Revenue and Customs (HMRC) as a charity. Recognition by HMRC provides a gateway to relief from income and corporation tax on monies applied to charitable purposes and to the ability to reclaim tax paid by donors on income applied through the gift aid scheme (Sections 466–493 Corporation Tax Act 2010, Sections 521–536 Income Tax Act 2007).[19] These tax reliefs also cover income generated from investments, land and property and from trading profits.[20] Charities are further exempt from capital gains tax, inheritance tax and stamp duty land tax and are entitled to relief at 80 % from business rates on non-domestic property used for charitable purposes and to relief on value-added tax on certain purchases (Section 256 Taxation of Chargeable Gains Act 1992).[21] There are no additional or specific taxation benefits afforded to charitable foundations.

[18] Trading will be caught by the wholly and exclusively charitable rule where it is not ancillary to the charity's primary charitable purpose.

[19] Gift aid allows charities to reclaim from HMRC the income tax paid by the donor on donations where the donor is a UK taxpayer.

[20] For a discussion, see Dawson (2000).

[21] VAT relief is available, for example, on advertisements, goods and services for disabled people and construction of buildings; see http://www.hmrc.gov.uk/charities/vat/purchases.htm

4.2.4 Funding and Reporting

As noted above, charitable foundations can be funded in a number of different ways from permanent endowment to covenanted annual allocation. Amendments put in place by the Charities Act 2006 allow the trustees of unincorporated charities (trusts and unincorporated associations) the power to spend the whole or part of the capital out of a permanent endowment fund free from the endowment restrictions (Section 43 Charities Act 2006, Section 281 Charities Act 2011). In order to exercise this new and flexible power, the charity's trustees must be satisfied that the purpose of the trust fund could be more effectively carried out if the capital as well as the income of the fund is spent (Section 43 Charities Act 2006, Section 281(4) Charities Act 2011). For charities where the endowment is greater than £10,000 with an annual income over £1,000, the approval of the Charity Commission is required; for charities with endowment and income less than these amounts, the power to spend capital can be achieved by resolution of the trustees (Section 43 Charities Act 2006, Section 282 Charities Act 2011).

Charities must prepare information returns (including reporting on public benefit) and provide an annual statement of accounts.[22] These financial statements are subject to differing levels of external scrutiny and audit according to certain income thresholds as set out in legislation (Sections 3, 41–43 Charities Act 1993, amended by the Charities Act 2006). Light-touch reporting requirements apply to charities with an income up to £25,000. Above this threshold, accounts must be filed with the regulator, the Charity Commission for England and Wales, and be subject to external scrutiny through independent examination. For charities with an income over £250,000, accounts must comply with the accounting guidance *Accounting and Reporting by Charities, Statement of Recommended Practice* (known by its acronym 'SORP' (Charity Commission 2005) and discussed further below). A threshold of £500,000 income triggers a full audit.

4.2.5 Supervision

As noted above, the Charity Commission for England and Wales is the charity sector regulator with responsibility for all charities whether registered or not, unless such charities are exempted and fall within the remit of another principal regulator. The Charity Commission has explicit statutory objectives and functions in relation to maintaining public trust and confidence in charities as well as ensuring compliance with charity law and promoting accountability and the effective use of charity resources (Section 7 Charities Act 2006, Sections 14–15 Charities Act 2011). Alongside a general power to advise organisations, the regulator has concurrent

[22] The rules set out in this section apply to accounts post 1 April 2008. For discussion, see Morgan (2010).

jurisdiction with the High Court in regard to the administration of charities (Section 69 Charities Act 2011).[23]

The Charities Act of 2006 strengthened the role of the regulator and with it the monitoring of charities. The new Act placed greater emphasis upon the Commission's statutory objectives and enhanced its already extensive powers to investigate and intervene in the management and administration of charities. Ensuring charity trustees' compliance with accounting and reporting requirements as well as the duties and powers, standards of care and skill and general good governance of organisations is within the remit of the regulator, which has broad powers to intervene and investigate charities through both informal and inquiries as well as to appoint or remove trustees, appoint interim managers, enter premises and seize documents and remove organisations from the register of charities (Sections 46–53, 83, 107 Charities Act 2011). Under new provisions of the Charities Act 2006, the Charity Commission can also make specific directions to protect a charity and its assets where, for example, there has been misconduct or mismanagement, or to direct application of charity property, where it appears that the trustees are unwilling to apply the property to the purposes of the charity (Sections 20–21 Charities Act 2006, Sections 84–85 Charities Act 2011). There are no special or separate provisions for the monitoring or supervision of charitable foundations, but the latter (untested) provision on the ability of the regulator to direct application of the trust property where it is necessary and desirable to do so (and which does not carry a requirement of bad faith or mismanagement on the part of the trustees) theoretically opens up the possibility that a foundation, like any other charity, could be compelled to disburse its funds in accordance with the charitable purpose.

4.2.6 Dissolution

Finally, the organisational structure of a charity also has a bearing upon its dissolution. For example, a charity established as a trust or unincorporated association will cease to exist once its assets are exhausted or, where the terms of the trust allow or via consent of the Charity Commission, when all the assets are transferred to another similar charitable organisation or through a cy-près scheme (Sections 15–18 Charities Act 2006, Sections 62–68 Charities Act 2011). By contrast, a charity established by incorporated form as a company will be dissolved when it is removed from the register of companies or when it is wound up. In these circumstances, the assets of the organisation will be dealt with according to the

[23] Section 16 covers, inter alia, jurisdiction over appointment and removal of trustees, establishing or implementing a scheme for the administration of a charity, vesting and transferring property. The general power to advise is set out in Section 29 Charities Act 1993, amended by the Charities Act 2006 and consolidated in Section 110 Charities Act 2011.

company's memorandum of association and articles of association, typically by transfer to another similar charitable organisation.

The above burdens and privileges apply to all charities, including foundations. We can see that foundations receive no special privileges nor are they provided with separate or light-touch regulation, nor indeed extra regulatory requirements. In this respect, charity law follows a 'one size fits all' approach, albeit that the Charity Commission as regulator has some discretion in application of the rules to the individual circumstances of charities whatever their hue. There are clear advantages of certainty and transparency in this regulatory framework. Nonetheless, it has left many foundations concerned at the operating burden of the regulatory regime and the lack of formal recognition in the rules as to their particular circumstances. This concern was vocally demonstrated in the run up to charity law reform, a lobby to which this chapter now turns.

4.3 To Reform or Not to Reform? Debates on the Regulation of Charitable Foundations in England and Wales

As noted above, the Charities Act 2006 updated the previous Charities Act 1993 and put in place a number of charity law reforms in England and Wales. This Act sought to provide comprehensive and cohesive legislation building on existing common law rules and provide a strong overarching supervisory and regulatory framework for all charities. In particular, the reform sought to modernise the legal framework for charities, extend the range of legal organisational forms available for charities, build public trust and confidence in charities through greater transparency and accountability and provide for independent, fair and proportionate regulation (Strategy Unit 2002, 8). The lengthy build-up to the Act involved widespread sector consultation, and it was a fertile period for debates on the propriety, extent and form of charity law reform.[24] Foundations and their umbrella body, the Association of Charitable Foundations, played a significant role in these debates. In particular, they lobbied for recognition of the importance of the role of foundations in funding the broader voluntary sector and, secondly, for separate status.

Although, at one level, the regulatory regime is not invasive (it does not, e.g. apply a disbursement rule[25]), the overarching concern of foundations was

[24] The reform process began in earnest with a report from the Treasury's Strategy Unit (2002), the proposals of which were supported by the Government in response; see Home Office (2003), eventually resulting in the Charities Act 2006.

[25] Although there are suggestions that one should be introduced similar to requirements in the legal regimes of the USA or Canada, see Driscoll and Grant (2009). Their research found a median payout of 3.5 % for 21 foundations in the study, alongside an overall increase in asset value above that necessary to maintain endowment.

with the operating burden placed upon them by the regulatory regime. By association, foundations also expressed concern about the effect that regime has upon philanthropy, both by discouraging wealthy donors from setting up foundations and by reducing the flexibility foundations have to distribute funds to a wide range of causes.[26] Research undertaken by the Association of Charitable Foundations published in 2004 had revealed that one-fifth of a small sample of philanthropists and their advisors who had set up a foundation in England and Wales had reservations about the regulatory burdens of doing so (Lloyd 2004).[27] This research underpinned the foundation lobby for a lighter regulatory regime. For example, the accounting guidance for charities in England and Wales in the *Accounting and Reporting by Charities, Statement of Recommended Practice* (SORP) was cited as a particular burden (Charity Commission 2005).[28] As noted above, the accounting regulations to which SORP is a recommendation of best practice require charities to submit accounts to the Charity Commission and which are subject to different levels of examination and audit depending upon the income threshold of the charity. The application of SORP highlights two principal but common problems with the regulatory regime: the first as an example of the hardening of best practice guidelines into a statutory requirement and the second as an example (along with reporting mechanisms such as information returns submitted by charities to the regulator) of a regulatory regime designed for fundraising charities but applied to all charities without nuance. The foundations' argument was that having a 'one size fits all' approach to all charities created a 'rigid and stifling regulatory parity' (Lord Hodgson, House of Lords Debate (Grand Committee), Hansard, Vol 669 col 301GC, 23 February 2005). In order to ameliorate this inflexibility, calls were made for lighter, more proportionate regulation,[29] to be served in part by placing an obligation on the Charity Commission as regulator to exercise its functions

[26] See in particular Joint Committee on the Draft Charities Bill (2004c, Memorandum from Nuffield Foundation DCH195), Joint Committee on the Draft Charities Bill (2004b, 16 June, Q138-139 (David Emerson, Chief Executive of the Association of Charitable Foundations)), Joint Committee on the Draft Charities Bill (2004b, Memorandum from the Association of Charitable Foundations, DCH23, paras 3, 6).

[27] They cited, in addition, monitoring by the Charity Commission and lack of privacy as disincentives. The commitment and motivations of the founder are important in discerning the real existence of a disadvantage to philanthropy from the regulatory regime. See the complaint by one that gift aid provides a better scheme because of the availability of tax relief without the burden of sifting through applications: 'Having a foundation attracts applications – somebody has to deal with them' cited in Joint Committee on the Draft Charities Bill (2004b, Supplementary Memorandum from the Association of Charitable Foundations, DCH276, Annex 2).

[28] For discussion, see Joint Committee on the Draft Charities Bill (2004a, para 132), Joint Committee on the Draft Charities Bill (2004c, Memorandum from Rayne Foundation DCH204, para 11.2–11.3, Memorandum from the Sainsbury Family Charitable Trusts DCH329). See now Charities (Accounts and Reports) Regulations 2008.

[29] Baroness Rawlings, supporting the views of Lord Sainsbury, put forward the view that proper regulation of grant-making foundations should simply be '*are the recipients of their donations proper charities, and are their expenses reasonable and legitimate?*' House of Lords Hansard Vol 668 pt 26, col 951, 20 January 2005.

proportionately and in a manner compatible with encouragement of charitable giving (Joint Committee on the Draft Charities Bill 2004a, para 137).[30]

Calls for regulatory sensitivity were considered by a Joint Committee of the House of Commons and House of Lords, set up to consider overall reform to charity law (Joint Committee on the Draft Charities Bill 2004a). The Association of Charitable Foundations argued before the committee for a regime for foundations which required no more than compliance with charitable objects and public benefit (Joint Committee on the Draft Charities Bill 2004b, Memorandum from the Association of Charitable Foundations DCH23). The argument for lighter regulation, however, was not unanimously held across the whole foundation sector. Arguments against light-touch regulation were put forward on the basis of the need for trust and confidence in the sector to be drawn from consistent regulation for all charities (Joint Committee on the Draft Charities Bill 2004c, Memorandum from Guy's and St Thomas' Charitable Foundation DCH154, para 4). These different views highlight the tension in the policy agendas underlying the law in this field: to encourage philanthropy but also to ensure accountability.

For its part, the Joint Committee did not recommend a separate regulatory regime for foundations, but focused more broadly upon the role that the Charity Commission as regulator can play in ameliorating regulatory burden. The Joint Committee recommended that the Commission be charged with an objective of increasing public trust and confidence in charities as well as stimulating philanthropy (Joint Committee on the Draft Charities Bill 2004a, para 139). Another recommendation was a further duty upon the Charity Commission to ensure that its regulation of foundations was 'reasonable, proportionate and fair' (Joint Committee on the Draft Charities Bill 2004c, Memorandum from Nuffield Foundation DCH195, para 6).[31] These proposals were primarily pushed forward by concerns over the treatment of grant-making foundations but also by a general concern with the bureaucratic and inflexible attitude of the Charity Commission towards regulation. The Government initially baulked at both of these recommendations from the Joint Committee on the basis that proportionality was already an inherent requirement in decision-making of public bodies (*Associated Provincial Picture Houses v Wednesbury Corporation* [1948] 1 KB 22) and that the achievement of stimulating philanthropy function could not be measured. Nevertheless amendments to the Charities Bill were passed which allowed the general duties of the Charity Commission, where reasonably practical, to contain a requirement when exercising its functions, to act 'in a way which is compatible with the encouragement of ... all forms of charitable giving' (Section 7 Charities Act 2006, Section 16 Charities Act 2011). In addition, the resulting Charities Act 2006 contains a requirement for the

---

[30] This was mooted before the Joint Committee by the Minister in charge of the sector at the time and taken up further in debates on the Bill. These duties are now set out in (Section 7 Charities Act 2006, Sections 16, 20 Charities Act 2011).

[31] This was vigorously debated in the passage of the Charities Bill; see, for example, House of Lords Debate (Grand Committee), Hansard, Vol 669 col 300–301, 304GC, 23 February 2005 (Lord Hodgson and Earl of Caithness).

Commission when exercising its functions and where relevant to have regard to the principles of best regulatory practice, viz. the principles that activities should be 'proportionate, consistent, transparent, and targeted only at cases in which action is needed' (Section 7 Charities Act 2006, Section 16 Charities Act 2011). Joined to these duties is a further one requiring the Charity Commission to have regard 'to the desirability of facilitating innovation by or on behalf of charities' (ibid).

These additional duties of the regulator are obviously significant for charitable foundations generally and grant-making foundations in particular and were taken to be a victory for foundations in the debate. However, context needs to be considered in terms of their breadth and impact. These statutory duties apply to the Charity Commission in carrying out its functions under the law. The Charity Commission's role is not as a principal law-making body, but as a regulator which applies the legislative and case law rules created by the executive and judiciary. The extent to which it can reverse existing and future legal requirements and practice is therefore circumscribed. The Charity Commission's application of the law falls under these statutory duties, but in light of the obligations on the Commission to apply the law, they give only a small margin for manoeuvre at the level of practice. Indeed, in the immediate implementation years post the Charities Act 2006, it is difficult to discern where and to what extent these duties have been specifically exercised by the Commission in favour of the regulation of foundations. It is in effect a symbolic legislative change rather than a substantive one, and, whilst regarded as an achievement by the charity foundation sub-sector, the concession in the legislation is not as extensive as such organisations may have hoped.

Two further specific legal issues affecting charitable foundations and creating a disincentive to philanthropy were raised in the Parliamentary reform debates, each championed in Joint Committee, Grand Committee and the House of Lords debates on the Bill by Lord Sainsbury, himself the founder of a foundation.[32] Uniting the two legal issues highlighted by Lord Sainsbury was the same overarching theme that both the legislation and its application by the Charity Commission as sector regulator were inflexible to the needs of foundations as a specific type of charity.

First, Lord Sainsbury made the point that the accounting disclosure requirements under SORP did not allow the details of a foundation's grant-making to be withheld from the public without receipt of special permission from the Charity Commission.[33] This was argued to be a disincentive to philanthropists wishing to create a foundation and who, for many reasons, may wish to retain anonymity. This was anomalous especially in light of the gift aid system which allows for public anonymity in giving and can equally be used to distribute funds efficiently and

[32] See, for example, House of Lords Hansard Vol 668 pt 26, col 902–905, 20 January 2005. See also Baroness Rawlings in the same debate at col 95 and House of Lords Debate (Grand Committee), Hansard, Vol 670 col 260-261GC, 8 March 2005.

[33] 'Of course the commissioners have full information, as must the Inland Revenue, but I believe that it is almost like a human right: you should be able to give money to a foundation and to make the give without drawing attention to yourself' House of Lords Debate (Grand Committee), Hansard, Vol 670 col 260-261GC, 8 March 2005 (Lord Sainsbury).

with much the same taxation effect. Of course, for planned giving, gift aid is only a partial solution, requiring donors to find recipients rather than receiving applications for grant-making, and it only permits tax relief on income rather than capital, but nevertheless on this point, gift aid permits anonymity for donors from public scrutiny of their donation choices.[34] In support, Lord Hodgson accepted that there needed to be balance between privacy and accountability, but rated more highly the need to protect the philanthropic urge to give to causes which a donor might not wish to be publicly linked.[35] Although Lord Bassam for the Government initially rejected an amendment to the Bill on the basis of full anonymity, the resulting Charities Act 2006 amended regulations for charitable trusts to allow non-disclosure during the lifetimes of the settlor (founder) or the settlor's (founder's) spouse or civil partner (Section 7 Charities Act 2006, Sections 132–135 Charities Act 2011).[36]

Secondly, Lord Sainsbury raised concerns about the requirements placed upon charity trustees to diversify and vary investment funds. He argued that many founders were able and had the desire to set up foundations through their own company assets and that a diversification rule, whilst sound investment practice, was unrealistic and a disincentive in these circumstances.[37] Lord Sainsbury was concerned that the requirements for diversification and variation of investments should not apply to a foundation which was using company stock, at least during the founder's lifetime. In fact, nuance in application of the diversification rules is already present in the law. Trustees of charities do not have separate duties and powers of investment, but fall under general trust law set out by the Trustee Act 2000. Under these provisions, trustees of all types of trusts have a broad statutory investment power to make any investments as if the trustees are entitled to the assets (Section 3 Trustee Act 2000).[38] This broad power can be excluded or restricted by the trust deed (Section 6 Trustee Act 2000). Powers of investment are subject to a duty of care under Section 1 of the Trustee Act 2000 requiring trustees to take such care and skill as is reasonable in the circumstances, a test interpreted in light of any specialist knowledge the trustee has or holds him/herself

[34] For a comparison of gift aid and foundations, see Siederer (2005).

[35] House of Lords Debate (Grand Committee), Hansard, Vol 670 col 268-269GC, 8 March 2005. Lord Sainsbury along with Lord Swinfen in the Grand Committee supported an unsuccessful proposal put forward by Lord Hodgson to allow charities the right to make anonymous donations; see House of Lords Debate (Grand Committee), Hansard, Vol 670 col 260-261GC, 8 March 2005.

[36] SORP does allow non-disclosure of grants in limited circumstances. The exceptions are currently set out in paragraph 200 and cover grants to individuals; grants made in the lifetime of either the settlor or the settlor's spouse/civil partner; grants which are neither material to the charities overall activities nor, if the grant is made to an institution, material to the context of institutional grants; and finally, where to disclose the grant would 'seriously prejudice either the grant maker or the recipient'.

[37] See House of Lords Hansard, Vol 672 pt 11, col 801, 7 June 2005. The point was also raised as a recommendation for change by Lloyd (2004).

[38] The exception is trustees of pensions trusts who fall under their own regulations: see Pensions Acts 1995 and 2004. For an examination of the practical barriers to investment, see Breeze (2008).

out as having, or which is reasonable to expect if he/she acts as a trustee in the ordinary course of business.[39] When exercising their investment powers, trustees should obtain and consider advice unless the trustee reasonably deems it unnecessary (Section 5 Trustee Act 2000). In addition, trustees must take into account the 'standard investment criteria' by considering the suitability of investments of the same kind and the need for diversification (Section 4 Trustee Act 2000). The standard investment criteria should be applied in a periodic review of the investments in which consideration should be given to diversification and variation. Under the legislative test, the standard investment criteria are to be applied as appropriate to the circumstances of the trust (a relevant consideration for grant-making foundations) and carried out subject to the duty of care.

In interpreting trustee duties, particularly trustees' duties on investment, the traditional approach has been to apply a 'best interests of the beneficiaries' test.[40] This test views the circumstances of investment from a beneficiary perspective, with the interest of the beneficiaries discerned from the purpose of the trust and a requirement that the benefit of an investment must not be too remote from that purpose. Existence as a grant-making foundation subject to and wishing to sustain the goodwill of the founder, especially where that founder is an existing or potential future donor, is a relevant consideration in the circumstances of the trust and can be considered alongside factors as the level of resources available to the trustees, rate and return; the long- and short-term requirements for a return on investment; and the needs of present and future beneficiaries (Charity Commission 2003, paras 57, 70–71, 73). Nevertheless, the duty of care under Section 1 of the Trustee Act 2000 applies to the deliberations of the trustees, and this consideration is simply one factor among many that can be taken into account. So, whilst considering the express wishes of the founder to retain company stock in one or a small number of investments is not unfeasible, it would need strong justification from the

[39] However, liability may be excluded by a trustee exemption clause; see Armitage v Nurse [1997] 3 WLR 1046. The Law Commission successfully recommended the adoption of a non-statutory rule of practice governing disclosure and explanation of exemption clauses: Law Commission (2006).

[40] See Cowan v Scargill [1985] Ch 270, Harries v Church Commissioners of England [1992] 1 WLR 1241. Examining investment from the best interests of the beneficiaries also means that trustees are somewhat limited in any ethical or social investment that they make, where the purpose of the investment is for market return. Charity trustees are less restricted than trustees of other types of trusts in applying ethical investment policies because they may more easily fall within the exceptions for non-financial criteria set out in Cowan v. Scargill [1985] Ch 270. For grant-making foundations, it may be harder to find a consensus amongst beneficiaries and so fall within one of the exceptions given the broad scope of their operations. Research from the Charity Commission suggests that only a small proportion of foundations employ an ethical investment policy, largely on the grounds of trustee caution to ensure maximum market returns; see Charity Commission (2009). Purpose-related investment where market returns are not the primary object of the investment are more common, and indeed, other research suggests that some foundations are manoeuvring within the investment parameters by using small proportions of endowment for purpose investment; see Bolton (2008).

perspective of the best interests of the beneficiaries rather than simply the best interests of the founder or the founder's company.

Amendments to the investment rules for endowed charitable trusts were later recommended by the Better Regulation Task Force (2005) set up to provide an independent review of the burden of regulation on charities. In its response, the Government accepted that trustees of grant-making charities may need to be better informed on the use and exercise of the diversity and variation requirements but held to the need for regulation to prevent possible abuse in the control of charitable assets (Office for the Third Sector 2006, 2). In a broader context, it is this focus upon protecting the interests of the public as well as donors and beneficiaries that make the recent call by the Association of Chief Executives of Voluntary Organisations (ACEVO) for the Charity Commission to be more encouraging in enabling charities to use a wider variety of financial vehicles including speculative financial ideas unlikely to reach fruition (ACEVO 2010, 19).

This position of the government on the overriding need for trust and confidence in the management of charities and in the charity sector more broadly underlined the debate on the Charities Act 2006, and it became a principal objective of the legislation to protect the 'charity brand' (Dunn and Riley 2004). As Lord Bassam noted, the 'spirit of the times' created an overriding need in the public interest for transparency and accountability to ensure public confidence in charities (House of Lords Debate (Grand Committee), Hansard, Vol 670 col 264GC, 8 March 2005) (Joint Committee on the Draft Charities Bill 2004b, Q985, Fiona Mactaggart, Parliamentary Under-Secretary for the Home Department). The regulatory framework for all charities, he argued, required a 'greater public interest' in transparency than privacy and the encouragement of philanthropy (Lord Bassam, House of Lords Debate (Grand Committee), Hansard, Vol 670 col 267GC, 8 March 2005). Thus, although important concessions were made for foundations in the Charities Act 2006 in setting out the statutory duties of the Charity Commission and tinkering at the edges on reporting requirements, specific foundation regulation (or indeed freedom from regulation) was ultimately rejected.

4.4 Conclusion

That the Charities Act 2006 did not provide far-reaching reform in favour of foundations is unsurprising given that to have done so would have involved a significant policy shift in the regulation of charities in England and Wales (so too given that it would also have been out of line with the regulation of charities in other parts of the UK). A consideration of if and how to separate out regulation of different types of charities or charitable purposes has not been part of the general charity law reform debate in England and Wales, and the law reformers were ill-prepared in this instance to have taken on the task. Lighter regulation was the best that foundations could have achieved, but even here the case for doing so was less evident in the face of a broader imperative for protection of the public through robust transparency and accountability mechanisms. This policy imperative highlights the difficulties charitable foundations face within the regulatory framework. The push for transparency and accountability was driven by a desire to ensure that the public have faith in and trust predominantly service delivery charities which are quite different in operation to foundations. The societal and regulatory challenges facing charitable foundations, viz. a need to encourage philanthropy through a less burdensome regime and to enable continued investment in and the sustainability of the sector, are longer-term concerns that are easily lost in the immediacy of other accountability-based policy and political incentives. This is not to say that the concessions that were made for foundations in terms of promotion of philanthropy through a duty upon the Charity Commission as sector regulator to act in a way that encourages charitable giving were not significant. But such concessions are hollow where the generalised nature of the duty will make it hard to apply and almost impossible to enforce.

Bibliography

ACEVO Taskforce on Better Regulation. 2010. *Public impact centred regulation for charities*. London: ACEVO.

Anheier, H., and D. Leat. 2002. *From charity to creativity: Philanthropic foundations in the 21st century, perspectives from Britain and beyond*. Stroud: Comedia.

Better Regulation Task Force. 2005. *Better regulation for civil society*. London: Better Regulation Task Force.

Bolton, M. 2008. *Mission possible: Emerging opportunities for mission-connected investment*. London: New Economics Foundation.

Breeze, B. 2008. *Investment matters: In search of better charity asset management*. London: Institute of Philanthropy.

Charity Commission. 2003. *Investment of charitable funds; Detailed guidance*. London: Charity Commission.

Charity Commission. 2005. *Accounting and reporting by charities, statement of recommended practice*. London: Charity Commission. http://www.charitycommission.gov.uk/Library/guidance/sorp05textcolour.pdf.

Charity Commission. 2009. *Firm Foundations: A snapshot of how trusts and foundations are responding to the economic downturn in 2009*. London: Charity Commission.

Clark, J., D. Kane, K. Wilding, and J. Wilton. 2010. *The UK civil society almanac 2010*. London: NCVO.

Community Foundation Network. 2010. Community Foundation Statistics 2008–09. http://www.communityfoundations.org.uk.

Daly, S. 2008. Institutional innovation in philanthropy: Community foundations in the UK. *Voluntas* 19: 219–241.

Dawson, I. 2000. Taxation of trades in the charities sector. In *The voluntary sector, the state and the law*, ed. A. Dunn, 177–192. Oxford: Hart Publishing.

Dawson, I., and A. Dunn. 2006. Governance codes of practice in the not-for-profit sector. *Corporate Governance: An International Review* 14(1): 33–42.

Driscoll, L., and P. Grant. 2009. *Philanthropy in the 21st century*. London: Alliance Publishing Trust.

Dunn, A., and C. Riley. 2004. Supporting the not-for-profit sector: The Government's review of charitable and social enterprise. *Modern Law Review* 67(4): 632–657.

Governance Code Steering Group. 2010. *Good governance: A code for the voluntary and community sector*, 2nd ed. London: Code Steering Group.
Home Office. 2003. *Charities and not-for-profits: A modern legal framework*. London: Home Office.
Joint Committee on the Draft Charities Bill. 2004a. Volume 1 minutes and evidence, HL167-I/HC 660-I.
Joint Committee on the Draft Charities Bill. 2004b. Volume 2 minutes of evidence, HL167-I/HC 660-I (16 June 2004).
Joint Committee on the Draft Charities Bill. 2004c. Volume 3 written evidence, HL167-I/HC 660-I.
Law Commission. 2006. *Trustee exemption clauses*. Law Com No 301, Cm6874.
Leat, D. 2001. United Kingdom. In *Foundations in Europe: Society, management and law*, ed. A. Schlüter, V. Then, and P. Walkenhorst. London: Directory of Social Change.
Lloyd, T. 2004. *Why rich people give*. London: Philanthropy UK, Association of Charitable Foundations.
Luxton, P. 2001. *The law of charities*. Oxford: Oxford University Press (new edition forthcoming 2012).
Morgan, G. 2010. The use of charitable status as a basis of regulation of nonprofit accounting. *Voluntary Sector Review* 1(2): 213–230.
Office for the Third Sector. 2006. *'Better regulation for civil society': The Government's response*. London: OTS.
Siederer, N. 2005. Is creating a foundation going out of fashion?. Funding for Change, London. http://www.good-foundations.co.uk/Writing/Downloads/Foundation%20creation.pdf.
Smith, J.A., and K. Borgmann. 2001. Foundations in Europe: The historical context. In *Foundations in Europe: Society, management and law*, ed. A. Schlüter, V. Then, and P. Walkenhorst. London: Directory of Social Change.
Strategy Unit. 2002. *Private action, public benefit*. London: Strategy Unit.
Traynor, T., and C. Chronnell. 2010. *The guide to the major trusts*, vol. 1, 2010/2011th ed. London: Directory of Social Change.
Wiggins, K. 2009. Aspinall Foundation sets up its own fundraising agency. Third Sector Online, December 2, 2009. http://www.thirdsector.co.uk/news/archive/971643/Aspinall-Foundation-sets-its-own-fundraising-agency/?DCMP=ILC-SEARCH.

Chapter 5
Foundations in France

Isabelle Combes

5.1 Introduction

This chapter deals with French foundation law and its potential need for change.

Firstly, it describes the historical background (Sect. 5.2) and explains the great evolution foundations have undergone, mostly in the last 30 years (Sect. 5.3).

Consequently, a reform of the rules applying to foundation is strongly needed and this chapter will examine the main issues that could be the focus of a new foundation law or code (Sect. 5.4).

5.2 The Historical Background

Throughout the Middle Ages, foundations developed in France as in other European countries, taking usually the form of hospitals or poorhouses under the auspices of the Catholic Church. Both the Church and monastic orders received important legacies and donations, in money and in kind, in order to create foundations.

After centuries, the wealth accumulated by foundations driven by the religious power drawn the attention and suspicion of the French monarchy which began to consider foundations not only as a meaning to evade royal taxes but also as concentrating wealth for the Church. Therefore, during the seventeenth and eighteenth centuries, the French kings began to limit the rights of existing foundations and to prohibit the creation of new ones (Pomey 1980).

The suspicion to foundations was reinforced during the French Revolution as the 1791 Le Chapelier Act established the state's monopoly on all activities performed

I. Combes (✉)
Expert Conseil Juridique et Fiscal, Fondation de France, 40 avenue Hoche, 75008 Paris, France
e-mail: Isabelle.Combes@fdf.org

C. Prele (ed.), *Developments in Foundation Law in Europe*, Ius Gentium: Comparative Perspectives on Law and Justice 39, DOI 10.1007/978-94-017-9069-7_5,

for the public benefit, this law being mainly directed against foundations, as well as against guilds and corporations. Moreover, during that revolutionary period, all the properties of the Church and of church-related foundations were confiscated, and many charitable institutions were obliged to close or were nationalised.

Napoleon enacted in 1804 the first Civil Code, which authorised individuals to make legacies and donations to public benefit institutions, subject to a formal state authorization in the form of a decree. Such a heavy procedure explains that during the nineteenth and the first half of the twentieth centuries, a very few number of foundations were created in France.

The first law on foundations was enacted only in 1987 and was completed by a second law in 1990 which introduced in France the new status of corporate foundations (*fondations d'entreprise*).

5.3 The Existing Situation and Its Evolution

5.3.1 The Legal Framework

In France, foundations are not ruled by the Civil Code, but are currently governed by the law of 23 July 1987 and the law of 4 July 1990. Until 1987, foundations were governed by general regulations applicable to a large range of non-profit organisations such as associations and were eligible for state recognition as a matter of administrative practice. But although existing as a specific legal form, they did not enjoy from a legally defined legal status. This is the reason why, in 2010, there were only around 2,300 foundations of various forms in France.

Why are there so few foundations in France? There are at least three reasons that have hampered the emergence of foundations in France (Lemaistre and other authors 2007).

First, an explanation that has often been given for the insufficient development of foundations in France is the state's stifling grip on the concept of public utility and its fear of seeing any private competition develop that might, by accumulating wealth, constitute a counterweight to its authority. This distrust, which took the form of the requirement for prior authorisation, lasted for centuries: the *Ancien Ré gime*'s distrust of institutions often linked to religious authority accumulating inalienable property, condemnation by the French Revolution, a persistent reluctance, even now, to encourage instruments perceived as being made to measure for the rich. The modern history of foundations is marked by the creation in the late 1960s of the Fondation de France, a general-purpose intermediate body entrusted with developing private philanthropy by allowing the establishment under its legal auspices of individual foundations of varying size. Nearly 890 foundations were set up under these auspices, of which 610 were still operating in 2007, providing a shot in the arm for private philanthropy.

The second explanation for the small number of French foundations is undoubtedly the huge success in France of non-profit associations. Much more recent than foundations, since they date from the well-known 1901 Act, these voluntary associations have developed enormously as a result of the freedoms they enjoy. Unlike a foundation, an association does not need resources or, consequently, any authorisation to be formed. Whereas in 2010, only 2,264 foundations have emerged from centuries of tradition (593 public utility foundations, 262 corporate foundations, 26 scientific cooperation foundations, 20 university foundations, 9 partnership foundations, 861 funds and foundations under the auspices of other public utility foundations, and 493 endowment funds), and in just a hundred years, more than a million associations have been set up. Given the constraints in creating a foundation and the freedom of associations, these figures do not perhaps properly reflect the reality of the situation. Overtime, as many voluntary associations have increased their resources and put their activities on a more professional footing, they have become endowed institutions, whose original democratic purpose has gradually faded, and are now in practice like foundations.

The third reason, less often put forwards and yet key to explaining the poor development of foundations, is French inheritance law. The French Civil Code contains a major obstacle to the development of private foundations: the reserved share of an estate, designed to protect the transmission of assets within a family. This public law provision stipulates that descendants automatically receive a share of the deceased's fortune: 50, 66 or 75 % of the estate, depending on the number of surviving heirs. In some cases, heirs who consider their interests to have been harmed by major donations made by the deceased during his or her lifetime are entitled to sue (even in the criminal courts) to have their proportional rights recalculated on the basis of the estate plus the contested donations. This recourse is available to direct heirs for 10 years after the testator's death. Whereas it is hard to imagine a child contesting their parents' philanthropic activities while they are alive, it is not certain that the same heir, once their parents are dead, will not be tempted to turn against an institution to which they owe nothing, especially when one considers that systems of family values may no longer be as homogeneous and permanent as they were some generations ago. The 23 June 2006 reform of inheritance law now allows the possibility, formerly prohibited, of concluding an "agreement on future succession": the protected heirs may now renounce in advance their right to contest the bequest. This "informed" renunciation may only involve one or more specified persons or entities, which includes an existing or pending foundation. This renunciation is possible only for adult protected heirs, must be concluded in the presence of two notaries, and may only be revoked in a limited number of cases. The purpose is to enable the donor to make a promise or express an intention in the full knowledge of his or her protected heirs, who may wish to associate themselves with the project. Without fundamentally changing the principles of French inheritance law, this opportunity makes the law more flexible in order to respect both the freedom of adult heirs and the generosity of the donor. In the absence of an agreement on future succession, the period during which an heir may contest the will was reduced from 30 to 10 years after the testator's death.

From the point of view of the beneficiaries, and consequently foundations, this provision secures major donations made during the founders' lifetimes and those of donors who are parents.

In 2008, the endowment fund was created with the ambition to help France to catch up in terms of private philanthropy. If we stick to the number of funds created, the result is instructive: in 3 years, 757 endowment funds were created. It seems clear that the endowment fund moves things in philanthropy in France. However, the actual financial impact of this new legal tool on private philanthropy should be relativised: many endowment funds have been created without any capital, sometimes with the purpose of collecting pledges and sometimes with the purpose of making fundraising.

The 23 July 1987 Act on the development of philanthropy defines foundation as "*the act by which one or more individuals or legal entities decide on the irrevocable transfer of goods, rights or resources for the accomplishment of a not-for-profit endeavour of general interest*". With the endowments they manage, foundations may provide services in various fields—hospitals, retirement homes, research centres, museums, social welfare services, etc.—or fund voluntary association projects, prizes or scholarships.

The French system of foundations is characterised by oversight by the public authorities, the irrevocable nature of the resources they receive and their long-term action and management procedures. These four points are the result of a long heritage and yet have gradually changed over the last 10 years.

When they began and during their lives, foundations were long closely bound by the guidance and direct monitoring of the public authorities. The French system of foundations still retains the hallmarks of practices begun under the monarchy: the creation of a foundation was subject to the prior approval of a competent authority. Royal authorisation was succeeded by government assent and then the assent of the Prime Minister in the form of a decree. For foundations with no legal autonomy, approval needs to be formally granted by the body requested to establish them under its auspices. For many years, the presence of state representatives on foundation boards was the French system's way of ensuring the public interest. However, the *corporate foundation* defined in 1990 and the *public utility foundation* of 2003 may have boards with no representatives of the public authorities. More recently, a new legal tool was implemented in France: the *fonds de dotation* or endowment funds, the creation of which is not subject to any prior authorisation from the government, but requires a simple declaration with the prefecture. Those recent developments clarify the relations with the state as guardian: while enshrining the private nature of foundations, it redefines the role of government oversight as an external guarantor of public utility.

The irrevocable nature of resources transferred to foundations is clearly stated in the 23 July 1987 Act on the development of philanthropy. There has been no challenge to it since then. The principle of long-term action was for many years a central element in specifically defining French foundations when compared with foundations in other countries. To plan for the long term, foundations must possess an endowment sufficient for their revenues to finance their annual budgets. For decades, all *public utility foundations* were designed on that condition. In 1990, the long-term requirement was first challenged by the creation of the *corporate foundation*, basically designed as a project of limited duration, funded by financial flows and not the revenues from a capital fund. This was the first step towards a radical modernisation of the instrument, confirmed by the redesign in 2003 of standard by-laws for *public utility foundations*: the model now accepts a variant with expendable capital. In actual fact, the Fondation de France has been accepting the establishment of *individualised foundations* under its guardianship since 1969, but because this procedure occurred within a structure that was itself permanent, it did not officially challenge the principle of long-term foundations.

Finally, while voluntary associations are institutions in which major decisions are made by a General Meeting of members, foundations and endowment funds are governed by smaller boards that do not necessarily represent all the contributions they receive.

5.3.2 Types of Foundation

In 2011, French foundations may be categorised in four main sorts and four specialist arrangements. The 1990 Act followed the intention of the philanthropy development act to protect the name "foundation" by restricting this term to three forms of organisation:

1. Public utility foundations
2. Corporate foundations
3. Sheltered foundations hosted by an approved body

In 2006 and 2007, parliament encouraged the development of foundations for research and higher education: three specialist arrangements emerged that were directly inspired by the first three types, to which has been added in 2009 a fourth one for hospitals:

(a) Scientific cooperation foundations
(b) University foundations
(c) Partnership foundations
(d) Hospital foundations

Finally, in 2008, the French government decided to create a new mechanism to develop philanthropy in France: the endowment fund, the legal definition of which clearly associates it to all pre-existing French foundations. The law for modernization of the economy of 4 August 2008 defines it as "*a non-for-profit legal entity which receives and manages assets and legal rights of any kind irrevocably transferred to it for free, and which uses income derived from their capitalization to perform public-benefit activities or to distribute them to other non-profit legal entities for the purpose of their own public-benefit activities*".

Public Utility Foundation

The creation of a public utility foundation requires state authorisation by Prime Ministerial decree, countersigned by the Minister of the Interior, after receiving the opinion of the Council of State.

The solidity and permanence of these autonomous foundations are based on their assets. In theory, the income from their endowment should cover their expenses and finance their social missions. To achieve long-term survival, they must also protect their assets against monetary erosion. The new model for foundations with expendable endowments, designed in 2003 for medium-sized and small endowments and projects, has in practice been strictly reserved by the Council of State for causes that are deemed to be limited in time and for research foundations.

Public utility foundations were for many years governed by a board of directors or trustees comprising roughly equal numbers of founders, representatives of the public authorities and eminent persons co-opted for their competence in the foundation's fields of action. Since 2003, it has been possible to opt for a dual system of governance (supervisory board and directorate) and to have a government commissioner as sole representative of the state, no longer as a joint decision-maker but as an observer entrusted with ensuring that the public interest is respected.

Corporate Foundations

In 1990, following requests from bodies in the corporate sector, French law instituted corporate foundations. Since a public utility foundation must have a permanent endowment, it was too rigid and complicated a structure for the philanthropic purposes of a for-profit enterprise subject to the ups and downs of business life and commercial strategy. A more flexible intermediate structure was consequently needed.

As a limited-period foundation with a budget based not on income from capital but from resources contributed annually by the enterprise, this new legal structure is established by a prefectoral decree in the department the corporate head office is situated. The founder must commit for a period of 5 years which is renewable and a minimum total endowment of 152,500 Euros. In return for the corporate foundation's right to bear the name of the company that established it, the law strictly limits its authorisation to raise funds from benefactors other than the company's own employees.

Since 2002, the requirement for an endowment has been removed for corporate foundations.

Sheltered Foundations

The 1990 Act creating corporate foundations also entailed the possibility of creating sheltered foundations with no legal status of their own, which consist of the "irrevocable transfer of goods, rights or resources for the accomplishment of a not-for-profit endeavour of public interest to a public utility foundation whose bylaws have been approved for that purpose". In reply to an enquiry from the Minister of the Interior, an opinion of the Council of State, issued by the Interior section at its 25 October 1988 session, confirmed that conditional transfers to the *Institut de France* could be called foundations.

As of 1 January 2011, there are 42 bodies in France that are legally entitled to shelter, or host, foundations, of which the most important are the *Institut de France*, *Fondation de France*, *Fondation du Judaïsme Français*, *Fondation Caisse d'Épargne pour les solidarités* and *Fondation pour le Protestantisme Français*. The purpose and operation of the foundations they host must comply with their own by-laws. For example, a "mother" foundation dedicated to health cannot host "daughters" concerned with the arts. Similarly, a grant-making organisation cannot really host sheltered foundations with an operational purpose: management of a museum, hospital, retirement home, provision of meals or clothes, etc.

In 2003, the French Parliament approved a historic increase in the tax incentives for philanthropy, and the state decided to speed up the collection of private funds for research and education. To that end, two further acts were passed for additional special arrangements for foundations dedicated to those purposes.

Scientific Cooperation Foundations

On the initiative of the Ministry of Research, the scientific cooperation foundation was created by the 18 April 2006 Programme Act on research. This new status is intended to relax the conditions for managing major research projects while not departing from the requirements of accounting transparency and the management of strictly public projects. The new type of foundation is dedicated to establishing and financing advanced research thematic networks (RTRA) linking public or private research or higher education establishments and private legal entities. These networks are intended to pursue projects of scientific excellence in one or more research areas, including corporate participation.

Partnership Foundations

The 1 August 2007 Act on universities' freedoms and responsibilities, known as the Pécresse Act, introduced the possibility for public scientific, cultural or vocational establishments to set up not-for-profit legal entities, to be called partnership foundations. This status authorises a variety of founders: universities and public research centres may work with enterprises.

University Foundations

The August 2007 Pécresse Act also authorises public scientific, cultural or vocational establishments—universities—to manage their own foundations with no legal status. These university foundations are the result of an irrevocable transfer of goods, rights and resources by one or more founders to universities for the accomplishment of one or more purposes or activities relevant to their missions. They are managed by the "parent" university in an individual manner, like foundations sheltered by public utility foundations or the *Institut de France*.

A forthcoming decree of the *Conseil d'Etat* will provide a more detailed framework for the operation of these foundations.

Hospital Foundations

The 21 July 2009 Act on hospital reform and on patients, health and territories authorises hospitals to set up not-for-profit legal entities, to be called hospital foundations.

Fonds de Dotations

In 2008, as the foundations framework appeared to have matured through a process of opening and relaxing, a new legal tool, the endowment funds (*fonds de dotation*), was created by the French government. Initially inspired by the Anglo-Saxon endowment funds (a capitalization fund whose income is used for public benefit), the French endowment fund was finally developed in a much wider aim. A French endowment fund may be, for example, a structure without any capital managing resource flows (collection, gifts, legacies, etc., eventually for a single designated beneficiary), a structure carrying out income-generating activities, a structure itself leading the activities of public benefit, etc. All forms previously taken by the foundations will be under this new status. What distinguishes the endowment from traditional foundations is the most radically liberal approach of the public benefit which it arises and, thus, the rupture it represents with a centuries-old French practice of guardianship by the public authorities.

Exclusively dedicated to the management of assets from private sponsors, the creation of endowment funds is freed from the control of the French administrative authorities. No prior authorization is required for their creation: like the association governed by the 1901 law, their creation is only subject to a simple declaration with the prefecture. No representation of the state is imposed in their governing bodies. The proposed framework for their governance is very flexible: only the existence of a board of directors of at least three members is required, as well as an Investment Committee when the endowment exceeds a certain amount. Their constitution and operating process are left completely free.

However, endowment funds are not fully freed from all public controls. The prefect is the controlling authority for endowment funds: he is deemed to control the regularity of their operation and may initiate procedure leading to their dissolution when their public benefit mission is no longer assured.

5.4 The Need to Reform Foundation Law and the Focus of a New Foundation Law or Code in France

5.4.1 The Need to Reform Foundation Law

Contrary to what exist in other countries such as in Italy, for example, the French Civil Code does not contain any provision relating to foundations. Moreover, whereas French associations are mainly ruled by one law, dated 1901, French foundations are governed by at least eight laws and more numerous decrees and administrative regulations. Moreover, many of the legal provisions applicable to foundations are not *special* ones, but are only an extension to foundations of regulations originally set forth with respect to associations only. Therefore, in many cases, those provisions appear as not being fully adapted to foundations.

In 1996 already, an official report published by the Conseil d'Etat (the highest administrative court in France) recognised that the 1987 and 1990 Acts, despite the obvious progress they represented, did not fully compensate the disadvantages of the lack of a single text (Conseil d'Etat 1997). In 2011, this observation is still valid; no common text having been adopted since the publication of this study.

The need for a single act (or a code) for French foundations results from various legal reasons.

First of all, it is not satisfactory that provisions as fundamental as the administrative control on some acts or on the terms of the dissolution of a foundation are ruled only by its by-laws, even framed in the *model statutes* proposed by the Conseil d'Etat.

Secondly, foundations do not have a statute of their own. In many cases, the law applicable to them is actually the more generally applicable to that broader category of institutions called *of public interest*. However, in some areas, the problems faced by foundations might be more easily solved by the rules applicable to commercial companies.

Thirdly, the adoption of a special law or of a code is necessary in order to clarify the legal status of foundations in the eyes of candidate founders. If the formation of foundations is a difficult exercise, it is largely due to the absence of a global text that precisely defines the conditions of creation. The *model statutes* are indeed published, but they are only indicative, even if over time, the Ministry of Interior and the Conseil d'Etat have interpreted them in an increasingly strict manner. In addition, these *models* exist only with respect to public utility foundations and are not necessarily adaptable to other categories of foundations or to endowment funds. It seems that it is for the law to set a minimum of mandatory rules; the right of foundations cannot remain indefinitely a mostly jurisprudential one.

It is also quite ironic that the French Parliament when adopting some new laws (such as on the occasion of the creation by law of the *Fondation du Patrimoine*) has referred to a *general status of foundations*, whereas such a general status is still only partially resolved by law.

The coexistence of eight different legal statuses could also become an obstacle to the development of foundations in France. Potential funders seem now quite lost and are no longer able to decide by themselves which of those statuses is the most adapted to their personal project. It could probably be more efficient for the development of the foundations sector to simplify the situation by limiting the number of such statuses to only four different ones: public utility foundations, corporate foundations, non-autonomous foundations and endowment funds, each of them corresponding to a specific need for founders.

In addition, the development of community foundations in France, linked or not to local authorities, will probably be another major issue in the future years.

5.4.2 Focus of a New Foundation Law or Code

In its 1996 study, which remains still relevant for a large part, the *Conseil d'Etat* classified its proposals into three categories: those under the law, those under a regulatory act and those under the model statute. Although we will not classify our own suggestions in the same manner, we consider that the following issues should be addresses by a unique law (or code) on foundations.

Purpose

All existing legal texts provide that the purpose of a foundation or an endowment fund must be of public utility, but this concept has not been clearly defined. It is generally considered that public utility corresponds to the interest of the community of citizens, opposing in it to the particular interests. An instruction issued on 10 October 2006 by the Ministry of Youth, Sports and Associative Life and sent to the *Préfets* responsible for the approval of associations confirms that "*generally speaking, is considered as of public utility the mission carried by a private person who has for object to return a bigger service, because it satisfies a need guaranteed by the Constitution or the law, because this service is useful for a definite public, or because its realization will have favourable direct or indirect impacts for the public generally*".

Besides this almost unofficial definition, it must be noted that, from a purely tax standpoint, the application of a favourable tax regime to French associations and foundations does not depend on the fact that they are of public utility, but on that fact that they are non-profit organisations performing their activities for "general interest". To that extent, the legislator, through article 200 and 238 bis of the French general tax code, considers as being of general interest actions carried out in the philanthropic, educational, scientific, social, humanitarian, sports or family fields, or which contribute to the development of the artistic heritage, to the protection of natural environment or to the circulation of French culture, language and scientific knowledge.

As the definitions of "public utility" and "general interest" do not coincide, it may happen that a foundation, although considered as performing public utility activities from a civil standpoint, is not regarded as being of general interest from a tax standpoint. This is notably the case for foundations performing microcredit activities.

It should then be necessary that such an issue be considered in a foundation law or code so as to harmonise the civil and fiscal approach of the public utility/general interest notions.

Endowment

In France, no legislative or statutory text brings precision on the minimum amount of the initial endowment for a foundation. The Conseil d'Etat, as the competent authority having drafted the model statutes for public utility foundations, estimates that this amount must be in coherence with the ambitions of the founders, which means that the initial endowment must produce income sufficient enough to fulfil the purpose of the foundation for perpetuity. In practice, the Conseil d'Etat has fixed the minimum amount of the initial endowment for public utility foundations to Euros 1.5 to –2 million, but this position is not an official one and may vary from one foundation to another.

It then appears necessary that such an issue be considered in a foundation law or code so as to officialise a minimum amount of initial endowment which would be accepted unanimously as being sufficient to ensure a perpetual life to public utility foundations.

Different Statuses

As already mentioned, eight different statuses exist now in France for foundations. Although this large offer enables any kind of persons (whether individuals, companies or even public or semi-public bodies) to act as founders, it may also be considered as confusing since some of those statuses explicitly refer to the rules applicable to other ones for their management and functioning. As an example, legal provisions relating to scientific cooperation foundations clearly refer to the legal rules applicable to public utility foundations. Similarly, partnership foundations are regulated by the same rules applicable to corporate foundations.

Therefore, one suggestion could be to reduce the number of the existing statuses to only four:

1. Public utility foundations
2. Corporate foundations
3. Sheltered foundations hosted by an approved body
4. Endowment funds

Partnership foundations, university foundations, hospital foundations and scientific cooperation foundations remaining only as under categories of those main statuses.

The common or specific rules related to each of these four statuses could be included within a unique text (law or code), which would govern all the aspects of the foundations law:

(a) Mode of creation
(b) Minimum initial endowment
(c) Duration
(d) Governance and control
(e) Rules of dissolution

The reform should then combine all existing laws related to foundations and entirely rewrite them in a unique legal document—whether a law or a code—and not merely correct some of their rules.

In addition, European decisions should also be taken into account. To that respect, all the work of EFC and of the European Commission regarding the proposal for a European Foundation Statute should be considered.

Governance

The various laws on French foundations do not contain any specific rule about the foundations' governance; they generally only deal with the need to appoint a board, a president and, in some cases, a treasurer or a financial committee. Therefore, no complete rule about the structure of the foundations' governance is contained in those laws; besides, the model statutes for public utility foundations as enacted by the Conseil d'Etat contain specific provisions to that respect, but they cannot be considered as legal provisions.

Once again, the adoption of a large law or code relating to foundations could make up the lack of such provisions and regulate all governance issues.

Merger

Neither French civil law nor French tax law allows a foundation to merge with another one. Up to now, a merger of two foundations may only be realised through the creation of new foundations by the founders of the two existing foundations, followed by the dissolution of such existing foundations and the devolution of their assets to the newly created one. It may also be observed that such an operation can be realised with no tax consequences only when the newly created foundation is a public utility one.

A major reform of foundation law could then include specific provisions allowing mergers of foundations and explain the tax regime applicable to such an operation.

Tax Regime

Finally, a reform of foundation law in France should also cover some tax issues. As an example, the performance of economic activities by a foundation is not regulated by civil law in France. It is thus not completely clear whether a French foundation may legally carry out economic activities or not, and if so, whether such economic activities must be subsidiary to its non-profit ones. The sole regulations of this issue derive from the provisions of the French tax code and from the related comments published by the tax authorities. Pursuant to those administrative comments, some French foundations may perform some related economic activities without challenging their non-profit status when such economic activities remain subsidiary to their non-profit ones and the profits derived from them do not exceed an annual ceiling of €60,000. However, this exception only applies to public utility foundations, corporate foundations and endowment funds, other foundations being excluded from this possibility although it does not sound logical.

Another example relates to the possibility offered to a French foundation to hold the majority of the capital of a corporation. The law of 2 August 2005 relating to the development of small and middle enterprises which has set up this possibility in its article 29, was clearly inspired by the situation existing in some European countries where most industrial companies are held by private foundations so as to limit the risk of aggressive takeover bids. The purpose of the law of 2005 was then to offer the same protection to French industrial companies.

However, in the same time, the French tax authorities published comments pursuant to which the fact for a foundation to hold the majority of the capital of a commercial or industrial company is regarded as the performance of an economic activity, resulting to the foundation becoming fully subject to commercial taxes.

Due to this restrictive approach of the French tax authorities, only one French industrial group has been transferred under the control of a French foundation since the implementation of the law of August 2005.

To be regarded as a non-profit entity from a tax standpoint, a French foundation is subject to a non-distribution constraint, that is, profits, if any, as well as investment income derived from the foundation's assets cannot be distributed to the founders or the directors, but must be dedicated to the foundation's scope and activity. However, this principle results only from the comments published by the tax authorities. French foundations would be in a more secured position if this principle is regulated by a legal text, a provision of a specific code for foundations.

5.5 Conclusion

In the 2000s, the French government has encouraged citizens—individuals, companies, associations, etc.—to invest in the philanthropic sector, with tax provisions but also by creating new tools, so that private donations and sponsorship become able to take over public financing in a context of declining public funding.

Nevertheless, the attitude of the French government towards foundations remains ambiguous. On the one hand, the government encourages and simplifies the creation of foundations by implementing numerous new statuses, among which the new status of endowment funds. On the other hand, in contrast to such encouragement, the government remains constantly suspicious of public utility foundations, by restricting their management and activities, although their status is the most controlled one.

With respect to taxes, several laws have encouraged donations as an income tax deduction of 66 % of the amount of gifts for individuals as well as a wealth-tax reduction of 75 % ceiled at € 50,000. However, since a few years, the French government is regularly considering to reduce tax advantages allowed to French taxpayers. Although the tax advantages related to gift and donations made to foundations have not been modified or reduced up to now, many managers of French foundations and associations dread that such a situation could occur within few months or years, and particularly after the 2012 elections. Then, it appears necessary that the tax regime applicable to gift and donations made to foundations is strengthened, such types of resources being the most important ones for foundations and associations.

The foundations sector in France is then in full development, but the money involved remains still very modest in comparison to the situation in other countries over the world. And even though a cultural revolution would occur to give a central position to sponsorship in France, philanthropy will probably never be substituted for state funding, which remain major in France.

Bibliography

About Foundations and Endowment Funds in France

Baron, E., and X. Delsol. 2004. *Fondations reconnues d'utilité publique et d'entreprise*. Paris: Juris Association.

Binder, O. 2005. *Guide juridique et fiscal du mécénat et des fondations à l'usage des entreprises et des entrepreneurs*. Paris: Admical.

Conseil d'État. 1997. *Rendre plus attractif le droit des fondations*. Paris: La Documentation Française.

Fondation de France. 2011. *Les fondations et fonds de dotation. Constitution-gestion-Evolution*. Paris: Juris Editions.

IFA. 2008. *La gouvernance des associations et fondations*. Paris: Eyrolles.

Lemaistre, D., E. Hannah, J. Le Marchand, A. Floret, and O. de Laurens. 2007. *Foundations in France in 2007, Founders, fields of action, economic weight*. Paris: Observatoire of the Fondation de France.

Pomey, M. 1980. *Traité des Fondations d'utilité publique*. Paris: PUF.

About Fondation de France

Broca, B. 2009. *La Fondation de France 1994–2008. Une aventure très humaine*. Paris: Perrin.

Fondation de France. 1992. *Histoire de cœurs. Portrait de trente et une foundations*. Paris: Fondation de France.

Pavillon, E. 1995. *La Fondation de France 1969–1994. L'invention d'un mécénat contemporain*. Paris: Editions Anthropos historiques.

Chapter 6
Resolved and Still Unresolved Problems in German Foundation Law

Birgit Weitemeyer

6.1 Historical Development in Civil Law Relating to Foundations

The legal preconditions for founding legal entities under German private law are shaped by their increasing *emancipation from governmental* collaboration (Schmidt 1998). For the majority of private law legal entities, for instance, for the AG (stock corporation), GmbH (limited liability company), cooperative society (*Genossenschaft*) and non-profit association (*Idealverein*), special legislation of HGB (*Handelsgesetzbuch* – German Commercial Code), GmbHG (German Act on Limited Liability Companies), GenG (German Act on Commercial and Economic Cooperatives), AktG (German Act on Stock Corporations) and BGB (*Bürgerliches Gesetzbuch* – German Civil Code) of 1900 replaced the concessionary system under which legal personality was granted by governmental licence, by a system of normative provisions. Under the normative system, the founders have a subjective right to be recorded in a register if the preconditions for registration stipulated by statute have been met. Up until today, this situation is only different for the commercial association pursuant to Sect. 22 BGB and for a foundation pursuant to Sect. 80 BGB. The historical legislator considered that the legal power enabled through the multi-purpose foundation in conformity with the common good (*gemeinwohlkonforme Allzweckstiftung*), namely, the legal power to dedicate assets to a wide range of possible objects for an unlimited period of time and thus to

The text is based on Chapter 1 of the work by Hüttemann et al. (2011). I would like to thank Dr. Christine Franzius for her valuable assistance in drafting the text.

B. Weitemeyer (✉)
Lehrstuhl für Steuerrecht, Institut für Stiftungsrecht und das Recht der Non-Profit-Organisationen, Bucerius Law School, Hochschule für Rechtswissenschaft, Jungiusstraße 6, 20355 Hamburg, Germany
e-mail: birgit.weitemeyer@law-school.de; http://www.law-school.de

C. Prele (ed.), *Developments in Foundation Law in Europe*, Ius Gentium: Comparative Perspectives on Law and Justice 39, DOI 10.1007/978-94-017-9069-7_6,

perpetuate both the wealth and also the objects of the foundation, constituted an extension considerably exceeding classical ownership powers that required state control (Reichstag Commission 1899, 961 et seq.; Reuter 2011 margin no. 3.1). This is the reason why the BGB made the legal personality of a foundation subject to *official approval* being granted (Sect. 80 BGB old version). Since under the constitutional law applying at the time, legislative competence for public law lay with the states of the German Reich, the BGB only provided that, in addition to the endowment transaction, the creation of a foundation with legal personality required the approval of the competent federal state, but it did not stipulate any preconditions for this. The *Länder* subsequently made very different use of the possibility of subjecting the private law relating to foundations to public law supervision (Reuter 2011 margin no. 3.3).

After the Second World War, the *Länder* of the young Federal Republic of Germany and also the *German Democratic Republic* gradually replaced the state foundation laws of the old German states (Weitemeyer and Franzius 2011 margin no. 2.1 et seqq.). Based on Art. 74 Sect. 1 of the old version of the GG (*Grundgesetz* – German basic law), the matter was subject to the concurrent legislation of the Federation for which the *Länder* only have regulatory powers if and to the extent that the Federation does not exercise them (Art. 72 (1) GG old version) and the establishment of equal living conditions throughout the federal territory or the maintenance of legal or economic unity renders federal regulation necessary (Art. 72 (2) GG old version). Thus in the 1960s already, the different structuring of public law powers for foundations triggered off the call for a reform of foundation law with greater exploitation of the legislative competence of the Federation. The 44th forum of the Association of German Jurists (*44. Deutscher Juristentag*) raised the question "Should foundation law be unified and reformed by federal law and if so, what should be the basic principles?" (Mestmäcker 1962; Ballerstedt and Salzwedel 1962).[1] The accompanying paper by *Ernst Joachim Mestmäcker* came out in favour of having *stronger privatisation and deregulation of the law relating to foundations* based on examinations of comparative law (Mestmäcker 1962). This went hand in hand with a discovery of charitable foundations as part of a third sector between the market and the state which were able to relieve the state of some of its own social duties by providing funding and through the founders' own initiatives (Jakob 2006, 18 footnote 53). Nonetheless, it still took more than 40 years for the *Reform of the German Law Relating to Foundations* to come into effect through the Act to Modernise the Law Relating to Foundations of 15.7.2002 which was enacted on 1.9.2002 (BGBl. I 2002). In 1974, an inter-ministerial working group on foundation law established by the federal government still had denied that there was any need for reform (Inter-Ministerial Working Group on Foundation Law 1977). And thus –

[1] In this respect and with respect to the historical development in general, see Reuter (2012) margin no. 56 et seqq.; Hüttemann and Rawert (2011) preliminary remark on §§ 80 et seqq. margin no. 63 et seqq.

although it failed to quell the debate on reform – it did bring the legislator's reform considerations to a standstill for a long period of time.

It was not until the bill to advance foundations was put forward by the parliamentary party *Bündnis 90/Die Grünen* in 1997 (BT-Drucks. 13/9320 1997) that political debate on a reform of foundation law was reinvigorated.[2] The bill was based on the consideration that effective advancement of foundations in Germany would have to prioritise the modernisation of the civil law relating to foundations basically stemming from the nineteenth century and fragmented between the Federation and the *Länder*, accompanied by tax relief some people considered to be necessary (BT-Drucks. 13/9320 1997, Explanatory Memorandum of the bill).

6.1.1 Act to Modernise the Law Relating to Foundations of 2002

Genesis of the Act

The Act to Modernise the Law Relating to Foundations of 15.7.2002 (BGBl. I 2002; came into effect 1.9.2002) only partially adopted the proposals put forward in the discussion on improving foundation law whilst other demands were not considered to require regulation. The demands not taken up included the transition from the concession system to a merely *judicial registration procedure* (BT-Drucks. 13/9320 1997). In a bill dating from 1999, the FDP parliamentary party had even demanded a system under which a foundation could be established merely by having the endowment transaction notarised in accordance with the *system of free establishment of corporations* (BT-Drucks. 14/336 1999; differently in the amendment motion BT-Drucks. 14/3043 2000 and in the further bill of BT-Drucks. 14/5811 2001). In a motion entitled *Modern Foundation Law for the 21st Century*, the CDU/CSU parliamentary party demanded a judicial registration procedure and sought for the supervision of foundations to be transferred to a self-management corporation similar to that of the English Charity Commission (BT-Drucks. 14/2029 1999, 8 et seq.). The following proposals were not put into effect either: the introduction of a uniform register of foundations for the whole of Germany with or without disclosure effect (BT-Drucks. 13/9320 1997), subjecting foundations to the general *accounting regulations* of Sect. 242 et seqq. HGB (BT-Drucks. 13/9320 1997), introducing a time limit for *family foundations* for family use (BT-Drucks. 13/9320 1997 on § 81 para. 2) and the explicit prohibition of foundations merely pursuing the purpose of continuing to operate an enterprise (*foundation where the enterprise itself is the only object of the foundation*

[2] With respect to the further development and the individual proposals, see Rawert (2001) p. 146 et seqq.; Hüttemann and Rawert (2011) preliminary remark on §§ 80 et seqq. margin no. 48 et seqq.

(*Unternehmensselbstzweckstiftung*)) in accordance with the legal concept of Sect. 22 BGB (BT-Drucks. 13/9320 1997).

The *Bund-Länder Working Group* set up by the German Federal Justice Ministry presented its report in October 2001 after hearing and consultation with associations and experts (Bund-Länder Working Group 2001). The procedure and composition of the working group, largely comprising as it did the heads of the *Länder* foundation departments, met with criticism. It was reproached for wishing to unilaterally uphold the status quo of supervision of foundations by the *Länder* (Burgard 2002, 697 et seq.; Rawert 2002; Reuter 2001; Hüttemann 2003, 38; Schmidt 2002, 145 et seqq.). In addition to the loss of influence on foundations, the *Länder* were presumably particularly fearful of incurring higher costs through the introduction of a foundation register with disclosure effect (Hüttemann 2003, 38; Rawert 2002). The only limited proposals for reform put forward by the working group were incorporated in the government bill (BT-Drucks. 14/8765 2001) and the bill of the coalition parliamentary parties (BT-Drucks. 14/8277 2002), which was put on the statute books almost unchanged[3] as the Act to Modernise the Law Relating to Foundations of 2002.

6.1.2 Overview of the Changes to the Law

The Act to Modernise the Law Relating to Foundations has regulated the conditions for the *formation of a private law foundation with legal personality* exclusively in the German Civil Code, BGB, thus eliminating the coexistence of federal and state legal requirements in this connection, some of which also varied considerably from one another at land level. The concession system has been retained in that the requirement for the creation of a foundation with legal personality under the new law is also for recognition by a state authority in addition to an endowment transaction under private law (Sect. 80 (1) BGB). But the terminology has changed. The Act now speaks of *recognition* instead of *approval*. In addition, in accordance with Sect. 80 (1) BGB, the founder has a legal right to recognition of the foundation because the provision stipulates a non-discretionary decision (*is to* be recognised as having legal personality).

There are three requirements for recognition of a foundation, all of which have to be met:

(a) The *endowment transaction* has to satisfy the requirements of Sect. 81 (1) sentences 1–3 BGB.
(b) Pursuant to Sect. 81 (1) sentence 3 BGB, the *charter of the foundation* has to contain certain provisions. If the charter fails to satisfy these requirements, the

[3] Cf. the recommendation for a resolution and the report of the law committee (BT-Drucks. 14/8894 2002) and the opinion of the Bundesrat and counterstatement by the German federal government, (BT-Drucks. 14/8765 2001, 13 et seqq.).

competent public authority may make additions to the endowment transaction pursuant to Sect. 83 sentence 2 to 4, 81 (1) sentence 4 BGB, but only if the founder has died.

(c) *An additional precondition for recognition* is, pursuant to Sect. 80 (2) BGB, for the long-term and sustained achievement of the objects of the foundation to appear guaranteed and the objects of the foundation not to endanger the common good. Pursuant to Sect. 80 (3) BGB, church foundations are subject to land legislation and church law partially deviating from this.

Pursuant to 87 (2) sentence 1 BGB, the conditions for *changing the objects of the foundation* have been restricted. If, pursuant to Sect. 87 (1) BGB, the objects of the foundation have become impossible to achieve, they may be altered as an exception. In this respect the intention of the founder should then also be taken into account, and, in particular, it should be ensured that the income of the foundation assets is maintained for the group of persons that it was meant to benefit, as intended by the founder. When the foundation ceases to exist, Sect. 88 sentence 2 BGB explicitly provides that the *property devolves* on the treasury of the land in which the foundation had its seat, if no other provisions have been made.

Statutory Changes in Detail

Approval Procedure

Prior to the reform, the condition for the formation of a civil law foundation with legal personality of Sect. 80 sentence 1 BGB old version was the *approval* of the federal state in which the foundation had its seat. Since the 44th forum of the Association of German Jurists, the demand had been made for the concession system, that is, legal personality afforded by means of official approval, to be replaced for foundations too, that is, for the situation to be regulated as it had been for the non-profit association since the BGB was first enacted, by virtue of being recorded in a register held by the courts (Mestmäcker 1962; Ballerstedt and Salzwede 1962; Reuter 2012, Before § 80 margin no. 56 et seqq.).

The legislator adhered to the *concession system* however (BT-Drucks. 14/8277 2002). Now, pursuant to Sect. 80 (1) BGB, it is necessary to have recognition by the competent authority in the *land* in which the foundation has its seat. This change is initially only one of terminology, since such recognition also constitutes official approval. In this the legislator adopted the recommendations of the Bund-Länder Working Group, according to which the ruling applying hitherto had stood the test (Bund-Länder Working Group 2001). If the local courts (*Amtsgerichte*) were to be responsible for registering foundations, this would lead to responsibilities and recourse to the courts being divided between the initial recognition and later supervision of foundations. Furthermore, the approval requirement was said to enable preventive advice to be given to potential founders (Bund-Länder Working Group 2001; Andrick and Suerbaum 2001, 248 et seqq.; Schwintek 1999, 25).

Above all this latter justification correctly met with criticism, creating as it does the impression that establishing a foundation is negotiated between the authority which later has to supervise it and the founder himself (Hüttemann 2003, 40). On the other hand, the danger of dividing responsibility between the unit approving and the unit supervising the foundation cannot be denied. The fact that after it has been established, a foundation – unlike an association for instance – requires constant supervision, not only has historic reasons which are now obsolete. Today too the supervision of foundations although they are subject to the application of the basic law is required. The concepts of the principal-agent theory developed in the economic analysis of law give a lucid explanation: A foundation is designed to achieve objects which lie beyond the interests of the founder and the members of the foundation's governing bodies. A foundation may not be guided by self-interest. The foundation's governing bodies decide on third-party assets without any natural persons being behind the foundation as its owner or members. Thus here there is an especially clear manifestation of the conflict between the principal and the board as agent (in this respect, Jakob 2006, 206 et seqq.). If one correctly regards the foundation itself as being the principal and not the founder, who, after all, does not participate in the foundation either with asset rights or with autonomous administrative rights (different view: Koss 2005, 206), it becomes clear that the foundation can form its will solely through its board, the agent. A guarantee for the correctness of the decisions made in the foundation is not therefore to be assumed, other than is the case with associations which have members. Internal control within the foundation is not sufficient on its own (similarly, Hüttemann and Rawert 2002, 2021; Pues and Scheerbarth 2004, 60; Hüttemann and Rawert 2011, §§ 80 et seqq. margin no. 2; Schulte 1996, 501; Jakob 2006, 95 et seq.; Richter 2001, 368). Whether or not external control absolutely still has to take the form of state legal supervision or whether it has to be supplemented by limited popular action for groups interested in the foundation along the lines of the model practised in the Netherlands or in other countries (Reuter 2012, § 85 margin no. 18 et seqq., Saenger and Veltmann 2005, 67; Hopt 2005, 250 et seq. on European Foundation; Reuter 2002, 172 et seqq.) is another question. As long as supervision continues to exist in its current form, however, then the approval function should also remain with the supervisory authority.[4]

Creation of a Legal Right to Recognition

Although the Act to Modernise the Law Relating to Foundations of 2002 has retained the concept of official approval, now called *recognition*, for a foundation to acquire legal personality pursuant to Sect. 80 (1) BGB (BT-Drucks. 14/8277

[4] Critically, Hüttemann (2003, 40); cf. also Reuter (2001, 40), who points out that the objection of divided responsibilities could also be eliminated by transferring supervision to voluntary jurisdiction. Tendency towards jurisdiction by courts of ordinary jurisdiction also, Schmidt (1998, 240).

2002, 5), in fact the approval has been largely approximated to the system of normative provisions, since Sect. 80 BGB grants the founder a non-discretionary right to recognition under sub-constitutional law, provided that the conditions have been met. If the endowment transaction satisfies the requirements of Sect. 81 (1) BGB, if the long-term and sustained achievement of the objects of the foundation appears guaranteed and if the objects of the foundation do not endanger the common good, a foundation *is to be* recognised (Hüttemann 2003, 40; Burgard 2002, 698; Kaper 2006, 57 et seq.; Schwarz 2002, 1720; Andrick 2003, 9; for the reactions in the land foundation laws, see Lucks 2005). The fact that the term *approval* familiar from administrative law has been replaced by the term *recognition* that has a friendlier ring to it can certainly be classified as being a purely cosmetic change of terminology (critically, Hüttemann 2003, 42 et seq. with further references; Hüttemann and Rawert 2011, § 80 margin no. 3).

Although the opinion had already previously prevailed that, contrary to the concept of the historic legislator, there was no further approval discretion by the approval authority, state concessions under the modern rule of law are not discretionary either but are subject to *duty-bound discretion* (Reuter 2012, § 22 margin no. 53; Rawert 1995, § 80 margin no. 28 et seq.; cf. Schmidt 1984, 60). The approval authority was therefore already previously bound by the legal stipulations, and the founder had an actionable claim for an examination of the decision made by means of recourse to the administrative courts pursuant to Sect. 42 Rules of the Administrative Courts (VwGO – Verwaltungsgerichtsordnung) (cf. OVG Münster 1995; Schmidt 1998, 233; Hüttemann and Rawert 2011, § 80 margin no. 2).[5] Whether or not, in addition to this, there is a right under the basic law pursuant to Arts. 2, 3 and 14 GG (Schmidt 1998, 237) to establish a foundation or whether the *land* authorities still had a certain low degree of approval discretion under the application of the old law had not been definitively clarified by jurisdiction or jurisprudence.[6] The modification of the law is therefore to be welcomed as a contribution towards legal certainty (BT-Drucks. 14/8765 2001, 8; in agreement Hüttemann 2003, 41).

Nonetheless, the recognition authority does have a certain degree of scope on account of the *ambiguous legal terms* contained in the elements of the rule. This relates to both the viability forecast and also to the question of endangering the common good. Since both terms require a great deal of specification by the authorities, the de facto scope for making decisions thus afforded to the foundation

[5] On the right of action of the founder if approval is refused, see Andrick (1998, 292 et seq.).

[6] Against a right to approval for a foundation, for instance, Sachs (1999, 957 et seqq.); in favour VG Düsseldorf (1994); reversed by OVG Münster (1995); the question is not addressed in the appeal ruling – BVerwG 1998; on the status of the discussion (Hüttemann 2003, 41; Hüttemann and Rawert 2002), preliminary remark on §§ 80 et seqq., margin no. 20 et seqq., who come out in favour of the freedom to donate assets, guaranteed by the ownership guarantee and by the right to have a decision on the recognition of a foundation as having legal personality free of discretionary error protected by the general freedom to act of Art. 2 para. 1 GG ("Stifterfreiheit"), margin no. 33 et seq.; similarly Rawert (2010).

authorities has met with criticism (Reuter 2012, Before § 80 margin no. 7; Jakob 2006, 99 footnote 567; Hüttemann 2003, 40 et seq.; Reuter 2001, 62; Burgard 2002, 699 et seq.). Ambiguous legal terms are, however, fully subject to examination by the courts (Maurer 2011, § 7 margin no. 36). This does not apply only if responsibility for establishing the uncertain legal concept is transferred to a committee of experts and the decisions concerned are decisions of a forecast nature which, according to the purpose of the provision, are only subject to limited examination by the courts (Maurer 2011, § 7 margin no. 40 et seq.). This is not the case here. On the contrary, they are fully verifiable conditions for the elements of the rule. Any regulation technique other than using a general clause is certainly not conceivable with regard to the forbidden objects of the foundation, since possible violations cannot be exhaustively enumerated, and even then, there would still be considerable scope for interpretation. Thus, under the law relating to associations, despite the narrow preconditions for prohibition set forth in Sect. 3 Association Act, the court of registration is also authorised, based on the freedom of association embodied in Art. 9 GG, to reject an application by a non-profit association to be recorded in the register of associations, also in the event of any other violations of the law (KG Berlin 2005). However, the provision has to be interpreted in a narrow way to the effect that recognition of a foundation may only be refused if achieving the objects of the foundation violate the common good, insofar as this has been made concrete by legislation.[7] It is thus not the authority which defines the common good but the legislator.

There is also uncertainty with respect to the second precondition for recognition, *the viability forecast*, as to what this means and what preconditions have to be satisfied by the foundation so that it appears to be viable in the long term. This is due to the fact that, on the one hand, a forecast is demanded of the authority. Nonetheless, this decision is fully verifiable by court, since responsibility for this forecast is not imposed on independent experts but on an administrative authority bound by law. On the other hand, jurisdiction and jurisprudence are called upon to develop reliable criteria.[8]

Preconditions for Recognition of a Foundation

Relationship to *Land* Law

By virtue of the Act to Modernise the Law Relating to Foundations of 2002, the conditions for recognising a foundation as having legal personality have been

[7] Reuter (2012, §§ 80, 81 margin no. 53 et seq). With criticism of the deviating ruling of the BVerwG on the "Republikaner-Stiftung", BVerwG of 12.2.1998; Hüttemann and Rawert (2011, § 80 margin no. 35); Hof (2009, § 6 margin no. 312 et seq.).

[8] Cf., for example, Hüttemann (1998, 2009, 89), on the question of funding with foundation assets; Reuter (2010) on the admissibility of the consumption foundation.

regulated in the BGB. Since concurrent legislative competence of the Federation exists for this, this provision supersedes contradictory or supplementary *land* law, if or to the extent that the provision is conclusive in this respect. This is a question of interpretation of the rule of law and thus of Sect. 80 (2) BGB. The conclusive character derives, on the one hand, from the wording, which makes the right to recognition dependent on three clearly evident conditions without any restriction or reservation with reference to *land* law. Furthermore, the divergent rulings of *land* law governing the conditions for approval were precisely the cause of criticism prior to the reform of the Act and were the reason behind the ruling (Mestmäcker 1962; BT-Drucks. 13/9320 1997, 7; Härtl 1990, 163 et seq.; Criticism also in Reuter 2012, Before § 80 margin no. 117 et seq.). Contradictory or even only supplementary rulings under *land* law are therefore, insofar as they still exist, formally unconstitutional and thus null and void (Andrick 2005, 156; Hüttemann and Rawert 2011, preliminary remark on §§ 80 et seqq. margin no. 16; on individual land rulings that are null and void, see Weitemeyer and Franzius 2011, margin no. 2.24 et seqq.).

Endowment Transaction

Content

The provision of the old version of Sect. 81 BGB only regulated the necessary written form for the endowment transaction and the possibility of revocation by the founder subject to certain preconditions. Through the amendment to the law, all of the requirements as to the content of the endowment transaction have been incorporated in the BGB, so that contrary *land* law is superseded (see above).

Pursuant to Sect. 81 (1) sentence 2 BGB, the *endowment transaction* must dedicate certain assets to objects of the foundation; moreover, the endowment transaction must give the foundation a charter (see below), which must, for its part, have certain provisions (Sect. 81 (1) sentence 3 BGB). The terminology is inconsistent. Whereas the Act refers to the fact that the endowment transaction must dedicate assets to and give the foundation a charter, in part only dedicating assets to a certain object is classified as being an *endowment transaction* (cf., for instance, OLG Stuttgart 2009; details in Hahn P 2010a, 336 et seqq.). Irrespective of the terminology, the explanatory memorandum of the Act assumes, however, that establishing a foundation requires a deed of foundation in which the founder gives a binding declaration to dedicate assets to achieve objects specified by himself in accordance with Sect. 80 (2) BGB (BT-Drucks. 14/8765 2001, 9). The term endowment transaction is thus to be understood as a *superordinate concept* in accordance with the wording of the Act encompassing both the act of dedicating assets and giving a charter so that one component under property law and one component under organisation law have to be distinguished from one another.

Dedicating Assets

Pursuant to the newly introduced provision of Sect. 81 (1) sentence 2 BGB, the founder has to make a binding declaration in the endowment transaction that he will dedicate assets to achieve objects specified by himself. According to the former ruling, Sect. 82 BGB merely contained, as the characteristic of the rule establishing the foundation, *the assets covenanted in the endowment transaction*. Thus previous prevailing opinion assumed that there was no need for the founder's promise to equip the foundation with certain assets. The founder merely had to specify that assets, insofar as they were available, were to be dedicated to certain objects and it had to be anticipated with a certain degree of certainty that the assets expected from the founder were available (Hüttemann 2003, 48; Reuter 2012, Before § 80 margin no. 20; Flume 1983, 140 et seq.; Hof 2009, § 10 margin no. 12; Wochner 1999, 1443; dissenting opinion Heinrichs 2002, margin no. 1; Neuhoff 2000, margin no. 14).[9] Thus the justified expectation that the foundation was to be supported by donations or external donations from third parties also sufficed for recognition of the foundation. A foundation could therefore be initially formed without any assets, even though this was not the normal case.

Through the change to the wording, it has become doubtful whether this previous opinion can be upheld (doubting therefore, Hüttemann 2009, 88). However, the explanatory memorandum of the Act provides no indication to suggest that establishing a foundation was to be rendered more difficult in this manner by the new regulation. On the contrary, the reform was above all intended to act to simplify foundation law. On the other hand, with regard to the forecast viability of the established foundation, the legislator allowed for it to suffice for the possibility of otherwise obtaining funding to be incorporated (BT-Drucks. 14/8765 2001, 9). But then it is an unnecessary formalism to demand an amount for the original funding of the foundation – however low and symbolic this may be (Hüttemann 2003, 48, 2009, 87 et seq.; Hüttemann and Rawert 2011, § 81 margin no. 19). The question of whether the foundation has to be adequately funded by the founder himself or by third parties rather has to be examined in the course of the examination of the foundation's viability.

Form

Pursuant to Sect. 81 (1) sentence 1 BGB, the written form suffices for a lifetime (inter vivos) endowment transaction as it did under the previous law. The legislator decided against stipulating mandatory notarisation.[10] One can regret this decision, since this means that there is no obligatory advice by an independent notary (Hüttemann 2003, 47 et seq.). However, this would have conflicted with the aim of simplifying foundation law and advancing the establishment of foundations.

[9] Insofar as land law – cf. for instance Art. 5 BayStiftG old version – sets more stringent conditions, such regulations have become ineffective by § 80 para. 2 BGB.

[10] Cf. § 82 para. 1 S. 2 BGB-E, BT-Drucks. 13/9320 1997, 10.

Furthermore, this puts an inter vivos endowment transaction rather on a par with a foundation established by testamentary disposition. For this, all kinds of last will and testament are admissible, thus also including the form of a handwritten testament (Reuter 2012, § 83 margin no.1). If notarisation had been introduced for an inter vivos transaction, this would also have had to be taken into consideration for foundations by testamentary disposition. However, practical examples do show that establishing a foundation by means of a handwritten last will and testament and without any legal advice can be prone to error (thus, e.g. OLG Stuttgart 2009).

The Foundation Charter

Minimum Content

In accordance with the newly introduced provision of Sect. 81 (1) sentence 3 BGB, the endowment transaction must give the foundation a *charter* with certain minimum provisions, including rulings on:

(a) The name of the foundation
(b) The seat of the foundation
(c) The objects of the foundation
(d) The assets of the foundation
(e) The composition of the foundation board

The founder must give the foundation a *name*. He is largely free in taking this decision and merely has to comply with a general right to a name and, if appropriate, any contradictory general personality rights of third parties (Hüttemann 2003, 51; Hüttemann and Rawert 2011, § 81 margin no. 34 et seq.). The concept of a "foundation" is not restricted to charitable foundations[11] nor is there any compulsion for a foundation to use a certain supplement for its legal form (cf. in this respect Bund-Länder Working Group 2001, 41). It is well known that associations or charitable companies with limited liability with a structure akin to that of a foundation may therefore also use the suffix *foundation*.[12]

Pursuant to Sect. 81 (1) sentence 3 no. 2 BGB, the charter must also specify the *seat* of the foundation. However, Sect. 83 sentence 3 BGB supplements this provision by specifying that the seat of a foundation is the place where the management is carried out, unless a seat is otherwise provided for. The seat of the management and the seat specified in the charter may also deviate from one another, however (Hüttemann and Rawert 2011, § 81 margin no. 37). Subsidiary to

[11] For a restriction of the term "foundation" to foundations "oriented towards the common good", motion by the parliamentary party CDU/CSU, BT-Drucks. 14/2029 1999, 6.

[12] On the admissibility of the component of the company name *foundation* in a GmbH foundation ("Robert Bosch Stiftung gGmbH") cf. OLG Stuttgart (1964); on the admissibility of the component of the company name "foundation" in an association cf. BayObLG (1972) and OLG Frankfurt (2000).

this, in accordance with Sect. 83 sentence 4 BGB, the last residence of the founder within the country is deemed the seat. These provisions applying to a foundation by testamentary disposition are also applicable to a foundation established inter vivos pursuant to Sect. 81 (1) sentence 4 BGB when the founder has died.

The principal characteristic of a foundation is the *objects* thereof, and these must therefore also be stated in the charter according to Sect. 81 (1) sentence 3 no. 3 BGB. The charter thus supplements the specification of the objects already contained in the endowment transaction (BT-Drucks. 14/8765 2001, 10). For a foundation established by testamentary disposition, it suffices for the endowment transaction to contain a designation of the objects that is adequately specific, to comply with the form stipulated under inheritance law and to refer to a formless charter (OLG Stuttgart 2009). The founder may largely use his own discretion in designating the objects of the foundation. The approval authority may not interfere in this decision with considerations regarding the pertinence but must restrict itself to merely exercising legal supervision.[13] However, on account of the examination of conformity with the common good, it must be evident which objects are to be achieved with which funds (Hüttemann 2003, 52; Hüttemann and Rawert 2011, § 81 margin no. 40 et seqq.; on the further objects of civic foundations Weitemeyer 2008).

Furthermore, pursuant to Sect. 81 (1) sentence 3 no. 4 BGB, the charter must contain rulings on the *assets of the foundation*. Even though it is not mandatory for the founder to fund the foundation with adequate initial assets (see above), this at least includes details on obtaining adequate assets. In addition, the founder should determine which present or future assets should remain permanently available and how the assets are to be employed to achieve the objects, for instance as an institutional (*Anstaltsstiftung*) or capital foundation (*Kapitalstiftung*) or as a mixture of both types. In addition, it is pertinent to stipulate whether external donations can be accepted since this would otherwise have to be ascertained by interpreting the endowment transaction (on external donations, Werner 2003; Rawert 2008; Hof 2009 § 9 Rn. 11 et seqq.; Hüttemann and Rawert 2011, preliminary remark on §§ 80 et seqq. margin no. 264 et seqq.).

Diverse stipulations by the founder regarding the assets are also conceivable, for instance on the question of the investment policy or the admissibility of redeployment of assets. In the absence of any specific stipulations, the board is only obliged within the framework of *due and proper asset management* to achieve as profitable and sustainable an achievement of the objects of the foundation as possible. In principle, the board does not have to pursue a particularly safe investment policy (Hüttemann and Schön 2007, 10 et seq.; Hüttemann and Rawert 2011, § 86 margin no. 24).

---

[13] Cf. BT-Drucks. 14/8765 2001, 10; Hüttemann 2003, 52; on the question of whether concealed company foundations as an object in themselves and family foundations for maintenance without any preconditions are admissible or whether they contravene the prohibition of *Selbstzweckstiftung*, see Hüttemann and Rawert (2011), preliminary remark on §§ 80 margin no. 150 et seqq. with further references.

Finally, pursuant to Sect. 81 (1) sentence 3 no. 5 BGB, the charter must regulate the *composition of the foundation board*. From the referencing of Sect. 86 BGB to the rule of law applying to associations of Sect. 26 BGB, it ensues that the foundation has to have a board as its statutory representative. Clearly, any other title can be selected for this, for instance, *governing body* (*Direktorium*), *administrative council* (*Verwaltungsrat*) or any similar title, provided that it is made clear that this is the body with the representative function of the foundation (Hüttemann 2003, 52; Hüttemann and Rawert 2011, § 81 margin no. 59). As a minimum requirement, the charter must stipulate the number of members on the board and the procedure for appointing and withdrawing such members (BT-Drucks. 14/8765 2001, 11). In addition, other advisory or supervisory bodies can be provided for the foundation. The explanatory memorandum of the Act points out that the details regarding such additional bodies must be consistent with those with respect to the foundation board (BT-Drucks. 14/8765 2001, 11). According to this, the foundation board must remain capable of acting, and the powers and duties of the bodies must be clear with respect to one another (cf. Hüttemann 2003, 53). The recognition authority may not undertake any considerations regarding pertinence with respect to setting up bodies of the foundation either but may merely advise the founder in this regard (Hüttemann and Rawert 2011, § 81 margin no. 60).

Further Content of the Charter

Apart from the minimum content stipulated in Sect. 81 BGB, the founder may provide for additional details in the charter pursuant to Sect. 85 BGB and should do so after having obtained careful advice. This includes, on the one hand, clauses on the extent to which changes may be made to the charter and *changes to the charter* which may become necessary at a later date (see comprehensively in Happ 2007, passim).

In addition, non-profit law demands additional details from charitable foundations in accordance with the standardised *sample charter for tax purposes* of Sect. 60 (1) sentence 2 AO in conjunction with Annex 1 to Sect. 60 AO.

The question of whether or not in addition to this, as could be derived from the wording of Sect. 85 BGB, the *land legislator* may provide for additional provisions on the constitution of the foundation is the subject of dispute. In the reform enacted in 2002, the federal legislator correctly sought to create uniform requirements for establishing a foundation and to open up a large degree of latitude for the founder in this respect (BT-Drucks. 14/8894 2002, 10). For this reason the regulation is also conclusive in this respect too and supersedes supplementary or conflicting *land* law (Hüttemann 2003, 50; Hüttemann and Rawert 2011, § 85 margin no. 3; Becker 2011; dissenting opinion Hahn S 2010b, 39).

Power to Supplement

The foundation authority can require the founder to supplement or amend a faulty or incomplete endowment transaction or respective charter if it would otherwise be impossible to grant the approval. If the founder is no longer alive, through the reference to Sect. 83 sentences 2 to 4 BGB, Sect. 81 (1) sentence 4 BGB creates the possibility for the competent authority to create or supplement a charter which is missing or incomplete. Pursuant to Sect. 83 sentences 2 to 4 BGB, this also applies directly to foundations established by testamentary disposition. This does not, however, encompass specifying the objects of the foundation as such or the provision of the foundation's assets (Hüttemann 2003, 54; Reuter 2012, §§ 80, 81 margin no. 35; Hüttemann and Rawert 2011, § 81 margin no. 68). Such basic decisions are made by the founder alone. This is expressed by the wording of the statute in that only if details are missing or incomplete in the charter is the competent public authority ordered, pursuant to Sect. 81 (1) sentence 3 BGB, to have the power to make additions. The authoritative content of the endowment transaction given in Sect. 81 (1) sentence 2 BGB, that is, specifying the objects and dedicating funds, is excluded from this.

This means that insofar as the details on the assets or objects contained in the charter are incomplete, but the decisive basic decisions on this are to be found in the endowment transaction, then a merely supplementary interpretation of the charter is conceivable. If, however, the founder did not make these structural decisions, then the endowment transaction did not become effective (Reuter 2012, §§ 80, 81 margin no. 35; Otte 2009; Hüttemann and Rawert 2011, § 81 margin no. 68).

Viability Forecast

The recognition authority must, as stipulated by Sect. 80 (2) BGB, decide on whether the long-term and sustained achievement of the endowment transaction appears guaranteed. According to the explanatory memorandum of the Act, this was intended, in conformity with the former legal situation, to guarantee the *long-term existence* of the legal entity of the foundation without any members in order to protect legal relations and for the legal form of the foundation to take into consideration that it is basically established for an indefinite period of time (BT-Drucks. 14/8765 2001, 8).

In partial deviation from hitherto prevailing opinion (Hüttemann 1998, 2003, 54 et seqq.; Rawert 1995, preliminary remark on §§ 80 et seqq. margin no. 8; Reuter 2010, 70 et seq., 2012, §§ 80, 81 margin no. 16 et seq.; Beuthien 2009, margin no. 33 et seq.), *Muscheler* recently therefore expressed the opinion that a *time-limited foundation* (*Zeitstiftung*) structured for a specific period of time or a *consumption foundation* (*Verbrauchsstiftung*) designed to consume the foundation assets was not admissible in the form of a foundation having legal personality (Muscheler 2009, 140 et seq.). This opinion is, however, controverted by the explanatory memorandum of the reform of foundation law of 2002. According to this, the concept of *long-term* employed in Sect. 80 (2) BGB was not to be understood as meaning that these forms of foundation for a limited term were to be forbidden in the future (BT-Drucks. 14/8765 2001, 8). Whilst a certain period of time was held to be necessary, this could also be combined with the timed end of the objects of the foundation, however. The decisive criterion was held to be the enduring specification of the objects and constancy *during* the existence of the foundation (BT-Drucks. 14/8765 2001, 8; BT-Drucks. 14/8894 2002, 10). This is correct. Whereas the numerus clausus of societal and legal forms demands that the conditions created by statute for the respective legal form be complied with and that no new forms be evolved by private autonomy; for foundations, this only means that they have to be of a certain duration. This could also be derived from the wording of the Act in Sect. 80 (2) BGB old version. The genetic interpretation of this provision by no means compels – nor does the interpretation of the purpose of the provision – the requirement for "perpetuity in foundation law". A foundation is, in fact, characterised by the feature that only in this legal form *can* objects be combined with certain assets for an indefinite duration in perpetuity. But this does not justify demanding it of every foundation. The speciality of the legal form of a foundation is rather to be found in the specification of objects which can no longer be changed by private autonomy *during the period of its existence*. This can also be meaningful for a foundation established for a limited term. A founder, who, for particular reasons, wishes to regard the objects as having been achieved, for instance, when a specific event comes to pass (e.g. the rebuilding of a historic monument or the concentrated employment of his assets within a certain time frame in the hope of thus achieving an objective such as eradicating a disease), must be provided with a legal form with which to do so and which he can rely on to reliably pursue these objects for the period of time stipulated by him even after his death (Hüttemann and Rawert 2011, § 81 margin no. 57 with further references). The same applies to collective foundations such as community foundations (*Bürgerstiftungen*) where a large number of donors or external donors wish to rely on objects being permanently pursued (Weitemeyer 2008). For these reasons the freedom of the founder to decide on the time frame for his foundation is only limited where the objects desired can no longer necessarily be striven for by a short-term donation or setting up collective assets (Hüttemann 2003, 55).

Only recently, this question was resolved by the Act to Enhance Volunteering of 21.3.2013 (BGBl. I 2013) which makes it clear that a foundation may also consume its entire assets after a given period of at least 10 years, by adding the following sentence to Section 80 (2) BGB: "In the case of a foundation established for a specific period of time and whose assets are to be consumed in pursuing the objects for which it was established (consumption foundation), then permanent compliance with the foundation's objects appears to be guaranteed if the foundation is to exist for a period of time specified in the endowment transaction which must be at least ten years". The explanatory memorandum of the Act points out that due to the discussion among legal scholars, the public authorities of some *Länder* previously disallowed the recognition of consumption foundations (BT-Drucks. 17/11316, 24).

Pursuant to Section 80 (2) BGB, the long-term achievement of the objects of the foundation has to *appear* guaranteed. This wording was intended to clarify that this is rather a forecast decision (BT-Drucks. 14/8894 2002, 10) in which funding for the foundation by possible external donations also has to be taken into account (see above). The degree of necessary probability of the viability of the foundation was not specified. If this *has to appear guaranteed*, then an overwhelming probability has to be assumed for this. It is therefore correct to regard a reference to later external donations which will only possibly be given by third parties or to public funding still conditional upon budgetary approval as being inadequate (Hüttemann 2003, 56; in this respect also Hüttemann and Rawert 2011, § 80 margin no. 20 et seqq.; Rawert 2002b, 56 et seqq.; Muscheler 2000, 394).

Objects of the Foundation

Multi-purpose Foundation in Conformity with the Common Good (Gemeinwohlkonforme Allzweckstiftung)

Pursuant to Sect. 80 (2) BGB, the objects of a foundation may not endanger the common good. Thus all conceivable objects are allowed for a foundation unless they endanger the common good. The legislator therefore confirms the opinion already previously prevailing, namely that a *gemeinwohlkonforme Allzweckstiftung* has to be recognised (BT-Drucks. 14/8765 2001, 9; in this direction hitherto already Reuter 2001b, margin no. 8 et seqq.; Rawert 1995, preliminary remark on §§ 80 et seqq. margin no. 13; Hof 1999, margin no. 56.).

The legislator did not restrict (BT-Drucks. 14/8765 2001, 8) the objects of a foundation to charitable objects within the meaning of tax law, excluding, for instance, *family foundations* for private use.[14] The following demand had been made for instance: "In future, when new foundations are established, an orientation towards the common good should be the precondition for the right to use the term foundation, in order to give esteem to the special character of civic involvement expressed in the final and irrevocable transfer of private assets for charitable purposes". A reference to tax law would have been problematical, however, as a genuinely civil law issue would have been transferred to the field of tax law, thus also resulting in the risk of conflicting decisions (Hüttemann 2003, 56).

The legislator did not exclude *foundations tied to enterprises (unternehmens-verbundene Stiftungen)* either. Merely, the condition of *altruism* (*Fremdnützigkeit*) applying to every foundation and already evolved based on the legal situation prevailing hitherto does limit the possible objects of a foundation. A foundation that only benefits the founder or has only been established for the purpose of maintaining its own assets (*Selbstzweckstiftung*, a foundation serving an end in itself) therefore remains forbidden (Bund-Länder Working Group 2001, 44 et seqq.; Hüttemann 2003, 58).

According to Sect. 80 (2) BGB, the objects of the foundation may not endanger the *common good*. The concept of *common good* is not easy to grasp. However, the common good is certainly endangered if the objects of the foundation are against the law (BT-Drucks. 14/8765 2001, 9; Hüttemann 2003, 58; Reuter 2012, §§ 80,

[14] Thus, the motion for decision by the parliamentary party CDU/CSU. BT-Drucks. 14/2029 1999, 6; for a restriction of admissible foundation objects, certainly also Schmidt (2002, 149).

81 margin no. 53 et seq.; Hüttemann and Rawert 2011, § 80 margin no. 35). Furthermore, the explanatory memorandum of the Act also refers to the ruling of the German Federal Administrative Court on the Schönhuber foundation case (BT-Drucks. 14/8765 2001, 9). This rules that common good is also endangered if the planned objects merely endanger constitutional legal interests (BVerwG 1998). This delimitation meets with criticism. A legal right to recognition could thus be undermined by the undetermined concept of endangering the common good having been selected and for endangering constitutional legal interests to already suffice for this (Hüttemann 2003, 59; Reuter 2001c, 144; Reuter 2001, 30 et seqq.; similarly Schwarz 2002, 1769; Reuter 2012, §§ 80, 81 margin no. 53 et seq.).[15] For reasons of sub-constitutional law and to protect the basic rights of the founder, it would have been better to only prohibit those objects of a foundation that violate applicable law (Hüttemann 2003, 59; Rawert 2002; Reuter 2012, §§ 80, 81 margin no. 53 et seq.). In any event, the wording of the recognition provision is to be interpreted in a restrictive way in the same vein (see above) (Burgard 2002, 700; Hüttemann 2003, 60; Reuter 2012, §§ 80, 81 margin no. 53 et seq.; Hüttemann and Rawert 2011, § 80 margin no. 35 with further references).

*Foundations Tied to Enterprises (*Unternehmensverbundene Stiftungen*)*

The Reform Act dispensed with having any special rulings for, still less a prohibition of, foundations tied to companies. Both those foundations which operate a business themselves (institutional enterprise foundations – *Unternehmensträgerstiftungen*) and also those which hold majority shares in enterprises (institutional shareholding foundations – *Beteiligungsträgerstiftungen*) are therefore admissible. The reform discussion had debated on whether foundations may only operate commercial enterprises to a limited degree, for instance, within the framework of the ancillary objects also permitted for a non-profit association (cf. on the discussion Hüttemann 2003, 60 et seq.; thus § 81 para. 1 BGB-E of BT-Drucks. 13/9320 1997, 9).

Even in the absence of any respective provision in the Act, it must be assumed, however, that the *prohibition of a foundation serving an end in itself* also limits foundations tied to enterprises. The objects of the foundation may not be restricted to permanently maintaining the assets committed within it without any altruistic purpose being pursued with such assets. The object of merely upholding the enterprise as the explicit or concealed objects of the enterprise is not therefore permissible (Hüttemann 2003, 61; Schwintek 2001, 49 et seqq.; Reuter 2012, §§ 80, 81 margin no. 90 et seqq.; Hüttemann and Rawert 2011, preliminary remark on §§ 80 et seqq. margin no. 150 et seqq.; in detail Rawert 1990; Hushahn 2009). Even the object of safeguarding jobs associated with every enterprise does not suffice as the principle altruistic object (Hüttemann 2003, 61). Altruistic enterprise foundations are, however, permissible if, through their operations, they serve charitable

[15] Such fears are held to be unfounded, however, by Andrick and Suerbaum (2002, 2908).

objectives, for instance by operating a hospital or by generating funding for charitable purposes (Hüttemann 2003, 62). When, however, extremely low asset distribution for charitable purposes for instance merely serves as a fig leaf for maintaining the enterprise as the actual object pursued has not yet been sounded out in practice (Hüttemann 2003, 61 with further references; Hushahn 2009, 75 et seqq.; Reuter 2012, Before § 80 margin no. 48; Reuter 2010-1).

Family Foundations

In accordance with what has been explained above, altruistic foundations which distribute their assets to the relatives and descendants of the founder are admissible. This form is classified as *family foundations – Familienstiftungen* (Bund-Länder Working Group 2001, 45). For reasons of regulatory policy, the right to create a legal form such as a foundation for permanently providing for the founder's descendents and thus withdrawing assets from the general economic cycle is seen critically.[16] After the reform of foundation law in 2002, there can no longer be any doubt, however, that a family foundation is fundamentally admissible (Wachter 2007, margin no. 4; Hüttemann and Rawert 2011, preliminary remark on §§ 80 f. margin no. 185 et seqq.).

6.2 Legal Policy Evaluation

Overall, the Reform Act of 2002 has largely moved in line with opinions prevailing hitherto on civil law foundations and has hardly created anything new (Hüttemann 2003, 65). A new initiative was only taken with regard to the conditions for recognising a foundation as having legal personality. The provisions have been simplified in this respect, and legal certainty has been created by establishing a uniform structure for the whole of the Federal Republic and resolving some questions of doubt. In addition, a number of problems have been addressed in the explanatory memorandum of the Act and have thus been resolved indirectly, at least when taking account of the subjective interpretation theory,[17] even if the statutory wording did not do so explicitly.

No revolutionary changes have been introduced. Within the meaning of an evolutionary development of the law, a stable basis has, however, been established for foundations of the current day. The task of jurisdiction and jurisprudence is now

[16] Thus § 81 para. 2 of the bill, BT-Drucks. 13/9320 1997, 10; on the prohibition of entailed estate (*Fideikommiss*) Reuter (2001, margin no. 37 et seqq., 2010-1, 318); on the radiation effects of inheritance law rulings on foundation law Rawert (1995), preliminary remark on §§ 80 et seqq. margin no. 132 et seqq.; Beckert and Rawert (2010); dissenting opinion Saenger and Arndt (2000, 15 et seqq.).

[17] In this respect in detail, Jestaedt (1999), in particular 332 et seqq.

to carefully observe what is put into practice and to counteract erroneous developments, also in the comparison of legal systems.

Bibliography

Andrick, B. 1998. Sachentscheidungsvoraussetzungen im stiftungsrechtlichen Verwaltungsprozeß. In *Stiftungen in Deutschland und Europa*, ed. A. v Campenhausen, H. Kronke, and O. Werner, 281–301. Düsseldorf: IDW-Verlag.

Andrick, B. 2003. Die Entwicklung zum modernisierten Stiftungsrecht. *ZSt* 2003: 3–13.

Andrick, B. 2005. Das modernisierte Stiftungsprivatrecht – eine Zwischenbilanz. *ZSt* 2005: 155–159.

Andrick, B., and J. Suerbaum. 2001. *Stiftung und Aufsicht, Hauptband*. Munich: C. H. Beck.

Andrick, B., and J. Suerbaum. 2002. Das Gesetz zur Modernisierung des Stiftungsrechts. *NJW* 2002: 2905–2910.

Ballerstedt, K., and J. Salzwedel. 1962. Thesen. In Ständige Deputation des des Deutschen Juristentages (ed) *Verhandlungen des 44. Deutschen Juristentages*, vol. II (Sitzungsberichte), G 89. Tübingen: Mohr Siebeck.

Bayrisches Oberlandesgericht (BayObLG) of 25.10.1972 – 2 Z 56/72. *NJW* 1973: 249.

Becker, F. 2011. Die Verteilung der stiftungsrechtlichen Gesetzgebungskompetenzen zwischen Bund und Ländern. In *Non profit law yearbook 2010/2011*, ed. R. Hüttemann, P. Rawert, K. Schmidt, and B. Weitemeyer, 31–48. Hamburg: Bucerius Law School Press.

Beckert, J., and P. Rawert. 2010. Kritik des Erbrechts: Im Würgegriff der toten Hand. Frankfurter Allgemeine Sonntagszeitung of 11.7.2010, issue 154, p 37.

Beuthien, V. 2009. § 77 Gesellschaftliche Bedeutung, Begriff und Art der Stiftung. In *Münchener Handbuch des Gesellschaftsrechts, volume 5 Verein – Stiftung des bürgerlichen Rechts*, 3rd ed, ed. V. Beuthien and H. Gummert, 1083–1174. Munich: C. H. Beck.

BGBl. (Federal Law Gazette) I. 2002. Gesetz zur Modernisierung des Stiftungsrechts of the 15.07.2002. BGBl. I 2002: 2634–2635.

BGBl. (Federal Law Gazette) I. 2013. Gesetz zur Stärkung des Ehrenamts of the 21.3.2013. BGBl. I 2013: 556–560.

BT-Drucks. (Official record of the German Bundestag) 13/9320 of 1.12.1997, StiftFördG. http://dip21.bundestag.de/dip21/btd/13/093/1309320.pdf. Accessed 12 Feb 2013.

BT-Drucks. (Official record of the German Bundestag) 14/2029 of the 9.11.1999, Ein modernes Stiftungsrecht für das 21. Jahrhundert – Motion for decision by CDU/CSU parliamentary party. http://dip21.bundestag.de/dip21/btd/14/020/1402029.pdf. Accessed 12 Feb 2013.

BT-Drucks. (Official record of the German Bundestag) 14/3043 of 23.2.2000, Änderungsantrag (amendment motion). http://dip21.bundestag.de/dip21/btd/14/030/1403043.pdf. Accessed 12 Feb 2013.

BT-Drucks. (Official record of the German Bundestag) 14/336 of 28.1.1999, Entwurf eines Gesetzes zur Reform des Stiftungsrechts (StiftRReformG). http://dip21.bundestag.de/dip21/btd/14/003/1400336.pdf. Accessed 20 Feb 2013.

BT-Drucks. (Official record of the German Bundestag) 14/5811 of the 4.4.2001, Entwurf eines Gesetzes für eine Reform des Stiftungszivilrechts (Stiftungsrechtsreformgesetz). http://dip21.bundestag.de/dip21/btd/14/058/1405811.pdf. Accessed 12 Feb 2013.

BT-Drucks. (Official record of the German Bundestag) 14/8277 of the 20.2.2002, Entwurf eines Gesetzes zur Modernisierung des Stiftungsrechts der Bundesregierung der SPD und Bündnis 90/Die Grünen. http://dip21.bundestag.de/dip21/btd/14/082/1408277.pdf. Accessed 18 Feb 2013.

BT-Drucks. (Official record of the German Bundestag) 14/8765 of the 11.4.2001, Entwurf eines Gesetzes zur Modernisierung des Stiftungsrechts der Bundesregierung. http://dipbt.bundestag.de/dip21/btd/14/087/1408765.pdf. Accessed 18 Feb 2013.

BT-Drucks. (Official record of the German Bundestag) 14/8894 of the 24.4.2002, Beschlussempfehlung und Bericht des Rechtsausschusses (6. Ausschuss). http://dip21.bundestag.de/dip21/btd/14/088/1408894.pdf. Accessed 18 Feb 2013.

BT-Drucks. (Official record of the German Bundestag) 17/11316 of the 6.11.2012, Entwurf eines Gesetzes zur Entbürokratisierung des Gemeinnützigkeitsrechts der Fraktionen der CDU/CSU und FDP. http://dip21.bundestag.de/dip21/btd/17/113/1711316.pdf. Accessed 30 Sep 2013.

Bundesverwaltungsgericht (BVerwG) of 12.2.1998 – 3C 55/96, BVerwGE 176: 177–186.

Bund-Länder Working Group. 2001. Report of the Bund-Länder Working Group on Foundation Law dated 19.10.2001. http://stwb.net/gesetze/288.pdf. Accessed 12 Feb 2013.

Burgard, U. 2002. Das neue Stiftungsprivatrecht. *NZG* 2002: 697–702.

Flume, W. 1983. *Die juristische Person, Allgemeiner Teil des Bürgerlichen Rechts*, vol. I/2. Berlin et al.: Springer.

Hahn, P. 2010a. *Die Stiftungssatzung: Geschichte und Dogmatik*. Tübingen: Mohr Siebeck.

Hahn, S. 2010b. *Die organschaftliche Änderung der Stiftungssatzung nach der Reform der Landesstiftungsgesetze*. Baden-Baden: Nomos.

Happ, A. 2007. *Stifterwille und Zweckänderung: Möglichkeiten und Grenzen einer Änderung des Stiftungszwecks durch Organbeschluss*. Cologne: Heymann.

Härtl, P. 1990. *Ist das Stiftungsrecht reformbedürftig?: Eine vergleichende Untersuchung der Landesstiftungsgesetze unter Berücksichtigung der Stiftungspraxis bei den staatlichen Stiftungsgenehmigungs- und –aufsichtsbehörden*. Baden-Baden: Nomos.

Heinrichs, H. 2002. § 80 BGB. In *Bürgerliches Gesetzbuch*, 61st ed, ed. O. Palandt, 54. Munich: C. H. Beck.

Hof, H. 1999. § 8 Stiftungszweck. In *Stiftungsrecht-Handbuch*, 2nd ed, ed. W. Seifart and A. v. Campenhausen, 151–186. Munich: C. H. Beck.

Hof, H. 2009. § 36 Unselbstständige Stiftung. In *Stiftungsrecht-Handbuch*, 3rd ed, ed. W. Seifart and A. v. Campenhausen, 593–630. Munich: C. H. Beck.

Hopt, K.J. 2005. Corporate Governance in Nonprofit Organisationen. In *Nonprofit-Organisationen in Recht, Wirtschaft und Gesellschaft*, ed. K.J. Hopt, T. von Hippel, and W.R. Walz, 243–258. Tübingen: Mohr Siebeck.

Hushahn, J. 2009. *Unternehmensverbundene Stiftungen im deutschen und schwedischen Recht: ein Rechtsvergleich zur Behandlung der Konstellation verdeckter Unternehmensselbstzweckstiftungen*. Cologne: Carl Heymanns.

Hüttemann, R. 1998. Der Grundsatz der Vermögensverwaltung im Stiftungsrecht. In *Festgabe für Werner Flume zum 90. Geburtstag*, ed. H.H. Jakobs, E. Picker, and J. Wilhelm, 59–98. Berlin: Springer.

Hüttemann, R. 2000. Das Gesetz zur weiteren steuerlichen Förderung von Stiftungen. *DB* 2000: 1584–1592.

Hüttemann, R. 2003. Das Gesetz zur Modernisierung des Stiftungsrechts. *ZHR* 167(2003): 35–65.

Hüttemann, R. 2009. Stiftungsgeschäft und Vermögensausstattung. In *Festschrift zum 70. Geburtstag des Jenaer Gründungsdekans und Stiftungsrechtlers Olaf Werner*, ed. I. Saenger, W. Bayer, E. Koch, and T. Körber, 85–101. Baden-Baden: Nomos.

Hüttemann, R., and P. Rawert. 2002. Der Modellentwurf eines Landesstiftungsgesetzes. *ZIP* 2002: 2019–2028.

Hüttemann, R., and P. Rawert. 2011. J. von Staudingers Kommentar zum Bürgerlichen Gesetzbuch, volume 1, Allgemeiner Teil §§ 80–89 (Stiftungsrecht) Neubearbeitung. Berlin: Sellier – de Gruyter.

Hüttemann, R., and W. Schön. 2007. *Vermögensverwaltung und Vermögenserhaltung*. Munich: Carl Heymanns.

Hüttemann, R., A. Richter, and B. Weitemeyer (eds.). 2011. *Landesstiftungsrecht*. Cologne: Dr. Otto Schmidt.

Inter-Ministerial Working Group on Foundation Law. 1977. Report. In *Deutsches Stiftungswesen 1966–1976*, ed. R. Hauer, H. Pilgram, and F. v. Pölnitz-Egloffstein, 359–428. Tübingen: J. C. B. Mohr (Paul Siebeck).

Jakob, D. 2006. *Schutz der Stiftung*. Tübingen: Mohr Siebeck.

Jestaedt, M. 1999. *Grundrechtsentfaltung im Gesetz: Studien zur Interdependenz von Grundrechtsdogmatik und Rechtsgewinnungstheorie*. Tübingen: Mohr Siebeck.

Kammergericht (KG) Berlin of 1.2.2005 – 1 W 528/01. *NZG* 2006: 557.

Kaper, A. 2006. *Bürgerstiftungen: die Stiftung bürgerlichen Rechts und die unselbstständige Stiftung als Organisationsformen für Bürgerstiftungen*, 1st ed. Baden-Baden: Nomos.

Koss, C. 2005. Principal-Agent-Konflikte in Nonprofit-Organisationen. In *Nonprofit-Organisationen in Recht, Wirtschaft und Gesellschaft*, ed. K.J. Hopt, T. von Hippel, and W.R. Walz, 197–219. Tübingen: Mohr Siebeck.

Lucks, C. 2005. Stiftungsgesetze der Bundesländer nach der Reform des Stiftungszivilrechts. In *Stiftungen in Theorie, Recht und Praxis: Handbuch für ein modernes Stiftungswesen*, ed. R. Strachwitz and F. Mercker, 269–280. Berlin: Duncker & Humblot.

Maurer, H. 2011. *Allgemeines Verwaltungsrecht*, 18th ed. Munich: C.H. Beck.

Mestmäcker, E.-J. 1962. Soll das Stiftungsrecht bundesgesetzlich vereinheitlicht und reformiert werden, gegebenenfalls mit welchen Grundzügen?, Referat. In Ständige Deputation des Deutschen Juristentages (ed) *Verhandlungen des 44. Deutschen Juristentages*, volume II (Sitzungsberichte), G 3–30. Tübingen: Mohr Siebeck.

Muscheler, K. 2000. Plädoyer für ein staatsfreies Stiftungsrecht. *ZRP* 2000: 390–395.

Muscheler, K. 2009. Die Verbrauchsstiftung. In *Festschrift zum 70. Geburtstag des Jenaer Gründungsdekans und Stiftungsrechtlers Olaf Werner*, ed. I. Saenger, W. Bayer, E. Koch, and T. Körber, 129–145. Baden-Baden: Nomos.

Neuhoff, K. 2000. Before § 80 BGB. In *Bürgerliches Gesetzbuch, Allgemeiner Teil*, vol. 1, 13th ed, ed. H.T. Soergel, W. Siebert, J.F. Baur, et al., 432–484. Stuttgart et al.: Kohlhammer.

Oberlandesgericht (OLG) Frankfurt of 20.11.2000 – 20W 192/00. *NJW-RR* 2002: 176–178.

Oberlandesgericht (OLG) Stuttgart of 10.6.2009 – 8W 501/08. *ZEV* 2010: 200–201 = *npoR* 2010: 83–84

Oberlandesgericht (OLG) Stuttgart of 12.2.1964 – 8W 229/63. *NJW* 1964: 1231–1232.

Oberverwaltungsgericht (OVG) Münster of 8.12.1995 – 25 A 2431/94 (n. rkr.). *NVwZ* 1996: 913–918.

Otte, G. 2009. Eine oktroyierte Stiftungssatzung – oder: Ist die Stiftungsaufsicht bei den Verwaltungsbehörden gut aufgehoben? In *Festschrift zum 70. Geburtstag des Jenaer Gründungsdekans und Stiftungsrechtlers Olaf Werner*, ed. I. Saenger, W. Bayer, E. Koch, and T. Körber, 75–84. Baden-Baden: Nomos.

Pues, L., and W. Scheerbarth. 2004. *Gemeinnützige Stiftungen im Zivil- und Steuerrecht*, 2nd ed. Munich: C.H. Beck.

Rawert, P. 1990. *Die Genehmigungsfähigkeit der unternehmensverbundenen Stiftung*. Frankfurt am Main: Lang.

Rawert, P. 1995. §§ 80–89 BGB. In *J. von Staudingers Kommentar zum Bürgerlichen Gesetzbuch*, volume 1, Allgemeiner Teil §§ 80–89 (Stiftungsrecht) 13. Bearbeitung. Berlin: Sellier – de Gruyter.

Rawert, P. 2001. Aktuelle Aspekte des deutschen Stiftungsrechts. In *Die Stiftung in der juristischen und wirtschaftlichen Praxis*, ed. H.M. Riemer, 123–175. Zurich: Schulthess.

Rawert, P. 2002. Was aber bleibet, stiften die Stifter – Mit Savigny gegen Rockefeller: Das neue Stiftungsgesetz, das an diesem Freitag vom Bundestag beschlossen wird, führt zurück ins 19. Jahrhundert. FAZ (Bücher und Themen) of 23.04.2002, 51.

Rawert, P. 2002b. Trägerschaften von Kultureinrichtungen im Rechtsformvergleich. In Bundesverband Deutscher Stiftungen – Kulturkreis der deutschen Wirtschaft im BDI (ed) Stiftungen als Träger von Kultureinrichtungen, 48–65. Berlin.

Rawert, P. 2008. Kapitalerhöhung zu guten Zwecken – Die Zustiftung in der Gestaltungspraxis. *DNotZ* 2008: 5–18.

Rawert, P. 2010. Die staatsfreie Stiftung. In *Festschrift für Klaus J. Hopt zum 70. Geburtstag am 24. August 2010*, ed. S. Grundmann, B. Haar, H. Merkt, et al., 177–194. Berlin: De Gruyter.

Reichstag Commission. 1899. Bericht der XII. Kommission v. 12. Juni 1896. In Die gesamten Materialien zum Bürgerlichen Gesetzbuch für das Deutsche Reich, volume 1: Einführungsgesetz und Allgemeiner Theil, ed. B. Mugdan, 948–975. Berlin: Decker.

Reuter, D. 2001. Neue Impulse für das gemeinwohlorientierte Stiftungswesen? Zum Entwurf eines Gesetzes zur Modernisierung des Stiftungsrechts. In *Non profit law yearbook 2001*, ed. H. Kötz, P. Rawert, K. Schmidt, and R. Walz, 27–64. Cologne: Carl Heymanns Verlag.

Reuter, D. 2001b. Vorbemerkung § 80 BGB. In *Münchener Kommentar zum Bürgerlichen Gesetzbuch*, 4th ed, ed. K. Rebmann, F.J. Säcker, and R. Rixecker, 804–854. Munich: C.H. Beck.

Reuter, D. 2001c. Stiftung und Staat. In *Stiftungsrecht in Europa: Stiftungsrecht und Stiftungsrechtsreform in Deutschland, den Mitgliedstaaten der Europäischen Union, der Schweiz, Liechtenstein und den USA*, ed. K.J. Hopt and D. Reuter, 139–158. Cologne: Carl Heymanns.

Reuter, D. 2002. Die Haftung des Stiftungsvorstands gegenüber der Stiftung, Dritten und dem Fiskus. In *Non profit law yearbook 2002*, ed. H. Kötz, P. Rawert, K. Schmidt, and R. Walz, 157–178. Cologne: Carl Heymanns Verlag.

Reuter, D. 2010. Die Verbrauchsstiftung. *npoR* 2010: 69–73.

Reuter, D. 2010-1. Gesellschaftsrecht oder Unternehmensverfassungsrecht? In *Recht des Wohnens – Gestalten mit Weitblick: Festschrift für Werner Merle zum 70. Geburtstag*, ed. C. Armbrüster, M. Becker, W.-R. Bub, D. Reiß-Fechter, and J. Wenzel, 309–328. Munich: C H Beck.

Reuter, D. 2011. Anwendungsbereich des Landesstiftungsrechts. In *Landesstiftungsrecht*, ed. R. Hüttemann, A. Richter, and B. Weitemeyer, 99–134. Cologne: Dr. Otto Schmidt.

Reuter, D. 2012. Juristische Personen (§§ 21–89 BGB). In *Münchener Kommentar zum Bürgerlichen Gesetzbuch*, 6th ed, ed. F.J. Säcker and R. Rixecker, 452–991. Munich: C.H. Beck.

Richter, A. 2001. *Rechtsfähige Stiftung und Charitable Corporation: Überlegungen zur Reform des deutschen Stiftungsrechts auf der Grundlage einer historisch-rechtsvergleichenden Untersuchung der Entstehung des modernen deutschen und amerikanischen Stiftungsmodells*. Berlin: Duncker & Humblot.

Sachs, M. 1999. Kein Recht auf Stiftungsgenehmigung. In *Freiheit und Eigentum. Festschrift für Walter Leisner zum 70. Geburtstag*, ed. J. Isensee and H. Lecheler, 955–972. Berlin: Duncker & Humblot.

Saenger, I., and I. Arndt. 2000. Reform des Stiftungsrechts – Auswirkungen auf unternehmensverbundene und privatnützige Stiftungen. *ZRP* 2000: 13–19.

Saenger, I., and T. Veltmann. 2005. Corporate Governance in Stiftungen. *ZSt* 2005: 67–74.

Schmidt, K. 1984. *Verbandszweck und Rechtsfähigkeit im Vereinsrecht. Eine Studie über Erwerb und Verlust der Rechtsfähigkeit nichtwirtschaftlicher und wirtschaftlicher Vereine*. Heidelberg: Decker & Müller.

Schmidt, K. 1998. Konzessionssystem und Stiftungsrecht. In *Stiftungen in Deutschland und Europa*, ed. A. v. Campenhausen, H. Kronke, and O. Werner, 229–242. Düsseldorf: IDW-Verlag.

Schmidt, K. 2002. Brave New World – Deutschland und seine Unternehmenserben auf dem Weg in ein Stiftungs-Dorado? *ZHR* 166(2002): 145–149.

Schulte, M. 1996. Die Mehrfachkontrolle von Stiftungen. *DÖV* 1996: 497–504.

Schwarz, G.C. 2002. Zur Neuregelung des Stiftungsprivatrechts (Teil I). *DStR* 2002: 1718–1725.

Schwintek, S. 1999. Stiftungsförderung durch Normativsystem? Anmerkungen zu gegenwärtigen Reformbestrebungen im Stiftungsrecht. *ZRP* 1999: 25–30.

Schwintek, S. 2001. *Vorstandskontrolle in rechtsfähigen Stiftungen bürgerlichen Rechts: eine Untersuchung zu Pflichten und Kontrolle von Leitungsorganen im Stiftungsrecht – insbesondere in Unternehmensträgerstiftungen*. Baden-Baden: Nomos.

Verwaltungsgericht (VG) Düsseldorf of 25.3.1994 – 1K 4629/93 ("Franz-Schönhuber-Stiftung"). *NVwZ* 1994: 811–815.

Wachter, T. 2007. § 22 Erbersatzsteuer für Familienstiftungen. In *Handbuch des internationalen Stiftungsrechts*, ed. A. Richter and T. Wachter, 541–606. Bonn: Zerb.

Weitemeyer, B. 2008. Die Bürgerstiftung – Rechtsform und Reformbedarf? In *Gedächtnisschrift für Jörn Eckert*, ed. A. Hoyer, H. Hattenhauer, R. Meyer-Pritzl, and W. Schubert, 967–984. Baden-Baden: Nomos.

Weitemeyer, B., and C. Franzius. 2011. Reform der Landesstiftungsrechte. In *Landesstiftungsrecht*, ed. R. Hüttemann, A. Richter, and B. Weitemeyer, 33–98. Cologne: Dr. Otto Schmidt.

Werner, A. 2003. *Die Zustiftung: eine rechtsdogmatische Untersuchung unter besonderer Berücksichtigung aufsichtsrechtlicher Genehmigungsvorbehalte und Anzeigepflichten.* Baden-Baden: Nomos.

Wochner, G. 1999. Rechtsfähige Stiftungen – Grundlagen und aktuelle Reformbestrebungen. *BB* 1999: 1441–1449.

Chapter 7
Foundation Law in Hungary

Zoltán CSEHI

7.1 Definition

7.1.1 Introduction

Foundations have had a long history in Hungary; however, during the 50 years of the communist-socialist era, this form of legal person was unknown and was not regulated.

The first foundations were established in the early period of the middle ages, and throughout the centuries, this legal form was devoted for asset for special purposes. The historical law of foundation in Hungary was customary law; it was neither codified nor laid down in written form. The historical foundation is a special endowment of the founder and is sustained by a third person (church, university, community, city council, etc.) for the purposes determined by the founder.

This law was partially accepted by case law of the courts, but in 1949 all foundations were nationalised. In the communist-socialist era, this form of legal personality was not accepted; the Civil Code of 1959 contained rules only on associations and other legal forms, but not on foundations. The communist-socialist idea did not acknowledge private initiatives for human help or social altruism. The state was governed by the idea that all social need was fulfilled by the state itself and any and all form of individual altruism was unnecessary. The Civil Code was amended only in 1988, and as a result the foundation as special legal form was regulated very broadly. The law on foundation is case law permanently developed for more than 20 years based on the regulations of the Civil Code.

Z. CSEHI (✉)
Chair of Department of Civil and Commercial, LawPázmány Péter Catholic University, Ugocsa 4b, H-1126 Budapest, Hungary
e-mail: csehi.zoltan@nt.hu

C. Prele (ed.), *Developments in Foundation Law in Europe*, Ius Gentium: Comparative Perspectives on Law and Justice 39, DOI 10.1007/978-94-017-9069-7_7,

7.1.2 Public Purpose

A foundation, as a legal person, can be established to pursue a permanent, long-term public interest, and it can conduct business only with the restriction that it should support its own main nonprofit activity (Section 74/A of the Civil Code). In practice, the requirement of "long-term public interest" is used and interpreted very broadly. Moreover, the foundation can also be registered if it supports only a small group of persons.[1] The foundation is registered at the state court register and it acts as a legal person from the date of its registration. The foundation has got a limited liability, limited to its asset. Neither the founder nor the officers (members of the management body) shall be liable for the obligations of the foundation, only the asset of the foundation shall secure its creditors.

7.1.3 Foundation Without Legal Personality

The Civil code of 1959 created a special foundation without legal personality. This special foundation is a special purpose asset given by the founder to pursue public interest in a way that the asset shall be managed to its purposes by a third party. This way the endowment does not create a new legal person, this is only a special legal act. This asset does not belong to the asset-manager, and it has only a broadly defined beneficiary. It is to be underlined that this endowment can be created only for public purposes and not for any special person or any identified persons. The asset-manager has to make decisions, taking into account the deed considering the nature and the way of help (money, tuition, recovery of costs, etc.) to be granted.

7.1.4 Nature of Foundation

Hungarian foundations are mostly fund-raising foundations that collect funds and distribute them within a very short period of time. According to Hungarian foundation rules, the asset of the foundation is not required to be kept, and it does not give limitation concerning the distribution of the capital, or original asset by the management for the purposes of the foundation. Basically the founder has a right to determine and regulate the asset management of the foundation, if the founder fails to provide detailed regulation of the asset management in the deed. The board has a broad discretionary power to dispose over the asset in the line of the purpose of the foundation.

[1] See the reported case law and its critique: Csehi (2006, chapter VII, 277).

7.1.5 *Foundation with Legal Personality*

There are two concepts on foundations in Hungarian legal theory. According to the older one, the foundation is described as an asset management for specific purposes where the foundation itself is the asset, the wealth. The new approach of foundations underlines that the legal person foundation is an organisation, having several organs like the founder, the management and the supervisory board, and the essence of the foundation is to pursue the goal of the foundation with the source of its asset. The asset itself cannot be the foundation, because in that case if all assets are spent, then the foundation would have to be ceased. Under Hungarian law, the foundation can exist without any asset, and it can collect and acquire new assets irrespective of its original asset.

If the founder is the state, the government or municipality of the city or a village, the foundation has to be elected in a special form with the foundation of public law. Foundation of public law cannot be established since 2006. Old foundations of the public law still exist; with some exceptions the rules on private foundations are applicable.

7.1.6 *Statistical Data on Foundations in Hungary*

Based on the overview of the Central Statistical Office, up to 2011 23,236 foundations were registered in Hungary, 42,325 associations, 2,834 nonprofit business companies, 2,606 trade unions and 299 chambers (profession chambers, scientific chambers).[2]

The total yearly income in 2011 of all nonprofit entities was HUF1,238,190 million (cca. € 4.2 million), from that HUF 240,797 million (cca. € 802 million) is related to foundations, which is around 19.4 % of the total income of the Hungarian nonprofit sector.

7.2 Purpose: Public-Benefit Requirement

7.2.1 *Public-Benefit Requirement*

A foundation can be established only for lasting public benefit. This limit is very clear in the Civil Code and the case law. The permanent public purpose can be very broadly described in the deed of the foundation, such as education, healthcare, environmental protection, cultural activity, sports, consumer protection or any kind

---

[2] Source: http://portal.ksh/hu/pls/ksh/docs/hun/xstadat/xstadat_eves/i_qpg005a.html

of charity. There are two lists of the charity activities. The nonprofit act, Act no. CLVI of 1997, as amended (the "NonProfit Act"), determines the activity as nonprofit within its scope. This list is binding for foundations only in cases where the foundation shall be registered in the charity register. This is not obligatory but a possibility to get some advantages as charity institution. A foundation not registered in the charity registration is still a foundation. The NonProfit Act lists 24 charity activities, broadly formulated, for example, health preservation, disease prevention, therapeutic and medical rehabilitation activities, social activities, family consulting, care for the elderly, scientific activities, research and so on.[3] The second list serves administrative purposes.

The New NonProfit Act of 2011 provides a more general concept of public benefit purposes. Section 2 no. 20 of the New NonProfit Act defines 'public benefit activity' as follows: "it shall mean all activities serving – directly or indirectly – the fulfillment of public functions specified in the instrument of constitution, with a view to facilitating the common interests of society and of the individual." In this concept the "public function" is also stated in the act under section 2 no. 19. as follows: "public function" shall mean statutory State or municipal government functions carried out by the body tasked thereof in the interest of the public, without aiming to make a profit, in compliance with the relevant statutory requirements and conditions, including the supply of public services to the general public, and the supply of infrastructure for carrying out such duties. The new concept of public benefit is linked to the task of the state and its bodies.

The filing of application shall refer to the permanent public purposes as defined in the Decree of the Minister of Justice no. 12/1990. The decree lists the public

[3] List of charities under the NPO Act (Subsection 26 (c) of NPO Act): (1) health preservation, disease prevention, therapeutic and medical rehabilitation activities; (2) social activities, family counselling, care for the elderly; (3) scientific activities, research; (4) school instruction and education, personal ability development, dissemination of knowledge; (5) cultural activities; (6) preservation of cultural heritage; (7) preservation of historical monuments; (8) nature preservation, animal protection; (9) environmental protection; (10) children and juvenile protection, children and juvenile advocate services; (11) promotion of equal opportunity within society for underprivileged groups; (12) protection of human and civil rights; (13) activities in connection with ethnic minorities living in Hungary and with Hungarian nationals living outside of Hungary; (14) sports, not including sports activities involving professionals and those performed under contract within the framework of a civil law relationship; (15) protection of public order and traffic safety, voluntary fire fighting, rescue, and disaster preparedness and response activities; (16) consumer protection; (17) rehabilitative employment; (18) promotion of employment and training for underprivileged groups in the labour market, including placement by the hiring-out of workers, and associated services; (19) promotion of the country's Euro-Atlantic integration; (20) services provided to and available solely for nonprofit organisations; (21) activities associated with flood and water damage control; (22) activities associated with the construction, maintenance, and operation of public roads, bridges, and tunnels; (23) prevention of crimes and protection of victims; and (24) providing electronic public services

purposes activities, similarly to the NonProfit Act.[4] Cultural activity, sport, education, health care, scientific research, environmental protection, development of settlements, political activity and others are listed in 16 points.

7.2.2 Case Law on Public Benefit

The case law elaborated some basic principles regarding the requirement of permanent public purposes. The foundation shall not pursue economic activity, and running a business cannot be the sole function of the foundation. The goal of the foundation cannot be only earning and generating profit, increasing the asset of the foundation. The activity cannot serve one person[5] or a closed circle of persons, for example, to support a sportsman in his sports carrier. The activity shall be based on solidarity, human sympathy and humanism. The operation of a broadcasting network was accepted by the court if the operation is not intended to make profit. The purpose of the foundation shall relate to the general interest of the society or of a smaller community. The public purpose is accepted if the foundation supports health care, education and similar activities, including religious activities. The foundation cannot serve religious activity; only the support of religious entities is allowed.

In practice, the meaning of public purpose covers the charity activities as defined by the NonProfit Act.

The Civil Code states that purpose of the foundation cannot be significantly modified (Section 74/B. (5) CC). The case law follows this rule which means that no change of the purpose is accepted. A new or additional purpose can be given to the older one, but in this case the founder shall provide additional assets for this new or additional purpose of the foundation.

---

[4] Guide of the Decree of the Minister of Justice no. 12/1990 (VI.13) on the Registration of Foundations.

The foundation can promote the following activities based on its goals laid down in its deed: (1) cultural activity (e.g. media, art, preservation of cultural heritage, folk art, care of traditions, care of minority and national cultures); (2) sport (e.g. supporting sport); (3) hobbies (e.g. old students, collections); (4) professional cooperation; (5) education (e.g. educational activity, support); (6) research (e.g. sciences, social sciences); (7) Health care; (8) social activity (e.g. protection of the family, support of the elderly); (9) civil protection, fire protection; (10) environmental protection (e.g. protection of the natural environment, protection of the built environment, animal protection); (11) development of settlements; (12) legal aid (e.g. human rights and consumer protection); (13) public security (e.g. rehabilitation of criminals); (14) international activities (e.g. international cultural exchanges); (15) political activities; and (16) others.

[5] Education of a child is not a public purpose, LB Kny.III.27.797/1997 [decision of the Supreme Court of Hungary].

7.2.3 *Frustration of the Purpose of the Foundation*

If the purpose of the foundation is fulfilled (Section 74/E (1) (a) CC) or the purpose is frustrated (Section 74/E (3) CC), the foundation shall be ceased. In special case, the founders can decide on the merger of foundations and keep its original purposes.

7.2.4 *Near Future: No Restriction, Private Purpose Will Be Allowed*

The New Civil Code does not require any public purpose for the establishment of a foundation. According to the new law, no business activity is allowed to be done by a foundation, and the purpose of the foundation cannot serve the interest of the founder and his family members. The goal of a foundation should not be linked to permanent public purpose.

7.3 Establishment of the Foundation and Change of the Deed

7.3.1 *Establishment*

Since 1987, it has been very easy to establish a foundation in Hungary. The founder shall sign a deed of foundation specifying the name, seat, goals, assets and the assets management of the foundation, the founder appoints the members of the board of the foundation, and the deed is filed with other attached documents at the court. Theoretically a foundation can be established without a board,[6] but in practice it is very unusual. The foundation is mostly established by the registration decision of the court.

7.3.2 *One or More Founders*

The foundation can be established by one or more persons, individuals and legal persons as well. Any legal person has the right and capacity to set up a foundation. In some cases, it is controversial whether a foundation can establish another

[6] See Section 74/C. (2) of Civil Code: The court shall order the appointment of a managing body if the founder has failed to provide for one or if the managing body declined to undertake to perform this task.

foundation. Basically it depends on the deed of the foundation. The public foundation cannot establish a private foundation; it cannot be a joinder and merger is excluded (Section 1 (2) b of Act no. LXV of 2006). Hungarian practice follows the rule that the foundation shall pursue its goals directly and immediately; in other words, the activity shall be performed by the foundation itself, and an intermediary person to transfer the support to the real beneficiary is exceptional. Therefore, a foundation cannot establish an additional foundation to pursue its original purposes, only if it is specified in its deed.

In case the foundation has more founders, all modification of the deed requires the consent of all the founders. This rule may cause difficulties, if one or more founder is not available or due to minor changes of the deed such as changes in addresses, etc. If one founder dies, his rights are not inheritable. If the legal person founder ceases to exist, the remaining founders can make decision in connection with the foundation.

7.3.3 Appointment of a Trustee

The founder has a right to appoint a person to exercise his founder's right. This appointment can be made for the case of the death of the founder or for any other event, subject to the decision of the founder (Section 74/C. (7) CC). The appointment of the trustee-founder is irrevocable after its registration at the court. It is disputed whether the trustee-founder has the right to appoint a further trustee-founder. In case law the right is not accepted, however, the wording of the Civil Code does not refer to any kind of restriction.

In case all the founders or the trustee-founders die or the legal person founder ceases, the rights of the founder will be exercised by the registration court (Section 74/C. (7) CC).

7.3.4 **Mortis Causa** *Foundation*

A foundation can be established in a will. In this case, the registration of the foundation will be managed by a trustee appointed by the public notary or the trustee of the estate (Section 74/D. (1) CC). The foundation can be the heir of the founder or legatee subject to the terms of the will. The registration of the foundation will occur only after the death of the founder based on the principle of inheritance law, and such a foundation cannot be inherited. The heir has to exist at the time of the inheritance, and a nonexisting person cannot inherit. The Civil Code states a special rule, a presumption, in case the foundation is established by will. The time of the registration of the foundation is the time of the death of founder (Section 74/D. (2) CC).

If the deed of the foundation cannot be accepted by the court and the registration of the foundation is refused, the endowment of the will for the foundation shall be spent for the public purpose defined as the purpose of the foundation (Section 74/D. (2) CC).

In Hungarian inheritance law, a common will is not allowed, so a foundation cannot be established by more persons in the same will.

7.3.5 *Deed of Foundation*

The Civil Code requires the following points to be set up in the deed of the foundation: name, address, purpose, the asset given by the founder and the management. The foundation's character can be fixed in the deed. An important feature to be mentioned is the so-called open foundation which means that the foundation after its registration may accept endowments from third parties; the so-called closed foundations have no such right, the closed foundation shall use its assets only, and no third-party endowment is allowed by the founder.

The name shall not harm the rights of third parties, and the address where the foundation is available. The statement of the use of address shall be filed at the registration court (lease, or property, or others).

The founder has the right to declare the branch or a unit of the foundation as independent legal person (74/.B. section (2) CC). In this case, the unit or branch shall have a management and separate assets shall be allocated by the founder to this branch or unit. This rule shall be used for larger foundations operating nationwide that have more branches physically far from each other where the branches are independent from each other.

There is no minimum capital requirement in the Civil Code; however, the provision on capital seems to be very clear: The assets of the foundation should be sufficient to pursue the goal of the foundation.[7] In spite of this requirement of the Civil Code, the courts tend to accept minimum assets of €1,000, or even less, for the registration of an "open" foundation.

According to the rules, if the founder fails to appoint a board in the deed of the foundation, the register court has the power to nominate a body to manage the assets (Section 74/C (2) Civil Code) and the activity of the foundation. This rule is not followed in practice. The establishment of a foundation requires the nomination of the members of the board, and the declaration on the acceptance of the board members is also filed at the court.

[7] The principle elaborated by the Supreme Court of Hungary BH 1992/350 – published decision no. 350 of 1992.

The court has the right to appoint a board if the foundation is already registered and the members of the board refuse to accept this position.[8]

7.3.6 *Open Foundations and Closed Foundations*

Open foundations are the ones where other contributions, grants and co-founder's endowments are donated to the foundation and the deed of foundation permits receiving other endowments of third parties. Closed foundations can only use their own assets for the operation; endowments from third parties are not possible.

7.3.7 *Change of the Deed*

The deed can be changed only with the consent of the founders. The name, purpose and asset of the foundation cannot be changed, and the asset cannot be reduced by the founder, only increased. The members of the board can be recalled by the founder only in case the management threatens the activity of the foundation. In the court practice, the reason of the recall or withdrawal of the member of the management shall be proved at the registration court. A special rule applies for public foundations. The state as founder has the right to recall a member from the management at its sole discretion without the consent of other founders if this member was appointed by the state (Section 5(1) Act no. LXV of 2006).

7.3.8 *Transfer of the Asset*

The founder shall transfer the assets to the foundation. Legally this is possible also after the registration of the foundation, but the registration court shall check the availability and the nature of the asset. Cash and securities shall be transferred to an escrow account of the foundation before filing the foundation; other assets shall be transferred to the future management of the non-registered foundation. The transfer of the assets shall be proved at the registration court: This is a condition of the registration of the foundation (attachment 2, section c of the Decree).

[8] Point 1 of the no. 5/2006 decision of the Supreme Court to unify the case law on the appointment of the management board of the foundation.

7.4 Registration and Court Supervision

7.4.1 Filing at the Court Register

The foundation, as an independent legal entity and legal person, is established upon the registration by the state court. Without registration the foundation is only a legal act. Any change of the deed of the foundation, the change of the board and other officers shall be filed at the court as well and the court shall pass a decision on the request as well.

7.4.2 Nature of Registration

Theoretically the state court has a limited power to check the establishment. The register court shall check the establishment documents only whether they comply with the requirements of law or not. The judge has no discretional power; he cannot demand more or others than required by the law. Hungarian law follows the registration principle for the establishment of legal person, like business companies or associations. Registration courts interpret the law, and if the rules are silent, the gap of the legislature can be developed by the registration courts. This is the origin of the case law of the foundation.

The first instance court decision is appealable by the persons who have legitimate interest and by the state prosecutor. The second instance court for registration matters is the court of appeal. The second instance court has a right to annul the former decision, to pass a new decision or to give additions to the former decision. This decision is final and non-appealable. In exceptional cases, a supervision request can be filed against the decision of the court of appeal for legal review of the decision of the second instance court by the Supreme Court of Hungary.

7.4.3 Non-registered Foundation

The will of the founder remains an undertaking only if the foundation is not registered. This undertaking may have legal relevance and consequences, if the undertaking complies with the requirements of the simple foundation without independent legal personality, governed by Sections 593–596 of the Civil Code. This is the case if the foundation was made in the will and its registration was refused by the registration court.

7.5 The Organisation of the Foundation

7.5.1 Organisation

The foundation, as a legal person, has a management body and a founder, and the decision-making power is split between the founder and the management. If the foundation is a registered charity foundation, a supervisory board shall operate. The operation of the foundation is supervised by the state prosecutor under a special law of legal supervision (Section 74(1) of the Civil Code).

A foundation has a very simple internal structure under Hungarian law: the board, in some cases a one-member board; the founder or the person appointed by the founder to exercise the founder's rights; and a supervisory board, if any. Case law does not allow for setting up any further organ within the structure of the foundation, not even an advisory board or a different control organ; however, some exceptions are known in practice. The founders shall make decisions unanimously, all founders have to agree and vote for a valid decision. If one founder disagrees, even if a founder does not give his consent, the decision of the other founders is invalid. Should the founder die or terminate (legal person), the founder's rights will be exercised by the court unless the founder appointed a person to exercise those founder rights. It is ambiguous whether the founder belongs to the structure of the foundation or whether his or her position is outside the structure.

7.5.2 The Founder

Judges take the view that a founder does not have any right to intervene or to determine the operation of the foundation and the foundation is primarily to be protected against its founder. This unique idea originates from the everyday abuses, especially in taxation and business, in the early 1990s, and since then the idea has been accepted and followed as case law.

The competence of the founder(s)[9]:

1. The change of the deed of the foundation, however the name and the purpose of foundation cannot be changed, and the asset of the foundation cannot be reduced or withdrawn by the founder. The change cannot threaten the public purpose of the foundation. The original goals of the foundation cannot be reduced later on by the founder.
2. He can file the deed of foundation at the register court.
3. The founder has a right to appoint a trustee-founder to exercise the founder's rights.

[9] Based on Csehi (2006, chapter VI).

4. He can nominate and withdraw the management of the foundation. The withdrawal of the management or any member of the management is restricted, only if the management threatens the activity of the foundation [Civil code Section 74/C (6)].
5. The founder has the right to set up the terms and conditions of the asset management.
6. The founder has the right to determine the terms and conditions of the acceptance of the endowment of third parties in case of "open foundations".
7. The founder has the right to determine the final beneficiary of the remaining asset in case the foundation ceases. If the foundation is terminated, the remaining asset shall be transferred to the person nominated by the founder in the deed. This person cannot be the founder itself, and the heirs of the founder are not entitled to receive the remaining asset either.
8. If the foundation's purpose is frustrated, the founder has the right to apply at the court for termination of the foundation (Section 74/E. section (3)(2) CC). In any other case, the founder has no right to wind up or to terminate the foundation.

The limit of the founder's right in case law[10]: The founder neither can waive its right finally nor to any third party, and cannot modify the deed in respect to the name and purpose of the foundation. The founder cannot represent the foundation. The founder does not have any right to revise the decisions of the management board. The founder and his family members cannot be the majority of the management board (74/C. section (3) CC).

7.5.3 Board

The board or one-member trustee is the everyday manager of the foundation. The management can be made also by a single individual, subject to the decision of the founder. The scope of the rights, powers and duties of the management is not defined by law. The founder has the right to define the competence and the power of the board, and the founder's rights cannot be transferred to the board. The board shall have competence in all matters that do not fall within the competence of the founder and the supervisory board.

The board of the management has three main tasks: (1) decision-making body, (2) management of the foundation and (3) representation of the foundation towards third persons.[11] The management board must be independent from the founder, and its decision shall pass independently from the founder in respect of the purpose of the foundation only.[12]

[10] Csehi (2006, 252).

[11] See the reasoning of the no. 2 statement of the College of the Judges for Administrative Cases of the Supreme Court, as amended.

[12] Lomnici (2008, 192).

The Supreme Court declared in a registration case the principle that the board of the foundation shall set up and the board members shall be selected in such a way that ensures the proper management of the foundation for a long term.[13]

According to case law, the board can be structured horizontally and vertically. It means the founder can split the competence among more boards, or it is possible to set up a supreme board and subordinated board or boards; the structure shall secure the proper allocation of competences and the tasks of the different boards.[14]

7.5.4 Control Instruments

The Civil Code does not provide any control organ over the management of the foundation; the state prosecutor has the right to supervise the activity of foundations (Section 74/F of the Civil Code). The internal control rules are not even mentioned by Civil Code only in the NonProfit Act. Some fragmentary practice was developed on the basis of nonprofit law, with the method so-called four-eyes principle.

The so-called four-eyes principle is applicable for foundations as well. Interestingly, this rule, Section 29(3) of the Civil Code, was adopted in the socialist-communist times as a general rule for all legal persons, both for (for-)profit (former state-owned enterprises) and nonprofit organisations. In the meantime company law has been codified by new rules, but still this old clause remains in the Civil Code valid as a general rule for all legal persons. In 2005 the Supreme Court of Hungary in its official position confirmed the validity and applicability of the *four-eyes principle* for all associations and foundations, saying that in any and all cases, two officers' signatures are required for a transfer from the bank account of the organisations mentioned.[15] But if only one officer is appointed or elected, how can the so-called four-eyes principle be followed? The Supreme Court declared that in any case at least two officers should be elected or nominated in order to comply with the *four-eyes principle* of the Civil Code.

The conflict of interests in respect of the officers of the foundation is not regulated by the Civil Code. Only Company Law provides fundamental corporate governance rules.

---

[13] Legf.Bír. Kpkf.II. 25.830/1993, Supreme Court case, quoted by Lomnici (1998, 210).

[14] Lomnici (1998, 236).

[15] 3/2005. KJE – decision of the special Chamber for Administrative Cases of the Supreme Court for unifying judicial practice

7.5.5 Supervisory Board

Civil Code does not refer to any supervision board in connection with the foundation; the court practice accepts – based on the pattern of the NonProfit Act – the establishment of the supervisory board. Due to the lack of legislation, the founder shall define in the deed of foundation the competence and rules of supervision.

If the foundation is registered in the charity register, and the yearly income of the charity foundation exceeds HUF 5 million (cca. € 19,000), an internal supervisory organ or body shall be set up to control the management of the foundation. The bylaw of the supervisory organ shall be passed by itself. The NonProfit Act states that the control organ supervises and monitors the operation and the financial management of the charity foundation (Section 11 NonProfit Act). The control body may request reports from the management and information from the employees of the foundation and has a right to inspect, review and audit the books and records of the charity foundation (Section 11 (1) NonProfit Act). The members of the supervisory organ have a right to attend in the meetings of the management board, or the law and/or the deed of foundation may require that their presence at the meetings is obligatory (Section 11 (2) NonProfit Act).

The supervisory organ shall notify the management body to convene a meeting of the board of managers if the foundation's operation breaches the law or the interest of the foundation was harmed or the personal liability of the board members should be discussed (Section 11 (3)(4) NonProfit Act). The supervisory organ shall notify the state supervision if irregularities are not cured by the management body properly (Section 11 (5) NonProfit Act).

7.5.6 Other Organs

It is controversial in the case law whether any other organs can be established or not by the foundation. This issue depends on the competence and scope of the activity of this organ. The founder's rights and the management's duties cannot be transferred to a third organ within a foundation. Usually the founder would like to set up an advisory organ, the register court examines the competence of such an organ, and if it does not interfere with the competences of others, like the supervisory board, this advisory organ is acceptable by the court.

7.5.7 Status of Co-founders and Joinders

The status of the joinders of the foundation is not regulated by law; this issue is dealt in practice only. Even the meaning of *joinder* is not defined by law. Joinder shall deem all persons contributing endowments to the registered foundations if he is not a founder. The joinder is not an organ of the foundation: His status is only a contractual link to the foundation, unless otherwise defined in the deed of foundation. The joinder and the foundation have entered into a contractual relation which is a gift under Hungarian law. In some special cases, the gift can be withdrawn under the rules of the Civil Code. The joinder's status will be regulated in the new Civil Code.

7.5.8 Status of the Beneficiaries

The foundation has a special character: It serves the economic interest of a third party appointed by the management board, the beneficiary. The foundation is an intermediary between the founder and the beneficiary where the proper allocation and use of the foundation asset is secured by the foundation.

The status of the beneficiary is not regulated by the law and it is not discussed by case law yet. The beneficiary does not belong to the legal structure of the foundation; however, I do not see any problem if the founder sets special rights for the beneficiary in the deed of the foundation. Such beneficiary's right can be, for example, right for certain information, access to certain data of the foundation or the beneficiaries can practice some advisory tasks. I can image that some limited control rights can be vested to the beneficiaries.

7.6 Asset of the Foundation

7.6.1 Legal Requirements for the Establishment

Without assets, a foundation cannot be established. We referred to the special interpretation of foundations such as asset management person for the benefit of third party. The asset given by the founder and its returns shall be spent to perform the purpose of the foundation. This asset has a beneficiary, which cannot be a defined person under Hungarian law. The beneficiary can only be described generally in the deed of foundation.

The asset is usually money, cash or banking money, transferable tangible and intangible asset with value, goods, real property and in some special cases consumable thing. The value of the asset shall be fixed by the founder; independent asset evaluation by an expert is not required.

The asset shall be transferred by the founder to the foundation after its registration. Cash and banking money shall be transferred prior the registration to an intermediary escrow account of the foundation, and the statement of the transfer shall be filed at the court.

7.6.2 *Rules on Asset Management*

The asset management is the duty of the board. The founder has a right to set up special rules of the asset management in the deed of foundation or in a separate by law. For example, the asset can be invested only by state bonds, or partially shall keep a bank account, or special goods, pictures, art objects cannot be sold to any third party. If the foundation is run as a nonprofit organisation, special rules of the asset investment are required (Section 17 NonProfit Act). The special by law of the investment shall be filed at the state court of the charities.

Otherwise the board has a wide discretionary right on the asset management. The board members have civil and criminal liability for the duty of their activities, especially the proper use and proper management of the asset. The final target of the asset management is set down by the founder in the deed of foundation, this is the authoritative purpose for the activity and decisions of the board.

7.6.3 *Consequences of the Loss of Asset*

Should the foundation lose its asset, this might endanger the activity of the foundation; in the worst case, this can lead to the cease of the foundation.

The beneficiary of the asset cannot be specified as a single person or persons; the deed shall define the public purpose, not the persons targeted directly. Somehow a general description of the persons is possible, like "students" or "homeless people" who need the services of the foundation.

7.7 Business Activity of the Foundation

Foundations can do business only as a secondary or subordinated purpose and activity in addition to its public interest. The foundation can conduct business only with the restriction that it should support its own main public purpose (Section 74/A of the Civil Code). The law does not state how this "second goal principle" should be interpreted and applied. The business activity is measured by income and expenses and based on accounting clearly shown. The charity activity cannot be verified and demonstrated this way. The charity can be performed by doing something, and those activities cannot be always shown in the balance sheet of the foundation.

In case law the judge is expected only to scrutinise the short description of the activity in the deed of foundation. If the description of the main activity appears to have business profile as the main goal of the foundation, or if the real intention of the founder is business, the judge refuses registration. Under the case law determined that associations cannot be founded for the operation of a cable television network,[16] purchasing and management of shares,[17] distribution of goods and services,[18] health care with natural methods and publishing books, newspapers and others.[19] Similar rules are applicable for foundations as well.

Special rules are applicable for registered charity foundations under the Non-Profit Act. In general nonprofit organisations can conduct business only in connection with and solely in the interest of their nonprofit purposes without endangering the nonprofit activity (Section 4(1) b of Nonprofit Act). The non-distribution constraint is a condition for an organisation to be filed in the nonprofit register, and this principle must be laid down in the deed of foundation. The NonProfit Act states further restrictions relating to the business of the charity foundations. A charity foundation may receive state subsidies only on the basis of a written agreement, except in case of so-called normative subsidies that are set forth in the yearly state budget act. The subsidy agreement sets forth the terms and conditions, as well as the methods of accounting for such subsidies (Section 14 (2) NonProfit Act.). The terms and conditions of the state subsidies must be published in the media.

The conditions of the services to be provided by a charity foundation must be made publicly available and accessible to all parties. A charity foundation must not provide any services to the board, to the management and to contributors, or to the relatives of such persons, with the exception of services which may be used by anyone without restriction and designated provisions provided, by virtue of membership, by nongovernmental organisations.

A charity foundation shall not issue any bill of exchange or promissory notes (Section 16 (1) NonProfit Act). Further restrictions relate to the business in a way that a charity foundation may not borrow business loans to the extent that it may jeopardise its public welfare activities; it may not pledge any subsidy received from the state budget as collateral for a loan and may not apply as loan payment (Section 16 (2) Nonprofit Act).

If a charity foundation wishes to invest its assets, it should draw up internal investment rules, which must be approved by its supreme body (Section 17 Non-Profit Act) and filed at the nonprofit court register.

---

[16] Legf. Bír. Kpkf.I.25.043/1993 – Supr. Court case, published in Lomnici (2006, 37–39)

[17] Legf. Bír. Kpfk.II.25.220/1992 – Supr. Court case, published in Lomnici (2006, 39–44).

[18] Legf. Bír. Kpfk.I.25.681/1993 – Supr. Court case, published in Lomnici (2006, 44–46).

[19] Fővárosi Ítélőtábla Kny.52.119/2004/3 – case of the Metropolitan Court as Court of Appeal, published in Lomnici (2006, 47–49).

7.8 Transparency, Reports

7.8.1 Annual Reports

Private Law

The status law of the foundation does not require any special reporting except the filing of the organisational and other changes of the data and other registered information in the court of registration and in the nonprofit registration.

Tax Law

Foundation shall file tax returns, but special rules were passed on bookkeeping and reporting of special organisations.[20] Special organisations include – among others – nonprofit organisations, foundations, associations, civil organisations and nonprofit companies. The operation and financial data, the turnover and assets of the foundation must be shown and prepared in an annual report. The business year is the calendar year; no alteration is allowed by law. If the foundation has made bookkeeping by single entry, the report can be a simplified report or a nonprofit simplified report; with double-bookkeeping it can be a simplified annual report or a nonprofit simplified annual report. A simplified report and annual report can be prepared if the yearly income of the foundation does not exceed HUF 50 million (cca. €180,000) in two consecutive years. If the income exceeds HUF 50 million (cca. €180,000), an annual report or nonprofit annual report needs to be prepared.

Charity foundations must register their revenues and expenses deriving from nonprofit and business activities separately (Section 18 (1) NonProfit Act).

Charity foundations shall prepare a nonprofit report simultaneously upon approval of the annual report (Section 19 (1) NonProfit Act). The approval of the nonprofit report falls within the exclusive competence of the management board of the foundation. The nonprofit report should contain the following: *(a)* the accounting report; *(b)* the utilisation of state subsidies; *(c)* a statement on the utilisation of property assets; *(d)* a statement on designated donations to beneficiaries; *(e)* the amounts of subsidies received from state organs, off-budget state funds, local governments or associations of community local governments, or from agencies of such; *(f)* the value or amount of any remuneration given to the board members or officers of the nonprofit organisation; and *(g)* a brief description of the nonprofit activities.

[20] Governmental Decree no. 224/2000 (XII.19).

The nonprofit reports of charity foundations are to be made available for review by the public, and anyone may make copies of such at his own expense (Section 24 (2) NonProfit Act). In addition, charity foundations are to publish their nonprofit report on their official website by 30 June following the year to which it pertains, or in some other forum that is accessible by the general public.

7.8.2 Audit

The audit is outside the scope of the status law and the foundation case law. The state-governed foundations of public law and the foundations, including charity foundations with a yearly income over HUF 100 million (cca. €400,000) and having more than 50 employees in the last 2 years average, must have their books and records, and the annual report audited. The audit can be performed only by auditors or audit companies registered in the Chamber of Hungarian Auditors.[21]

The annual report of the foundation (non-charity foundation) does not fall under the publicity requirement of deposit or that of publishing of its data and operation. The only requirement is that the annual report has to adopt by the management body.

7.8.3 Disclosure

Disclosure of data of the operation of foundation is not regulated by the law. Only the NonProfit Act refers to the possibility that the registered NPO will provide grants through public tender. The terms and conditions of tendering are decided by the charity foundation.

Any modification of the deed of foundation, the board and supervisory members, or any other data registered in the register must be notified and filed with the registration court. These are the only requirements in the material rules. The data and the documents filed at the register court are to be made available for public.

The charity is given by registration by the state court. The following issues should be taken into consideration: As long as the charity foundation does not use any third-party contribution and does not collect funds, and does not use public collections but uses only its own resources, no further disclosure is really needed. If the charity foundations were to distribute state or municipality subsidies, raise funds via advertising from the public, or use of third-party contributions, the disclosure may be expanded in different ways.

[21] The duty and tasks of the auditor are regulated in the Act C of 2000 on Accounting (*Accounting Act*) and in Act LV of 1997 on the Chamber of Hungarian Auditors and Auditing Activities. The auditor must be independent from the foundation.

Some special rules deal with this issue in the NonProfit Act, but this relates only to the services rendered by the registered nonprofit organisations, charity foundations.

7.8.4 Creditor Protection

Creditor protection is a serious deficiency of the law, including case law. The foundations are outside the bankruptcy law. Only the general rules of creditor protection of private law, some rules of the law of contract are applicable, for example, the *actio Pauliana*.[22] The rule of *actio Pauliana* is very exciting and controversial in connection with the foundations because the main activity of the foundation is a free donation to a third party, without any consideration. Creditors might refer to this old rule: Until the foundation has no sufficient reserves for creditors' claims, it cannot provide grants and donations free to third party, because it would diminish the basis of the operation of the foundation.

The NonProfit Act states a special creditor protection rule; however, it is not clear what sanctions should be applied if this rule is breached. This special provision states that upon termination of the nonprofit status by the court, a charity foundation is liable to settle all its outstanding public debts and to perform its other contractual obligations for public services (Section 20 NonProfit Act).

7.9 Supervision

7.9.1 State Prosecutor Supervision

State Prosecutor Control

The Civil Code states that the state prosecutor's office, in accordance with the special rules, has general supervisory competence over all foundations (Section 74/F (1) CC).

[22] Section 203 of Civil Code: (1) A contract by which the assets for covering a third person's claim have been deprived entirely or in part shall have no legal force in respect of such third person if the other party acted in bad faith or had a gratuitous advantage from the transfer of the assets. (2) If a person enters into such a contract with a relative, a business organisation in which such relative is involved by way of concentration, a member or executive employee of the business organisation or one of their relatives, bad faith and/or gratuitous promise shall be presumed. Bad faith and/or gratuitous promise shall also be presumed when such a contract is concluded between business organisations that are not directly or indirectly connected by way of concentration, but are controlled by the same person or the same business organisation. (3) A party who has lost the gratuitous advantage originating from a contract in a manner for which he is not accountable shall not be held liable towards the third person.

The public prosecutor's office is officially informed about all registrations of foundations and all registered modifications of the deed with the copy of the order of the registration court (Section 74/A (5) Civil Code). The state prosecutor's office has the right to bring a legal action against the foundation if the ordinary operation of the foundation cannot be otherwise ensured. In this case, this is a legal procedure, the plaintiff is the state prosecutor, and the defendant is the foundation.

The Civil Code provides for two additional possibilities to bring a legal action by the state prosecutor's office: (1) The court will order to wind up the foundation and to delete it from the register if the state prosecutor files a claim that the objectives of the foundation have been frustrated, or should the registration of the foundation be refused due to a change in the law, and (2) the court may make a decision to terminate the foundation if the management threatens the purpose of the foundation and the founder fails to dismiss the management and appoint new board members contrary to the court order (Section 74/E (4) Civil Code).

We mentioned before that Hungarian foundations do not fall under the bankruptcy law; special procedural law is applicable for winding up and nonvoluntary dissolution without securing the creditor's right and interests.

The NonProfit Act prescribes that the state prosecutor shall supervise nonprofit activity of the registered charities, including the charity foundations (Section 21 of NonProfit Act).

Rules of the State Prosecutor's Control

Act no. V of 1972 on the state prosecutor's office regulates the tasks, duties and competence of the state prosecutor's office of the Republic of Hungary. Section 13 of this act provides for a very broad supervision power over governmental agencies and other private entities, including but not limited to foundations and charity foundations. The general supervision rights of the state prosecutor's office include the following (Subsections 13 (3) (c), (e) and (f) of the Act no. V of 1972):

- Initiate actions to issue, modify or cease the illegal operation by laws, rules or internal rules
- Inspect and review the decisions of the foundation
- Conduct an investigation to review the legality of the operation and enter the offices and other rooms of the foundation
- Call management to provide documents, files and information

The state prosecutor may investigate the operation of the foundation; based on the result of such an investigation, the state prosecutor's office may start a legal action against the foundation or order other measures.

It used to happen quite often that the state prosecutor's office filed an appeal against the order of the court that registered the foundation, for the modification of the statute of the foundation, or for the articles of association in order to get a higher court order in case of debated or unclear legal interpretations of the law.

7.9.2 Register Court Supervision

The registration court, and in case of charity foundations the charity registration court (in practice this is the same court), shall have a limited supervision power in connection with the registration of the foundation. The new data, the modification of the deed, is subject to the judicial review and registration.

According to the case law, the court will order the foundation's management to restore the lawful operation of the foundation by fixing a specific deadline in case a legal action is filed against the foundation by an interested person. This third person can be not only the state prosecutor but the co-founder or in special cases the joinder as well. The case law emphasises that a legal procedure shall start to discontinue the foundation.[23] The court will decide on discontinuing the foundation if the management fails to comply with the order of the court in due time or the founder fails to withdraw the board and appoint the new board members (Section 74/E (4) Civil Code).

Disagreeing with the case law in my opinion, no legal procedure shall be brought if the foundation's purposes have been frustrated and the founder has failed the winding up of the foundation (Section 74/E (3)(2) Civil Code).

7.9.3 State Supervision with Regard to Tax Matters

Foundations doing business are generally required to file tax returns concerning corporate tax following the relevant tax year (this is always the calendar year for nonprofits). Corporate tax is not paid in advance; VAT and personal income tax deducted from employee salaries and other payments for individuals are required to be accounted for on a monthly basis.

Tax audits are planned by the Hungarian tax authorities on the basis of an internal audit plan. The general objective is for foundations and other nonprofit organisations to be checked if they would like to receive the 1 % funds from the personal income tax of the taxpayers. In the Hungarian tax law, the taxpayers have a right to appoint a foundation or charity institution to receive 1 % of the personal income tax paid to the state. The foundation or charity institution shall comply with the requirements of the law to receive these endowments from the state.

7.9.4 State Supervision of State Subsidies

The state subsidies provided to the registered charity foundations are controlled by the State Audit Office.

[23] Lomnici (2008, 376–377).

7.10 Dissolution

7.10.1 Winding Up

The foundation ceases with the deletion from the court register. The rules on winding up are only generally formulated, both of material and procedural aspects. The Civil Code states that a foundation can be discontinued if its goal has been fulfilled, or if the time set in the deed has expired, or if the condition precedent put into the deed occurred (Section 74/E (1) section of the Civil Code).

7.10.2 The Founder

The founder has the right to file a request in the register court to delete the foundation from the register if the purpose of the foundation has been finally frustrated (Section 74/E (4) of the Civil Code). The founder cannot terminate the foundation for any other reason and founder cannot define any other reason of the deed of the foundation for dissolution. The founder has no right to close the foundation; the founder's power is reduced to make a decision on the merger of the foundation with another foundation (Section 74/E (6) Civil Code.).

7.10.3 Merger

Merger of foundations is allowed if the purposes of the foundations are in harmony with each other (Section 74/E (6) Civil Code). In practice the original purposes of all foundations shall be kept in the new deed of the foundation. The consent of every founder is required for the merger of foundations. No procedural aspect of demerger or a split of the foundation is regulated by the Civil Code.

Since 2010, special rules have been applied for state-controlled foundations.

7.10.4 State Prosecutor

The state prosecutor has a right to bring legal action against the foundation if the purpose of the foundation is frustrated or if the registration of the foundation – due to a change in legislation – is refused (Section 74/E (3) of the Civil Code). The court has discretional power to discontinue the foundation if the board of the foundation threatens the activity of the foundation and the founder fails to withdraw the members of the board or fails to appoint new board members. A further possibility for the court to terminate the foundation is based on the claim of the state prosecutor if the proper activity of the foundation cannot be ensured (Section 74/F (2) of the Civil Code). In practice, the state prosecutor will first try to use other methods to stop the violation of the law; legal action against the foundation is only a final solution.

7.10.5 *Bankruptcy*

The creditors and third parties are informed about the procedure of the winding up of the foundation, so the creditors and other third parties of the foundation are protected by law as of January 2012.

The law on bankruptcy is not applicable to foundations, as of January 2012.

7.11 Future

The new Civil Code Act no V of 2013 will restate the rules on foundations and provide much more detailed regulations on the operation of the foundations. Based on the new law, the foundation's activity will be no more restricted to public purpose, but also private purposes will be allowed. Recently in statutory and case law, the founders have been able to exercise their rights only jointly; all decisions and all modifications of the deed of foundation shall be adopted unanimously by the founders. This has made it very difficult to manage the foundation in some cases. The new law gives more flexibility to the foundation established by more than one founder. If the founders agree in the deed, a majority decision-making can be used. The status of the co-founder and joinder, as well as his rights and obligations, can be regulated by the founder very broadly in the deed; also the new law gives much more freedom to the founder to define the structure of the foundation, the competence of the board and the rights of the co-founders. The founder itself can be beneficiary in case the goal of the foundation is the long-term management of the scientific or artistic works of the founder. The founder can transfer his founder rights to a third person, but these rights are out of the scope of succession, and cease to exist with the death of the founder, unless a third person has been appointed. The new law entered into force on 15 March 2014 and it shall apply for the newly established foundations. The deeds of the old foundations shall adjust to the new law until 15 march 2016.

Bibliography

Csehi, Z. 1991. Das Stiftungsgeschäft im deutschen Bürgerlichen Gesetzbuch. Heidelberg 1991. Magisterarbeit, published in: Csehi (2005) *Diké kísértése* [Temptation of Diké], 376–452. Budapest: Gondolat.

Csehi, Z. 2006. *A magánjogi alapítvány* [The private law foundation]. Budapest: Gondolat.

Csehi, Z. 2007a. *A civil társadalom szervezeteinek joga Magyarországon* [Nonprofit law in Hungary]. Budapest: Gondolat

Csehi, Z. 2007b. Gemeinnützigkeits- und Spendenrecht in Ungarn. In *Spenden- und Gemeinnützigkeitsrecht in Europa*, ed. R. Walz, L. von Auer, and Th. von Hippen, 511–570. Tübingen: Mohr Siebeck.

Csehi, Z. 2007c. Vázlat a nonprofit szféra státus-szabályozásáról és a kutatás irányairól [An outline of the Hungarian nonprofit law and the directions of the research]. *iustum aequm salutare (IAS)* III(2007/4): 5–53.

Csehi, Z. 2010. Nonprofit organisations in Hungary. In *Comparative corporate governance of nonprofit organizations*, ed. Klaus J. Hopt and Thomas von Hippel, 325–378. Cambridge: Cambridge University Press.

Egriné, R.M., and Z. Pettendi. 1995. *Az alapítványok* [Foundations]. Budapest: Közgazdasági és Jogi Könyvkiadó.

Gadó, G. 2010. Vázlatok a magánjogi alapítvány jövőbeli szabályozására [Sketches on future regulation of private foundations] *Gazdaság és Jog*.

Kecskés, L. 1988. Az alapítványi jog fejlődéséről [The development of foundation law]. *Magyar Jog* 35: 104–116.

Kecskés, L. 1999. *Magyar polgári jog. Általános rész II. A személyek joga.* [Hungarian private law. General Part II. Law of persons]. Budapest/Pécs: Dialóg Campus.

Lomnici, Z. 1998. *Alapítványok és közalapítványok kézikönyve*. Budapest. [Handbook of foundations and foundations of public law] – A collection of case law by topic, 5th ed. Budapest 2008.

Lomnici, Z. 2006. Az egyesületek. 2. bőv. kiad. [Associations, 3rd. enlarged ed.] – A collection of case law by topic. Budapest.

Nemes, A. 1994. Az alapítványi jog változásai [Changes in the law of foundations]. *Jogtudományi Közlöny* XLIX(1994/3): 135–140.

Szécsényi, T. 1996. Alapítók, csatlakozók [Founders and co-founders]. *Ügyészek Lapja sz.* IV (1996/4): 21–24.

Chapter 8
In Search of Terre Firma: The Unpacking of Charitable Foundations in Ireland

Oonagh B. Breen

8.1 Introduction

The emergence of the foundation sector in Ireland is still an unfolding story. Rated in 1999 as the smallest foundation sector in Europe with just 0.7 grant-making foundations per 100,000 inhabitants (European Foundation Centre 2005, 2), the influence of the Celtic Tiger led to a phenomenal growth of foundations in the following 6 years when the number of public foundations rose from 30 in 1999 to 107 in 2005 – an increase of 257 % (European Foundation Centre 2008, 8). However, the size of Ireland's foundation sector still lags behind the European average of 20 foundations per 100,000 inhabitants. Latest figures published in 2009 reveal that foundations contribute €85 million annually to philanthropic giving in Ireland (Forum on Philanthropy 2009).[1] Although there are approximately 30 active grant-making foundations in Ireland,[2] more than 85 % of the annual aggregate grant-making budget is attributable to three large limited life foundations. All three will have ceased to exist by 2016, which means that foundation funding is set to decrease dramatically in the future to less than €13 million per annum if no new foundations enter the philanthropic marketplace in the next 5 years (McKinsey and Company 2009, 9).

It is important at the outset of this chapter to set out the political and cultural contexts in which foundations operate in Ireland. Setting the scene in this manner also provides a better basis for predicting whether the climate is now right for

The author wishes to thank Niall O'Sullivan, Patricia Quinn and Alison Dunn for their assistance with the preparation of this chapter. All views expressed and all errors remain those of the author.

[1] Cited in McKinsey and Company (2009, 5).

[2] This number compares poorly with the estimated 8,000 active grant-making foundations operating in the United Kingdom. See McKinsey and Company (2009, 8).

O.B. Breen (✉)
Sutherland School of Law, University College Dublin, Belfield, Dublin 4, Ireland
e-mail: oonagh.breen@ucd.ie

C. Prele (ed.), *Developments in Foundation Law in Europe*, Ius Gentium: Comparative Perspectives on Law and Justice 39, DOI 10.1007/978-94-017-9069-7_8,

foundation growth or whether the next decade will find further stagnation and decline of an already vulnerable sector. Government support of the non-profit sector in Ireland is substantial, accounting for over 60 % of the sector's income (Centre for Nonprofit Management 2006, 47). Such dependency on government, however, creates its own difficulties both for the non-profit sector and its beneficiaries when economic priorities shift within government. The current economic climate has resulted in significant cuts in government funding for the community and voluntary sector, valued at an estimated loss to the sector of €25 million alone in 2010 (2 into 3 2010, 6). Political encouragement of philanthropic funding outside of government that may be more stable in times of recession and allow for multi-year funding would thus seem to be a sine qua non. More than a decade ago, the government recognised the need for greater foundational involvement in funding projects in a manner that was not a replication or replacement of state funding but actually amounted to additional funding. To this end, the government has supported the creation of a national civic endowment fund and facilitated local government in the creation of similar funds at regional level. The success of such ventures, however, is dependent upon the achievement of financial critical mass such that an endowment produces sufficient income to have an impact at community level. As will be explored below, the concept of strategic long-term giving which is inherent in philanthropy and thus distinguishes it from charity is a relatively new concept in Ireland, and the recent economic downturn will adversely affect the potential for growth of such giving in the near future.[3]

Culturally, the foundation sector can be functionally categorised in Ireland into grant-making foundations, community foundations and operating foundations. As indicated above, the grant-making foundation sector in Ireland remains one of the smallest in Europe and is set to decrease in size in the coming years. Few Irish companies have corporate foundations as a tangible indicator of corporate social responsibility.[4] The community foundation movement is small but growing. The first such foundation, the Community Foundation for Ireland, was established in 2000. In 2012 the value of its pooled endowment was €28 million, and over the past decade, it has made grants of over €14 million on behalf of its donors.[5] In terms of operating foundations, there are many service providers and fundraising arms of

[3] The effect of the global downturn on foundation wealth in Ireland is evident in the financial accounts for 2010. The JP McManus Charitable Foundation's investments fell from €41 m to €36million in 2010, resulting in payments totalling €1.9 million being made to 139 charities in 2010 as compared with payments valued at €10.6 million to 143 good causes in 2009 (Source: Business Section, The Sunday Times, July 10, 2011).

[4] A notable exception to this general trend is the Vodafone Foundation Ireland. The Vodafone business model approach to CSR has led to the creation of 27 Vodafone foundations in the countries in which Vodafone operates. In Ireland, since its creation in 2003, the Vodafone Foundation, which is a company limited by guarantee which enjoys charitable tax-exempt status, has given an average of €1.5 million to charitable causes each year.

[5] See http://www.foundation.ie/images/uploads/file/CFI%20ANN%20REP%202013%20F-A%20COMP%20L-R.pdf (Accessed May 20, 2014).

non-profit organisations that style themselves as foundations. Thus, most hospitals, universities and cultural bodies have foundations specifically set up to raise funds for those bodies. Service providing foundations typically operate in the fields of health, education and provision of counselling services. These operating foundations typically will not enjoy endowed or permanent funding, as is more common with civil law foundations, and indeed, at times, it may be difficult to differentiate these entities from other non-foundation non-profit organisations.

8.2 Mapping the Foundation Landscape in Ireland

Perhaps one of the defining features of foundations in Ireland is that categorisation of an entity as a foundation does not confer a legal status on the organisation independent of the legal vehicle used to create the foundation in the first instance. As a consequence, the use of the word 'foundation' in the title of an organisation provides no guarantees as to the structure, purpose or funding of the entity.

8.2.1 Legal Structure

In terms of legal structure, generally a founder wishing to establish a foundation in Ireland will choose between a company limited by guarantee (and thus enjoying limited liability) or a trust (with liability being personal to the trustees) as the legal vehicle for the foundation. Occasionally, foundations enjoy a statutory basis, as is the case with the Science Foundation of Ireland, a body corporate with perpetual succession, established under the Industrial Development (Science Foundation Ireland) Act 2003 to promote and develop world-class research capability in strategic areas of scientific endeavour that concern economic and social benefit and long-term competitiveness.

Whereas in some jurisdictions the laws governing foundations make it clear that foundations are a recognisable and separate legal vehicle from other legal vehicles such as associations or corporations, the attribution *foundation* has no such legal consequences in Ireland. More commonly, the title *foundation* may be used to signal organisational legitimacy or credibility. The branding of an organisation as a foundation lends a populist gravitas to the body, which may be beneficial to it in its fundraising endeavours (Donoghue 2004, 9). To this end, it is quite common to find fundraising arms of cultural bodies labelled as foundations. Similarly, university fundraising bodies and hospital fundraising bodies tend to classify themselves as foundations. In all of these latter cases, typically there is no permanent fund or endowment that vests upon the establishment of the entity. Rather, it is the goal of such organisations to garner the necessary financial support from donors on an ongoing basis.

8.2.2 *Purpose*

A more critical issue than structure for the founder will be the purpose of the foundation and whether it will qualify for charitable tax exemption. Not all foundations are charitable foundations. A cross-referencing of the current Revenue listings of charitable tax-exempt organisations with the word *foundation* in their title and a *foundation* keyword search of the companies register reveals the existence of foundations engaged in public benefit work that do not enjoy charitable tax-exempt status.[6] To be eligible for the latter, the founders must satisfy Revenue that the objects of the foundation are exclusively charitable and its charitable purposes provide sufficient public benefit. The determination of these issues is subject to common law and remains unaffected by recent statutory reforms to charity law.[7]

More recently, Ireland has reformed its charity law with the introduction of the Charities Act 2009. This Act sets down for the first time a statutory definition of charitable purpose and provides some statutory guidance on meeting the public benefit test.[8] When fully commenced, the Act will bring about the establishment of a new statutory regulator, the Charities Regulatory Authority (CRA). The CRA will be responsible for setting up a public register of charities and for adjudicating on applications from organisations to be registered as charities.[9] The CRA will oversee the governance of charities and will scrutinise their financial probity. Charities, including charitable foundations, which already have charitable tax-exempt status at the date of the establishment of the Charities Register, will be *deemed* to be registered as charities.[10] New charities established after the creation of the Register will need to apply directly to the CRA for registration as a charity. They will also need to apply separately to the Revenue Commissioners for the granting of charitable tax-exempt status.

---

[6] See, for instance, the Malmar Foundation, established by Forward Emphasis International as its vehicle for corporate social responsibility; the World Wildlife Foundation which styles itself as a charity although it does not enjoy charitable tax-exempt status; and the FairFund Foundation, which is primarily dedicated to economic investment, economic growth and stability in the developing nations of the world and, in particular, in the Commonwealth member countries, the Anglophone and the Francophone countries. None of these foundations are charitable tax-exempt entities in Ireland.

[7] Charities Act, 2009, s.7 provides that nothing in the Charities Act shall operate to affect the law in relation to the levying or collection of any tax or the determination of eligibility for exemption from liability to pay any tax. Section 7(2) also provides that the Revenue Commissioners shall not be bound by a determination of the Charities Regulatory Authority as to whether a purpose is of public benefit or not in the performance by them of any function under or in connection with the tax acts.

[8] Charities Act, 2009, s.3.

[9] Charities Act, 2009, s.39.

[10] Charities Act, 2009, s.40.

8.2.3 Foundation Funding and Endowment

With regard to foundation funding and endowment, the use of the descriptor *foundation* does not always coincide with the traditional understanding of a permanently endowed institution, as is more commonly the case in civil law countries or in the United States. According to West's Encyclopaedia of American Law (West's Encyclopaedia of American Law 2011), a foundation may be defined in the following terms:

> A permanent fund established and maintained by contributions for charitable, educational, religious, research, or other benevolent purposes. An institution or association given to rendering financial aid to colleges, schools, hospitals, and charities and generally supported by gifts for such purposes.

This legal definition is a useful starting point since it contains many of the elements that lawyers and academics alike from both common law and civil law jurisdictions generally associate with the concept of foundation. Thus, a foundation typically comprises assets most usually in the form of a permanent fund of private money. This fund often begins life as an initial endowment that may be topped up by subsequent additional gifts or contributions. The fund's income (although sometimes also its capital) is then commonly used to financially support charitable or benevolent public purposes either through the making of grants to bodies engaged in these pursuits or through the actual provision of programmes or services directly by the foundation itself. Despite the frequency of use of the term *foundation* in Ireland, its appearance in the name of an organisation does not automatically signal that one is dealing with either a permanent fund or indeed an endowed fund that is available for charitable purposes.

Ireland does not have a long tradition of well-endowed philanthropic foundations built upon either personal fortunes or corporate wealth. Various rationales for this absence have been advanced. Absence of critical mass in indigenous wealth in the past is commonly cited as a factor, with much wealth being newfound during the reign of the Celtic Tiger.[11] Donoghue submits that economics alone, however, cannot explain the disparity in foundation numbers that exists between Ireland and its European neighbours especially since, as a nation, Ireland's wealth in recent years would have exceeded that of Spain, Portugal or Greece and yet these countries have a significantly higher percentage of foundations than Ireland (Donoghue 2004, 39). Rather, Donoghue (2001, 160) attributes the under-development of foundations in Ireland to a combination of past financial penury and the experience of being a colonised nation as opposed to a colonising power (like Spain or Portugal).

Another possible explanation for the low level of foundation growth in Ireland draws on similar Italian experiences and the trends that saw many Irish donors, just like their counterparts in Italy, more inclined to give directly to the Catholic Church

[11] See Barclay's Wealth (2010, 7) citing O'Sullivan of the Community Foundation of Ireland to the effect that wealth in Ireland is to a large degree only one step removed from working or middle class.

and its associated charitable arms in the past rather than establishing their own independent foundations (Donoghue 2001, 160). The trend towards greater establishment of independent foundations in Ireland in the first decade of the 2000 may in part be attributable to a greater secularisation in Ireland.

8.2.4 The Cultural Context of Large-Scale Philanthropy in Ireland

Finally, the culture of large-scale philanthropy and planned giving is not well established in Ireland. The noted absence of intermediary organisations to assist donors in planned giving and philanthropic estate planning in Ireland has meant that professional advice in this regard has been a relatively undeveloped area. In this regard, McKinsey and Company (2009, 10) report that philanthropy is not a high-priority topic for Irish professional advisors with 50 % of those surveyed never having a discussion with their clients about philanthropy. Moreover, legal vehicles readily available in the United States that facilitate planned giving, such as charitable remainder trusts and charitable lead trusts, are not recognised in Ireland as permissible under tax law.

The charitable landscape is changing in this regard, however. The aforementioned creation of the Community Foundation for Ireland in 2000 brought home the possibilities of philanthropy to a broader section of the donating public. It introduced the possibility of moving beyond charity to philanthropy through the use of pooled endowed funds and enabled more efficient management of those funds through the Community Foundation, thanks to economies of scale, than might otherwise be feasible or economic through multiple independently established foundations. In this way, Ireland's late entry into the foundation field coupled with the emergence of the Community Foundation for Ireland may help it to avoid the situation prevalent in jurisdictions such as Germany and the United Kingdom of too many small foundations that find it difficult to achieve their mission or hire staff given their low levels of funding.[12] The Community Foundation also acts as the Irish partner in the Transnational Giving Europe Project (TGE), which facilitates tax-efficient cross-border charitable giving within Europe.[13] The TGE network currently covers 16 countries and places the Community Foundation for Ireland in the same circle as well established and prestigious foundations such as Fondation de France; the King Badouin Foundation, Belgium; and the Charities Aid Foundation in the United Kingdom.

---

[12] McKinsey and Company (2009, 9) noting that 80 percent of foundations in Germany and 60 percent of foundations in the United Kingdom have an annual budget of less than €250,000.

[13] See http://www.transnationalgiving.eu/tge/default.aspx?id=219948&LangType=1033 (Accessed October 21, 2011).

In terms of intermediary organisations, a notable development was the establishment of Philanthropy Ireland in 1998, a funders' forum with charitable tax-exempt status and boasting more than 28 grant-making foundations and trusts amongst its members. Philanthropy Ireland has as its mission the goal of 'increas [ing] the level of philanthropy in Ireland and expand[ing] the community of engaged donors who are regular, strategic, long-term contributors to good causes'.[14] The organisation seeks to assist funders and grant seekers by acting as a bridge between the two and is responsible for Ireland's yearly country report on foundations to the European Foundation Centre.[15]

Philanthropy Ireland was centrally involved in the 2006 Forum on Philanthropy. The forum, a government initiative chaired by the Secretary General of the Department of An Taoiseach, included representatives from the Department of Finance, Philanthropy Ireland and a number of other philanthropic organisations. The forum was set up to promote philanthropic culture, and a working group, led by Philanthropy Ireland, was responsible in 2008 for establishing a baseline report for philanthropy in Ireland. The resulting report provided an empirical basis for estimating the value of individual, foundational and corporate giving for the first time in Ireland. Although the report was never formally published, the research findings were used in the compilation of the McKinsey report on philanthropy in Ireland in 2009 (McKinsey and Company 2009).

8.3 Government Involvement in Foundation Establishment and Development

Government involvement in foundation development and support has ebbed and flowed over the past decade. In 1998, the government in a joint venture with the major employer bodies established the Foundation for Investing in Communities. The foundation was set up with three main aims: (a) to support voluntary-community-based projects through the provision of additional funding; (b) to continue the development of local enterprise networks under the auspices of 'business in the Community' and (c) to find new ways to address the needs of disadvantaged children. With initial funding of €1.3 million, the foundation was challenged to create an endowment fund through corporate and private donations and bequests.[16] Three separate foundations were subsequently set up under the

[14] See http://www.philanthropy.ie/our-partners/ (Accessed May 21, 2014).

[15] The European Foundation Centre provides annual status reports on the health of foundation law and regulation throughout the European Union. Reports, which are presented in template form for ease of country comparison, are compiled by national experts and made available online. For the most recent Report on Ireland, see http://www.efc.be/programmes_services/resources/Pages/Legal-and-fiscal-country-profiles.aspx (Accessed May 21, 2014).

[16] See Vol. 535 Dáil Debates, Written Answers – Foundation for Investing in Communities, Tuesday May 1, 2001.

umbrella of the Foundation for Investing in the Community, namely, the Community Foundation for Ireland, Business in the Community and the National Children's Trust, the last of which was later subsumed into the Community Foundation for Ireland.

In its 2000 White Paper on Supporting Voluntary Activity the Government specifically acknowledged the important role that community foundations and trusts play in other countries, referencing its own involvement in the establishment of the Foundation for Investing in Communities (Department of Social, Community and Family Affairs 2000, 153). Legislative support for the creation of further endowed funds came in the Local Government Act 2001, which provided for the creation of 'community funds' for the purposes of supporting community initiatives. Local authorities can establish the funds and contribute directly themselves or they can accept contributions by any voluntary, business or community group, other local authority or public authority or other person.[17] Money from the fund can then be used to provide or improve amenities, recreational, cultural or heritage facilities, the protection or the enhancement of the environment and programmes to promote social inclusion and community development. Although information as to the existence of this scheme is available from the relevant department[18] and regulations were passed in 2002 to bring it into force,[19] there is little tangible evidence available of use of this innovative legislative provision (Combat Poverty Agency 2007, 50).

There remains scope, however, for the growth of both philanthropy and the foundation sector in Ireland. The Times Rich List for 2014 reveals that the wealth of Ireland's richest 250 exceeds €47.26 billion, an increase of 11 % on the 2013 figures (Sunday Times 2014). In a 2010 survey of global philanthropic giving by high net worth individuals ('HNWI'), Ireland led the way in terms of donating time and money with 20 % of its surveyed HNWI spending more than 5 h per week on charity (tying for first place with India in this respect) and 30 % of its surveyed HNWI stating that philanthropy was one of their top three spending priorities (Barclays Wealth 2010, 9). Building on this growth in June 2011, the Minister for Local Government, Environment and Heritage launched a new expanded Forum on Philanthropy with a strong foundation presence. The forum's mandate is to develop a strategy to create the optimum environment to develop charities' fundraising capacity and to expand philanthropy in Ireland.[20] The forum launched its report in

[17] Local Government Act 2001, s.109.

[18] See http://www.environ.ie/en/LocalGovernment/LocalGovernmentAdministration/LocalGovernmentFinance/#Current%20Expenditure (Accessed July 11, 2011).

[19] Local Government Act, 2001 (Commencement) (No. 2) Order, 2002, SI 213 of 2002.

[20] See http://www.communityfoundation.ie/news/news/philanthropy-forum-re-established (Accessed July 11, 2011). The forum now includes amongst its members: The Community Foundation for Ireland, Philanthropy Ireland, The Ireland Funds, ICTR, Business to Arts, Atlantic Philanthropies, The One Foundation, Dept of Finance, Dept of Environment, Community and Local Government, Fundraising Ireland and Dept of Foreign Affairs, giving foundations and their intermediaries 5 out of 11 seats on the forum.

2012, setting out key recommendations to increase philanthropic activity in Ireland.[21] Publication of the Forum's report marked an important step in benchmarking the progress of foundational and philanthropic development in Ireland as well as charting future directions for growth. On the giving side, the report proposed a National Giving Campaign to increase private giving (subsequently launched as the 'One Percent Difference' campaign in 2013) and it recommended fiscal and infrastructural measures to promote the creation of structured vehicles for major gifts. From a funding perspective, it put forward proposals to build fundraising capacity through education and training and recommended the creation of a €10 million Social Innovation Fund leveraging state funds to align matching private philanthropy for social enterprise activity.

8.4 The Statutory Framework for the Regulation of Charitable Foundation Activity in Ireland

8.4.1 Creation

The creation of a foundation may be by trust or through the establishment of a company limited by guarantee. In either case, the founder may continue involvement with the foundation through his/her appointment as a trustee of the trust or a director of the company. There is no law specific to foundations in Ireland. In the case of a charitable foundation, although the founder may continue to be involved in the running of the foundation, he/she must relinquish ownership and control entirely over any assets given to the foundation as a condition of obtaining charitable status.

According to s. 2 of the Charities Act 2009, a charitable organisation is one that promotes a charitable purpose only and that under its constitution is required to spend all its assets (both real and personal) in furtherance of that purpose except for monies spent in the operation and maintenance of the body including remuneration of the staff. Officers of the foundation, however, cannot be paid for their services to the foundation except in accordance with s.89 of the Charities Act, relating to additional non-trustee services rendered to the charity. With regards to activities, a charity cannot promote a political cause, unless the promotion of that cause relates directly to the advancement of the charitable purposes of the body.[22]

---

[21] http://www.philanthropy.ie/information/forum-on-philanthropy/report-of-the-forum-on-philanthropy-and-fundraising/. Accessed May 18, 2014.

[22] Charities Act, 2009, s.2.

8.4.2 *Registration*

A charitable company upon establishment must register with the Companies Registration Office (CRO) and provide a copy of its Memorandum and Articles of Association as well as details of its directors. If the foundation is incorporated, it must file annual returns with the CRO. As companies limited by guarantee are public companies, they do not benefit from the audit exemption and must file audited accounts each year, regardless of turnover. These returns are publicly available.

Pending the full commencement of the Charities Act 2009, there is no requirement for registration of a charitable trust deed with any statutory authority upon establishment, other than Revenue, of course, if charitable tax-exempt status is sought. If the governing instrument of the foundation is a trust, at present, such a foundation is under no legal obligation to make its annual accounts publicly available. It must prepare annual accounts, and where its annual turnover exceeds €100,000, these accounts must be audited and made available to the Revenue Commissioners upon request.

With the introduction into force of the Charities Act 2009, procedures for the registration of new charities will change. New charitable foundations, regardless of legal structure, will be required to register with the Charities Regulatory Authority under s.39 of the Charities Act. Section 39(5) sets out the requirements for registration, which include the provision of, inter alia, detailed information on the charitable purposes to be undertaken, details as to whether the charity is established in the state or has its principal place of business here, information on charitable funds held and on proposals for raising further funding; and financial accounts relating to the foundation in respect of the period of 12 months immediately preceding such application. Failure to register will constitute an offence under the Charities Act if the unregistered foundation causes the public to believe either through its activities or its promotional literature that it is a charity.[23]

Whereas, in the past, it was only possible for charities established in Ireland to apply for charitable tax exemption, changes dictated by European law have resulted in the recognition of charities established anywhere in the EEA for both regulatory and tax purposes.[24] Under s. 39(5) and (7) of the Charities Act 2009, provision is made for the registration of charities established in the state with a principal place of business in Ireland and for the registration of charities established anywhere else in the EEA with their principal places of business located outside Ireland. Equally, the Finance Act 2010 makes provision for Revenue to recognise charities established in an EEA/EFTA and to enable them to seek a determination entitling

[23] Charities Act, 2009, s.46.

[24] See C-386/04 Centro di Musicologia Walter Stauffer v Finanzamt München für Körperschaften [2006] E.C.R. I-8203; C-318/07 Hein Persche v Finanzamt Lüdenscheid [2009] ECR I-359. See also Houlder (2009).

them to tax relief on any income incurred in Ireland equivalent to the relief granted to an Irish charity.[25]

Neither company law nor trust law impose at present any additional requirements on charitable foundations. Rather, company law facilitates their operation. Under Section 24 of the Companies Act 1963, the Minister can license a limited liability company formed for the purposes of promoting, inter alia, art, religion, science or charity which intends to apply its profits to these ends and which prohibits any payment of dividends to members to dispense with the word 'limited' from its name. There are no minimum capital requirements imposed under Irish law for the creation of new foundations. Nor is state approval required for the establishment of a new foundation.

8.4.3 *Taxation*

If the foundation wishes to avail of charitable tax exemption, it must receive the approval of the Revenue Commissioners. Although officially only concerned with fiscal matters, in practice, the Revenue Commissioners have filled a regulatory void and acted as de facto charity regulators. In addition to scrutinising the governing instruments of organisations seeking charitable tax-exempt status to ensure that their objects and powers are so framed that every object to which their income or property can be applied is charitable, in the absence of a charity regulator, Revenue have overseen (albeit reluctantly) the governance of charities.

The granting of charitable tax-exempt status is extremely valuable to a foundation. A charity for the purposes of tax law is exempt from income tax[26] or corporation tax in the case of companies,[27] capital gains tax,[28] capital acquisitions tax,[29] deposit interest retention tax,[30] stamp duty[31] and dividend withholding tax.[32] A tax-exempt charity may further apply to Revenue to qualify as an 'eligible charity'.[33] This status confers extra tax benefits on a qualifying organisation since it entitles the charity to reclaim from Revenue the tax paid on a donation received from an individual tax-paying donor once the sum donated exceeds an annual

[25] Finance Act, 2010, s.23 inserting ss. 208A and 208B into the Taxes Consolidation Act, 2007. See also Revenue Commissioners Guidance (2010).

[26] Taxes Consolidation Act, 1997, ss. 207 and 208.

[27] Taxes Consolidation Act, 1997, ss. 76 and 78.

[28] Taxes Consolidation Act, 1997, s. 609.

[29] Capital Acquisitions Taxes Consolidation Act 2003, ss. 17, 22 and 76.

[30] Taxes Consolidation Act, 1997, s. 266.

[31] Stamp Duties Consolidation Act, 1999, s. 82.

[32] Taxes Consolidation Act, 1997, Chapter 8A, Part 6.

[33] Taxes Consolidation Act, 1997, s. 848A provides for a scheme of tax relief for certain *eligible charities* and other *approved bodies* in respect of donations received on or after 6 April 2001.

threshold amount, currently valued at €250 per annum. In effect, the charity therefore receives a grossed up donation, with Revenue repaying to the charity the tax already paid by the individual on the donation made. In the case of a corporate donation to an eligible charity, the corporate donor can claim a deduction for the donation as if it were a trading expense, thus reducing the overall cost of the donation to the charity.

Revenue publishes a quarterly list of organisations that enjoy charitable tax-exempt status. The June 2011 list contains the names of over 7,900 charities of which 238 include the word 'foundation' in their title. The list, however, does not reveal the charitable purposes of these foundations nor in many cases does it indicate the legal structure used by the foundation. Cross-referencing the Revenue listings with the Companies Registration Office's public records reveals that of the 238 self-identified charitable foundations, 73 % are companies limited by guarantee. The remaining 27 % are unincorporated and may be assumed to be trusts.

These figures provide a rough guide to the current size of the charitable foundation sector in Ireland. However, they are not comprehensive for two reasons. First, a further cleaning of the Revenue data reveals that organisations self-identified as trusts rather than as foundations on the Revenue website refer to themselves as foundations in their dealings with the public.[34] Second, a search of the CRO database reveals that there are in excess of 420 companies with the word *foundation* in their title and an address in Dublin. A review of this list, even allowing for the inevitable incorrect use of the word *foundation* for our purposes, reveals a far broader list of foundations than that represented by the charitable tax-exempt list.[35]

Foundations seeking charitable tax-exempt status in Ireland are required to demonstrate that the income and property of the charity will be applied solely towards the promotion of their main charitable objects as set out in their governing instruments. Any changes to the governing instrument of the organisation may only be made following receipt of advance approval in writing from Revenue.

8.5 Issues Related to the Non-distribution Constraint

During the charity's lifetime, Revenue requires a commitment by the charity to the non-distribution constraint, including the insertion of an express clause in the governing instrument to the effect that no director, trustee or officer shall receive

[34] A good example of this is Wexford Festival Trust, a tax-exempt charity that operates as the fundraising arm for the world famous Wexford Opera Festival. In its dealing with sponsors, the media and the public, however, the word 'trust' is shed and the organisation is referred to publicly as the Wexford Festival Foundation.

[35] This assumption is confirmed by Patricia Quinn, former CEO of INKEx who kindly ran data keyword searches on my behalf in the beta version of INKEx, an Irish non-profit database. See http://www.irishnonprofits.ie/ (Accessed May 21, 2014).

any remuneration or other benefit in money or money's worth from the exempted body. The Charities Act 2009, while otherwise respecting the non-distribution constraint,[36] will allow for such persons or those connected to them to be paid for additional services rendered to the charity (i.e. beyond the role of trusteeship) when payment does not exceed what is reasonable and proportionate having regard to the service provided, provided the agreement is in writing and approved by the other charity trustees.[37]

Moreover, when a charity intends to accumulate funds over a period in excess of 2 years, it must seek advance approval from Revenue, specifying the reasons why such funds are being accumulated rather than applied for charitable purposes. This requirement would have a special resonance for charitable foundations. There is, however, no legal or revenue requirement in Ireland for a charitable foundation to disburse a certain percentage of funds in any given year.

Upon dissolution of the charity, Revenue applies the Cy Près Doctrine, requiring that any remaining funds or property must be transferred to some charitable body having similar main objects to the dissolved charity, or failing that, to some other charitable body. Notification of winding up must be forwarded to the Revenue Commissioners together with a final set of accounts and details of how any residual funds at the time of dissolution were distributed. The constraints imposed upon dealing with charitable assets upon dissolution are also echoed in the Charities Act. Section 92 provides that when a charitable organisation is dissolved, the property, or proceeds of the sale of the property, of the charitable organisation shall not be paid to any of the members of the charitable organisation without the consent of the Authority, notwithstanding any provision to the contrary contained in the constitution of the charitable organisation.

8.5.1 Economic Activity

Charitable foundations wishing to engage in trading must apply for a separate tax exemption from the Revenue Commissioners.[38] The trading exemption covers trading income derived by a charity in pursuit of its charitable objects and is not granted automatically to a charity with general charitable exemption. Although trading by charities may take on a number of forms, exemption covers only two types, namely, (1) trades which are exercised in the course of the actual carrying out of a primary purpose of the charity or (2) trades carried on by the beneficiaries of the

[36] See Charities Act, 2009, s.3(3), which provides that a gift will not be for the public benefit unless it is intended to benefit the public or a section of the public and (b) in a case where it confers a benefit on a person other than in his or her capacity as a member of the public or a section of the public, any such benefit is reasonable in all of the circumstances, and is ancillary to, and necessary, for the furtherance of the public benefit.

[37] Charities Act, 2009, s.89.

[38] Taxes Consolidation Act, 1997, s.208.

charity. In both cases the profit of the trade must be applied solely for the purpose of the charity (Breen 2010).

8.6 Governance of Charitable Foundations

8.6.1 The Emerging Regulatory Framework

The Charities Act 2009 and the Companies Acts 1963–2010 prescribe the governance requirements for charities. The Charities Act sets out the obligation to keep proper books of account, to file an annual report and, where relevant, audited annual returns with the CRA and to ensure that those running the charity are qualified to do so. There is no mention of duties of care or any reference to the fiduciary duties of charity trustees in the Act.

The Companies Bill 2012, which will overhaul entirely the legal framework for company law in Ireland when enacted, is much stronger on corporate governance requirements for public companies limited by guarantee. Part B4 includes an entire chapter on corporate governance standards (chapter 4) and specifies the duties of directors and other officers in chapter 5. Given that 73 % of charitable foundations are companies limited by guarantee, when enacted the Companies Bill 2012 will have a major impact on the running of these foundations.[39]

Trust law in Ireland requires serious reform and has not been the subject of statutory revision in many years. Despite a Law Reform Commission Report on Trust Law calling for reform of this area in 2008 (Law Reform Commission 2008),[40] no reform has taken place to date and the principal legislation remains the Trustee Act 1893. Great reliance is thus placed on common law jurisprudence in ascertaining the fiduciary standards to which charitable trustees are held.

A new Governance Code for non-profit organisations was developed by the non-profit sector in 2012. The Governance Code is a voluntary code of practice designed for use by community and voluntary organisations in Ireland.[41] The Code provides five key principles[42] that apply to all organisations before breaking down all organisations into one of three category types[43] (grouped according to size,

---

[39] For further details on the Companies Bill, see http://www.clrg.org/ (Accessed May 21, 2014).

[40] See also Law Reform Commission (2006) for earlier efforts by the Law Reform Commission to bring to light anomalies and short falls in the particular area of charitable trusts and legal structures for charities.

[41] See www.governancecode.ie (Accessed May 21, 2014).

[42] The principles relate to the provision of leadership within the organisation, the exercising of control over it, being transparent and accountable, working effectively and behaving with integrity.

[43] Comprising volunteer only organisations, emergent and small single-staff membered organisations, and larger, more complex organisations with 10 or more members of staff.

function, staff members and maturity) and setting out how each type should go about effectively implementing these principles. The Governance Code currently has 78 compliant signatory organisations with a further 409 organisations listed as being on the journey towards adoption of the code.[44]

There is no specific reference to foundations or issues particularly pertinent to them in any of these codes or statutes. The absence of a vocal foundation movement in Ireland, equivalent to the United Kingdom's Association of Charitable Foundations, coupled with lack of charity regulation requirements in the past have contributed to this void. It may be that when the new Charities Act is brought fully into force that grant-making foundations in particular will find issue with the regulatory requirements to which they will then be subject from both a regulatory burden perspective and a disclosure perspective.[45]

8.6.2 Transparency and Reporting Requirements

At present, there is minimal regulatory review of charitable activities on a systematic basis. Revenue reviews the financial accounts of all new charities within 18 months of the date that exemption was first granted. Thereafter, a charity remains subject to periodic review by Revenue to ensure that the income of that body continues to be applied for charitable purposes only. However, with more than 8,000 organisations enjoying charitable tax-exempt, Revenue's role, given limited resources, is more reactive than proactive. The other existing statutory body, the Commissioners of Charitable Donations and Bequests, plays a facilitative role, assisting charities in situations in which their governing instruments do not provide them with the necessary powers to achieve their charitable missions. Although the Charities Acts 1961–1973 envisaged an investigatory and quasi-enforcement role for the Commissioners, the lack of enforcement powers in those statutes has rendered these provisions nugatory (Breen and O'Halloran 2000).

The Charities Act 2009 goes a long way towards introducing greater accountability and transparency in relation to charities. It requires all charities, whatever their legal structure, to be registered with the CRA. It will be an offence under the Charities Act for a body (other than a registered charitable organisation) to hold itself out as a charity or to describe itself or its activities in terms that would cause members of the public to reasonably believe that it is a charitable organisation.[46] Once registered, all charities will be required to prepare an annual report for submission to the CRA.[47] Unincorporated charities will be required to submit

[44] The Governance Code at http://www.governancecode.ie/about.php (Accessed May 21, 2014).

[45] See Dunn (2013) on the regulatory issues that currently arise in the United Kingdom for foundations subject to the UK's Charities Act 2006.

[46] Charities Act, 2009, s.46.

[47] Charities Act 2009, s. 52.

with their annual report an annual statement of accounts, which depending on their size may be audited or examined.[48] Incorporated charities which already file annual statement of accounts with the CRO will be required to submit only the annual report, the contents of which may be tailored by regulation to enable the CRA to extract the same level of relevant information from all charities. These reports will be made available to the public.

An exception to this procedure is provided for in Section 54 of the Charities Act. According to Section 54, the rules relating to public inspection shall not apply to the reports and accounts of private charitable trusts. A private charitable trust is defined in Section 54(3) as a charitable trust that is not funded by donations from the public. Thus, although a private individual or an institution that establishes and endows a charitable foundation by way of trust deed must still prepare and file an annual report and statement of accounts with the CRA, these documents will not be made publicly available. This provision is likely to facilitate the privacy of a small number of family foundations that are operated by way of trust. A review of the Revenue Listings of named foundations enjoying charitable tax-exempt status as at June 2011 reveals 64 foundations that are unincorporated and thus presumably established by way of trust. Of these foundations, the vast majority represent fundraising foundations that actively seek public funding and so will be unable to avail of Section 54. However, a percentage of these bodies are endowed family foundations or trusts associated with HNWIs and thus will benefit from the privacy provided by Section 54.[49]

8.7 Conclusion: The Future for Foundations in Ireland

The new regulatory framework in Ireland for charities does not give specific consideration to charitable foundations. This oversight is understandable given the relatively undeveloped size of the Irish foundation sector and perhaps, to a degree, the absence of comprehensive and cohesive charity regulation in the past. It is likely that when the Charities Act 2009 is fully commenced in 2014 and the CRA established under it is operational, issues may arise for charitable foundations requiring further attention or lobby for reform. The revamped Forum for Philanthropy holds out the greatest potential for invigorating the growth of the sector, bringing together as it does, the appropriate officials from the Department of Finance along with a strong foundation representative presence. The joint capacity of state and sector to deliver on the ambitious targets set in the Forum's 2012 Report

[48] Charities Act 2009, ss.48–51.

[49] Thus, the O'Reilly Foundation, the One Foundation, the Naughton Foundation, the Quinn Family Foundation and the Charles McCann Charitable Foundation are amongst those foundations likely to benefit from this exemption from public scrutiny.

to grow private philanthropy should provide some indication as to the viability and likely sustainability of foundations in Ireland.

Bibliography

2 into 3. 2010. Steering your non-profit organisation through the storm actions a board and CEO can take to deliver the promise in tougher times, Dublin.

Barclay's Wealth. 2010. *Global giving: The culture of philanthropy*. London: Barclays Wealth.

Breen, O. 2010. Holding the line: Regulatory challenges in Ireland and England when charity and business collide. In *Modernising charity law: Recent developments and future directions*, ed. Lowndes McGregor and K. O'Halloran. Aldershot: Edward Elgar.

Breen, O., and K. O'Halloran. 2000. Charity law in Ireland and Northern Ireland: Registration and regulation. *Irish Law Times* 18(1): 6–14.

Centre for Nonprofit Management. 2006. *The hidden landscape: First forays into mapping nonprofit organisations in Ireland*. Dublin: Trinity College Dublin.

Combat Poverty Agency. 2007. *Mapping social inclusion in local authorities*. Dublin: Combat Poverty Agency.

Department of Social, Community and Family Affairs, Supporting Voluntary Activity. 2000. *A white paper on a framework for supporting voluntary activity and for developing the relationship between the state and the community and voluntary sector*. Dublin: Stationery Office.

Donoghue, F. 2001. Ireland. In *Foundations in Europe: Society, management and the law*, ed. Then Schluter and P. Walkenhorst, 156–163. London: The Directory of Social Change.

Donoghue, F. 2004. *Foundations in Ireland*. Dublin: Centre for Nonprofit Management, Trinity College Dublin.

Dunn, A. 2013. Regulation absent: The chimera of charitable foundation law in England and Wales. In *Developments in foundation Law in Europe*, ed. C. Prele. Dordrecht: Springer. chapter 5.

European Foundation Centre. 2005, April. *Foundation facts and figures across the EU – Associating private wealth for public benefit*. Available at http://www.efc.be/programmes_services/resources/Documents/Facts_Figs_publication.pdf.

European Foundation Centre. 2008, May. *Foundations in the European Union: Facts and figures*. Report on work by EFC research task. Available at http://www.efc.be/programmes_services/resources/Documents/EFC-RTF_EU%20Foundations-Facts%20and%20Figures_2008.pdf.

Forum on Philanthropy. 2009. *Baseline report*. Dublin: unpublished.

Houlder. 2009. Restricted charity tax breaks ruled unlawful. *The Financial Times*, January 27, 2009.

Law Reform Commission. 2006. *Report on charitable trusts and legal structures for charities*. Dublin: LRC 80–2006.

Law Reform Commission. 2008. *Report on trust law: General proposals*. Dublin: LRC 92–2008.

McKinsey and Company. 2009. *Global philanthropy initiative: Philanthropy in the Republic of Ireland*. Dublin: McKinsey and Company.

Revenue Commissioners Guidance. 2010. Non resident charities (Resident in and Operating in an EEA/EFTA State) Seeking a Determination, DCHY1, June 2010.

Sunday Times Rich List. 2014. *The Sunday Times*, May 18, 2014.

West's Encyclopaedia of American Law. 2011. At http://www.enotes.com/wests-law-encyclopedia/foundation. Accessed 30 June 2011.

Chapter 9
The Civil Code and the Special Laws Ruling Foundations in Italy

Chiara Prele

9.1 Introduction

This chapter starts with a brief outline of the evolution of foundations in Italy, mostly happened in the last 30 years.

Afterwards, this chapter examines Italian foundation law. This differs when contained in Civil Code (general rules) or in special laws (special rules).

Section 9.4 deals with Civil Code regulations, while Sect. 9.5 deals with special laws and particularly with the two most important special foundations: opera-theatre foundations and foundations of banking origin, a very special kind of foundation existing in Italy.

Section 9.6 deals with tax law.

Section 9.7 outlines possible developments of foundation law, based on the current situation.

9.2 The Evolution of Foundations in Italy

Italian law and Italian society has not considered the non-profit sector to be very important and useful until the 1970s, when foundations started to grow in number and in importance.

Previously, the Italian approach to foundations was a hostile one. One reason is that foundations' rules are in Civil Code, which was adopted in 1942 during the totalitarian regime. This regime held itself a hostile approach to associations and foundations and therefore inspired the Code rules to a strong government's

C. Prele (✉)
Independent legal scholar and consultant on foundation and non-profit organization, Turin, Italy
e-mail: chiaraprele@yahoo.it

C. Prele (ed.), *Developments in Foundation Law in Europe*, Ius Gentium: Comparative Perspectives on Law and Justice 39, DOI 10.1007/978-94-017-9069-7_9,

oversight towards foundations. Foundations mostly started by an individual's will or testament.

Soon afterwards, in 1948, the Constitution entered into force, establishing democracy in Italy again. A more favourable approach started to non-profit entities takes place.

However, foundations' growing in number and in importance happened in the last 30 years. In this time, foundations have become very different both from the foundations that started previously and from one another.

This great change is due to several reasons. Civil society increased its work in several fields; the state turned to a favourable approach to foundations; fiscal incentives for non-profit organisations were introduced. Nowadays, non-profit organisations play a relevant, though not subsidiary, role in helping the state in many fields, such as culture, education, health and research. In fact, Italian welfare state has faced a financial crisis in recent years.

In 2001, Constitutional Law No. 3/2001 introduced the so-called *principio di sussidiarietà* in the Italian Constitution (art. 118). According to it, private citizens and organisations can conduct activities for public and general interest, and the states, regions, counties, and municipalities allow these activities.

Several laws about non-profit sector were passed during the last decades. These laws do not specifically refer to foundations but affect them.

In fact, laws passed during the last decades focus on fiscal incentives and on activity more than on juridical form. While in the past the law focused on a specific entity (e.g. a foundation), today the activity is much more important, whatever juridical entity conducts it.[1] Most of these rules introduce advantages, mostly fiscal, for the non-profit sector.

Not only the approach is different, but also some features in the more recently started foundations are different from foundations in older times.

9.3 Foundations Ruled by the Civil Code or by Special Laws

Until approximately three decades ago, the only Italian rule about foundations was the Civil Code, First Book. These rules are general rules and regulate any foundation, whatever its type and mission.

Laws related to a specific non-profit sector establish special requirements for its entities. In most cases, foundations operating in specific sectors observe both the Civil Code and special requirements related to their activity.

Moreover, Italian foundation world includes other outstanding types of foundations which are ruled by special laws.

[1] Scholars call this phenomenon '*netralization of juridical forms*' (Manes 2004, 267).

This phenomenon started around 1990 and has been followed since then. As a result, several foundations were established and ruled by laws different from one another. Any special law refers to a special type of foundation and cannot be applied to a different one. Civil Code rules are residual for special foundations.

Laws ruling special foundations inspired to a favour towards foundations. In fact, they created foundations in fields traditionally cared by different entities, mostly public entities. In recent years, the state has considered the foundation as a flexible juridical entity and adapted it to different needs. These laws, in most cases, inspire to modern principles, such as transparency and accountability, introduced in Italian system in recent years.

Civil Code rules and special laws have different limitations and restrictions and thus diverse impacts on foundations. This is due to the opposite principles that inspire them and to their different adoption eras.

9.4 The Foundation in the Civil Code

The Italian Civil Code, First Book, contains few rules about foundations; some of them are common to associations.[2]

Since 1942, foundation law has been modified in several aspects. Some regulations were cancelled. Thus, foundation law is today less organic than its original version.

The Code does not contain any definition of foundation. Scholars provide one, based on the two principal foundation's characters: endowment and scope. A foundation is 'an endowment that must be used to pursue the foundation's scope and cannot be re-appropriate by the founder'.[3] Thus, endowment and scope are strictly related, and the first should suffice to pursue the latter.

The Code requires two elements to start a foundation: an act and a registration.

The act may be a testament (foundation *mortis causa*) or a notarial deed (foundation *inter vivos*).

[2] The Roman law-based difference between foundation and association lies in focusing the entity on endowment (foundation, *universitas bonorum*) or on people (association, *universitas personarum*). More recently, the difference has become weaker, and association's characters are present in several foundations, too. In fact, organisation (that refers to people) is now an outstanding feature in foundations. In a special type of foundation, the so-called *fondazione di partecipazione*, founders can join the foundation later or participate with their expertise and work instead of endowment.

[3] According to the importance organisation has gained in present foundation, some scholars suggest to include organisation in foundation's definition (Galgano 1989, 1; Bianca 2002, 312).

9.4.1 Registration

The most important change of the Civil Code, First Book, is the registration, which was modified by Decree No. 361/2000. The central government or the regional government registers the foundation, depending on operating the foundation in the whole country or only in the region.

The decree introduced a less discretionary procedure, though not cancelled discretionary choice. In fact, Decree No. 361/2000 states that the foundation's endowment should be sufficient for its scope but does not fix its amount.

Therefore, registration procedure is at present a restriction to foundations. Registration completely depends on the supervising authority's choice. Normally, this reflects jurisprudence, which requires a sufficient endowment to pursue the scope[4]; at times, it registers a foundation with a small endowment and certain future contributions, as it frequently happens in *fondazione di partecipazione*.

On the contrary, actual needs require a non-discretionary procedure, because of different reasons. First, the autonomy and widely agreed importance of non-profit sector do not justify a discretionary choice any more. Secondly, in the last 10 years, at least, a simplified procedure was introduced in many fields, for instance, for corporations by article 32 Law No. 340/2000.[5] Lastly, foundations and corporations are becoming more and more similar, in particular in their activity. This is a reason to suggest the same simplified non-discretionary registration for foundations.

A less discretionary registration procedure requires rules about endowment, similar to the existing ones for corporations, e.g. a requirement about the minimum endowment. Such a rule would be clear and would make it easier to start a foundation, too. The registration authority would just check that the existing endowment corresponds to the rule, with no discretion at all.

At present, registration completely depends on the supervising authority's choice. Normally, this reflects jurisprudence, which requires a sufficient endowment to pursue the scope.[6]

With registration, a foundation becomes a legal entity with legal personality, which means limited liability for its administrators.

The possibility of a foundation not being registered, and therefore not being a legal entity, is mostly excluded in Italy by legal scholars and jurisprudence (De Giorgi 1982, 260–262; Bianca 2002, 355–357).[7]

---

[4] Consiglio di Stato, 23.4.1958, no. 316, 10.7.1970, no. 473, 7.12.1993, no. 1628.

[5] This solution was proposed in 1993 by a Commission studying the topic (Gruppo di Studio Società e Istituzioni). The Commission evaluated that this type of registration respects the founder's choice, and if good rules are stated, it is safe for beneficiaries and creditors.

[6] Consiglio di Stato, 23.4.1958, no. 316, 10.7.1970, no. 473, 7.12.1993, no. 1628.

[7] Cass. Sez. 1, 24.8.1979, n. 4681; App. Trento, 27.5.1974; App Trieste, 30.4.1975; Trib. Napoli, 26.6.1998; T.A.R. Friuli-Venezia Giulia, 25.3.1996, n. 143). On the contrary, the following affirm the possibility of a foundation with no legal personality: Galgano (1963, 172 and following, 1989, 2 and 8) and Costi (1968, 29 and following).

As it was said, starting a foundation requires two acts: a notarial deed or a testament by the founder, the registration. With no registration, no foundation exists.

Registration is an important moment also for limitations to the founder. In Italian foundation, the founder starts the foundation, gives the endowment and can designate the very first board. He can revoke his will, until he has made the foundation's activity start, or the foundation has been registered (art. 15 Civil Code).

9.4.2 Characters of Foundations: Endowment and Scope

The most important elements in a foundation are endowment and scope. Even more important is the relation between the two. The endowment shall be solely used to pursue the scope and be sufficient to this as well. As written in par. 10.4.1, the law does not fix an amount for the endowment.

In case of dissolution, the founder cannot receive the foundation's endowment back. Giving the endowment to the foundation when creating it, the founder shows his will to devote the endowment to an *external* scope.

As far as the scope is concerned, Italian jurisprudence requires that the foundation's scope should not be generic.[8]

The Civil Code just requires the scope be indicated in the deed; Decree No. 361/2000 states that the scope should be possible and allowable (art. 1). However, jurisprudence and traditional legal scholars require a public utility scope. Only public utility can justify that an endowment is forever devoted to a scope, in contrast with the principle of economical resources' best usage. This can be the only reason for devoting an endowment to a perpetual scope.[9] According to a different opinion, foundations can follow a private interest as well, since no rule denies it; this opinion can be even stronger now that foundations conduct economic activities.[10]

Actually, a foundation in Italy can currently pursue both public (i.e. of interest to many people) and private (i.e. of interest to a limited number of people) scopes.

The scope is outstanding, while it is not the activity, i.e. the ways to fulfil the scope. The Civil Code does not deal with the foundation's activity; on the opposite, as already said, recent laws focus on it. Nevertheless, this technique seems to be quite unusual for a general law as the Civil Code; it can be useful for a classification of foundations, but this is not what the task of the Civil Code is. Also, the foundation's autonomy should be granted as much as possible, and a clear

[8] Consiglio di Stato, Sez. II, 27.7.1979, n. 1228.

[9] For this opinion: Cass. 10.7.1979, n. 3969; De Giorgi (1982, 262), Bianca (2002, 314) and following; Galgano (1996, 37).

[10] For this opinion: Ferrara (1958), Costi (1968, 13), Rescigno (1968, 811 and following), Zoppini (1995, 13 and following and 54 and following), Ponzanelli (2000, 76).

statement about its scope should suffice. Therefore, activities can be stated in statute or decided, or at least influenced, by the board.

A final issue about the foundation's scope concerns the possibility of whether or not modification is possible, which it is presently not. However, the topic is worth considering because of the evolution that foundations have undergone, such as conducting economic activities, which require some adaptability to special needs (Rescigno 1967 828; contra, Zoppini 2005, 273). Additionally, governance and the decisions of the boards have grown in importance (Vittoria 1975, 312).

The real character of a foundation, as with any non-profit organisation, is the non-distribution constraint, which means that profits cannot be distributed to the members but should be devoted to the foundation's scope and activity. Whatever is the scope of the foundation, the non-distribution constraint is the very nature of foundations, as it is for any non-profit organisation. It can even be affirmed that other characteristics of the foundation's purpose are additional to the non-distribution constraint. However, the Italian Civil Code does not specify whom non-distribution constraint applies to (Zoppini 2005, 373).

It is important to affirm that the non-distribution constraint does not mean that a foundation cannot gain profit or conduct profit-making activities, such as economic or enterprise activities, which are currently more and more important for a foundation. Therefore, there is no doubt that a foundation can conduct economic activities, which is another important issue (see below).

9.4.3 Governance

The Civil Code does not contain a specific rule about the governance; it just deals with board members' liability and rule limitations to the representation of the foundation (arts. 18 and 19).

The only recognised entity is the board.

When Civil Code was adopted, in 1942, foundations were mostly considered to be endowments. Over time, governance has increased in importance, and the modern foundation shows a great change as far as the governance is concerned.

Actually, modern foundations have introduced other committees, such as an audit committee. Some foundations, such as *fondazioni di partecipazione*, which are similar to Italian associations, sometimes have an assembly, which is the typical board for associations, but not for foundations.

An audit committee could be needed in order to control the foundation's activity. The Civil Code does not rule any audit committee; on the opposite, it states a strong external oversight, such as government's control, which is in contrast to foundation's autonomy.

At the same time, regulations show no limitations in terms of introducing bodies. As already mentioned, in *fondazione di partecipazione*, whose characters belong both to foundation and to association, an assembly (a typical association body) is present as well.

9.4.4 Supervision

The supervising authority (state or region) also imposes limitations referred to the whole foundation's life. During foundation's life, the authority controls acts from the legal point of view and can annul acts (art. 25 Civil Code).[11]

In case of foundation's dissolution, a decision of the authority is needed (art. 27 Civil Code). Therefore, even if dissolution's reasons are ruled,[12] the foundation itself cannot decide to extinguish, and any board decision will be useless.[13]

The Civil Code deals with state or region supervision and focuses on control on acts. On the opposite, recent trends focus on controlling the whole activity, not singular acts. In fact, transparency is now a principle in Italian law.

However, while transparency has been an outstanding principle since 1990 for the state and the public administration, and later for corporations, there is no provision of it for foundation ruled by the Civil Code. As a result of this lack, foundations suffer from limitations, for instance, in fund raising that is more and more important when the initial endowment is little and, especially at present, when the state and the public sector devolve less and less money to foundations (as cultural foundations), because of lack of resources. Citizens and corporations quite hardly give money in case they cannot see reports, especially financial reports. The absence of reporting can cause a limitation in a foundation's successful activity.

9.4.5 Dissolution

The foundation dissolves when it has fulfilled the purpose or the purpose has become impossible, or not more useful, and in any case stated in statute or deed. In most cases, it can be transformed as well.

Dissolution is stated by the supervising authority.

The destination of the residual endowment after dissolution is ruled by the will and the statute. In case these acts contain no rule, the decision is taken by the supervising authority (art. 31 Civil Code).

Therefore, the board cannot take any decision about the foundation's residual endowment. Moreover, most scholars identify a restriction in the impossibility of the founder to return the given endowment. In fact the statute states the person or

[11] The supervising authority can also remove board members in case of inactivity and designate a person in charge of adopting specific acts, before a board is designated.

[12] Dissolution causes are purpose's achievement, impossibility to achieve the purpose (in case the entity has lost its endowment or this has become insufficient); in cases stated by the deed or the statute; purpose becoming scarcely useful (art. 27 Civil Code).

[13] After the decision of the supervising authority of extinguishing the foundation, board members cannot take decisions anymore; if they do, they are personally liable (art. 29 Civil Code).

entity to whom the residual endowment will be devolved after the foundation's dissolution (Galgano 1989, 8–9; contra Costi 1968, 29).[14] This argument is based on the very nature of foundation: starting a foundation, the founder cannot dispose of the endowment any more (unless until the foundation's registration); the foundation is a legal entity and personal entity, completely separate from the founder, with separate liability on foundation's endowment. Because of the essence of foundation itself, the endowment cannot return to the founder nor to his heirs.

The supervising authority can state different solutions to dissolution as well. Since the supervising authorities vary in different parts of the country, decisions can be different. Most state authorities, however, admit only the transformation, which is the only solution regulated by the Civil Code beyond dissolution (art. 28 Civil Code). Therefore, most supervising authorities do not admit merging of foundations nor homogeneous transformation decided by the board (i.e. into a different non-profit entity). On the contrary, many scholars and jurisprudence admit it now,[15] after corporation reforms introduced heterogeneous transformation (i.e. from non-profit to profit entity and vice versa) in the Civil Code (art. 2500-septies, art. 2500-octies Civil Code).

9.4.6 The Economic Activities

Modern foundations often conduct economic activities. The Civil Code does not rule this issue, which was introduced in foundations' operation later on.

Certainly, in modern Italian foundations, economic activities can be considered as a useful income, in particular for foundations in cultural fields, which often have problems related to lack of resources.

At present, with no rule on this issue in the Civil Code, both legal scholars and jurisprudence express different opinions. The topic is strictly linked to the non-distribution constraint as the main characteristic of the foundation and the actual foundation's scope, while the economic activity generates profits.

The different opinions are focused on the possibility for a foundation of leading economic activity only as a non-dominant activity, or also as the dominant activity, until being the economic activity is the foundation's sole activity.

The opinion that denies the possibility of conducting economic activity as the dominant foundation's activity is based on being the foundations non-economic entities, without the publicity and supervision that enterprises have to observe.[16] A minority of legal scholars agree today with this opinion.

[14] Costi, in fact, admits that the foundation has egoistic purpose.

[15] See Fusaro (2004, 300), Baralis (1999, 1110), Vittoria (1992, 1148) and Corte di Cassazione, 7.3.1977, n. 925.

[16] For this opinion:Bianca (2002, 344–345).

On the contrary, the majority of legal scholars affirm now, with no doubt, that a foundation can conduct economic activity, either as dominant or non-dominant.[17] This opinion is based on the observation that the Civil Code rule which defines the entrepreneur (art. 2082) does not mention the profit purpose[18]; moreover, present legislation allows other entities, different from corporations, to conduct economic activities.

In the absence of rules, legal scholars and jurisprudence affirm that the foundations which conduct economic activities should be enrolled to the enterprises register, and to foundations whose dominant activity is the economic one the rules of Civil Code referred to commercial enterprises should be applied (art. from 2188 to 2221).[19] In cases when the economic activity is non-dominant for a foundation, there are different opinions.[20] The more recent opinion affirms that the rules of Civil Code referred to commercial enterprises should be applied.[21] There is a clear need of definitive rules.

The jurisprudence allows the foundations to conduct economic activities, both as dominant and as non-dominant activities. Nevertheless, it requires this activity to respect the statute and the public utility foundation's scope[22]: the economic activity should be related to this scope. Otherwise, the economic activity cannot be considered a foundation's activity and people who act are liable.[23]

Foundations can even be a holding, conducting economic activity in order to distribute profits to another entity, which pursues the foundation's scope. This is allowed by both legal scholars and jurisprudence.[24,25]

Therefore, foundations conducting economic activity are one of the most important issues nowadays. Many foundations can grow conducting these activities; opinions of scholars and jurisprudence differ between each other; there are no definitive rules.

---

[17] For this opinion are the authors who have firstly studied this topic, some decades ago. They are Rescigno (1967, 812–47) and Costi (1968, I) and, more recently, Galgano (1989, 6) and De Giorgi (1999, 305).

[18] This point has been affirmed by jurisprudence as well (Cass., Sez. L, 28.8.2003, n. 12634).

[19] Cass., Sez. 1, 18.9.1993, n. 9589; Cass. Sez., 1, 19.2.1999, n. 1396; App Milano, 7.4.1989.

[20] See Cass., 9.11.1979, n. 5770 and 17.1.1983, n. 341; Galgano (1989, 6), Costi (1968, 27) and Rescigno (1968, 812–13).

[21] For this opinion: Campobasso (1994, II, 590 and following), Zoppini (1995, 176 and following) and Ponzanelli (2000, 163).

[22] Jurisprudence still requires a public utility purpose, in contrast with the opinion of most legal scholars, as mentioned in this study.

[23] Cass. Sez. L, 1.9.1994, n. 17543; Cass., Sez. L., 29.10.1998, n. 10826; Cass., Sez. L, 26.1.2004, n. 1367; App. Milano 25.2.1981; App. Roma 28.10.1986; App. Milano, 7.4.1989; Trib. Milano, 27.1.1988, 16.7.1988 e 17.7.1994.

[24] Consiglio di Stato, Sez. I, 12.12.1961, n. 2186; Trib. Chiavari 11.7.1959.

[25] For larger considerations on this topic, see Prele (2007a).

9.5 Foundations Ruled by Special Laws

As mentioned above, since the 1990s, the state has created foundations, by either transforming public institutions into foundations or starting new foundations. This study considers the best known cases of both types: the opera-theatre foundations and the foundations of banking origin, generally and more concisely called banking foundations. It deals with these foundations' characters. Any special law deals with a special type of foundation and cannot be applied to other foundations.

Italian special foundation laws are quite recent and thus inspired to modern principles. Therefore, special rules differ from Civil Code rules for many aspects.

It is important to underline that not only laws related to special foundations contain most of the rules about these foundations but also create the foundations. In fact, in most cases, no acts are required for these foundations to start.

Around 1990, Italian government started a significant *privatisation* process. The state preferred foundations to public institutions, and it often offered incentive to corporations and non-profit organisations to participate in these foundations. Foundations grew in number; however, most of newly created foundations differ from the foundation as regulated by the Civil Code.

9.5.1 Opera-Theatre Foundations

In 1996, Decree No. 367 transformed opera-theatre from public entities into foundations. It stated that not only the state and other public entities (region, municipality) but also corporations and non-profit organisations participate in these foundations.

Decree No. 367/1996 served as a model for later transformations of other public entities into foundations.

It should be observed that partnership between the state or other public entities and private entities started quite recently in Italy, and opera-theatre foundations are one of the first cases. Generally speaking, philanthropy is a quite recent phenomenon in Italy, and the state has introduced fiscal incentives only in recent years, contemporary to its need for resources.

In any foundation, or other legal entity, where the state acts with private partners, the state offers incentives to private partners, such as corporations and non-profit organisations, to participate in these foundations, but also maintains control on the foundation. This is a typical Italian feature, which makes it really hard to recognise public entities and foundations.

Opera-theatre foundations show this character. The state holds an oversight on foundations, both on its most important acts and on the board. Each foundation must adopt its own statute; however, since the statute must respect the Decree No. 367/1996, foundation's autonomy is quite restricted.

The opera-theatre foundations are regulated by the special law and by the Civil Code in residual parts. These foundations' governance is similar to the one now in use by foundations ruled by the Civil Code (president, board, board of auditors on financial reports), while it differs from foundations of banking origin's governance, which is inspired by modern principles.

The decree states that opera-theatre foundations can conduct economic activity: it expressly requires that profits are totally devolved to the foundation's purposes and cannot be distributed (art. 10). Economic activities are an interesting opportunity for these foundations, like for any cultural foundations: a theatre or a museum can receive income from their bookstore, cafeteria and accessory services. The economic activity's accounting shall be separated from the foundation's.

Entities different from the state and other public entities have limits regarding their presence on boards, since the majority of members are nominated by the state or other public administration (Decree No. 367/1996, art. 10).[26] Referring to this aspect and many others, which show the control and strong presence of the state, and public entities in general, in all the foundations created by the state itself, many legal scholars affirm that this is a *false privatisation.*[27]

These foundations' rules are very similar to the previous entities' ones; also, they are strongly connected with public administration and public institutions. In these foundations' boards, public institutions (such as region or municipality) are well represented, much more than private citizen or entities who donate money to the foundation; the state supervises the foundations.

Though the law considers these foundations as private entities (therefore ruled by quite free rules when compared to public entities, i.e. rules about procurement), they seem to have characters belonging to public entities (e.g. state control, state or region representative in board). This issue is important, and it is related to some European Commission decisions about competition.

According to the definition provided in article 1(9) of directive 2004/18/EC of the European Parliament and of the Council of 31 March 2004 on public procurement, a body 'established under public or private law.....financed for the most part by the State, or regional or local authorities, or other bodies governed by public law, or subject to management supervision by those bodies, or having an administrative, managerial or supervisory board, more then half of whose members are appointed by the State, regional or local authorities or by other bodies governed by public law' is a *public-equivalent body.*

Therefore, it was a *false privatisation.*[28]

[26] The president of opera-theatre foundation is the city mayor, as it used to be when the theatre was a public entity.

[27] The statement is affirmed by several scholars: Basile (1996, 103), Marasà (2005, 199), Consiglio Italiano per le Scienze sociali (2002, 27), Guarino (2005, 67) and Prele (2006).

[28] Marasà (2005).

These entities are *foundations* just by name. In some cases, the Italian Courts affirmed the public nature of such foundations and their duty to observe rules about public procurement.[29]

Other laws created foundations, mostly in cultural fields or in scientific research, many of which follow the above-mentioned model.

Actually, more than 10 years after their creation, these foundations mostly failed to attract private partners and resources. As a matter of fact, the biggest problem of privatisation in Italy is due to the fact that the state offers incentives to corporations and non-profit organisations to participate in these foundations but also maintains control on the foundation's board.

Therefore, the effects of *privatisation* look very much limited. Nevertheless, these foundations have characters proper of foundation as well: their definition by law, non-distribution constraint; their organisation; and the state control. Some scholars[30] observed they are *atypical* foundations, firstly because of their creation by the state.

The opera-theatre foundations are an interesting case of *fondazione di partecipazione*.

In *fondazione di partecipazione*, partners should not necessarily participate in the foundations from its creation and with money. As already mentioned, this type of foundation, which was created by legal scholars (Bellezza and Florian 1998), has some characteristics typical of associations. Its endowment is progressively formed during the life of the foundation; members can join the foundation not only at the beginning but also later and still be called founders. Also, they can participate in the foundations with any kind of contribution: money, work or expertise. If applied to foundations ruled by Civil Code, later contribution might cause problem for registration, since the endowment sufficient to the scope is required.

9.5.2 Foundations of Banking Origin

The most outstanding type of foundation ruled by a special law are foundations of banking origin, also called banking foundations.

These foundations were created by steps. Before this long process, banks were public institutions.

Law No. 218/1990 and Decree No. 356/1990 separated banking activity, conducted by a corporation, and shareholdings in it, belonging to another entity, which most scholars considered to be a foundation.

This was clearly stated later, by Law No. 461/1998 and Decree No. 153/1999, which introduced new rules.

---

[29] Cass., Sez. Un., 8,2.2006, n. 2637, related to Santa Cecilia Academy.

[30] For this opinion: Guarino (2005, 116), Freni (1996, 1115) and Marasà (2005, 192).

By deadlines, banking foundations should no more hold major shareholdings in the banking corporations. They pursue social utility scopes and the promotion of economic development in fields indicated by the law itself.[31] Banking foundations can run activities only in these fields. Among them, the foundation, every third year, selects no more than five fields and devotes to them at least 50 % of its revenue. The fields of activity are written in the foundation's statute. A minority of scholars (Fiorenzano 2004, 1923) consider this as a limitation to foundation's autonomy in selecting and planning their activity. According to major opinion,[32] the fields' list serves just as a purpose's specification. Since the banking foundation's scope has a social utility, it often refers to an activity that the state or other public organisation conducts, too. Consequently, the banking foundation has an integrative role, besides the state's one in times of lack of public resources (Guarino 2005, 62–63).

The law about foundations of banking origin also considers the activity, whereas the Civil Code just deals with foundation's scope.

Banking foundations are mostly grant making. They have great endowment and must invest it in order to obtain adequate profit (art. 7 Decree No. 153/1999). Modern trends suggest that foundations of banking origin's grants are based on projects' evaluation. Normally today banking foundations issue call for projects and then select the best ones, while in previous times grant-making activity did not follow any selection nor evaluation.

Because of their large endowments, foundations of banking origin really changed the realm of non-profit Italian universe.

Previous selection to grants is not a restriction to banking foundations: actually, it is mostly stated in statutes or foundations' internal regulations; banking foundations themselves started, in their practice, to issue call for projects and then selected. Nor is this a restriction for foundations which receive grants, these foundations are simply invited to present projects; the selection offers them a sort of protection, also in terms of possibility to appeal the decision that is discretionary.

Besides the larger grant-making role, foundations of banking origin are sometimes today operating foundations. They can do so, since the law does not contain any limitation about their being grant-making or operating foundations.[33] On the contrary, article 3, Decree No. 153/1999 states that these foundations pursue its scope in any possible way according to their legal status.

As any foundation, the foundation of banking origin can conduct economic activity.

[31] Fields are family, education, training, volunteering, philanthropy, religion, elderly assistance, civil rights, prevention of crimes and public security, food and agriculture security, social housing, buyers' protection, civil protection, health, sports activities, drug abusage, mental illness, scientific and technological research, environment, art, cultural beauty and public works.

[32] Also in more recent jurisprudence: Corte costituzionale no. 300 and 301/2003.

[33] In Italy, the majority of foundations are operating; however grant-making Italian foundations are quite a big universe since the creation of foundations of banking origin. In fact, these foundations with large endowments are considered to be grant making.

Article 3 Decree No. 153/1999 contains, however, a limitation: this activity must be related within the foundation's scope as specified by statutes and in fields of the foundation's activity.[34] The same limitation is stated for banking foundation's shareholdings in corporations whose sole activity is the economic one related to the banking foundation, as specified above (art. 6). Moreover, foundations of banking origin cannot conduct banking activity.

In contrast with foundations ruled by the Civil Code, in foundations of banking origin, the economic activity has the above-mentioned limitations.

These foundations can conduct related economic activity directly, or indirectly, through a corporation, linked to the foundations which own its shareholding. This issue has been examined several times by European Court of Justice,[35] and Italian Courts as well. In fact, fiscal incentives to foundations that conduct economic activities can distort competition, as in contrast with article 87 (1) EC.[36] About banking foundations, the Court stated that 'the mere fact of holding shares, even controlling shareholdings, is insufficient to characterise as economic an activity of the entity holding those shares, when it gives rise only to the exercise of the rights attached to the status of shareholder or member, as well as, if appropriate, the receipt of dividends, which are merely the fruits of the ownership of an asset. On the other hand, an entity which, owning controlling shareholdings in a company, actually exercises that control by involving itself directly or indirectly in the management thereof, must be regarded as taking part in the economic activity carried on by the controlled undertaking and must therefore itself, in that respect, be regarded as an undertaking within the meaning of Article 87 (1) EC'.

As far as economic activity is concerned, some scholars (Baratti 2005, 63–69) observe a limitation in requiring the foundation to choose its fields of activity every third year. This limitation of time can fit the foundation's grant-making activity while can disincentive or cause problems to economic activity. In fact, economic activity needs an organisation requiring large investments of money. This problem could be solved selecting the same field of activity after the third year. Actually, as the Corte Costituzionale[37] noticed, the selection of fields of activity for 3 years is not a restriction, since a foundation's activity programme should be based on many years. On the contrary, such programmes allow the foundation to gain profits and use them in the most effective way.

Restrictions and limitations mentioned above for foundations ruled by he Civil Code are unknown to banking foundations. In fact, laws referred to them are quite recent and therefore inspired to different principles: favour to foundations and transparency.

---

[34] This rule is in accordance with jurisprudence, which requires that economic activity is related to the foundation's purpose.

[35] Many decisions, e.g. 10.1.2006, C-222/04.

[36] Article 87 (1) EC prohibits aid which affects trade between member states and distorts or threatens to distort competition.

[37] Decision No. 301/2003.

Decree No. 153/1999 describes banking foundations' governance. It distinguishes three different functions (setting strategies and programmes, managing the activities, auditing) governed by three different bodies. Therefore, banking foundations have a board of governors, which determine strategies and programmes and verify results of the activity, being responsible for the pursuit of the foundation's purposes; moreover, it has some specific functions, such as modifying the statute; an executive committee, which acts according to the board of governors' decisions and manages the foundation's operations; an auditing committee, whose functions are not specified by the law.

Special requirements are needed for membership. Members should be honourable, professional and cannot be invested of the same office both in the foundation of banking origin and in the banking corporation. These restrictions ensure transparency and accountability. Banking foundations' statutes must contain and clarify the meaning of these requirements and might introduce more requirements as well.

Article 4 Decree No. 153/1999 has had some modifications since the original version. It states that board of governors must include members representing the area where the foundation of banking origin operates. However, this restriction cannot go too far. In fact, a more recent rule[38] required that the municipalities, provinces and regions of the area are represented in the board; the Constitutional Court[39]corrected the rule, stated that any local entity, and not only territorial local entities, should be represented. In fact, the restriction in Law No. 448/2001 would have allowed territorial local entities' influence on the foundation's choices through their political representatives.

Actually, 20 years after the most recent law on foundation of banking origin was adopted in 1999, all over the country, these foundations are strongly influenced by politics. It is well known that foundations' boards are formed by decision of territorial political representatives. As a consequence, politics and mostly territorial local politics can influence the banking foundation's choices.

Governance should respect the rules about decision making and consequently should be accountable for it. This provision is not really a restriction: on the contrary, the need for transparency requires it. In fact, laws about foundations of banking origin, differently from foundations ruled by the Civil Code, do not lack regulations, and not necessarily regulations are restrictions.

Decree No. 153/1999 expressly defines the non-distribution constraint within foundations of banking origin (art. 8). In particular, this rule refers to all the people, especially members of boards, to whom non-distribution constraint applies. It excludes the remuneration that these people receive for their activities.

According to article 10 Decree No. 153/1999, the Minister of Economy supervises foundations of banking origin until the First Book of the Civil Code is reformed and until the foundation of banking origin remains the major shareholder or maintains the control, directly or indirectly, of bank corporations. This second

---

[38] Law No. 448/2001, which modified article 4.11., Decree No. 153/1999.

[39] Decision No. 301/2001.

condition does no more exist today. However, a more recent rule[40] affirms that foundations of banking origin will be overseen by the Minister of Economy until the Civil Code reform, though they are not a bank corporation's major shareholder. This is the real restriction to banking foundations.

Actually, these foundations are non-profit organisation and do have the correspondent legal status and legal personality. The nature, private or public, of foundation of banking origin has been debated for years,[41] until the Constitutional Court affirmed its nature of non-profit organisation.[42] Therefore, supervision of Minister of Economy seems to be in contrast with the foundation's nature and autonomy. Also, the existence of an internal control, such as the auditing committee, makes external supervision less necessary.

Scholars and jurisprudence affirmed that the Minister's supervision should be as small as possible, at any rate it should consider only legitimacy. On the contrary, today the Minister's power goes far beyond: the Minister can revoke the executive committee and the auditing committee that act in contrast with the law.

Except from the Minister of Economy's supervision, the special law about foundations of banking origin contains restrictions and limitations inspired by transparency, accountability, reporting and effectiveness, which are not in contrast with present trends.

9.6 Tax Law

Some quite recent special laws have an impact on foundations, though not expressly referred to them.

As mentioned above, recent laws mostly refer to the activity, whatever the legal entity conducting the activity is. In most cases, the law regulates the activity, since it is worth having fiscal incentives because of its social utility.

Recent Italian non-profit law mostly introduced fiscal incentives. This is a very important issue for the life and work of a foundation.

However, it may be difficult to match recent fiscal law with outdated civil rules.

Moreover, fiscal laws introduced fiscal entities, which should be combined with civil entities.

On the opposite, an organic legislation needs to fix forms, characters and categories first, and afterwards state fiscal regulations. This method was quite recently followed in Italy to reform corporation law.

An example will be useful to explain the case.

---

[40] Article 52, Decree No. 78/2010, converted into Law No. 122/2010.

[41] Some scholars: Rescigno (1992, 398–99), Merusi (1993, 15), Cassese (1991, 34) and Belli and Mazzini (2000, 310).

[42] Decisions No. 300 and 301/2003.

Decree No. 460/1997 introduced Onlus, i.e. non-lucrative organisations with social utility.

Different legal entities (foundations, registered associations, non-registered associations) can be registered as Onlus if they show the characters required by the decree. Requirements are mostly related to the activity: the Onlus must conduct a social utility activity in a field mentioned by the decree (social assistance, health assistance, charity, education, scientific research, sports, art and culture, environment, civil rights).[43] Restrictions to Onlus are the exclusive public utility scope; non-distribution constraint; to devolve profits to Onlus' purpose; to conduct exclusively an activity in the above-mentioned fields and activities directly related to it; after Onlus' dissolution, to devolve endowment to other Onlus; limitations to the economic activity in its proportion to the Onlus main activity; reporting. Any entity having these characters can be registered as Onlus whatever its legal status is. Onlus benefit of a special fiscal treatment. The above-mentioned characters are required throughout the entire Onlus' life. In fact, Onlus are registered in the Onlus register and overseen by the Agenzia per le Onlus. Registration as Onlus does not imply any discretionary decision: the entity should only show the characters required by the law.

When compared to foundations, restrictions and limitations to Onlus look stronger. Actually, an Onlus can be either a foundation or an association, registered or non-registered, or a different legal entity. Requirements as Onlus are related to fiscal incentives; requirements as foundation, or association stated in the Civil Code, are related to their regulation as a legal entity. If a foundation, Onlus must register both on the Onlus register at Agenzia per le Onlus and as a foundation, according to the Decree No. 361/2000 (paragraph 9.4.1).

The foundation Onlus has both the characters of a foundation and the above-mentioned characters as an Onlus. When compared, some characters are similar, though more clearly stated for Onlus. So in non-distribution constraint, that is the very essence of foundation's purpose according to scholars, and it is expressly stated by article 10, Decree No. 460/1997 about Onlus. Actually, decree about Onlus is inspired by modern principles of favour and transparency. In fact, reports and audits are required. When compared to foundation, Onlus looks more regulated. It seems to be more restricted (e.g. reports or audits are required); however, most times the law states a requirement in order to benefit for fiscal advantages.

The impact of the decree about Onlus is outstanding. Many non-profit organisations register as Onlus in order to receive fiscal advantages. As a result, a great number of Onlus exist today in Italy. They have the same fiscal treatment and the same characters required by Decree No. 460/1997; however, they may have a different legal entity according to the Civil Code. In this approach, the fiscal treatment deserves prime consideration. An Onlus is firstly identified by its activity.

---

[43] The list includes almost all public utility fields. Therefore, it is a mere specification of the public utility idea.

9.7 Conclusion

A general overview over Italian foundation law shows different features in Civil Code and in special laws. The first inspires to updated principles, the latter to modern ones. The first starts statements by considering legal entities, the latter by considering the activity. Impacts on foundations are therefore completely different.

Civil Code rules look outdated, and Italian foundations today are mostly different from the time when the Civil Code was adopted in 1942. At that time most foundations were created through a person's will and testament; on the contrary, today foundations are mostly started by institutions (corporations and the public administration or the state itself). In 1942, most foundations did not have big endowment and their beneficiaries were well established; modern foundations often have a broad scope and countless beneficiaries. Foundation's endowment was considered the most relevant issue; today foundations sometimes initially start with a small endowment and receive periodical contributions to finance their activities.

The above-mentioned changes were possible because of the lack of detail in regulations about foundations in the Civil Code, which permitted the supplementation of the rules through statutes.

It is worth mentioning that the need to reform the Civil Code, First Book, has been affirmed for many decades. More recently, the Commission which studied corporate law reform (Civil Code, Fifth Book, 2003) observed that non-profit entities urge a reform as well. Various ministers and deputies proposed bills, which never came into a law. It is likely that a reform will not pass in the near future.

When considered from the strictly legal point of view, the impact of the whole foundation law is not organic, because of the existence of rules having different approaches. Also, considering legal entities quite irrelevant creates a disorder in a Civil law system.

However, special laws applying to different legal entities contain innovations worth being introduced, as non-distribution constraint regulations, reports and audits. They could serve as an example to a forthcoming Civil Code reform.

Foundations ruled by the Civil Code may be regulated by more recent laws as well, e.g. because they are Onlus. If not, reports, audits and transparency are not compulsory, unless their statutes inspire to modern principles. Still, a Civil law system must provide fair update rules for any entity, leaving supplementation to bylaws only where the law is clear and not weak.

Bibliography

Baralis G. 1999. Enti *non profit*: profili civilistici. *Rivista del notariato* I.

Baratti, G. 2005. Fondazioni di origine bancaria e imprese strumentali. In *Le imprese strumentali delle fondazioni di origine bancaria*, ed. A. Stefanelli. Milano: Giuffrè.

Basile M. 1996. Sono davvero fondazioni le casse di previdenza dei liberi professionisti trasformate in <<fondazione>>?. *Nuova giurisprudenza civile commentata*. I.

Bellezza, E., and F. Florian. 1998. *Le Fondazioni nel Terzo Millennio*. Firenze-Antella: Passigli.

Belli, F., and F. Mazzini. 2000. Term "Fondazioni bancarie". In *Digesto delle discipline privatistiche, Sezione Commerciale*. Torino: UTET.

Bianca, C.M. 2002. *Diritto civile. Vol. I. La norma giuridica, I soggetti*, 2nd ed. Milano: Giuffrè.

Campobasso, G.F. 1994. Associazioni e attività d'impresa. *Rivista di diritto civile*, II.

Cassese, S. 1991. La ristrutturazione delle banche pubbliche e gli enti conferenti. In: ACRI. *La legge 30 luglio 1990, n. 218.*

Consiglio Italiano per le Scienze Sociali. 2002. Libro Bianco sulle Fondazioni in Italia. Queste Istituzioni, no. 127.

Costi, R. 1968. Fondazione e impresa. *Rivista di diritto civile* I.

De Giorgi, M.V. 1982. Le persone giuridiche in generale. Le associazioni e fondazioni. In: *Trattato di diritto privato*, vol. II, dir. P. Rescigno. Torino: UTET.

De Giorgi, M.V. 1999. Il nuovo diritto degli enti senza scopo di lucro: dalla povertà delle forme codicistiche al groviglio delle leggi speciali. *Rivista di diritto civile* I.

Di Majo, A. 1997. Le neo-fondazioni della lirica: un passo avanti e due indietro. *Il corriere giuridico* 1.

Ferrara, F. 1958. Le persone giuridiche. In: *Trattato di diritto civile*, dir. F. Vassalli, Reprint. 2nd ed. Torino: UTET.

Fiorenzano, S. 2004. Le fondazioni di origine bancaria nuovamente al cospetto della Corte costituzionale: alla ricerca di un duplice equilibrio tra autonomia privata e tentazioni neo-dirigiste. *Giurisprudenza italiana.*

Freni, E. 1996. La trasformazione degli enti lirici in fondazioni di diritto privato. *Giornale di diritto amministrativo.*

Fusaro, A. 2004. Trasformazioni eterogenee, fusioni eterogenee ed altre interferenze nella riforma del diritto societario sul<<terzo settore>>. *Contratto e impresa.*

Galgano, F. 1963. Sull'ammissibilità di una fondazione non riconosciuta. *Rivista di diritto civile* II: 172–188.

Galgano, F. 1989. Term "Fondazione I, Diritto civile". *Enciclopedia giuridica dell'Istituto dell'Enciclopedia Italiana* XIV: 1–9.

Galgano, F. 1996. *Le associazioni. Le fondazioni. I comitati*, 2nd ed. Padova: CEDAM.

Guarino, G. 2005. Le fondazioni tra Stato, società e mercato. In: *Le fondazioni e le fondazioni di origine bancaria*, Atti dei convegni Lincei 219. Roma.

Manes, P. 2004. Le nuove prospettive in materia di fondazioni. *Contratto e impresa.*

Marasà, G. 2005. *Fondazioni, privatizzazioni e impresa: la trasformazione degli enti musicali in fondazioni di diritto privato. La riforma di società, cooperative, associazioni e fondazioni.* Padova: Scritti.

Merusi, F. 1993. Dalla cassa di risparmio alle fondazioni. Metacon.

Ponzanelli, G. 2000. *Gli enti collettivi senza scopo di lucro*, 2nd ed. Torino: Giappichelli.

Prele, C. 2002. *Il privato partner per la cultura.* Torino.

Prele, C. 2006. Le fondazioni nell'evoluzione della società. *Economia pubblica* 3–4: 71–85.

Prele, C. 2007a. L'esercizio dell'attività d'impresa da parte della fondazione. Giurisprudenza piemontese, 1.

Prele, C. 2007b. *La fondazione. Evoluzione giuridica di un istituto alla ribalta.* Torino: Fondazione Giovanni Agnelli.

Prele, C. 2010. Legal issues considered for changing Italian foundation law. ISTR conference working papers, vol VII, Istanbul Conference 2010.

Prele, C. 2011. The impact of legal restrictions and limitations on Italian foundations. In: Foundations in Europe: Legal contexts, legal aspects. Giving: 59–73.

Rescigno, P. 1967. Fondazione e impresa. *Rivista delle società*: 812–847.

Rescigno, P. 1968. Term "Fondazione c) Diritto civile". *Enciclopedia del diritto,* XVII: 790–814.

Rescigno, P. 1992. *La fondazione e I gruppi bancari.* Banca, impresa, società.

Vittoria, D. 1975. Le fondazioni culturali ed il consiglio di amministrazione. Evoluzione della prassi statutaria e prospettive della tecnica fondazionale. *Rivista del diritto commerciale e del diritto generale delle obbligazioni*, I.
Vittoria, D. 1992. Il cambiamento del tipo per gli enti del I libro del codice civile. *Contratto e impresa*.
Zoppini, A. 1995. *Le fondazioni. Dalla tipicità alle tipologie*. Napoli: Jovene.
Zoppini, A. 2005. Problemi e prospettive per una riforma delle associazioni e fondazioni di diritto privato. *Rivista di diritto civile* II: 365–377.

Chapter 10
The Foundation Governance under Liechtenstein Foundation Law

Francesco A. Schurr

10.1 Competition amongst Foundation Jurisdictions in Europe

10.1.1 Boom of Foundations

The foundation industry is currently experiencing a boom across Europe for the most varied social and economic reasons. With regard to common-benefit foundations, the enormous number of new formations (and also additional endowments) can be explained by the fact that – due to the current financial situation – the public purse in many EEA countries is being tightened, increasingly leading to spending cuts in areas typically falling within state competence (e.g. culture, science, etc.).

The trend towards the formation of new private-benefit foundations is due to the foundation's suitability as an instrument for succession planning – possibly as a supplement to or a replacement for a testament/trust. The likely largest generation change is presently taking place in Europe. To survive this transition, many small- and medium-sized businesses require the stabilising effects of a succession planning vehicle.

10.1.2 Criteria for Choosing a Location for Foundations

Individuals wishing to use a foundation to realise their personal common- or private-benefit goals will have to take numerous factors into consideration in order to be able to identify the ideal location in which to realise their projects. In practice, advisors use a variety of criteria to determine the suitability of a location.

F.A. Schurr (✉)
Institute for Financial Services, University of Liechtenstein, Fürst-Franz-Josef-Strasse, 9490 Vaduz, Liechtenstein
e-mail: francesco.schurr@uni.li; http://www.uni.li/gesellschaftsrecht

C. Prele (ed.), *Developments in Foundation Law in Europe*, Ius Gentium: Comparative Perspectives on Law and Justice 39, DOI 10.1007/978-94-017-9069-7_10,

The first significant criterion is the impact taxation will have on a foundation and on its beneficiaries. Besides these tax considerations, increasingly more importance is being attributed to purely civil law factors in deciding upon a location. In this regard, emphasis is often placed on the degree of flexibility associated with determining the foundation's purpose: for example, the option of transforming a common-benefit foundation into one with private-benefit purpose and vice versa. It is striking that issues concerning foundation governance are currently the subject of particularly fierce debate at all levels of European foundation law (i.e. during legislative processes, in the judiciary and in academic literature on the topic).

A general trend is emerging in advisory practice: Where the selection of a location for a foundation is concerned, attention is increasingly being paid to the issue of governance. In this respect, a return to the roots and the origins of the foundation can be detected. According to the European understanding of foundations, a foundation is an entity holding ownerless assets. It is ultimately only subject to the will of its founder, as originally expressed by him/her on the formation of the foundation (Universität Heidelberg 2008). Compliance over decades or even centuries with a foundation's purpose requires a careful balance to be struck between its administration and supervision. The fact that foundations lack a corporate element, a characteristic present in other legal entities, highlights the fact that foundations are considerably more susceptible to abuse than any other legal entities. It also illustrates that the quest for an ideal form of foundation governance is more complex than a comparable form of corporate governance for companies.

The modern approach in advisory practice is to look for jurisdictions which provide a high degree of legal certainty with regard to pursuing the foundation's purpose over a long period of time; the greatest degree of freedom possible for the founder in establishing the internal organisation of the foundation; confidentiality concerning the formation of the foundation; and a high degree of expertise amongst the official authorities and courts involved. From these criteria, a link between structure and function – that is, the inextricable connection between a foundation's governance and its purpose – stands out. In today's globalised world, where it is possible to actively choose a legal system in which to establish a legal entity, the triumphant jurisdictions will be those with a mixture of hard and soft law geared towards fulfilling the requirements of this modern advisory approach.

10.1.3 ECJ Case Law on the Freedoms of Establishment and Capital

Competition amongst the various jurisdictions in the EU (and thus also in the EEA) was strongly stimulated by the European Court of Justice's case law on the free movement of capital[1] and its case law on the freedom of establishment.[2]

---

[1] ECJ Case C-384/06 Stauffer [2006] ECR I-08203; ECJ Case C-318/07 Persche [2009] ECR I-359.

[2] ECJ Case C-212/97 Centros [1999] ECR I-1459; ECJ Case C-208/00 Überseering [2002] ECR I-9919.

At the end of the first decade of the twenty-first century, it is now clear that – on consistent application of the basic freedoms – a prospective founder is able to freely choose a jurisdiction (in which to form a foundation) from the many legal systems in the EEA which recognise the institution of the foundation. In the future, such jurisdictions will follow a trend previously set in company law with regard to limited liability companies. They will adapt their tax and civil law legislation to make it as attractive as possible in order to entice prospective founders from other EEA countries. An excellent example of this is the complete reform undertaken in Liechtenstein of its foundation law, which was completed in 2008. This reform brought the Principality's foundation law in to line with modern standards and requirements.[3] Since entering into force on the 1st of April 2009, the new provisions (Art 552 §§ 1ff) provide Liechtenstein with an ideal basis upon which to hold its own in an ever harsher competitive environment. A question which will be discussed below is the extent to which legal requirements of foundation governance enshrined in national law and their enforcement by courts play a decisive role for prospective founders in choosing a jurisdiction. In addition to considerations concerning hard law, issues regarding self-regulation (soft law) are also are gaining greater importance in relation to foundations and are thus no longer restricted to company law.

10.2 General Considerations for Governance Concepts

10.2.1 Corporate Governance

Current trends in company law indicate that regulatory frameworks are becoming a central criterion for corporate supervision. *Corporate governance*, a term originating from the academic study of business, has become relevant due to the practical consideration that a company should be protected from any misconduct on the part of its management bodies. This leads to the requirement of establishing an adequate monitoring system. In this respect, reference is made to the conflict-prone relationship between the company's management and its shareholders (Müller and Fischer 2009, 112). The so-called principle-agent relationship (Kreutz 2007, 51) can in principle be subjected to regulation by both hard and soft law. However, existing mandatory law, found in both legislative acts and case law, is often not an adequate means of getting to grips with the complex situations which arise in the context of modern business management. It is for this reason that numerous corporate governance codes have been produced across the world. These codes set out good

[3] See the Law of 26 June 2008 on the Amendment of the Persons and Companies Act, Liechtenstein Law Gazette 2008, No. 220 (*Gesetz vom 26.06.2008 über die Abänderung des Personen- und Gesellschaftsrechts, LGBl. 2008, Nr. 220*); in this context, see Schauer (2008, 7); with regard to its historical development, see Tschütscher (2008, 79).

management practice as well as internal corporate control mechanisms for the protection of share- and stakeholders and thus follow economic models. They are normally voluntary codes based on the '*comply-or-explain*' principle (von Werder 2003, 15ff; Jakob 2008, 83). The use of corporate governance codes leads to a standardisation of business management standards and their monitoring. This demonstrates that soft law can also bring about legal harmonisation (Hopt 2003, 32 ff).

10.2.2 Foundation Governance

In European legal tradition, foundations are more or less the only type of legal entities which exist without a so-called *corporate element*. As a result, the legal concept of shareholders is completely missing from its realm. This is because a foundation constitutes a special purpose fund which belongs to itself and is subject only to its own purpose. The autonomous nature of the special purpose fund requires the establishment of an organisational structure by means of which the long-term pursuit of the foundation's purpose – even long after the death of the founder – is rendered possible (Schauer 2008, 28). The logical consequence of this is that tighter control mechanisms are ultimately necessary for foundations than for companies (Müller and Fischer 2009, 114). Having said that, it is imperative that the realisation of the purpose is not hampered by complicated regulatory bureaucracy or insufficient expertise on the part of the regulators. Therefore, every foundation finds itself on a fine line between the rigidity usually associated with regulation and the flexibility needed to pursue its purpose.

Looking at a map of Europe, it is striking that some jurisdictions leave the task of monitoring foundations to public institutions. In Germany, for example, public administrative bodies deemed competent by the respective foundation law of each federal state are given the responsibility of supervising the foundations within their state (Richter 2007, 789ff). Other European jurisdictions (e.g. Austria) have placed the responsibility for the supervision of foundations within the ambit of the courts, as an independent force in the country (Briem 2009, 14). Effective supervision is assured by the fact that beneficiaries play an active role in the process and have a right to petition the court (Kalss 2008, 50). The system in Liechtenstein represents a combination of the systems in place in Austria and Germany. It is much more sophisticated and distinguishes between the supervision required for common-benefit foundations, which are subject to state supervision, and for private-benefit foundations, which are supervised by courts acting in response to petitions (Kerres and Proell 2009, 322). This combined system of governance could certainly be taken as a prototype for the future development of a supranational foundation law in Europe.[4]

[4] With regard to the prospects of inclusion of the possible structures of governance in a future system of foundation governance, see Jakob and Studen (2010, 93ff).

10.2.3 *Normative Entrenchment of Foundation Governance*

The general development towards legal entities regulating themselves, which first began in the context of listed companies, is increasingly being extended to foundations (Jakob 2009, para. 444). In this regard, the Swiss Foundation Code should be noted as an example. Like other voluntary codes on foundations in Europe, it is intended to contribute significantly towards closing any lacunae in hard law by means of a suitable system of soft law (Sprecher et al. 2009).

As experience from company law shows, it is not rare for principles from self-regulatory standards to be taken into consideration in legislation and case law and ultimately be written into mandatory law. This was the case in Liechtenstein when its foundation law underwent a complete reform and valuable governance principles, originally only contained in voluntary codes, were integrated into hard law.

10.3 Structures of Governance under the New Liechtenstein Law

10.3.1 *Internal and External Governance*

In comparison to other foundation laws in Europe, the new Liechtenstein law can be categorised as especially innovative. This is because it offers governance structures for which statutory law has been *optimised*. The legal provisions concerned are in many cases optional, such that the governance structures *can be adapted* still further by founders.

It is necessary to distinguish between two very different types of legal instruments governed by the same set of provisions (Art 552 §§ 1ff PGR): common- and private-benefit foundations. It is only the first category of foundations which is subject to supervision by the foundation supervisory authority (STIFA); private-benefit foundations are not subject to compulsory supervision by this public administrative body. For the latter type of foundations, a considerable emphasis is placed on the beneficiaries as constituting an internal control body (Jakob 2009, paras. 453ff; Schauer 2008, 31ff).

The fact that family foundations, for example, can exist completely independently of state supervision clearly gives Liechtenstein a definite competitive advantage over other jurisdictions. Merely by determining the purpose of the foundation on its formation, it is possible to ascertain whether the future foundation will be subject to supervision by the STIFA (Jakob 2009, para. 448).

The Definition of Common Benefit

Pursuant to Art 552 § 29(1) PGR, the foundation supervisory authority (STIFA) is responsible for supervising common-benefit foundations. Common-benefit foundations are understood as foundations whose purpose is of benefit to the general public. This is taken to be the case when a foundation's activity serves the common good in a charitable, religious, humanitarian, scientific, cultural, moral, social, sporting or ecological sense (Art 107(4a) PGR). In Liechtenstein, there is also a special feature which should be mentioned: A common good is also deemed to be served even if only a specific category of persons benefits from the foundation's activity (H.S.H. Prince Michael of Liechtenstein 2008, 111). The definition of common benefit in Liechtenstein, as relevant for determining the governance structure applicable, is liberal in comparison to other European jurisdictions. In accordance with the principle of private autonomy, the founder may pursue common-benefit goals by dedicating assets, even if this is not authorised by the foundation's management. This is because the founder's goals will be deemed to be of sufficient common benefit when these are compatible with the common good (Hopt and Reuter 2001, 10).

Voluntary External Governance for Private-Benefit Foundations

A unique feature in the Liechtenstein system is that external governance is not restricted exclusively to common-benefit foundations. Private-benefit foundations can choose to be placed under such supervision – by so determining in the foundation deed (i.e. by opting in). This means that public administrative bodies can also become involved in monitoring more than just the philanthropic sector (Hammermann 2008, 69).

If, on forming a Liechtenstein private-benefit foundation, no choice is made to opt in, the foundation's internal governance structure will form the basis of supervision. In such cases, it is left to the foundation participants (Art 522 § 3 PGR) to exercise their supervisory functions (Jakob 2009, paras. 474ff).

Multidimensionality in Comparison to Other Systems of Foundation Law

On international comparison, Liechtenstein stands out with its combination of external and internal governance, which has been in place since the reform of its foundation law. The same applies to the approach of combining supervision by the STIFA with that of audit authorities. This approach has been borrowed from Switzerland, where Art 83c ZGB also provides for co-operation between the audit authorities and the supervisory authority.

In contrast, supervision of private foundations in Austria is undertaken by the courts – and not by any administrative authorities. This approach has the advantage that the judiciary is politically independent. The opposite approach is taken in Germany, where the supervision of foundations lies within the ambit of public administrative bodies. These individual approaches were merged into a unique multidimensional governance structure in Liechtenstein (see above).

10.3.2 *Official Supervision of Foundations*

The mandatory provisions concerning state supervision contained in Liechtenstein foundation law are tempered by the fact that the foundation supervisory authority and the courts co-operate with one another where punitive measures are required. This almost completely prevents the work of the STIFA from being influenced by political considerations. Following the reform of Liechtenstein's foundation law, responsibility for foundation supervision has been transferred to the Office of Justice (which is responsible for land and public registration) (Art 552 § 29 (2) PGR). This means that the STIFA is now independent of the Liechtenstein government. The new foundation supervisory authority is very impressive; it has extensive expertise and an excellent range of services for current and prospective foundations.[5]

With regard to the duties and responsibilities of the foundation supervisory authority as set out in the new Liechtenstein foundation law, a distinction must be made between areas requiring preventative and punitive measures.

Preventative Measures

The second sentence of Art 552 § 29(3) governs the scope of the preventative measures available. Under this provision, the foundation supervisory authority is entitled to request information from a foundation and to order an inspection of a foundation's books and documents, which is to be carried out by an audit authority (Jakob 2009, para. 460). The appointment of an audit authority may be dispensed with for financial reasons (Art 552 § 27(5) PGR together with Arts 4 and 5 of the Regulation of Foundations Act).[6] In such cases, the foundation supervisory authority may itself inspect a foundation's books and documents.

[5] With regard to the foundation supervisory authority's duties and responsibilities as well as its organisational structure, see Hammermann (2008, 67ff).

[6] Merkblatt betreffend die Befreiung von der Revisionsstellenpflicht aufsichtspflichtiger gemeinnütziger Stiftungen gemäß Art 552 § 27 Abs 5 PGR iVm Art 5 und Art 6 Abs 2 b StRV, see www.llv.li/files/aju/pdf-llv-aju-newsletter_2010_02.pdf.

Punitive Measures

The fourth sentence of Art 552 § 29(3) PGR governs the scope of the punitive measures available. Under this provision, the STIFA can ensure that executive bodies are dismissed, special audits are carried out or resolutions passed by the executive bodies are set aside, if these are to the benefit of a foundation. Such measures may, however, not be carried out by the STIFA itself. Instead, a petition must be filed in court within the framework of special non-contentious civil proceedings.[7] The new foundation law has thus introduced a combination of two models, which leads to a so-called supervision of the supervisors: Ongoing state supervision in the form common to Switzerland is combined with supervision by the courts, which only act on the basis of petitions. The Austrian Private Foundation Act only contains the latter model of court supervision (Jakob 2009, para. 461).

At the moment, it is still difficult to determine whether the mixture of state and court supervision will stand the test of time – and perhaps even serve as a model for other jurisdictions in Europe. Concerns are increasingly being raised by the industry that the establishment of two levels of supervision is leading to a considerable increase in bureaucratic work. This critical view is also supported by economic considerations. The high expenditure required for involving two public institutions (administrative authorities and courts) can ultimately only be justified using the argument that abuse will be completely eliminated by this sophisticated system of governance and that this in turn will contribute greatly to creating trust and confidence in the system. Considering the current competition amongst jurisdictions, a dual system of supervision could become an essential criterion for ensuring that Liechtenstein, rather than another jurisdiction, is chosen as the location of preference for an international foundation.

A Combination of Internal and External Governance for Common-Benefit Foundations

As far as common-benefit foundations in Liechtenstein are concerned, internal governance has also been given due consideration. An audit authority within the meaning of Art 552 § 27 PGR is of relevance in this context. Where an audit authority is established, some of the STIFA's duties and responsibilities are delegated to this internal body. In this respect, there are similarities between the legal approaches taken in Liechtenstein, Switzerland and Austria (Arts 83b, 83c, 87 1bis ZGB and § 20(3) PSG). Courts are also involved in appointing an audit authority: A court makes the appointment of an audit authority on recommendation by the founder concerned (Art 552 § 27(3) PGR). In making such appointments, the potential for any obvious conflicts of interest (especially of holding multiple posts

[7] See Act of 21 April 1922 on non-contentious procedure, Liechtenstein Law Gazette 1922 No. 19 (*Gesetz vom 21.04.1922 betreffend das Rechtsfürsorgeverfahren, LGBl. 1922, Nr. 19*).

in the foundation, Art 552 § 27(2) PGR) must be considered. Such conflicts of interest are clearly present where members of another executive body of the foundation, employees of the foundation, people with close family connections with members of executive bodies of the foundation, and beneficiaries of the foundation are involved (Jakob 2009, paras. 390f).

Conclusion

As far as common-benefit foundations in Liechtenstein are concerned, the STIFA and audit authorities work together in respect of preventative measures, while the STIFA works together with the courts within the framework of special non-contentious civil proceedings in respect of punitive measures. With regard to the new approach involving collaboration between the STIFA and the courts, the Liechtenstein legislature itself refers to it as a so-called key provision of the new system (Bericht und Antrag 2008, 111).

10.3.3 Altering the Purpose as a Measure of Governance Structures

Effective long-term foundation management often requires altering a foundation's purpose. It should be highlighted that, for this purpose, the foundation supervisory authority may apply to the court within the framework of special non-contentious civil proceedings pursuant to Art 552 § 33 PGR, if one of the following conditions is fulfilled: the purpose has become unachievable, impermissible or irrational or if circumstances have changed to the extent that the purpose has acquired a quite different significance or effect. The idea behind this provision is to prevent a foundation from becoming detached from the intention of its founder. Any amendment of the purpose must be consistent with the presumed intention of the founder concerned (Rick 2009, paras. 14ff). In such cases, the presumed intention of the respective founder must be established by applying the interpretative rules of the theory of intimation (in German, *Andeutungstheorie*) (OGH 03.08.2000, LES 2000, 240; OGH 06.03.2008, LES 2008, 354ff). This doctrine requires two steps to be taken: The intended purpose must be determined by analysing the facts of the specific case and the statements made by the founder in that case; thereafter, the question of whether a commensurate intimation of the intended purpose has been achieved must be answered (Bösch 2005, 493f).

Pursuant to Art 552 § 33(3) PGR, foundation participants are also entitled to file a petition in court for the amendment of a foundation's purpose. If no such application for amendment is made by the STIFA, foundation participants may petition the court in place of the STIFA (Rick 2009, para. 19).

The foundation supervisory authority may also file a petition for the amendment of other contents of a foundation deed or a supplementary foundation deed in accordance with Art 552 § 34(1) PGR. Foundation participants are also entitled to petition the court to this effect pursuant to Art 552 § 34(2) PGR (Schurr and Büchel 2009, 115). This is because an order for supervisory measures may be issued by the court on the basis of a petition filed by either the STIFA or the other foundation participants. Both the STIFA and other foundation participants can therefore act as applicants in special non-contentious civil proceedings. Under Art 552 § 3 PGR, founders, entitled beneficiaries, prospective beneficiaries, discretionary beneficiaries, ultimate beneficiaries, the executive bodies of foundations and members of these executive bodies are deemed to be foundation participants. It would of course be possible to regard subsequent donors as foundation participants in spite of their exclusion from the exhaustive list provided in Art 552 § 3 PGR. Ultimately, the decision rests with the courts. They must determine on a case-by-case basis whether such people holding an interest in filing petitions as provided for in Art 552 § 29(4) or Art 552 § 35(1) PGR also qualify as petitioners, despite not being included in the definition of participants in Art 552 § 3 PGR (Jakob 2009, para. 468f).

10.3.4 Supervision of Private-Benefit Foundations

Foregoing Mandatory External Governance

As indicated above, it is possible for private-benefit foundations to exist under Liechtenstein law without being exposed to any type of external governance whatsoever. While private-benefit foundations may choose to place themselves under the supervision of the state as carried out by the STIFA, this is a voluntary act. Public authority influence on foundations is thus reduced to any action taken by the courts on the basis of petitions filed. Courts may only issue court orders if a petition has been filed by foundation participants or in very rare and clearly defined cases ex officio. Clearly, the internal governance structures are paramount in private-benefit foundations. In this respect, Liechtenstein's private-benefit foundations resemble their Austrian equivalents.

Beneficial Owners as the Mainstay of Internal Governance

As far as non-officially supervised foundations are concerned, responsibility for supervision lies with the beneficial owners of the foundation (Zollner 2009, 77). It is therefore ultimately the beneficiaries who are the mainstay of the internal governance structure. The beneficiaries have their own separate interest in ensuring that the foundation's purpose as outlined in the foundation documents is in fact pursued (Schauer 2008, 33; OGH 23.07.2004, LES 2005, 392). The strong role played by beneficiaries as a body enforcing compliance with the foundation's purpose represents a significant advantage of the legal situation in Liechtenstein in respect of foundation governance. This distinguishes the approach taken in Liechtenstein foundation law from that of some other jurisdictions. In Germany, for example, there are no legislative provisions governing beneficiary rights as such, nor have these been considered in case law. On the other hand, there are other countries which take an approach similar to the one taken in Liechtenstein. In Austria, for example, beneficiary rights have actually been enshrined in the Austrian Private Foundation Act. Under Swiss law, beneficiaries may lodge complaints with the foundation supervisory authority against acts or omissions on the part of the executive bodies.[8] Looking back to the time preceding the reform of Liechtenstein's foundation law, it becomes clear that supervision by the beneficiaries of a foundation was not always as well regulated as it has been since the reform (Lins 2008, 84). In particular, the previous reference in Art 552(4) of the former PGR to the Trust Enterprise Act (*Treuunternehmengesetz*) was a source of great legal uncertainty. To overcome this problem, the decisions made in case law pertaining to beneficiaries as a control mechanism were incorporated into legislation (Bericht und Antrag 2008, 15, 56ff).

On examination of the structural design of the new Liechtenstein law on foundations with regard to private-benefit foundations on the whole, it becomes clear that the supervisory vacuum left by the lack of official supervision is filled by the active role undertaken by beneficiaries. It is, however, not entirely clear how beneficiaries falling within the framework of the foundation governance regulation can be compared to participants in listed companies under corporate governance. Ultimately, the beneficiaries cannot assume the same functional role held by shareholders or stakeholders of companies. This is because shareholders represent a corporate element which would be incompatible with the foundation's character as an ownerless fund (Jakob 2008, 87). Nevertheless, the beneficiaries do to some extent hold a legal position similar to that of an owner. Drawing a comparison between foundation beneficiaries and equitable owners of trusts cannot be justified dogmatically; on a functional comparison, however, it becomes clear that they have equivalent legal functions.

10.3.5 The Mechanisms and Dynamics of Supervision by Beneficiaries

A beneficiary's entitlement to supervise is primarily shaped by supervisory rights. Pursuant to Art 552 § 9(1) PGR, beneficiaries are entitled to inspect the foundation deed, the supplementary foundation deed and any regulations. Furthermore, they may request the disclosure of information, reports and accounts. For this purpose,

[8] A comparative law overview is provided by Jakob (2009, para. 475).

beneficiaries have the right to inspect business records and documents and to produce copies and also to examine and investigate all facts and circumstances, in particular the accounting, personally or through a representative (Art 552 § 9 (2) PGR). At the same time, the supervisory rights delineate the boundaries of beneficiaries' rights. Beneficiaries may not, for example, assume management of the foundation. Supervision by the beneficiaries is also restricted in other ways which will be discussed below.

Classification into Categories of Beneficiaries

Beneficiaries are not all equally entitled to conduct supervision. Beneficiaries are systematically classified into categories in Art 552 § 5f PGR. First, there is a limitation in place according to which beneficiaries only have a right to information insofar as their legitimate interests are concerned. In this context, beneficiaries with vested interests have a right to supervision under Liechtenstein law (Art 552 § 5 together with § 6(1) PGR). In addition, prospective beneficiaries also qualify for entitlement to supervise if they hold an interest in a future benefit (Art 552 § 5 together with § 6(2) PGR) (Schurr 2010, 865). Ultimate beneficiaries have a legal claim; the supervisory entitlement arises on the dissolution of the foundation (Art 552 § 5 together with § 8 and § 9(3) PGR). Holding an expectation of acquiring a benefit, but without any legally enforceable claims to entitlement, leads to being classified as a discretionary beneficiary. By way of this classification, discretionary beneficiaries have a legitimate interest in receiving information about the foundation and are therefore entitled to a supervisory role. Clearly, discretionary beneficiaries should be viewed as a particularly effective supervisory body as they ultimately could stand to lose their future interests and therefore are more attentive: Any decision made by the foundation council which could have a negative impact on the extent of the discretionary beneficiaries' benefit could become an occasion for preventative supervision (Jakob 2009, para. 479).

Any beneficiary who only holds a contingent expectation to a discretionary future benefit is excluded from claiming any entitlement to supervise. Therefore, only beneficiaries falling within the categories of discretionary beneficiaries and above may gain the status of being supervisors (Lorenz 2009, para. 12).

Restriction by Using Private Controlling Bodies

In the case of predominantly private-benefit mixed foundations within the meaning of Art 552 § 2(3) and (4) PGR, the rights of common-benefit beneficiaries to information are not precluded by Art 552 § 12 PGR. For such cases, it is important to ensure that alterative governance structures are created when forming a foundation. This will prevent common-benefit beneficiaries from exercising their supervisory rights in order to paralyse a foundation and hinder its work. The establishment of a private controlling body is one possible option in this regard (Art 552 § 11 PGR).

Restriction to Cases of Present Interest

Beneficiaries' supervisory rights are also restricted by the requirement of a so-called present interest. The use of this element leads, however, to a certain degree of legal uncertainty. The existence of present interest is put into doubt when a request for information made by a beneficiary pertains to an incident which occurred prior to a person gaining his/her status as a beneficiary. In this context, a beneficiary is only awarded an entitlement to obtain information in very specific exceptional cases. This includes circumstances where incidents have occurred prior to a person gaining his/her status as a beneficiary, which, however, have a direct effect on his/her current beneficial interest. If every beneficiary were awarded a right to obtain information about events occurring prior to receiving beneficial rights, it would disturb the balance achieved in governance and lead to a considerable increase in bureaucratic work, which it is not possible to justify on its merits (Jakob 2009, paras. 487f; Bericht und Antrag 2008, 64).

Restriction for the Protection of the Beneficiaries

Pursuant to the fourth sentence of Art 552 § 9(2) PGR, the rights of beneficiaries to information and disclosure may be denied under exceptional circumstances where this would serve to protect the beneficiaries. For example, if there are vast foundation assets, a restriction may be put in place to protect the beneficiaries from the so-called spoiling effect (Lins 2008, 93).

Balancing the Foundation's Interests in Confidentiality against the Beneficiaries' Interests in Transparency

Under exceptional circumstances, the right of supervision may also be restricted where the need to protect the foundation outweighs the interests of the beneficiaries in obtaining information. Abuse, in particular, should be prevented (third sentence of Art 552 § 9(2) PGR). In accordance with this provision, rights to information and disclosure must not be exercised with dishonest intent, in an abusive manner or in a manner which conflicts with the interests of the foundation or other beneficiaries. It is not entirely clear when a beneficiary's right of supervision can be denied due to the existence of a foundation's fundamental and conflicting interest. A foundation's interests in maintaining confidentiality alone will be unlikely to suffice; otherwise, every private-benefit foundation not falling under the supervision of the STIFA would be able to exist without any supervision whatsoever. It is for this reason that high benchmarks must be set when allowing any conflicting interests to prevail

(Bericht und Antrag 2008, 62; OGH 23.07.2004, LES 2005, 392ff). For the purpose of ensuring effective supervision, a decision in favour of beneficiary rights should be made in cases of doubt when examining the conflicting interests involved (i.e. the foundation's interests in protecting its privacy and the beneficiaries' interests in receiving information). This is due to the fact that a founder is able to strip down or minimise beneficiaries' information rights by implementing the use of other control mechanisms. On drawing up a foundation, he/she is able to do this, if necessary, to pursue the specific privacy interests involved. If this institutionalised option to minimise the information rights of beneficiaries had not been provided to founders under Liechtenstein law, the foundation would certainly not enjoy the same level of protection as it currently does (OGH 07.02.2008, LES 2008, 272).

Exclusion by Voluntarily Involving the STIFA

In accordance with Art 552 § 12 PGR, beneficiaries can be denied their information rights if a foundation is voluntarily placed under the supervision of the foundation supervisory authority (Bericht und Antrag 2008, 61). With regard to the mutually exclusive options of supervision being exercised either by the STIFA or by beneficiaries, one point should be highlighted: Beneficiaries often feel compelled to check the work done by the foundation supervisory authority. This is true for both common-benefit foundations subjected to compulsory supervision and private-benefit foundations subjected to voluntary supervision. Moreover, a beneficiary's entitlement to receive information cannot be denied where the STIFA omits to carry out its information duties as this would lead to the manifestation of a supervisory vacuum. In this situation, beneficiaries are granted a so-called emergency right of supervision. In practice, however, this situation only arises in extremely exceptional circumstances because the foundation supervisory authority in Liechtenstein usually fulfils its supervisory duties efficiently.

10.3.6 Private Controlling Body

Bundling the Beneficiaries' Rights to Information

Submission to supervision by the foundation supervisory authority is of course not the only method used to circumvent beneficiaries' rights to information. Under Art 552 § 11(1) PGR, an option is provided to reduce the beneficiaries' rights to a bare minimum by appointing a private controlling body. In such cases, beneficiaries are not entitled to receive information regarding the assets in a foundation's ownership or regarding any payments which have been made to other beneficiaries (Bericht und Antrag 2008, 68). Instead, the rights of beneficiaries to information are bundled into a private controlling body; in this respect, a private controlling body acts in lieu of any beneficiaries. Where there is a complex beneficiary structure, it makes sense to bundle the efforts of controlling institutions within a foundation and unite these in a private controlling body. Experience gained in the industry shows that the information rights of beneficiaries are often exercised in a vexatious manner. This is because the interests of beneficiaries often conflict with those of the foundation (Zwiefelhofer 2008, 130). It is not rare in practice for the information rights of a beneficiary to be asserted in order to prevent payments being made to another (co-beneficiaries).

Organisation of Private Controlling Bodies

It should be noted that a private controlling body can take the shape of an audit authority, a representative with sufficient expertise or a founder personally (Art 552 § 11(2) PGR).

If an audit authority is to act as a private controlling body, it must be appointed by court. Furthermore, the provisions governing conflicts of interest (fourth sentence of Art 552 § 27(2) PGR) must be observed (Zwiefelhofer 2008, 136f). In court proceedings dealing with the appointment, the foundation supervisory authority clearly has no standing, as is also the case with the appointment of an audit authority for common-benefit foundations. Pursuant to point 2 of Art 552 § 11(2), a founder's representative may be appointed as a private controlling body. In such cases, an appointment by the court is not required; however, the appointee must be a natural person (Zwiefelhofer 2008, 139f). In accordance with point 3 of Art 552 § 11(2), a founder may personally act as a supervisory body provided that he/she is not also one of the beneficiaries (Bericht und Antrag 2008, 24).

If a private representative is appointed as a controlling body for the purpose of curtailing beneficiaries' information rights, a situation arises resembling the one on appointment of a protector under common law trust laws. As regards the enforcement of rights through supervision by appointment of a private controlling body, the following points may be made. Beneficiaries supervise the supervisors in such instances. This means that a foundation must demonstrate that a private controlling body exists and has been set up properly if it wishes to be able to shield itself against beneficiaries' claims for information (Jakob 2009, para. 510). If, in such a case, a foundation demonstrates that a founder has been personally appointed as the supervisory body pursuant to point 3 of Art 552 § 11(2) PGR, proof must be provided that he/she is not also a beneficiary. In case an audit authority is set up, for the appointment of which the court is instrumental, a court order making the appointment is sufficient to deny beneficiaries their entitlement to information or to reduce this to a minimum.

10.3.7 Special Non-contentious Civil Proceedings

Like the participants involved with common-benefit foundations, those involved with private-benefit foundations have a right to petition the court within the framework of special non-contentious civil proceedings (Art 552 § 35(1) PGR). Involving the courts is in this regard the only method of being able to verify the external governance structures existing for private-benefit foundations. The involvement of the courts in response to a petition filed by foundation participants leads to a state supervisory body (the courts) having direct effect on foundations. Courts may intervene ex officio in very rare cases, for example, where the Office of the Public Prosecutor or the foundation supervisory authority issues a communication to this end (Hammermann 2009, para. 10).

10.4 Conclusion

By introducing new provisions on foundation governance, Liechtenstein has taken a route which will stand out for its highly nuanced approach. Under the new Liechtenstein foundation law, there is now an option which enables every foundation to tailor its governance structure to the personal demands of its founder. The public authority supervision by the STIFA, which is only mandatory for common-benefit foundations, is considerably tempered – especially in regard to punitive measures – by the involvement of the courts by means of special non-contentious civil proceedings. In this respect, Liechtenstein is an ideal, neutral location for realising international philanthropic projects. The involvement of the courts, or rather the possibility of involving them, hinders any political influence from being exercised on the work of a foundation by the government via the STIFA. The independence of the judiciary ultimately safeguards a foundation's ability to act entirely autonomously in this context. A drawback of this system of supervising the supervisors is the considerable increase in bureaucracy. The involvement of beneficiaries as controlling bodies of common-benefit foundations is kept to a minimum. Under exceptional circumstances, the courts are, however, able to grant beneficiaries a right to supervise when the foundation supervisory authority does not fulfil its duties and responsibilities as a supervisory institution.

As far as private-benefit foundations are concerned, beneficiaries hold the reigns to supervision. They are therefore the mainstay of foundation governance for such foundations. In this regard, a similarity to the situation under Austrian law can be noted. It should of course be borne in mind that it is possible to preclude supervision by beneficiaries when a private-benefit foundation is placed under the supervision of the STIFA. In such cases, the governance principles developed in relation to common-benefit foundations will apply. With regard to common-benefit foundations, it should be mentioned that placing important supervisory powers in the hands of an audit authority in its capacity as an internal governance body is a welcome step. An audit authority's proximity to a foundation council enables it to exercise its supervisory functions with more efficiency and less bureaucracy. Where private-benefit foundations are concerned, it should further be noted that beneficiaries' rights can also be significantly circumscribed through the appointment of a private controlling body – even if this is not an audit authority; it can take the form of a protector or a founder personally.

The main benefit of the new governance system under Liechtenstein law is its multilayered approach to the individual supervisory institutions. The uncertainty which has arisen due to the novelty of these provisions should not be overexaggerated. Despite the initial confusion caused by the implementation of the new foundation law, the positive merits of the new provisions should always be borne in mind.

In comparison to other European jurisdictions, Liechtenstein provides a multidimensional system of governance which will significantly contribute to its competitiveness. Whereas Germany and Switzerland rely on a heavily administrative-oriented foundation supervisory system and Austria relies on a heavily court-oriented one, Liechtenstein's system combines the best of both worlds. In this respect, Liechtenstein is an ideal setting for founders wishing to pursue both private- and common-benefit purposes. The new and innovative tools of foundation governance represent a groundbreaking development in Europe.

Bibliography

Bericht und Antrag. 2008 Bericht und Antrag der Regierung an den Landtag des Fürstentums Liechtenstein betreffend die Totalrevision des Stiftungsrechts Nr. 13/2008.

Bösch, H. 2005. *Liechtensteinisches Stiftungsrecht*. Bern: Stämpfli.

Briem, R. 2009. Corporate Governance der Privatstiftung unter dem Blickwinkel der aktuellen Judikatur. *GesRZ* 1: 12.

H.S.H. Prince Michael of Liechtenstein. 2008. Die konkreten Einsatzmöglichkeiten einer gemeinnützige Stiftung. In *Das neue liechtensteinische Stiftungsrecht*, ed. Hochschule Liechtenstein, 111. Zurich: Schulthess Verlag.

Hammermann, B. 2008. Die beim Grundbuch- und Öffentlichkeitsregisteramt in Vaduz angesiedelte neue Stiftungsaufsichtsbehörde. In *Das neue liechtensteinische Stiftungsrecht*, ed. Hochschule Liechtenstein. Zurich: Schulthess Verlag.

Hammermann, B. 2009. Art 552 § 29. In *Kurzkommentar zum liechtensteinischen Stiftungsrecht*, ed. M. Schauer. Basle: Helbing Lichtenhahn Verlag.

Hopt, K.J. 2003. Die rechtlichen Rahmenbedingungen der Corporate Governance. In *Handbuch corporate governance*, ed. P. Hommelhoff, K.J. Hopt, and A. von Werder, 32. Cologne: Schmidt.

Hopt, K.J., and D. Reuter. 2001. Stiftungsrecht in Europa: Eine Einführung. In *Stiftungsrecht in Europa*, ed. K.J. Hopt and D. Reuter, 10. Cologne: Heymann.

Jakob, D. 2008. Das neue System der Foundation Governance – interne und externe Stiftungsaufsicht im neuen liechtensteinischen Stiftungsrecht. *LJZ* 4: 83.

Jakob, D. 2009. *Die liechtensteinische Stiftung*. Vaduz: Liechtenstein-Verl.

Jakob, D., and G. Studen. 2010. Die European foundation. *ZHR* 174: 61.

Kalss, S. 2008. Grenzen der Einflussnahme von Begünstigten in der Privatstiftung. *JEV*: 48.

Kerres, C., and F. Proell. 2009. Das neue liechtensteinische Stiftungsrecht. *Ecolex* 4: 321–324.

Kreutz, M. 2007. Verhaltenskodices als wesentliches Element von Corporate-Governance-Systemen in gemeinnützigen Körperschaften. *ZRP* 40: 50.

Lins, A. 2008. Die Begünstigtenrechte, ihre Ausgestaltungsmöglichkeiten und Auswirkungen. In *Das neue liechtensteinische Stiftungsrecht*, ed. Hochschule Liechtenstein, 83. Zurich: Schulthess Verlag.

Lorenz, B. 2009. Art 552 § 9. In *Kurzkommentar zum liechtensteinischen Stiftungsrecht*, ed. M. Schauer. Basle: Helbing Lichtenhahn Verlag.

Merkblatt betreffend die Befreiung von der Revisionsstellenpflicht aufsichtspflichtiger gemeinnütziger Stiftungen gemäß Art 552 § 27 Abs 5 PGR iVm Art 5 und Art 6 Abs 2 b StRV. www.llv.li/llv-gboera-home.htm.

Müller, K., and M. Fischer. 2009. Wieviel (Corporate/Foundation) Governance braucht die Privatstiftung?. *ZfS* 3: 3.

Richter, A. 2007. Länderbericht Deutschland. In *Handbuch des internationalen Stiftungsrechts*, ed. Richter, A., and T. Wachter, 763. Angelbachtal: zerb verlag.

Rick, M. 2009. Art 552 §§ 33–35. In *Kurzkommentar zum liechtensteinischen Stiftungsrecht*, ed. M. Schauer. Basle: Helbing Lichtenhahn Verlag.

Schauer, M. 2008. Grundelemente des neuen liechtensteinischen Stiftungsrechts und die rechtsvergleichende Perspektive. In *Das neue liechtensteinische Stiftungsrecht*, ed. Hochschule Liechtenstein , 7. Zurich: Schulthess Verlag.

Schurr, F. 2010. Auskunftspflichten der Begünstigten im liechtensteinischen Stiftungsrecht nach der Totalrevision. In *Analyse und Fortentwicklung im Arbeits-, Sozial- und Zivilrecht. Festschrift für Martin Binder*, ed. H. Barta, T. Radner, L. Rainer, and H.T. Scharnreitner, 857. Vienna: Linde.

Schurr, F., and S. Büchel. 2009. Überlegungen zur Anpassung und Änderung des Stiftungszwecks durch den Stifter bzw ein Organ der Stiftung. *Liechtenstein-Journal*: 110–117.

Sprecher, T., P. Egger, and M. Janssen. 2009. *Swiss Foundation Code 2009 mit Kommentar*. Basle: Helbing Lichtenhahn Verlag.

Tschütscher, K. 2008. Das neue liechtensteinische Stiftungsrecht – Entstehungsgeschichte und Gesamtüberblick. *LJZ* 4: 79.

Universität Heidelberg. 2008. Feasibility study on a European foundation statute. http://ec.europa.eu/internal_market/company/eufoundation/index_en.htm.

von Werder, A. 2003. Ökonomische Grundfragen der Corporate Governance. In *Handbuch Corporate Governance*, ed. P. Hommelhoff, K.J. Hopt, and A. von Werder, 3. Cologne: Schmidt.

Zollner, J. 2009. Das Informationsrecht der Begünstigten als Baustein der Foundation Governance. *PSR* 2: 77.

Zwiefelhofer, T. 2008. Die Kontroll- und Überwachungsorgane einer Stiftung und ihre Aufgaben. In *Das neue liechtensteinische Stiftungsrecht*, ed. Hochschule Liechtenstein, 130. Zurich: Schulthess Verlag.

Chapter 11
The Development of the Law on Foundations in the Netherlands

C. Helen C. Overes and Tymen J. van der Ploeg

11.1 Introduction

In this chapter, we will outline the development of the law on foundations in the Netherlands. After an introductory section on the history of the law on foundations in general (Sect. 11.2), we examine the characteristics of the foundation, in particular its purpose and composition. Given that the law imposes no positive requirements in respect of these aspects, the requirements are of a negative nature: the non-distribution constraint and the no-members constraint (Sect. 11.3). Section 11.4 deals with the requirements for setting up and registering a foundation. Section 11.5 examines governance and the specific requirements for governance of foundations involved in the fields of education, public housing, etc. In Sect. 11.6, we examine a number of specific aspects in more detail: amendment of articles of formation, transformation, merger and demerger, and dissolution. Section 11.7 focuses on external supervision, with a role for the Public Prosecutor, stakeholders and the courts. This includes a look at the external supervision resulting from sector-specific legislation. Our concluding remarks are set out in Sect. 11.8.

11.2 A Historical Perspective on the Regulation and Use of the Foundation

The first law establishing the foundation as a legal entity is the Act of 31 May 1956, Stb. 327 (the Foundations Act (*wet op stichtingen*)). That does not mean, however, that before this date the foundation was an unknown legal entity in the Netherlands. As far back as the Middle Ages, there were foundations in the Netherlands: rich

C.H.C. Overes • T.J. van der Ploeg (✉)
Faculty of Law, Vrije Universiteit, Amsterdam, The Netherlands
e-mail: c.h.c.overes@vu.nl; t.j.vander.ploeg@vu.nl

C. Prele (ed.), *Developments in Foundation Law in Europe*, Ius Gentium: Comparative Perspectives on Law and Justice 39, DOI 10.1007/978-94-017-9069-7_11,

citizens would act on their religious faith to establish foundations to care for the sick, for example, or to provide for widows or orphans. The capital supplied for such purpose was thus separated from the personal capital of the founders, and creditors of such founders would have no claim against the separate money reserved for the foundation.[1] Later foundations were established not only for religious reasons but for purposes of more public benefit. The relationship between the founders, the church (following the reformation the Dutch Reformed Church) and the government was generally close. The articles of formation of such a private foundation for public benefit would often stipulate that if its directors could no longer be appointed in accordance with the articles of formation (e.g. because the family had died out), then the municipality should appoint the directors. In this way, municipal governments became practically directors of all manner of foundations for public benefit.

With the codification of our civil law, using the model of the French Civil Code following the French occupation of the Netherlands, draft laws of 1816 and 1820 originally set out regulations for the foundation. Since the Dutch Civil Code also had to be suitable for the Belgians – Belgium had been incorporated into the Netherlands by the Treaty of Vienna – and the Belgian delegates preferred to remain close to the French Civil Code, this approach was dropped in favour of a new code more in line with the French system. As a consequence, the foundation remained unregulated. Under the Civil Code it was clear that the foundations that predated it had the right of continued existence, but it was unclear whether and, if so, how new foundations could be created. In 1882, the Dutch Supreme Court confirmed what had already been assumed in practice, namely, that under Dutch law, even without legislation, that is, according to customary law, it was possible to create a foundation with a separate legal identity.[2] The requirements that a foundation had to satisfy were limited. There had to be an organisation as described in articles of formation, but it was debatable whether there had to be capital.[3] The articles of formation had to be in writing but not necessarily drawn up within a notarial deed.

Between 1855, when the Association and Meeting Act (*wet op vereniging en vergadering*)[4] came into force, and 1956 the foundation was the only generally useful legal entity that could be created other than by notarial deed and for which there were no requirements governing its creation.[5] This resulted in foundations operating in all kinds of fields, not only for charitable purposes, for which it had

[1] Up to the nineteenth century, the question was whether the foundation could be regarded as a separate legal entity or the directors of the foundation could be regarded as trustees of the foundation's capital. See Asser-Van der Grinten-Maeijer (1997, 458–459).

[2] Dutch Supreme Court 30 June 1882, W. 4800.

[3] See the literature cited in Asser-Rensen III* (2012/212–213).

[4] Act of 22 April 1855, Stb. 32.

[5] This applied also to the legal entity church community, but this could only be used by religious organisations.

been used for centuries, but also in commercial and financial spheres, and by the government. Many foundations were created at both municipal and national level to perform the governmental activities that the governments wanted to make less dependent on politics. Foundations were used in the socio-economic sphere to bind entrepreneurs to centrally imposed socio-economic regulations enforceable with the threat of high penalties. Before the Second World War, it was realised that foundations were growing without control and that statutory regulation was necessary. In 1937, a draft law to regulate the foundation was presented, but this was not debated in public. The draft law included the requirement regarding capital for the creation of a foundation – an issue that was somewhat contested. After the end of the war, a review of the Civil Code was undertaken. In 1954, Professor E. M. Meijers submitted a draft act relating to the first four books of the Civil Code. Book 2 concerned the legal entities, within which context the foundation was also regulated. Given the strongly felt lack of statutory regulation, the Foundations Act was passed in 1956 as a precursor to the revised Civil Code. This Act was more or less based on current practice. The purposes for which a foundation could be created remained – as before – without restriction. Only one limitation was stipulated: the *non-distribution constraint* (see Sect. 11.3.1). As regards its composition, there were few rules, just the *no-members constraint* (see Sect. 11.3.2). However, a number of supervisory powers were given to the courts to keep foundations in line, mostly exercised on the application of either the stakeholders or the Public Prosecutor (see Sect. 11.7.1 and following).

It is significant that the Foundations Act did not originally apply to government and church foundations, pension funds and benevolent institutions. As regards government foundations, this exception was reversed in 1963,[6] and the other exceptions were reversed by the introduction of Book 2 of the Civil Code in 1976.[7] All foundations[8] currently fall within the regulations of Book 2 Title 6 of the Civil Code.

The 1956 regulation of the foundation was included virtually unchanged in Book 2 of the Civil Code in 1976 and there have been no further significant changes to the law affecting the foundation since then. It is still a useful construct in numerous areas, because the law does not prescribe specific aims. There are commercial foundations, management foundations, cultural foundations, public service foundations, pension foundations and more.[9] The government also still uses the foundation. An argument expressed in favour of this is that this is a legal form that is more recognisable by the citizen. Whilst this may be true to some extent, it is

[6] Act of 10 July 1963, Stb. 297.

[7] See Article 53 et seq. of the New Dutch Civil Code Transitional Act.

[8] Church communities may create 'ecclesiastical foundations' as a separate – legal – entity of the church community, which is then governed solely by ecclesiastical law. Cf Dijk and Van der Ploeg (2013, par. 2.2.7).

[9] See Duynstee (1978, 60 et seq.) and Wessels (1996, 1 et seq.).

however not clear to the citizen who is behind a foundation and to this extent a foundation is not transparent.

Unlike for foundations in general, however, further requirements are laid down in sector-specific legislation with regard to the governance and financial accountability of foundations (and any other legal structures) operating in those particular societal sectors. These requirements are often linked to subsidies made available by the government in these areas.

Mention should be made here of a draft law on social enterprises from 2008, by which associations and foundations that provide a service focused specifically and exclusively on the societal interest thereby served may apply for permission to use the designation *social enterprise*. It was the hope of the Cabinet that this would strengthen the position of the clients of these service providers and reduce government monitoring. The draft was withdrawn in 2010 because there was no need for the proposed legal form.[10] At European level there is work on the introduction of a European foundation.[11] The plan is for such a foundation to be intended for public benefit. It is questionable whether a need will arise in the Netherlands for a subcategory of foundation with a public benefit purpose. To date, we mostly rely in the Netherlands on category-based legislation in which specific requirements are set out, rather than link such requirements to a specific legal form or sub-category thereof.

11.3 The Characteristics of a Foundation

Book 2 Article 285 of the Dutch Civil Code reads as follows:

> 1. A foundation is a legal form created by juridical act, without members, and that aims to achieve a purpose specified in its articles of formation, by using capital which has been introduced for this purpose.[12]
> 2. If the articles of formation grant any person(s) the power to fill vacancies in a body of the foundation, then this fact alone does not mean that the foundation has members.
> 3. The purpose of a foundation may not include the making of distributions to its founders or to those who participate in its bodies or to others, except, in the latter case, where these distributions are made for charitable or social purposes.

[10] Parliamentary Papers II, 2008–2009, 32 003, nr. 2 (draft law on corporate social responsibility), Parliamentary Papers II, 2010–2011, 32 417, nr. 47 (announcement of withdrawal of draft law).

[11] See Hopt et al. (2006, 78 et seq.).

[12] See Section 3.1 regarding the capital requirement.

11.3.1 The Purpose

With regard to the purpose, Book 2 Article 285 (3) of the Civil Code only prescribes constraints on distributions that may be made. It does not specify any other constraints. Of course, there is also the general constraint upon legal entities that they may not have a purpose, or perform activities, that is in breach of public order: see Book 2 Article 20 of the Civil Code.

Foundations are thus not constrained by the type of business they may operate or in their purpose to make profits. If someone wishes to invest risky capital in a business, then he must do this through a public or private limited company ('NV' or 'BV', respectively), which can make dividends, and not through a foundation. A further reason for this constraint is that those involved in the formation or management of a foundation are more likely to put their own interests before those of the foundation if the foundation is able to make distributions to them.

The extent to which a business of a foundation may be transferred is, however, constrained. The least complicated situation is one where the current directors wish to hand their seats to the directors of the legal entity acquiring the foundation.[13] The directors who are standing down will seek compensation for this. Provided that this compensation is met out of the pockets of the new directors themselves or from the purse of the legal entity of which they were already directors (the new parent entity), there can be no objection to this. However, if those acquiring the foundation pay this compensation from the funds of the foundation being taken over, then this is a prohibited distribution.[14] In practice, there are all manner of parent subsidiary, operating and support foundations where the non-distribution constraint threatens to be a nuisance.[15]

It is fairly generally accepted that a payment by a foundation to someone pursuant to a reciprocal contract is not a prohibited distribution. This would apply, for example, to employees and directors of the foundation – whether or not forming part of the management of the foundation – who are paid a reasonable sum for the work they do for the foundation.[16] Other examples include the payment of interest on loans and distributions of a pension.[17] The distribution of a profit share to someone who has supplied capital is, however, prohibited.[18]

[13] In addition, the foundation can be transformed into a BV or the business can be split-off as a BV. See Sect. 12.6.

[14] See Court of Utrecht 1 December 2010, JOR 2011, 69 commentary from J.M. Blanco Fernández.

[15] See De Kluiver (1988, 176 et seq.), Van der Ploeg (1989, 95 et seq.) and Hendriks (1994, 111 et seq.).

[16] Rechtspersonen, Overes (Art. 285, note 7).

[17] Book 2, Article 304 (2) of the Civil Code specifically states that pension distributions are not prohibited distributions.

[18] *Contra*: Pitlo-Raaijmakers (2006, 674).

11.3.2 Composition/No-Members Constraint

The formal composition of a foundation is subject to the *no-members constraint* which distinguishes a foundation from an association. The word *member* here is not intended to apply to the people involved in the foundation. In practice, the word *member* is also sometimes applied to persons with a contractual relationship with the foundation. This is not prohibited. What is prohibited for a foundation is to have a body alongside its management board that has (virtually) the same powers as the general meeting within an association.[19] The law also permits, per se, a body other than the management board to have the right under the articles of formation to appoint members of the management board or members of another body, such as a supervisory board (see Book 2 Article 285 (2) Civil Code). This appointing body will usually also have the right to dismiss. The articles of formation may also give this appointing body the power to amend the articles of formation or the right for any amendment of the articles of formation to be subject to its approval. If the body other than the management board does in fact exercise control in the foundation, this is in breach of the no-members constraint. This can be avoided by allocating the various powers to the different bodies that have been differently drawn up. See also details of the management structure of the foundation in Sect. 11.5.

Given that the law is rather unclear and not all commentators take the same view, Dutch notaries remain cautious in allocating decision-taking rights within a foundation to anyone but a director. Over the past few years there has been a lack of jurisprudence on this matter.

11.4 Formation and Registration

11.4.1 Formation

A foundation is a simple legal entity to form. The legal steps to formation can be taken by one party, whether a natural person or a legal entity. The foundation must be formed by notarial deed. No administrative approval is required for its formation, as is the case in other countries.[20] The notarial deed must be drawn up in Dutch and set out the foundation's articles of formation.[21] In addition to being formed by specific notarial deed, a foundation can also be created by will drawn up by notarial deed, in which case the foundation's articles of formation are contained in the

---

[19] Asser-Rensen III* (2012/333 and 344) and Dijk and Van der Ploeg (2012, par. 2.3.2).

[20] Van der Ploeg (1999, 55).

[21] Book 2, Article 286 of the Civil Code, unless the foundation has its registered office in the province of Friesland, in which case the deed can be drawn up in Frisian.

notarial deed containing the will. If a testator has bequeathed something to a foundation that he has created by will contained in a notarial deed, the foundation is the beneficiary according to the nature of the bequest (Book 4 Article 135 Civil Code). The foundation comes into being upon the death of the testator. After formation the foundation acquires rights and obligations and has the same rights and obligations regarding property as a natural person, unless the law provides otherwise.

The articles of formation of the foundation must include (a) the name of the foundation, which must include the word 'foundation'; (b) its purpose; (c) the means of appointment and dismissal of its directors; (d) the municipality in the Netherlands in which it has its registered office; and (e) the allocation of the surplus following the winding up of the foundation or the manner in which this allocation will be decided. The notary must ensure that the articles of the foundation comply with the law. If the articles of foundation do not comply with the law, then the formation is defective (Book 2 Article 21 (1) (b) Civil Code). However, the foundation will still be validly formed even if the notarial deed is not formally authenticated, although this will constitute a defect in its formation. The same applies if the juridical steps towards formation performed by a natural person or legal entity prove to have been invalid.

If there are defects in the formation of the foundation, its articles of formation do not comply with the law or the legal entity thus created does not satisfy the statutory description of a foundation (see Sect. 11.3), this can only be a step towards dissolution of the foundation. The court may grant the legal entity a period of time in which to remedy its defective formation, including by converting the foundation into another form of legal entity (see Sect. 11.6). The court will dissolve a foundation on the application of any stakeholder or the Public Prosecutor. It is not possible, in general, to give an indication of who qualifies as a stakeholder for the purposes of applying for dissolution (see Sect. 11.7 on stakeholders).

Although the statutory description of the foundation refers to 'the allocation of capital', there does not need to be capital involved when the foundation is formed. The foundation may be dissolved, however, if following formation the capital available is insufficient to realise the intended purpose and it is improbable that the capital will become sufficient within a foreseeable period (Book 2, Article 301 (1) (a) Civil Code).

The notary is responsible for ensuring the foundation is validly formed by ensuring that the articles of formation comply with the law.[22] He must ensure that the foundation does not have any purpose that is in breach of the non-distribution constraint and that the allocation of the surplus after winding up of the foundation as specified in the articles of formation does not result in any prohibited distribution. If the articles of formation do not comply with the law, the notary may decline to assist in its formation. The parties wishing to form the foundation have no right of appeal against this decision.[23] Since 2008 the notary

[22] Van der Ploeg(2011, 83).

[23] Art. 21 (2), 16a of the Dutch Notaries' Act, see Van der Ploeg (2011, 85).

must also carry out a client investigation for the purposes of the formation if there are any indications that the foundation will be used for money laundering or for financing terrorism.[24] Additionally, where relevant, it is necessary to identify the *ultimate beneficiary*, the person with actually control or someone who benefits from the foundation by 25 % or more of its capital.[25] The notary may not act in a professional capacity on behalf of the relevant parties without a client investigation or if any doubt regarding the client's intentions regarding the foundation remain.

The notary must also report any unusual transactions performed by or for the benefit of the foundation at the time of its formation. An unusual transaction (including any transaction involving more than EUR 15,000) must be reported to the Financial Intelligence Unit-Netherlands.[26] The notary can face an administrative-law penalty for any breach of this law. We assume that if such circumstances were to arise, the notary would not assist in the formation of the foundation in question.[27]

In the deed of formation, the founders can directly bind the foundation to the acts of formation insofar as these are juridical acts that are closely tied to such formation, such as the appointment of directors.[28] In respect of a juridical act carried out on behalf of a legal entity yet to be formed, the statutory provisions of Book 2 Articles 93 and 203 (1) of the Civil Code similarly apply to other legal entities.[29] This means that rights and obligations for the foundation arise from juridical acts carried out on behalf of the foundation yet to be formed only if the foundation expressly or impliedly confirms these juridical acts following its formation.

11.4.2 Registration

Following its formation, the directors of the foundation must register it in the commercial register.[30] In addition to the registration of the foundation and the disclosure of the first names, family names and home addresses of the founder or founders, a certified copy or extract of the deed of formation containing the articles of formation must be filed at the office of the commercial register.

---

[24] Art. 3 of the Dutch Prevention of Money Laundering and Financing of Terrorism Act (the results of the client investigation must be kept for 5 years).

[25] Art. 1 of the Dutch Prevention of Money Laundering and Financing of Terrorism Act.

[26] The Monitoring of Legal Entities Decree 2011, Art. 6 (e). Monitoring is carried out by the FIU with the aim of preventing money laundering and the financing of terrorism.

[27] Van der Ploeg (2011, 86).

[28] Dijk and Van der Ploeg (2013, par. 3.8).

[29] Dutch Supreme Court 24 January 1997, NJ 1997/399.

[30] Art. 6 Commercial Register Act 2007, if the foundation operates a business, the registration of the business also counts as the registration of the legal entity.
(Art. 7 Commercial Register Act 2007).

Registration is not a requirement for formation. But until the first registration has been effected and the documents have been filed, every director is jointly and severally liable alongside the foundation for any juridical act to which he binds the foundation (Book 2 Article 289 (2) Civil Code). Article 29 of the Commercial Register Decree 2008 further specifies what information must be registered by the foundation. It is especially important for third parties to know who the directors of the foundation are; whether they are individually, or only in combination with others, authorised to represent the foundation; which other persons have such authority; and what the extent of that authority is. A third party may assume the accuracy of the information included in the register. It can be no defence against a claim of a third party in good faith that any particular person is no longer a director or no longer has authority to represent the foundation or that the articles of formation have been amended, if this information is not included, or is inaccurately recorded, in the commercial register.[31]

11.5 Governance: Management Board, Supervision of the Management Board and Other Bodies

11.5.1 Governance

Governance refers to the performance of the management and supervisory tasks and the way in which these are accounted for. It involves a system of *checks and balances*, which is particularly important in the case of foundations because in Dutch law, there are virtually no rules at all concerning the internal supervision of the management of a foundation.[32] Alongside the way in which management and the supervision thereof is structured, the discussion over the governance of foundations also covers accountability to stakeholders, known as *horizontal accountability*. The requirement to account to stakeholders is dictated by the changed attitude of the government towards foundations that, in particular, supply services in the areas of welfare, education and housing.[33]

The organisation and management structure of foundations can vary widely, depending on the purpose and nature of the foundation. The management structure of a professional institution (hospital or educational institute) maintained by a foundation is of an entirely different order to that of a small service-providing institution, a family foundation or capital fund. The statutory regulation of the foundation is not aimed at foundations that run an institution or business.

[31] Book 2 Article 6 of the Civil Code; Art. 25 Commercial Register Act 2007.

[32] Wessels (1998, 45–46), Slagter (1999, 47), Van Veen (2007a, 755–766).

[33] Parliamentary Papers II, 2008–2009, 32 003, no. 3, Groeneveld (2004, 47).

The significance of the governance of foundations is increased by developments such as increases in scale, professionalisation of the organisation and a change in government attitude towards voluntary organisations in the various sectors. When an organisation grows in size and complexity, a management board of unpaid volunteers is no longer adequate: a professionalisation of the management structure is required. Various management models have been developed in practice, in which more detailed form is given to both the relationship between the management board and the day-to-day management of the organisation and to the supervision of the management board. Furthermore, governance codes have been drawn up for sector and umbrella organisations providing more detail about the tasks of the management board and supervisory body and regulating the position of the stakeholders.[34] These codes may be seen as a form of self-regulation filling the lacuna left by Book 2 of the Civil Code with respect to the structure of internal supervision. The codes are not generally binding regulations. Foundations that are not affiliated to the relevant sector or umbrella organisations are not bound by the codes at all. To a large extent, compliance with the codes is a matter for the institutions themselves.[35]

The legislature pays attention to the governance of foundations that operate especially in semi-public sectors such as education, welfare and housing.[36] For the initiative to include a regulation specifically for these foundations (*social foundations*) in Book 2 of the Civil Code, see Sects. 11.2 and 11.5.3.

11.5.2 The Management Board of the Foundation

The Tasks of the Management Board

The management board is the only body that is prescribed by law for a foundation. The law states that the management board is responsible for the management of the foundation, subject to limitations imposed by the articles of formation (Book 2 Article 291 (1) Civil Code). The law is otherwise silent about the substance of such management. In practice, the management board is responsible for realising the purposes of the foundation, the acquisition of funds, the management and

[34] *Code Goed Bestuur voor Goede Doelen, Zorgbrede Governancecode* (2010), *Code Goed Bestuur in het primair onderwijs* (PO-raad, Utrecht 2010), *Code Goed Onderwijsbestuur in het voortgezet onderwijs* (VO-raad Utrecht 2008), Governance Code Woningcorporaties 2007, *Code Cultural Governance*, Branchecode Maatschappelijke Onderneming (NTMO) (example codes setting out governance requirements for foundations in the fields of welfare, education and housing).

[35] The main principle for compliance with the codes is 'apply or explain'.

[36] ECORYS, *Governance in semi-publieke instellingen: welke lessen kunnen we leren uit het buitenland*? Final report commissioned by the Ministry for Economic Affairs, Rotterdam 2010; *Algemene Rekenkamer, Goed bestuur in uitvoering, De praktijk van onderwijsinstellingen, woningcorporaties, zorgorganisaties en samenwerkingsverbanden*, Den Haag 2008.

spending of these funds and the representation of the foundation. Management involves the governing of the foundation and – if the foundation is one that runs a business or institution – the governing of the said business or institution. This includes determining general policy. In carrying out such tasks, the management board must have regard to the interests of the foundation. Its tasks may be restricted by the articles of formation; for example, the requirement for prior approval for certain significant decisions of the management board, whilst certain management tasks can be assigned to another body.

Although the law does not say so in so many words, in principle the management board must act collectively. Management tasks are regarded as the responsibility of the whole board. The fact that a management board consists of more than one person is, to some extent, a guarantee of careful management.[37] The management board is liable to the legal entity for the proper performance of its tasks (Book 2 Article 9 Civil Code). Improper performance can result in individual directors being held liable insofar as their conduct is seriously at fault.[38]

The authority to bind the foundation to any third party is unlimited and unconditional insofar as the law does not specify otherwise (Book 2 Article 292 (3) Civil Code). Any restrictions of this authority under the articles of formation, such as the requirement for prior approval of another body for certain juridical acts, has no external effect, except for the juridical acts specified by law concerning the acquisition and encumbrancing of real property and the guaranteeing of third-party debts (Book 2 Article 291 (2) Civil Code).

The Appointment and Dismissal of Directors

By law, the appointment and dismissal of directors is a matter for the foundation's articles of formation (Book 2 Article 286 (4) (c) Civil Code). If the management board is the only body within the foundation, then the appointment of directors is mostly made initially by the founder and, subsequently, once the foundation has been formed, by cooption. Authority to appoint can also be assigned under the articles of formation to one or more natural persons or legal entities, whether specified in the articles or not.[39] An example would be assignment to a supervisory board established by the articles of foundation or to a government body that awards a subsidy to the foundation. According to the law, this is not in conflict with the no-members constraint (Book 2 Article 285 (2) Civil Code). The decision to appoint creates an organisational relationship in law, but not a contractual one, between the director and the foundation. A contractual relationship with the foundation can exist alongside this organisational relationship, however, where the director is also employed by the foundation (see under 'Management Models'.).

[37] Dijk and Van der Ploeg (2012, par. 3.8), Overes (2011b, 63).

[38] Dutch Supreme Court 10 January 1997, NJ 1997/360 (Staleman/van de Ven).

[39] Dijk and Van der Ploeg (2013, par. 8.5.1.b).

As with an appointment, any dismissal of a director must be regulated by the articles of formation. In the context of its statutory supervision of foundations, the court has power to dismiss a director who acts in breach of the law or the articles of formation or who is guilty of mismanagement; see Chap. 7. There is debate as to whether a director can be dismissed if the articles of formation are silent on this point. Our view is that if a director is appointed through a system of cooption, then he can be dismissed by the management board.[40] We believe that unless the articles of foundation specify otherwise, a director can be dismissed by the body or organisation authorised to appoint directors.[41]

Management Models

Book 2 of the Civil Code assumes a standard type of foundation in which the (voluntary) board of management is the only body: it was not written with a foundation that runs a professionalised institution or business in mind. A management board consisting of volunteers is unable to provide the day-to-day management of an institution or business. Various management models have been created in practice to formulate the relationship between the management board of the foundation and the day-to-day management of the business. The greater the size and complexity of the business, the more likely is the choice for a professional management structure in which the directors are also employees of the foundation (see models c. and d.). In practice, there are four management models:

(a) The classic (or *instruction*) model

Here the (voluntary) management board has ultimate responsibility for both general and day-to-day policy. Day-to-day management of the business is conducted by a director or board of directors. The director or members of the board of directors is/are not directors of the foundation but employees of the legal entity. The board of directors prepares policy and implements the policy drawn up by the management board. The position of the board of directors is not governed by the articles of formation; instead, its powers are usually set out in instructions to the board of directors. The board of directors exercises management authority on behalf of, and under the responsibility of, the management board.

(b) The executive board model

In this model, the management tasks and powers are divided between the management board and the board of directors and are set out in the articles of

---

[40] Dijk and Van der Ploeg (2013, par. 8.5.1.b).

[41] This observation is in line with the fact that the right of appointment implies a relationship of trust between the person making the appointment and the director whereby – unless the contrary is specified – the power to dismiss must apply at such time as the appointer has lost trust in the director .Dijk and Van der Ploeg (2013, par. 8.5.1.b).

formation.[42] The management board, referred to as the executive board, is the management as prescribed by the law. The executive board determines general policy, whilst the board of directors is responsible for the day-to-day management of the business. The difference between this model and the classic model is that here the powers of the board of directors are set out in the foundation's articles of formation. Powers conferred on the board of directors by the articles of formation cannot be exercised by the executive board. The board of directors is no longer an extension of the management board but instead a body of the foundation. The board of directors is not a management body as defined by law and its members are not appointed as directors of the foundation. The executive board has ultimate responsibility for the performance of management functions, even that part of which are delegated by the articles of formation to the board of directors (Book 2 Article 9 Civil Code). To be able to assume this responsibility, the executive board has authority to give the board of directors guidelines and instructions concerning the way in which it should exercise its powers. There is something absurd about the executive board model in that the management board can be held liable to the legal entity for the exercise of powers that the management board does not itself possess. There is also debate as to whether the board of directors could not also be held liable under the law relating to legal entities for that part of the management tasks for which it is responsible by virtue of the articles of formation.[43] In our view, this is not the case because the board of directors does not exercise its powers autonomously, since such exercise is limited by the policy framework set by the management board.

(c) The general management board/executive board model

Under this model, the day-to-day management of the business is exercised by an executive board that – unlike the board of directors in the executive board model – is a management body of the foundation. In this model, the management tasks are divided between general management tasks and executive tasks, whether or not exercised by two separate bodies. The executive board is responsible for the day-to-day management of the foundation and the business it operates, as well as for the preparation and implementation of decisions of the general management board. An exhaustive list of the tasks of the general management board is set out in the articles of formation and includes adoption of the budget and annual accounts, the adoption of the policy plans drawn up by the executive board and approval of significant decisions such as amendment of the articles of formation, dissolution, collaboration, merger and demerger. Members of the executive board are usually professionals, that is, as well as being directors they are also employees of the foundation. The general management board and the executive board each have their own tasks and powers and in this respect are liable to the legal entity (Book 2 Art. 9 Civil Code). The general management board does, however, supervise the executive

[42] Gitmans, Van Wersch (1976, 116).

[43] Groeneveld-Louwerse (2001, 9).

board and to be able to escape liability must intervene if the executive board is not performing its tasks properly in order to avoid any harmful consequences affecting the foundation.

Where the executive board forms a part of the general management board, the model is similar to a one-tier model. In such a case, one might ask how far this model is compatible with the statutory principles governing collective management responsibility. To remove any uncertainty regarding the consequences for collective management responsibility of dividing tasks within the management board, the one-tier model was recently regulated by statute for private and public companies.[44] Under this law, the articles of association may divide management tasks between one or more non-executive directors and one or more executive directors. This one-tier model is not statutorily regulated for a foundation and – strictly speaking – such regulation is not required for its application. The statutory regulation of the one-tier model for public and private companies offers no new understanding regarding the consequences for the responsibility (and liability) of the management board and individual directors of the division of tasks. The principle of the law remains that a division of tasks set out in articles of association does not affect the collective responsibility of the management board and the individual responsibility of the directors for the exercise by the management board of its tasks.[45]

(d) The supervisory board model

In this model the (professional) management board is responsible for the management of the foundation and the business operated by the foundation. Under this model, alongside the management board the foundation also has a supervisory board. Given that Book 2 of the Civil Code contains no provisions regarding supervision of the management board of the foundation, the tasks and powers of the supervisory board are set out in the articles of formation. Book 2 of the Civil Code allows the foundation complete freedom regarding the composition of the supervisory board. The provisions in the articles of formation regulating the tasks and powers of the supervisory board, however, are generally in line with those set out in Book 2 governing other legal entities.[46] The tasks of the supervisory board are to supervise the policy of the management board and the day-to-day affairs of the foundation and its business operations, as well as to advise the management board. In fulfilling its tasks, the supervisory board must act in the interests of the foundation and of the business it operates. The supervisory board has authority to appoint and dismiss members of the management board who are also employees of the foundation, and are also authorised to determine their remuneration. Under the articles of formation, the approval of the supervisory board is required for management decisions such as amendments of the articles of formation, dissolution, collaborations, mergers and demergers, the taking out of loans and the making of

[44] Act of 6 June 2011, Stb. 2011, 275.

[45] Verdam (2011, 28).

[46] Book 2 Article 57 (cooperation), 140 (NV) and 250 (BV) of the Civil Code.

significant investments. Adoption of the budget and annual accounts may also be made subject to the approval of the supervisory board. Within this model the management board and the supervisory board have their own tasks and authority. Within the limits to its authority set by law and the articles of formation, the management board is autonomous. The supervisory board has no authority to instruct the management board. The management board is liable to the legal entity for the proper exercise of its management tasks pursuant to Book 2 Article 9 of the Civil Code.

This model has seen enormous growth. As their business have grown larger and become more complex, many foundations have on their own initiative adopted the management structure set out under the supervisory board model, but sector-specific legislation that sets a requirement for a supervisory body as a condition for the grant of a subsidy or for recognition has also contributed to this growth. The majority of welfare institutions have a management structure based on this supervisory board model.[47] By virtue of welfare legislation, a requirement for the recognition of welfare institutions is that they create a body to supervise the general or day-to-day management of the institution.[48] Housing associations must also have a supervisory board.[49] However, the mandatory requirement for a supervisory board need not necessarily lead to the creation of a management structure in accordance with the supervisory board model. In practice, we also see a three-tiered structure, that is, a management board, a board of directors and a supervisory board.[50] In higher education the supervisory board model is the rule.[51] Since 1 August 2010, primary and secondary education institutions have been required by law to separate management and supervisory tasks. The manner in which they do

---

[47] See the report Governance en kwaliteit van zorg, Raad voor de Volksgezondheid en Zorg, Den Haag 2009.

[48] Art. 6.1 Recognition of Welfare Institutions Act Implementation Decree. Being prepared is the Welfare Client Rights Act that more specifically requires the creation of a separate supervisory body in the interests of a clear separation of tasks and powers (Parliamentary Papers II, 2009–2010, 32 402, art. 40).

[49] Art. 7 Management of Social Housing Decree in conjunction with Art. 70 of the Housing Act, where a requirement for recognition is that the articles of formation provide for a body, a board of supervisory directors, to supervise the management board and that is authorised to take such steps as are necessary to exercise that supervision. The structure and working methods of the board of supervisory directors are not otherwise described, although such detail will be contained in the draft legislation submitted to the Dutch Lower House in May 2011(Parliamentary Papers II, 2010–2011, 32 769).

[50] Report entitled Goed bestuur in de zorg, Ministry of Public Health, Welfare and Sport, Den Haag 2006, p. 15.

[51] The creation of a supervisory board is the starting point (Art. 10.3d Higher Education Act ('WHW') (technical universities) and 9.8 (special universities) whereby from a philosophical standpoint one could choose for a functional separation of powers (Art. 10.3d (7)/9.51 (3) WHW). In secondary education, institutions may choose between a supervisory board and a one-tier model (Art. 9.1.8. WEB).

this is left to the institutions themselves; large school boards (foundations that run more than one school) in particular select the supervisory board model.[52]

11.5.3 Internal Supervision

Internal supervision, supervision by a body of the legal entity, is based on the division of tasks and powers within the organisation, ensuring a system of checks and balances within the organisation. There is no form of internal supervision prescribed by law in the case of a foundation. Unless the articles of formation specify otherwise, the management board is not accountable to any other party. The Public Prosecutor and the courts are empowered to exercise some kind of control over the management board of a foundation (see Sect. 11.7). This external supervision is restricted to a control of the lawfulness of the management and policy. In addition to controlling the lawfulness of the management (whether acts by the management board comply with the law, the articles of formation, regulations and decisions of the foundation), the internal supervision also checks efficiency (whether the management board has set the right priorities, whether resources have been used as efficiently as possible, etc.).[53] Whether on their own initiative or in compliance with regulations applying to their particular sector, many foundations have already established some form of internal supervision. The form taken by this internal supervision is usually the creation of a supervisory board, whether or not the supervisory board model is adopted. The supervisory tasks do not necessarily have to be assigned to a separate supervisory board and it is sufficient to make a functional separation between management and supervision without the need for two separate bodies (see general management board/executive board model).

The necessity for arranging some form of supervisory role arises because directors of foundations are frequently responsible for managing the funds of other people or public funds. They should be periodically accountable for this management and must continually have regard to this repeated duty in their acts and omissions as directors.[54] Although the need to implement a system of internal supervision is generally advocated, there is absolutely no requirement for this under Book 2 of the Civil Code. The greatest stumbling block for the introduction of uniform statutory regulations governing internal supervision is the large diversity of foundations.[55] The management structure of a foundation is largely its own business and the structure that is best suited to a foundation depends heavily on the size

[52] Art. 17a (1) Primary Education Act, Art. 24d Secondary Education Act, see Overes (2011a), Turkenburg (2009, 88).

[53] Dijk and Van der Ploeg (2013, par. 10.1).

[54] Lubbers (1983, 8).

[55] See Overes (2011b, 71–72) and the literature quoted therein.

and complexity of the institution. The proposal for the introduction of a specific legal form for social enterprises (especially in the areas of welfare, education and housing) stumbled on similar objections. The introduction by the draft law of a *foundation for operating a social enterprise* included a mandatory supervisory board and stakeholders board and laid out in detail the composition, tasks and powers of these boards. Although the proposal had been introduced as a codification of the developments in the management of institutions in the semi-public sector and a significant part of the proposal had been set aside for codes of conduct, there was simply no need for the proposed new legal entity.[56]

Institutions in the various sectors had already established the desired management structure on their own initiative, having regard to the regulations set by sector-specific legislation and to the codes drawn up by their own sector and umbrella organisations.

The codes set out to a greater or lesser degree of detail the tasks and procedures of the management board and supervisory body contain rules regarding the composition of the bodies and the appointment, suspension, dismissal and remuneration of directors. They also contain rules regarding conflicts of interest. The codes do not prescribe a particular management model, although those regulating welfare, education and housing institutions do specify a two-tier model (management board and supervisory board) as a principle.[57]

The rules contained in sector-specific legislation regarding internal supervision are somewhat different from each other. Incidents within certain housing associations, welfare and education institutions have resulted in the rules governing internal supervision being tightened up.[58] As a consequence, each sector is introducing its own rules governing the tasks and powers of supervisory bodies.

In our view, this is not a development to be welcomed. General rules governing internal supervision and rules regarding the allocation of powers between the bodies of the foundation and the organisation of the foundation should be included, in our view, in Book 2 of the Civil Code. Given the diversity of the foundations and the fact that its management structure is primarily a matter for each individual foundation, the foundation must be left with the choice of how to structure its internal supervision. Our preference would be for a basic statutory regulation of internal supervision. This regulation should at least include rules governing the composition of the supervisory body, the incompatibility of functions, the description of and method of performing, tasks, the authority to appoint, suspend and

---

[56] Van Veen (2007b, 30) and Van der Ploeg (2008, 147).

[57] *Governance Code Woningcorporaties 2007*, *Zorgbrede Governancecode 2010*, *Branchecode Governance Hogescholen* (HBO raad, s-Gravenhage 2006) and *Goed bestuur in de bve-sector* (MBO raad, Woerden 2009).

[58] Additional, detailed standards are imposed upon the supervisory bodies of welfare institutions, Parliamentary Papers II, 2009–2010, 32 402, nr. 2, Art. 39 et seq. (draft law on welfare clients' rights). Likewise for housing associations, for which it was planned to make a legal form of social enterprise compulsory, the detailed rules governing the supervisory body were included in the draft law 'Amendment law on the recognition of public housing institutions' (Parliamentary Papers II, 2010–2011, 32 769, nr. 2, Art. 22–39).

dismiss directors, a provision covering conflicts of interest, additional provisions regarding tasks and powers and the right to information.[59] Additional rules can be adopted on a sector-wide basis as required for that sector, with or without the codes drawn up by the relevant sector and umbrella organisations.

11.6 Amendment of Articles of Formation, Dissolution, Transformation, Merger and Demerger

11.6.1 Amendment of Articles of Formation

The foundation's articles of formation provide the general ground rules for the work and structure of the foundation and are evidence of the existence of an organised body, that is, rules that are fundamental to the foundation.[60] Under the law (Book 2 Article 293 Civil Code), the articles of formation can only be amended if the articles themselves allow for this possibility. This rule ties in with the original characteristic of the foundation, namely, that its founders contribute capital assets to achieve the purpose of the foundation. It is for the founders to decide for themselves how to use the capital they have contributed. If the articles of formation permit their amendment, including a change to the foundation's purpose, then they must specify which body is authorised to take the decision to amend the articles of formation and what requirements the decision to amend must satisfy. The authority to amend the articles must be interpreted narrowly.[61] If a decision to amend includes a radical change to the purpose of the foundation whereby the interests of third parties are disregarded, the decision may be made void as being contrary to the principles of reasonableness and fairness. Furthermore, amendments that result in the situation that the foundation no longer satisfies its statutory description or that the statutory provisions governing the essential characteristics of the foundation (no-members and non-distribution constraints) are breached, be revoked by the court on the application of the foundation, the Public Prosecutor or a stakeholder. The same applies to an amendment of the articles of formation as a result of which the court may dissolve the foundation if it has insufficient capital to meet its amended purpose or if the amendment creates an unfeasible purpose (Book 2 Article 301 Civil Code).

Amendments to articles of formation must be made by notarial deed; otherwise, they will be void. It is expected that the notary will not only investigate whether the proposed amendment complies with the law and the articles of formation

[59] For more details, see Overes (2011b, 74–81).

[60] Dijk and Van der Ploeg (2013, par. 4.3).

[61] Asser-Rensen III* (2012/364–365), Dijk and Van der Ploeg (2013, par. 12.3.1).

themselves, but also take some care to with regard to any third-party interests that could be affected by the amendment of the articles.[62]

The founders of the foundation and those who after its formation are authorised to amend the articles of formation may decide that some provisions of the articles of formation may be excluded from the authority to amend, such as those of the provisions that describe the purpose and basis of the foundation as are important for the existence and operation of the foundation. If *not* amending the articles would lead to consequences that could not reasonably have been desired at the time the foundation was formed, and the articles do not include the possibility for amendment or the body competent to amend refrains from doing it, then the court may amend the articles of formation on the application of a founder, the management board or the Public Prosecutor (Book 2 Art. 294 (1) Civil Code). It is up to the court to judge whether a situation that leads to consequences that could not reasonably have been desired at the time the foundation was formed has arisen. Here the court takes an independent position, whereby the (assumed) wish of the founder is an important point of reference.[63] In amending the articles of formation, the court must change as little of the existing articles as possible. If a change in the purpose of the foundation is sought, the court must specify a related purpose. The court is not bound here by any amendment proposed by the applicants or by the Public Prosecutor.[64] If the court dismisses the application to amend the articles of formation, then it can of its own motion dissolve the foundation.[65]

11.6.2 Dissolution

If the foundation ceases to function as an organisation to achieve the purpose set out in its articles of formation, it can be dissolved. The dissolution of a foundation can be based on a provision of the articles of formation, a decision of a body of the foundation, a court order, a decision of the Netherlands Chamber of Commerce or a provision of law. The law states that the foundation's management board has power to take the decision to dissolve the foundation unless the articles of formation specify otherwise (Book 2 Art. 19 (1) Civil Code). The articles of formation may give this authority to another body, such as a supervisory board.

The foundation will automatically be dissolved if a circumstance that – according to the articles of formation – will result in dissolution occurs. These

[62] Court of Rotterdam 23 December 2009 RN 2010/38, in which the court held that the notary had acted unlawfully by assisting in the amendment of articles of formation by which third-party rights were harmed.

[63] Van der Ploeg (2011, 91).

[64] See Appeal Court of Arnhem 9 March 2006, JOR 2006, 121, in which the court held that the amendment proposed by the management board was insufficiently connected to the existing purpose.

[65] Book 2 Art. 301 (2) Civil Code; see Supreme Court 12 May 2000, NJ 2000, 439.

are grounds for dissolution that occur other than as a result of a decision taken by a body of the legal entity.[66] The court will make an order as to whether, and if so the date on which, the foundation is dissolved in response to an application by the management board, a stakeholder or the Public Prosecutor (Book 2 Art. 19 (2) Civil Code). For involuntary dissolution, It should be noted that according to book 2, art. 17 Civil code a legal person is established for indefinite time.

Dissolution does not mean an immediate end to the foundation. Only if at the time of dissolution the foundation has no capital ceases to exist. If at the time of dissolution the foundation does, however, have capital, then the foundation must first be wound up. The foundation then only ceases to exist once winding up has been completed (Book 2 Art. 19 (6) Civil Code). If the foundation's assets exceed its liabilities, leaving a credit balance, then this balance must be transferred by liquidators in accordance with the law to those entitled to it by virtue of the articles of formation. Whether there are those who are so entitled depends on that foundation's articles of formation. The non-distribution constraint applies here, too, which means that a credit balance may not be paid out to founders, to those who are members of the foundation's bodies or to others, unless in the latter case, such payments are of a philanthropic or social nature. If there are no persons designated by the articles of formation or the authorised body or if the implementation of the provision in the articles of formation is not possible in practice, then the liquidators must pay the credit balance to the State, which will then spend the money as far as possible in accordance with the foundation's purpose.[67]

11.6.3 *Transformation, Merger and Demerger*

Transformation

A reason for converting the foundation may be that the foundation no longer meets the statutory requirements for a foundation[68] as a result, for example, of its structure under the articles of formation or its actual operation whereby the foundation does have members or does make distributions in breach of the non-distribution constraint of Book 2 Article 285 (3) of the Civil Code. A transformation often occurs as a result of a legal merger or demerger, since a legal merger or demerger is only possible if the legal entities involved have the same legal form (see hereafter). A transformation of the foundation may also be indicated by a wish to carry out work on commercial basis. The foundation may be converted to any other legal form.[69]

[66] Dijk and Van der Ploeg (2013, par. 14.1.2).

[67] Art. 23b (1) see Dijk and Van der Ploeg (2013, par. 14.4.4).

[68] See Sect. 11.7.

[69] Association, cooperative, NV and BV.

Transformation does not end the existence of the legal entity, which remains the same legal entity in a different legal form.

A transformation of a foundation requires a decision to convert taken by the body authorised to amend the articles of formation. No decision can be taken to convert if the articles of formation do not allow the possibility for their amendment. In such a case, a founder or the management board must apply to the court to amend the articles of association. The court only has power to do this if, as set out in paragraph 11.6.1, the result of not amending the articles of association could lead to consequences that could not reasonably have been intended at the time the foundation was formed.

In addition to a decision to convert, a decision to amend the articles of formation is required from which it is clear that the articles of association of the converted foundation satisfy the material characteristics of the new legal form. In addition, the law requires that the articles of association of the converted foundation specify that the capital of the foundation existing at the time of the transformation and the income generated therefrom may only be spent in the manner specified before the transformation, unless the court allows otherwise (Book 2 Art. 18 (6) Civil Code). The purpose of the law here is to provide a guarantee that the equity in the converted foundation will not be improperly distributed by the new legal form or spent otherwise than in accordance with the articles of formation of the converted foundation. To avoid a merger or demerger leading to the capital of the converted foundation being spent otherwise, the law specifies that the capital of the foundation remains tied up even if the converted foundation goes through a legal merger or demerger. The articles of association of the legal entity that acquires the capital of the foundation (or the income therefrom) by virtue of a merger or demerger must specify that this capital may not be allocated to a different purpose without the consent of the court. However, the law does not specify what is meant by the capital of the foundation at the time of the transformation. In the context of proceedings concerning annual accounts, the Supreme Court held that – given the protective function of Book 2 Article 18 (6) of the Civil Code – the capital includes the balance of the assets and liabilities and not all (individual) assets and liabilities of the converted foundation.[70] Where the foundation has a more specific purpose, for example, the preservation of a special area of nature or special collection of paintings, such a business economic approach of the term 'capital' provides, in our view, an insufficient guarantee that the capital of the foundation cannot be spent in a different way from that prescribed prior to the transformation.

The tying up of the capital also plays a significant role in the transformation of the foundation to a NV or BV. The question here is whether the capital of the foundation can be used to pay in full for the shares in the company. If one were to accept that this could be the case, it is then important as to who the shareholders in the BV are, since a foundation may not distribute capital to founders, members of

[70] Supreme Court 21 January 2011, NJ 2011, 352 with commentary by P. van Schilfgaarde and H. Beckman.

the foundations bodies or others unless such distribution has a philanthropic or social purpose. Shareholders in the BV are entitled to receive dividends: in other words, a distribution of the income from the foundation's capital. Case law establishes that a payment for the shares in the BV made from the foundation's capital is lawful if the shares are acquired directly or indirectly by a foundation with the same purpose as the converted foundation.[71] If the shares are not acquired directly or indirectly by a foundation with the same purpose as the converted foundation, then a payment in full for the shares in the BV from the foundation's capital is not permitted. In such a case a reserve can be formed pursuant to the articles of association for the purpose for which the foundation was created, together with a provision in the articles of association that in the event of liquidation of the company, the reserve will be spent in accordance with the purpose of the former foundation.[72]

The transformation of a foundation requires the prior authorisation of the court.[73] The court will refuse authorisation if a decision that is required for transformation is void, if there is a claim for the decision to be avoided pending before the court, or if insufficient regard has been paid to the interests of those with voting rights who have voted against the transformation or of others. It is perfectly possible that insufficient regard is paid to third-party rights. Unlike the merger or demerger of a foundation, there is no need to publicise its impending transformation. It is entirely plausible that stakeholders do not learn of the transformation until after the authorisation of the court. An appeal against the decision to authorise the transformation may be filed within a period of 3 months.[74]

The transformation must be contained in a notarial deed setting out the new articles of formation. The transformation comes into effect once this notarial deed is executed.

Merger

The law defines a merger as a juridical act in which at least two legal entities are combined whereby one of these legal entities acquires the capital of the other entity (entities) under universal title or whereby the merging legal entities form a new legal entity that acquires the capital of each of them under universal title. To be able to merge in this way, the merging entities must have the same legal form.[75] As a

---

[71] Court of Zwolle 7 February 2003, JOR 2004/2.

[72] Court of Arnhem 14 May 1992, NJ kort 1992/45, Court of Zwolle 21 November 2003, JOR 2004/68.

[73] Court of Amsterdam 28 April 1998, JOR 1998/105.

[74] Art. 996 (b) Code of Civil Procedure.

[75] There are two exceptions to this rule applying to the foundation: a foundation may merge with a NV or BV in which it holds all the shares, and it may merge with an association, cooperative ormutual association of which it is the sole member.

result of the merger, the capital of the merging foundations transfers to the acquiring foundation, and the merging legal entities cease to exist. To achieve a legal merger, the merging foundations must satisfy a number of requirements. The merging foundations must set out their plans in a merger proposal that must be made available for inspection at the office of the Commercial Register. The fact that the documents have been filed for inspection must also be publicised in a national daily newspaper. In this way, interested third parties and creditors can find out about the proposed merger. Creditors have the right to object to the merger if they believe that the capital situation of the acquiring foundation offers insufficient guarantee that their claims will be satisfied.

The decision to merge – like the decision to convert a foundation – must be taken in the same way as a decision to amend the articles of formation, unless the articles of formation specify otherwise. If the foundation's articles of formation do not allow the possibility of amendment of the articles, then the law provides that the management board has authority to take the decision to merge. If the foundation's articles of formation do not enable all provisions of those articles to be amended, then the decision to merge also requires the approval of the court. This approval will be refused if the merger is in conflict with the interests of the foundation. Given the importance of the merger for the functioning of the organisation, we believe that in determining whether the merger is in conflict with the interests of the foundation the court must have regard to the standard set by Book 2 Article 294 (1) of the Civil Code.[76] The foundation ought to have to demonstrate that continuing the articles of formation in their current form would lead to consequences that could not reasonably have been intended when the foundation was formed. In reaching its decision, the court must give consideration to the interests of the founder (the application of the capital he contributed for the purpose of the foundation) and the interests of third parties with a stake in the foundation. The law states that stakeholders, unlike creditors, have no right to challenge the merger. If not all provisions of the foundation's articles of formation can be amended, then they have to be heard in proceedings in which the approval of the court is sought for the decision to merge. They can also appeal an approval of the court for the decision to merge. However, the court will have no involvement if all provisions of the articles of formation can be amended, and in this situation, the protection of the interests of the stakeholders is insufficiently guaranteed.

Demerger

Demerger is an important instrument to enable legal entities to reorganise or restructure their activities. The law governs both spin-offs and split-ups. A split-up occurs where a foundation splits up its entire capital to at least two acquiring foundations. The foundation performing this split-up then ceases to exist. In the

[76] See Dijk and Van der Ploeg (2013, par.13.8).

case of a spin-off, the demerging foundation continues to exist. The demerger can involve all or any part of the foundation's capital. The statutory regulation of demergers is in many ways similar to that for mergers.

For a demerger there is in principle a requirement that the demerging parties have the same legal form. An exception here is the split-off of capital to a NV or BV created as part of the demerger in which the demerging foundation is sole shareholder (Book 2 Art. 334b Civil Code). As with a merger, capital is transferred under universal title. Since the demerger involves a demerger of legal entities and not merely a split-off of capital, the law states that a demerger involves a change of structure. A 'change of structure' means the creation of a new legal entity or the dissolution of a demerging legal entity. In a split-up of a foundation, the demerging foundation always ceases existence. The same is not true of a spin-off, where the demerging foundation continues to exist. For a spin-off by a foundation at least one of the acquiring foundations must have been created by the spin-off. It is not possible for a foundation to spin-off its capital solely to an already existing foundation.

The procedure for a demerger is almost the same as that for a legal merger. However, a demerger is not a merger in reverse. For creditors, a demerger has far greater consequences than a merger. Capital is not brought together: on the contrary, it is divided up. In addition to the right of creditors to object to the demerger, the law also provides a number of guarantees intended to protect the interests of the creditors.[77] As with a merger, the management board is authorised to take a decision to demerge and in a situation where the foundation's articles of formation do not allow all of its provisions to be amended, the demerger requires the approval of the court (Book 2 Art. 334 m Civil Code). The protection of the foundation's capital and the interests of the stakeholders as described above regarding merger apply equally in the case of a demerger.

11.7 Supervision of Foundations

Since there is no statutory requirement for internal supervision (see Sect. 11.5.3), it is necessary for reasons of achieving the purpose set out in the articles of formation and thus in the interests of the founders (including testators) and creditors that there be supervision of the foundation during its existence. The legislature deliberately decided against administrative supervision but gave a supervisory role to the courts. This civil-law supervision is discussed in Sect. 11.7.1. In Sect. 11.7.2, we examine the supervision focused on abuse and breach of public order, in other words, public-law supervision.

[77] Book 2 Art. 334j, 334 t, 334 s of the Civil Code.

11.7.1 *Civil-Law Supervision*

Supervision by the Public Prosecutor and the Court

The Public Prosecutor is designated by law as the authority charged with investigating whether there are reasons for taking supervisory measures. The law authorises the Public Prosecutor to request information, where there is at least serious doubt as to whether the law or the articles of formation are being complied with, and authorises the court to order the Public Prosecutor to inspect documents if such an application is made (Book 2 Art. 297 Civil Code). Accordingly, the Public Prosecutor does not have direct access to the information it needs.

In circumstances where a foundation is not functioning, or threatens not to function, properly, the Public Prosecutor has authority to seek measures from the court:

(a) Amending the articles of formation (Book 2 Art. 296 Civil Code)
(b) Dismissing directors (Book 2 Art. 298 Civil Code)
(c) Appointing directors (Book 2 Art. 299 Civil Code)
(d) Dissolving the foundation (Book 2 Art. 301 Civil Code)[78]

The court will assess whether the request to take such measures satisfies the statutory conditions and is appropriate. In the context of supervision, the authority of the court to dismiss a director for an act or omission that is in breach of law or the articles of formation, or for mismanagement is the most far-reaching measure next to dissolution (Book 2 Art. 298 (1) Civil Code). Several times the Supreme Court has stated that the term *mismanagement* relates to financial mismanagement and not to mismanagement in a wider sense.[79] The court can also dismiss a director who is in breach of the law or the articles of formation, although the breach must be serious.[80]

During the investigation the court may take interim measures and suspend the director. This appears to give the court sufficient powers to prevent further loss by the failing director(s).

Stakeholders and Supervision

Given its role in protecting the public interest, it seems obvious that the Public Prosecutor should have this task in the context of the supervision of foundations. However, it is so heavily focused on combating crime that civil breaches by

[78] The Public Prosecutor may also request the court to dissolve the foundation if its purpose or work is in breach of public order (Book 2 Art. 20 Civil Code) or if there are any defects in the way in which the foundation was formed or is structured (Book 2 Art. 21 Civil Code).

[79] Supreme Court 3 January 1975, NJ 1975, 222 commentary by G.J.S. (*Stichting vorming werkende jeugdigen Ede e.o.*) and Supreme Court 23 April 2004, JOR 2004, 160.

[80] See Dijk and Van der Ploeg (2013, par. 10.3.2.c).

foundations receive hardly any attention at all. The fact that the Public Prosecutor in reality fails to exercise its powers here is down to chance. The legislature has therefore also given stakeholders the authority to apply to court for supervisory measures to be taken.[81]

The law does not further define the term ‘stakeholder’ nor can this be elicited from the legislative history.[82] Over time, the term has been interpreted in rather different ways.[83] Originally it was a requirement that to qualify as a stakeholder – if the relevant party did not belong to the organisation of the foundation – you had to suffer a concrete, specific disadvantage with regard to the foundation.[84] The term was subsequently interpreted more widely and in case law is also used if the relevant party is involved in the decision in his own interests or if he was closely involved in the matter in hand.[85]

Ban on Directorships

A sanction following from his dismissal by the court is that the relevant director cannot be a director of a foundation for a period of 5 years following his dismissal (Book 2 Art. 298 (3) Civil Code). There is also a ban on directorships by directors of foundations and other legal entities under criminal law[86] (see Sect. 11.7.2).

The Investigation Process for Large Foundations

Large foundations, that is, foundations that run a business and are required by law to have a works council (namely, those with at least 50 employees) are subject to the rules regarding the investigation process (Book 2 Art. 344 et seq. Civil Code). In this procedure the Enterprise Chamber of the Amsterdam Court of Appeal will, on the application of a trade association that has members working for the foundation or others given such authority under the articles of formation, appoint persons to investigate the policy and business operations of the legal entity. This application will be allowed if there are substantive reasons for doubting that the policy has been correct (see Book 2 Art. 350 Civil Code). This is not the place to deal with this procedure in detail. But it is worth noting that the Enterprise Chamber may take immediate measures at any time for the duration of the proceedings. If the

[81] This is not the case where articles of formation are amended (Book 2 Art. 294 Civil Code).

[82] In the law not the word ‘stakeholder’ is used, but the word ‘belanghebbende’, which means ‘interested person’. The translation ‘stakeholder’ seems however adequate.

[83] See Dijk and Van der Ploeg (2013, par. 10,3,3).

[84] Supreme Court 25 October 1991, NJ 1992, 149.

[85] See Supreme Court 10 November 2006, NJ 2007, 45 and Supreme Court 29 June 2007, LJN AZ7705.

[86] See Doorenbos (2010, 422 et seq.).

investigation reveals that there has been mismanagement, the Enterprise Chamber may, at the request, inter alia, of the original applicants, take steps such as the suspension or revocation of decisions, the suspension or dismissal of directors or supervisory directors, the temporary appointment of directors or supervisory directors, the temporary amendment of the articles of formation and, as a last resort, dissolution of the legal entity. Although initially this procedure was introduced with regard to companies, it has already been applied a few times to foundations.

Supervision of Amendment of Articles of Formation, Transformation, Merger and Demerger

The notary is responsible for ensuring that an amendment of the articles of formation, transformation, merger or demerger complies with the law and with the articles of formation. In certain cases, the approval of the court is also required. See Sect. 11.6.

Supervision of Finances

Most foundations are only required to keep financial accounts and to draw up a balance sheet and profit and loss account within 6 months following the end of each financial year (Book 2 Art. 10 Civil Code). Generally there is no requirement for a foundation to publish its accounts.

Large foundations – having a net turnover of more than € 4,400,000 – are subject by virtue of Book 2 Art. 360 (3) of the Civil Code to the annual accounts rules of Title 9, which require, inter alia, that their annual accounts must be set out in accordance with Book 2 Title 9 of the Civil Code, that their accounts are audited by an accountant or auditing consultant and that their accounts are filed with the Commercial Register (Book 2 Arts. 393 and 394 Civil Code).

In summer 2010, however, a draft law was issued by the Ministry of Justice for consultation concerning the publishing of balance sheets and profit and loss accounts of foundations in general.[87] An additional obligation was included with regard to the profit and loss account, namely, that it must include the assets acquired by inheritance, charged benefit, gift and natural obligation and those acquired because an administration on those goods ended (see book 4, art. 164(1) a and c Civil code. These measures comply with the requirements of the international Financial Action Task Force. They enable one to discover whether the foundation is financed by large donors wishing to use the foundation for unlawful purposes. The annual accounts need not give the names of the large donors, etc., but the

[87] See Klaassen (2010, 257 et seq.).

foundation must keep this information.[88] By publishing information, supervisors can perform their tasks better.[89] The Public Prosecutor and stakeholders may enforce compliance with these two obligations. The draft has yet not been discussed in Parliament.

There are no further requirements dictating the content of the foundation's annual accounts. The reason for this is that the burdens would otherwise be too great. Whilst publication leads to a certain transparency, there is as yet no real governmental supervision. There would be a supervisory element if an audit were to be compulsory. However, it is understandable that this is not required for, nor proposed for, all foundations since it would be disproportionately onerous on small foundations.

Dissolution by the Netherlands Chamber of Commerce

It should lastly be noted that the Netherlands Chamber of Commerce may, under certain circumstances, dissolve a foundation.

If a foundation has failed to pay the annual contribution to the Chamber of Commerce for a year, and no directors are named in the Commercial Register or the named directors have died or cannot be contacted, the Chamber of Commerce may dissolve the foundation (Book 2 Art. 19a Civil Code). If a foundation is subject to the duty to publish – see paragraph on "Supervision on finances" above – then failure to do so for a period of a year can form a ground for dissolution by the Chamber of Commerce.[90]

The persons involved in the foundation may appeal against a decision of the Chamber of Commerce to the Appeal Court for Commerce (CBB). This court has held that dissolution by the Chamber of Commerce is not appropriate if the legal entity is demonstrably continuing to carry out activities.[91]

---

[88] We cannot deal here with the issues regarding regulation of the supervision of fundraising in this context.

[89] See Explanatory Memorandum for the draft law, p. 3.

[90] In Book 2 Art. 19a (2) of the Civil Code to the words 'in Section 1 (b)' can be added the words 'or Section 1 (c)'.

[91] See most recently on theme CBB 27 March 2008, LJN: BC8398.

11.7.2 Public-Law Supervision

International and National Developments

As recently as 2000, the Minister was of the view that greater supervision of foundations than provided for in the Civil Code was inappropriate.[92] That view has since drastically changed. The terrorist attacks on the Twin Towers in New York as well as later such episodes have given rise to a huge international effort to combat terrorism and money laundering as efficiently as possible. They have led, for example, to UN Convention against Transnational Organised Crime (15 November 2000, Trb 2001, 68) and the Financial Action Task Force on Money Laundering (report dated 11 October 2001). These in turn have been reflected in Dutch legislation, in particular the important roles played by the Prevention of Money Laundering and Financing of Terrorism Act that came into force on 1 August 2008[93] and the Control of Legal Entities Act of 2010.[94]

Central Registration with the Ministry of Security and Justice

By requiring registration with the Ministry of Security and Justice, the Control of Legal Entities Act 2010 has created another source of information for the Public Prosecutor. All manner of bodies, including the Netherlands Chamber of Commerce, the legal profession, insurance companies, banks, etc. must report risks to the Ministry of Security and Justice. *Justis* (Justice Information Service)[95] keeps a register of founders, supervisory directors, members with management functions, directors and representatives of legal entities, as well as other persons who (help) determine the policy of the legal entity (see art. 4).[96] Art. 2 states that the Minister shall check legal entities to try to prevent and combat their abuse, including the commission of crimes and breaches of financial-economic regulations by, or by means of, such legal entities.[97] There is another hotline intended solely to combat

---

[92] See Van der Ploeg (2005, 8).

[93] Act of 15 July 2008, Stb. 303. The Service Provider Identification Act ('WID') and the Unusual Transactions Act have been revoked (Art. 49 Prevention of Money Laundering and Financing of Terrorism Act).

[94] Act of 7 July 2010, Stb. 280, which, by Royal Decree dated 21 April 2011, Stb. 194, came into effect on 1 July 2011.

[95] Formerly the *Centrale Justitiële Documentatie* (cf. Art. 3 (2) (a) Companies Documentation Act).

[96] Further data can include names of spouse, registered partner or life partner, parents, children and grandchildren of the said persons if this is necessary in connection with an analysis of the Legal entity's network of directors (Art. 4 new Section 3). For implementation and risks, see *Toelichting op Besluit controle van rechtspersonen*, Stb. 2011, 180, p. 10 et seq.

[97] A large amount of information is collated by the Ministry. The question is whether a correct balance has been struck between protecting privacy and combating crime. Cf Doorenbos (2010, 470–471).

money laundering and the financing of terrorism – the Financial Intelligence Unit-Nederland (FIU) – to which lawyers, banks, etc. must report unusual transactions as well as carry out client investigations if there are indications that such clients could be involved in money laundering or the financing of terrorism (Art. 3 of the Prevention of Money Laundering and Financing of Terrorism Act).

The said laws are not directly focused on civil-law consequences.

Ban on Directorships Under Criminal law

It has recently become possible for the court to remove from his directorship a director of a legal entity (and others) who is guilty of any form of embezzlement set out in the Dutch Criminal Code.[98]

Someone banned from being a director under civil or criminal law may not be nominated to fill a vacancy on the management board of a foundation. Whilst this ban is at first sight clear and sensible, in practice it is hard to uphold, since there is no centrally accessible list of directors who have been banned as directors under criminal or civil law. Since there is central registration of, for example, directors of foundations at risk under the Supervision of Legal Entities Act, then such a registration of banned directors should be possible.[99]

Prohibition and Dissolution of Foundations in Breach of Public Order

When the actual work of a foundation is in breach of public order, it can be declared prohibited and dissolved: see Book 2 art. 20 (1) of the Civil Code. If it is only its purpose that is in breach of public order, then only dissolution will occur (see Book 2 art. 20 (2) of the Civil Code). The procedure for the declaration of prohibition and dissolution of a foundation (or other legal entity) where its work is in breach of public order is difficult for the Public Prosecutor to succeed in. The courts have imposed strict standards for attributing the deeds of members and management board members to the organisation itself.[100]

---

[98] See Art. 194 (refusal/untrue information filed with insolvency), 205 (foreign military service), 235 (2) (forging documents, untrue declarations, breach of duty to supply information) and 349 (prejudicing of creditors) Dutch Criminal Code.

[99] Cf Van der Ploeg (2011, 90).

[100] See the failed cases in the Appeal Court of Amsterdam 5 January 2006, JOR 2006, 200 and Court of Leeuwarden 6 March 2007, LJN AZ9940 against chapters of the Hell's Angels, Supreme Court 26 June 2009, JOR 2009, 222. See also Schmieman (2008, 44 et seq.). The public prosecutor succeeded in Supreme Court 18 April 2014, ECLI:NL:HR:2014:948 regarding the association Martijn.

Civil-Law Consequences of Public-Law Registration?

It is clear that the legislation that involves further supervision and an attempt to combat money laundering and terrorism by the government provides much more data than the civil-law registration with the Netherlands Chamber of Commerce, which before then existed alone. It does seem that the existing civil-law registration and supervisory regulations could be improved. It remains to be seen whether the additional information about foundations obtained though the new services provided by the Ministry of Security and Justice can also be used for civil-law supervision. There are problems lurking here with regard to privacy.

11.7.3 Other External Supervision

The above provides just a limited overview of government supervision. In all sorts of areas, supervision is being differently exercised. Foundations that have a purpose or perform work in the area of public service or that otherwise operate for the public good are subject to governmental administrative supervision intended to specifically supervise a particular field, such as housing foundations, pension funds, healthcare institutions and education institutions. The government has drawn up specific rules in these fields in order to guarantee that the quality offered by these services is of good quality and that the finances of these foundations are properly managed, but is less focused on the structure and functioning of the legal entity, unlike the supervision described in Sect. 11.7.1.

Since the government also mostly grants subsidies to organisations operating for the public good, the organisations receiving such subsidies must produce annual reports and demonstrate that they have satisfied the conditions under which the subsidy has been granted.

Special mention should also be made of the supervision of charitable organisations – mostly foundations – by the tax inspectorate for the province of Noord Brabant in 's-Hertogenbosch. To be eligible for tax benefits, the foundation must be registered with the tax and customs authority as an institution for the public good (an *anbi*) 90% of the activities have to be directed at the charitable purpose. The *anbi* must, for example, submit annual accounts and a policy document each year. Since 1 January 2014 the anbi should publish its policy document and other data on its public website.

Lastly, it is interesting to note how the supervision of 'government foundations' is regulated. In principle, a ministry may only create a foundation in exceptional circumstances, but in reality such foundations are created even when there is not strictly any need. Since a government body is usual involved in the formation, it will ensure that it is entitled under the articles of formation to appoint directors or members of the supervisory board and the right of prior approval of any important decisions, such as the adoption of a budget or the annual accounts. This, in effect, is an example of internal supervision.

The Netherlands Court of Audit recently examined the formation of government foundations and their supervision.[101] It proposed greater consideration of the question whether a foundation was actually needed and to include summaries of the foundations with which the relevant ministry is involved in these ministries' budgets. The Minister of Finance is of the view that current practice has been sufficiently considered, but promises to strive for greater transparency of government foundations.

Furthermore, in many fields, such as in the arts world, or in the provision of social services, libraries and fundraising, supervision exists on the basis of self-regulation.

11.8 Concluding Remarks

The control over the creation of foundations and the juridical acts they perform has been considerably encouraged by recent legislation. The purpose of this control is intended, however, to deal with (the threat of) criminal acts. In principle, this control has no direct effect on the validity of the formation and functioning of the foundation. Thus, one can still conclude that despite this legislation setting out controls on foundations, the law on foundations in the Netherlands remains liberal. A foundation is formed in the presence of a Dutch notary without the need for any approval of its administration. There is substantial freedom with regard to its purpose and management structure. The only restriction is the non-distribution constraint, and whilst there is also a no-members constraint, it is not clear what is covered by this. The law relating to management structures is in development, but in practice is developing alongside the law. There is supervision by the court at a certain distance. However, often disputes will not actually get to court. In many cases, there are methods of control via self-regulation or government supervision based on specific legislation and policy in various social fields. There appears to be no need to develop particular regulations for subcategories within existing legislation on foundations. Additional regulations that need to be applied to foundations (and other legal forms) in specific fields can be better introduced in categorical legislation.

[101] Netherlands Court of Audit, *Zicht op overheidsstichtingen;achtergrondstudie*, April 2011; Parliamentary Papers II 2010–2011, 31 887, nr. 4.

Bibliography

Asser, Van der Grinten-Maeijer. 1997. *II 2 (De rechtspersoon)*, 8e druk. Deventer: Tjeenk Willink.

Maeijer en de Kluiver. 2012. *Asser-Rensen III* Rechtspersonenrecht; overige rechtspersonen*, 9e druk. Deventer: Kluwer.

de Kluiver, H.J. 1988. Steunstichting, fondsenwerving en overheid. *S&V*, 176–182.

Dijk, P.L., and T.J. Van der Ploeg. 2013. *Van vereniging en stichting, coöperatie en onderlinge waarborgmaatschappij*, 6e druk. Deventer: Gouda Quint.

Doorenbos, D.R. 2010. Controle op (misbruik van) rechtspersonen. *Ondernemingsrecht*, 465 et seq.

Duynstee, J.A.T.J. 1978. *Beschouwingen over de stichting naar Nederlands privaatrecht*, 2e druk. Deventer: Kluwer.

Gitmans, W.J.M., and P.J.M. van Wersch. 1976. *Knelpunten in de bestuursstructuur van het algemene ziekenhuis*. Deventer: Kluwer.

Groeneveld, J.G. 2004. *Publieke wenselijkheid of private beleidsvrijheid*, diss VU. Deventer: Kluwer.

Groeneveld-Louwerse, J.G. 2001. Voorwaarden voor het delegeren van bevoegdheden bij vereniging en stichting op grond van de bepalingen van Boek 2 BW in het licht van enkele bestuursmodellen. *S&V*, 9.

Hendriks, R.W.F. 1994. *De stichting in concernverband*, diss KUB. Deventer: Tjeenk Willink.

Hopt, K.J., W.R. Walz, T. von Hippel, and V. Then (eds.). 2006. *The European foundation*. Gütersloh: Bertelsmann Stiftung.

Klaassen, A.G.H. 2010. Maatregel ter verbetering van het toezicht op stichtingen, *Ondernemingsrecht*, 257 et seq.

Lubbers, A.G. 1983. *Bestuur en toezicht, keerzijden van een medaille*. Deventer: Kluwer.

Overes, C.H.C. 2006. *Rechtspersonen* (loose leaf), De stichting, art. 285 et seq.

Overes, C.H.C. 2011a. Een zorgplicht voor goed bestuur in het onderwijs. In *Zorgplichten in publiek- en* privaatrecht, red. Janssen, C.E.C. e.a. Den Haag: Boom.

Overes, C.H.C. 2011b. De stichting en governance: Bestuur en toezicht. In *De stichting; Kritische beschouwingen over de wettelijke regeling voor een veelzijdige rechtsvorm*, eds. M.-L. Lennarts and Zaman Van Veen, 63 et seq. Deventer: Kluwer.

Pitlo-Raaijmakers. 2006. *Ondernemingsrecht*, 5e druk. Deventer: Kluwer.

Schmieman, E. 2008. De stand van zaken bij het toezicht op stichtingen. *TvOB*, 44 et seq.

Slagter, W.J. 1999. Corporate governance bij stichting en vereniging. *S&V*, 47 et seq.

Turkenburg, M. 2009. Ready, willing and able? Schoolbesturen over goed bestuur, intern toezicht en horizontale verantwoording. *NTOR*, p. 88ff.

Van der Ploeg, T.J. 1989. Vraagtekens bij steunstichtingen. *TVVS*, 95–98.

Van der Ploeg, T.J. 1999. A comparative legal analysis of foundations, aspects of supervision and transparancy. In *Private funds, public purpose*, ed. H.K. Anheier and S. Toepler, 55–78. Kluwer-Plenum.

Van der Ploeg, T.J. 2005. Verscherpt toezicht op stichtingen en het algemeen belang. *FTV*, 5–10.

Van der Ploeg, T.J. 2008. De juridische inkadering van de 'maatschappelijke onderneming'. In *Preadvies van de Vereeniging 'Handelsrecht'*, 103–148. Deventer: Kluwer.

Van der Ploeg, T.J. 2011. Overheidstoezicht op stichtingen. In *De stichting. Kritische beschouwingen over de wettelijke regeling voor een veelzijdige rechtsvorm*, eds. M.-L. Lennarts and Zaman Van Veen, 55–78. Deventer: Kluwer.

Van Veen, W.J.M. 2007a Corporate governance for non-profit organisations; a legal approach. In *Zwischen Markt und Staat, Gedachtnisschrift für Rainer Walz*, eds. H. Kohl, F. Kubler, C. Ott, and K. Schmidt, 755–766. Berlin/München/Köln: Carl Heymans Verlag, pp. 755–766.

Van Veen, W.J.M. 2007b. Een nieuwe rechtsvorm voor 'de' maatschappelijke onderneming? Wenselijkheid en noodzaak (onder meer) vanuit een rechtspersonenrechtelijk perspectief. In *Maatschappelijke ondernemingen*, ed. T.J. Hoekstra, 17–32. Deventer: Kluwer.

Verdam, A.F. 2011. Collectieve en individuele bestuursverantwoordelijkheid. In *Hoe verder met collegiaal bestuur in Nederland? Bestuurstaak, bestuursverantwoordelijkheid en bestuurder-saansprakelijkheid volgens het nieuwe art. 2:9 BW*, J.B. Huizink e.a. Red. Deventer: Kluwer.

Wessels, B. 1998. 'Corporate' governance: niet voor beursvennootschappen alleen. *S&V*, 45–46.

Wessels, B. 1996. Profiel van stichtingen en vereniging in Nederland. *S&V*, 1–6.

Chapter 12
The New Portuguese Law on Private Foundations

Rui Hermenegildo Gonçales

12.1 Introduction

On July 9, 2012, the Portuguese Parliament approved, with minor amendments, the Law 24/2012, which was submitted by the Portuguese Government and comprised both a new framework-law (*lei-quadro*) on foundations and modifications to the chapter on legal persons of the Civil Code, more specifically to the articles relating to private foundations. This reform was a result of a recommendation contained in the Law 1/2012, of the 3rd of January, which apart from an instruction for the Portuguese Government to propose a new law on foundations provided for the realization of an inquiry to all foundations operating in Portugal, regardless of nationality or field of activity, in order to assess both their respective cost/benefit and financial viability and decide on their continuation or liquidation, the continuation, reduction, or termination of public financial support and finally on the maintenance or cancellation of their public utility status, when applicable.[1] Although one of the argued reasons to conduct this inquiry was the self-proclaimed lack of empirical knowledge about the Portuguese foundation sector, the Law 24/2012 was approved before the release of results of the referred inquiry, which happened only the 2nd of August 2012.

In turn, both laws, 1/2012 and 24/2012, were a direct result of the Memorandum of Understanding of the program of economic and financial assistance to Portugal, concluded between the Portuguese Government, the European Union, the Interna-

[1] The Portuguese law separates or distinguishes between the legal personality of a foundation and its eventual public utility status which can be granted only in certain conditions to a foundation which is considered to cooperate closely with the state in addressing pressing social needs. Only foundations with public utility status are eligible for tax privileges.

R.H. Gonçales (✉)
Calouste Gulbenkian Foundation, Av. de Berna 45-A, 1067-001 Lisbon, Portugal
e-mail: rgoncalves@gulbenkian.pt

C. Prele (ed.), *Developments in Foundation Law in Europe*, Ius Gentium: Comparative Perspectives on Law and Justice 39, DOI 10.1007/978-94-017-9069-7_12,

tional Monetary Fund, and the European Central Bank on 17 May 2011.[2] Or at least this conclusion could be extracted from the explanatory statement of the government proposal for the new law on foundations (Law 24/2012), which disappeared in the final version approved by the parliament. Indeed, in the referred explanatory statement, we could have read that the Memorandum of Understanding, with the aim of optimizing public costs, recommended the strict control of "the incorporation of new foundations" and "the adoption of a legal framework for its establishment, operation, monitoring, reporting, performance evaluation and extinction," In my opinion here lays one of the major faults of the new law, because nowhere in the Memorandum of Understanding is possible to read any reference to private foundations. In fact, in point 3.44 of the Memorandum of Understanding (1st version), containing the only explicit reference to foundations, we can only read that the government should "Regulate by law the creation and the functioning of foundations, associations, and similar bodies by the central and local administration." This means that only the foundations instituted by the state, that is, public foundations at large, were mentioned in the Memorandum of Understanding and not all foundations, which was the main argument of the Portuguese Government to both perform the inquiry and submit a new law on foundations to the Portuguese Parliament.

This preliminary explanation is important, not because the law on private foundations should not have been reformed but to understand some or the majority of the rules enacted by the new law which are state oriented and imbued with an unbalanced tendency for state supervision and monitoring instead of alternative private supervisory mechanisms. Indeed, some of the norms that most strikingly affect private foundations although reasonable for public bodies are, in my opinion, totally inappropriate for private institutions and represent an interference of the State in the management of private philanthropic institutions with which is difficult to agree, especially in a moment when, due to public budget constraints, social pressure and demand on these institutions are likely to increase.

This said, this chapter is going to be exclusively or mainly focused on private foundations and how the new Portuguese law affects their formation, governance structure, activities, reporting, and supervision.

12.2 Brief Historical Background

Foundations or similar bodies have existed in Portugal almost since the birth of nationality (in the twelfth century), having their first apogee during the fifteenth and sixteenth centuries and the second in the last quarter of the twentieth century when

---

[2] The first version of the Memorandum of Understanding on Specific Economic Policy Conditionality, of 17 of May 2011, can be accessed here http://www.portugal.gov.pt/media/371369/mou_20110517.pdf

the majority of the almost 500 foundations operating in Portugal[3] were incorporated. Despite their social impact, they lack public appraisal of their economic and social significance which somehow resonated in the inadequacy of the former legal regime, which was commonly considered as outdated, state driven, and not properly translating neither the foundation's private nature nor their contribution to the public good. The new law did not change this context; on the contrary, it increased the traditional mistrust towards foundations. Only social interest foundations are allowed under Portuguese law, and available data demonstrates that they have been a long-lasting and ongoing social innovation engine in the civil society arena.[4]

Foundations,[5] despite their typology and mission's diversity, have always been – and continue to be – the subject of passionate debates. This could be attributed to the social paradox they convey, regardless of the discussion about the specific purposes they address or the missions envisioned by their founders and which translates, very simplistically, in the universal Man's desire for immortality.[6] Among its detractors and its defenders or even within each of these groups, foundations have never merited consensual opinions but rather have been the target of infatuated appraisals, in both directions, which only increases the difficulty of any scientific research on the phenomenon.

Pomey defends the universality of foundations' definition, both historical and geographical, noting that these correspond to a timeless aspiration of men, without geographical boundaries, as they allow the founder to survive in a long-lasting work or even perpetual, affecting assets for the benefit of the community. That is, it is the history and geography of foundations that confirm their universal concept.[7]

---

[3] The number comes form the recent inquiry conducted under the mentioned Law 1/2012 of 3rd of January.

[4] For a general view about the evolution of foundations in Portugal, see Themudo (2003). In a more broad perspective, about the evolution of the nonprofit sector, see Campos Franco (2005).

The National Statistic Agency (www.ine.pt) published in 2011 the satellite account of the nonprofit sector, with data from 2006. According to this report, which does not disaggregate nonprofit institutions by type, there are in Portugal more than 45 000 nonprofit institutions, representing 2.2 % of the national gross added value and responsible for 4.4 % of paid jobs (http://www.tcontas.pt/pt/actos/rel_auditoria/2011/2s/audit-dgtc-rel001-2011-2s.pdf).

[5] The word *"foundation"* finds its etymological roots in Latin, *fundatio-ionis*, which has to do with *fundus*, meaning "fund" or stock of goods and the verb *fundare*, that is, the ability to lay the basis or the foundations of something (cfr. Alli Turrilas 2010, 46 e 47).

[6] Pomey (1980, 30–31) states that, as foundations allow their founder to remain in a work that transcends his/her lifetime, in principle, perpetually channeled for the common good, they respond to a universal human aspiration, which would explain the universality of the notion of foundation, as well as its history and its geography.

Emphasizing the characteristic of human nature that, in our view, underlies in the origins of foundations, we do not ignore their modern use by collective persons, whether public or private. This phenomenon thus is more recent and, without impairing the above assertion, is related to the pointed evolution ability of foundations.

[7] Pomey (1980, 31): "En tant qu'elles permettent au fondateur de se survivre dans une oeuvre durable et même, en principe, perpétuelle, tout en faisant le bien de ses frères, les fondations répondent à une aspiration de l'homme de tout temps, en tous pays, de biens a affecter ainsi, après

We must therefore analyze the context in which foundations, as assets earmarked for purposes of collective or social nature, emerged in first place and how they developed in both social and legal terms.

In historical terms, one can state that foundations are a legal category that has been able to circumvent the different political, social, and economic upheavals of, at least, the last twenty-five centuries,[8] having survived periods in which almost disappeared or were legally extinct. In order to prevail though they were often forced to adapt in terms of typology, concept, and mode of operation in the legal environments where their existence was challenged. To illustrate this trend, we could mention that foundations, for instance, were not included in the regulatory text that inaugurates the modern movement of civil codes, the Napoleon Code, from 1804. This absence earned them the epitome of "*illegitimate daughters of the* Code Civile."[9]

The history of foundations in Portugal, like the rest of Europe,[10] is intertwined with the history of either the social assistance or the penetration of the Catholic Church in the country.[11] We could define social assistance in general terms, as mentioned by Lopes (2009, 19), as "any organized activity, public or private, channeled to the satisfaction of material and moral needs of the population, especially the most deprived and socially unprotected." Since the founding of the nation, in 1143,[12] there were such institutions and charities, like the medieval guilds, brotherhoods, or confraternities, which combined the defense of professional interests with the pursuit of goals for mutual or spiritual assistance. While some of these institutions were directly linked with the Catholic Church, others were privately created institutions, and others were undertaken by the royal power itself or with its institutional or personal support.[13] A paradigmatic example, in the

---

lui, à la collectivité. C'est dire l'universalité de la notion de fondation; ce que confirment aussi bien l'histoire que la géographie."

[8] According to Liermann *apud* Blanch Nougués (2007, 109), the most ancient (Greek) foundation is from the fifth century B.C. It was incorporated by *NIKIAS*, an Athenian magistrate who, while living, assigned to the Delphic temple of Apollo properties with a charge to the clergyman, with its revenue, to organize banquets to praise for the well-being of the founder.

[9] The sentence belongs to Zoppini (1995, 28). Imbert (1988, 47) estimates that all foundations that existed in France during the *Ancien Régime* were either extincted or modified, by a joint action of the *Code Civile* or the laws of confiscation of the eighteenth century.

[10] Hopt et al. (2006, 45) acknowledge the "common historical roots" of foundations in Europe.

[11] In this sense, see Schlüter et al. (2001, 215), to whom "As in other European countries the first foundations in Portugal appeared under the influence of the Catholic Church." For Campos Franco (2005, 4), we must understand the role of the Roman Catholic Church in the formation of the country and national identity in order to understand its penetration in society "not only in terms of the provision of spiritual support, but also in terms of the provision of social and educational services to the population" (pp. 4).

[12] Some authors defend that even before the founding of the nation there were institutions similar to foundations. Carlos Monjardino states that the creation of a foundation is attributed to D. Teresa (died 1130), the mother of Afonso Henriques, Portugal's first king.

[13] For a description of the different types of institutions during this period, see Campos Franco (2005, 5–6).

reign of King Dinis, thrust away by his Queen Saint Isabel, is the establishment of fraternities, especially those that call upon the Holy Spirit, denouncing a nature equally Christian (Lopes 2009, 20).

These institutions were not foundations in the modern sense and had a more distinctive associative or membership nature, as the crafts corporations, which were characterized by the reunion of members with the same profession or from various professions for the pursuit of common goals. They were, however, even incidentally, endowed with some assets for the pursuit of charitable functions and of social assistance, namely, to provide assistance to the members affected by diseases, which involved, for instance, the establishment of hospitals. The fraternities and sororities had, instead, a more charitable nature or just spiritual, for the devotion or to worship, which would afterwards lead to the creation of the houses of mercy.

Although with a reference of scarce legal significance,[14] foundations were not explicitly contemplated in the first Portuguese Civil Code, of 1867, which was, like other European codifications of the nineteenth century, influenced by the French Civil Code. The current Civil Code, which entered into force in 1967, finally restored the historical injustice and established foundations as an explicitly corporate legal form of private collective persons, along with associations and corporations.[15] This provision, however, disregarded and continues to ignore the concept modernization that depicts the legal evolution of foundations during the second half of the twentieth century, which only demonstrates the traditional lack of interest by Portuguese legal scholars about foundations.[16] Indeed the Portuguese Civil Code portrays a concept of foundations that no longer correspond to the social dynamics that throughout Europe were and are being assigned to foundations.[17] Indeed, the conceptual criteria established by the Portuguese Civil Code reveal foundations as destination endowments, generally in perpetuity, to pursue goals of social interest and whose legal personality depends from the state approval which evaluates not only the nature of the purposes set by the founder but also the sufficiency of the disposed assets to achieve them.

[14] Caetano (1967, 6) states, however, that the Code has been unfairly accused of following the guidance of the highly individualistic Code Napoleon, when "the Viscount de Seabra not only withdrew from the French coding system, as respected as much as possible the Portuguese legal traditions and tempered the prevailing individualism of that time," with a title about moral persons in the chapter on the legal capacity. As for foundations, Caetano (1967, 28) however confirms that the Code had only one accidental reference, in Article 37, "and nothing more."

[15] According to Article 157.º of the Code, the chapter in question, on the collective persons', shall apply, in addition to the associations that have not the economic profit of their associates as a mission and, when the analogy of the situation so warrants, the corporations, to foundations of social interest.

[16] For example, it is noteworthy that the last deep monograph in Portugal about foundations and the law dates back to 1962 and belongs to Caetano (1962).

[17] About this evolution, see Lopez Lacoiste (1965, 567 and following) or Rescigno (1989, 469 and following).

12.3 Current Legal Provisions

The Portuguese framework-law on foundations establishes the principles and rules by which foundations should stand, being compulsory and prevailing over other laws that specifically address any other matters or types of foundations (Article 2º, 2). According to the transitional and final provisions of the Law 24/2012, Article 6.º, the modifications to the Civil Code and the rules of the framework-law indeed apply to the private foundations already incorporated, in the process of being recognized or already recognized, except when in contradiction with the will of the founder, in which case the later shall prevail. Within a maximum period of 6 months from the law's approval, private foundations with public utility status must adapt theirs statutes and governance structure according to the framework-law or else face loosing that status, unless the adaptation is in contradiction with the will of the founder.

12.3.1 Types of Foundations

Private foundations correspond, in Portugal, to a legal category typically enshrined in the law that seeks to address certain metajuridical interests[18] and whose formation process requires the verification of a set of elements and includes certain predetermined stages legally established which culminate with the acquisition of the legal personality. The general legal provisions regarding private foundations are inserted, as referred above, in the current Portuguese Civil Code, of 1967, with the modifications introduced by the Law 24/2012, which also approved a new framework-law on foundations. This framework-law includes the different types of either private foundations or foundations incorporated by the state. Nonetheless, the articles of the Civil Code which apply to private foundations, although modified, were not abrogated and are reproduced in the framework-law in the part concerning private foundations (Article 14.º ss). This is the reason why we still can say that the Civil Code contains the general legal provisions regarding private foundations. I will continue therefore to use the Civil Code as the general regime for private foundations in Portugal and will only refer to the framework-law when its regime diverges from or adds something not foreseen in the Civil Code.

Foundations, in Portugal, represent therefore one of the possible legal classified collective persons under the Civil Code chapter devoted to "legal persons" (Article 157 et seq.). Thus, this chapter, along with the nonprofit associations, includes the so-called foundations of social interest. According to Article 157º, the chapter in question is applicable, in addition to the associations which do not seek the

[18] De Oliveira Ascensäo (2000, 217) refers in this respect that "in the case of foundations, based on an endowment, only the granting of legal personality allows a polarization of interests that otherwise would not find adequate support."

economic profit of their members, and corporations, when the analogy of the situation so warrants, to foundations of social interest. Paragraph 2 of Article 158º states, in turn, that foundations' legal personality is acquired by a specific act of an administrative authority, designated *reconhecimento* (state approval). According to Law 24/2012, this act is currently a competency of the Prime Minister (Article 20.º).

Apart from these *foundations of social interest*, which constitute the general legal type of foundations of private origin in Portugal, other types of private foundations can be instituted under specific legal frameworks, depending on their aims. The Statute of Social Solidarity Private Institutions (*Estatuto das Instituições de Particularidade Social*, Law 119/83, of 25 of February) foresee the incorporation of social welfare foundations (*fundações de Solidariedade Social*), which are foundations specifically designed to address issues of social welfare, like social justice or public health.[19] These foundations are supposed to collaborate very closely with the state and benefit therefore from an exceptional legal and fiscal framework. The foundations of social welfare are incorporated within the Ministry of Social Solidarity, are exempted from the income tax since their registration, but it is the prime minister who is responsible for the recognition (Article 40.º of the framework-law). Other types of private foundations in Portugal are foundations for cooperation and development, foreseen in the Statute of the Non-Governmental Organizations on Cooperation for Development, or foundations whose objectives include the creation of higher education institutions, created under Law no. 62/2007 of September 10. The competence for the recognition of either the foundations for cooperation and development and the educational foundations, since the framework-law, belongs to the prime minister (Articles 43º and 46.º, respectively), who has the residual competence for the recognition of private foundations.

Another specific category of private foundations, with an autonomous legal regime, is the religious foundations. The legal status of these foundations is inserted, in general, in the Law on Religious Freedom (Law 16/2001 of 22 June), paragraph 3 of Article 22, which provides that churches and other registered religious communities can autonomously establish or recognize local or regional churches, religious communities, entities of consecrated life, or other institutions, with the nature of associations or foundations. Foundations with a religious mission incorporated under the conditions of the Law on Religious Freedom acquire their legal personality merely by registration in the religious collective persons' record created in competent government department (see Article 33. of the same law).

Note of mention are the *public or state foundations*, which have seen an increasing growth in the last decade in Portugal, a phenomenon described by the use (or abuse) of private law by the state, normally as a mean to offset the procurement constraints of public law but also to benefit of the potentialities of private law mechanisms or institutions like foundations. Public foundations will be those foundations established by public legal persons, usually by a legislative act,

[19] For a general introduction to these types of foundations, see Amado Gomes (1999).

for the pursuit of public purposes.[20] Public foundations can be incorporated under public law, and therefore considered as a subtype of public entities, or incorporated as private institutions governed by private law (*private foundations of state origin*). These foundations have their genesis in a public asset allocation, single or repeated, and set themselves apart in many ways from the typical private foundations, particularly on what concerns supervision, governance, and reversibility of the assets that formed the initial endowment and subsequent financial provisions. In the intersection of public and private law, there is another type of foundations in Portugal that we could designate as public-private foundations as they result from public-private partnerships where normally the state gets a minority stake therefore loosening the public interference in the foundation's governance and management. Established inter vivos or by legislative act, in the public-private foundations, the state and individuals, natural or legal persons, come together for the establishment of a new legal person. Sousa Ribeiro (2001) frames the emergence of these foundations as a direct result of a new paradigm of state functions and the nature of its relations with civil society.[21]

Since the framework-law, these types of public foundations, except the public-private foundations, have a specific legal regime. Indeed Article 4.º of the framework-law contains the different types of foundations admitted in Portugal: private foundations, public foundations of public law, and public foundations of private law. Private foundations are considered to be those foundations instituted by one or more private persons (individual or collective persons), in partnership or not with public collective persons, provided that these do not have a dominant position in the foundation. The dominant position occurs when the endowed assets are predominantly public or the state has the right to appoint or remove the majority of the management board of the foundation. On the other hand, public foundations are those created exclusively by public collective persons and are considered public bodies. Finally, public foundations of private law are those instituted by one or more public collective persons, in partnership or not with private persons (individual or collective persons) provided that the public bodies have a dominant position in the foundation.

The referred typology of foundations clearly demonstrates the public inclination of the framework-law, as it admits the incorporation of *private* foundations in

---

[20] The criteria for the distinction between public foundations and private foundations are a controversial matter. Blanco De Morais (1995, 565) defines a public foundation as "any entity created, in general, by a public act by the state or other public body, with the power to do so, affecting an endowment suitable for the autonomous performance, although guided, of administrative functions."

[21] According to this author (p. 265), "Now, the state intervenes as a founder, participating 'within' the initiative of creation and the life of many foundations. Responsible for broad social functions that do not want to resign, but not claiming (or not being able) to perform them exclusively, the state actively seeks the cooperation of private individuals to carry them out. The foundation appears to us here as an institutional partnership between public entities and private entities: the first takes the initiative, provide the seeding conditions of the organization, but seek the involvement of individuals in the project, encouraging them through additional tax benefits."

partnership with *public* collective persons, this way, in my opinion, undermining the private nature that historically and conceptually informs the notion of foundations. Private foundations should be *private*, and if the state and private persons wish to institute foundations in a public-private partnership, even if the public bodies do not have a dominant position, to use the expression of the law, these foundations should not be considered as "private foundations." They should have a different designation that could raise the awareness of those dealing with them, signaling their different nature and status.

12.3.2 Foreign Foundations

Article 5 of the framework-law provides for the applicable regime to foreign foundations operating in Portugal. According to the Portuguese law, then, a foundation which has been created under a law other than the Portuguese and intends to steadily pursue its purposes in Portugal, must have a permanent representation in the Portuguese territory (Article 5. º 1).

An exception to the aforementioned rule is the foundations covered by the European Convention on the Recognition of the Legal Personality of International Non-Governmental Organizations. This convention only applies, however, to foundations which satisfy the following conditions: have a nonprofit-making aim of international utility, have been established by an instrument governed by the internal law of a party, carry on their activities with effect in at least two states, and have their statutory office in the territory of a party and the central management and control in the territory of that party or of another party (Article 1. of the Convention, ratified by Portugal by Presidential Decree No 44/91 of September 6). The legal personality and capacity of foundations established in these terms shall be automatically recognized on the territory of other state parties to the Convention (Article 2.º), having only to prove the acquisition of legal personality and capacity through the presentation of their statutes or other formation acts (Article 3.º).

Article 5.º applies to a foreign foundation that does not meet the requirements of the Convention, because of its purposes or because it does not pursue effectively its activities in two states that have ratified the Convention, for example, and wishes to steadily pursue its purposes in Portugal. The densification of the concept of *steadily pursue* the statutory purposes of the foundation will determine, in turn, the mandatory or optional nature of the opening of a permanent representation on the part of a foreign foundation.

Without prejudice to the obligation or not to open a permanent representation, however, foreign foundations when developing their purposes in Portugal, even incidentally, are subject to registration under the law (Article 8., 3).

12.3.3 Foundations of Social Interest and Public Utility

We are going to focus mainly in the *foundations of social interest*, as they constitute the standard model of foundations in Portugal. Social interest is not equivalent though to public interest, and some argue if the Portuguese legal system admits foundations of private interest. If we define foundations of private interest as organizations instituted for the realization of any lawful aims, then we have to conclude that they are not allowed under the current Portuguese legal system, even if Article 191.º of the Civil Code admits the possibility for the founder to encumber the foundations' endowment, for instance, with a liability to pay some stipendium to the founders or their family,[22] as long as this burden does not compromise or constitute an absolute impediment for the fulfillment of the foundation's main goal. In our opinion, to the effect of the Portuguese Civil Code, social interest does not imply that the foundation pursuits aims of public interest or of public relevance, only that the aims are of a disinterested nature or individual, providing primarily a certain benefit to the society at large, and that there is a link between the community and the permanent aims of the foundation.[23] In favor of this opinion, one should note that foundations of social interest do not benefit from any tax exemptions or special privileges. Only foundations declared of public utility, granted as an additional legal status, are eligible to a more favorable tax treatment.

The new framework-law approved a specific regime for foundations to be granted public utility status, separated from the Legal Regime of Public Utility Legal Persons (*Regime Jurídico das Pessoas Colectivas de Utilidade Pública*), which applies to all not-for-profit legal persons, except foundations, another active legislative discrimination towards foundations. According to Article 24, private foundations can be granted public utility status when the following cumulative conditions are fulfilled: not-for-profit development of relevant activities for the benefit of the community in areas of social value (as described in a closed list); being properly constituted and with statutes prepared in accordance with the law; not pursuing, primarily, economic activities in competition with other entities which cannot benefit from the public utility status; and finally, having the adequate human and material resources to fulfill their statutory purposes. The public utility status is granted (and cancelled) by the prime minister for renewable periods of 5 years but can only be required by foundations after 3 years of effective and relevant activities, except if the founder or the majority of the founders already have the public utility status. This regime is significantly different from the one that applies for the other not-for-profit organizations which can immediately require the status after their incorporation, provided that they are active nationwide or show evident social relevance, and when granted the status is permanent.

[22] The Portuguese Supreme Court, for instance, ruled that the founder can restrict the use of the foundation assets to maintain the founder himself, his spouse, and descendents, which could be considered, partially, as a family foundation (Supreme Portuguese Court, 24 October 1996).

[23] With this opinion, Blanco De Morais (1995, 573).

Foundations of social interest declared of public utility must apply for the Ministry of Finance in order to obtain the income tax exemption. This exemption does not comprise, however, the business income derived from commercial or industrial activities performed outside the statutory purposes of foundations. On the other hand, its maintenance is subject to the compliance with the following requirements: (a) exclusive or predominant realization of activities aimed at achieving the purpose for which their status as public utility entities was granted, (b) use in the purposes just mentioned of at least 50 % of the overall net income that would be subject to taxation by the end of the 4th year following that in which it was obtained, and (c) absence of self-dealing activities.

12.3.4 Incorporation of a Foundation

The incorporation of a foundation of social interest involves a procedural *iter* comprising two key moments or acts chronological separated: an act of private law, the incorporation of the foundation, by public deed or by a testamentary disposition, that is, the foundational agreement (Article 186. of the CC); and an act of public law, which follows chronologically the previous one and corresponds to an administrative act of granting the legal personality or state approval, named the recognition (Article 188. of the CC). According to the law (Article 185.º, 3), the incorporation of a foundation becomes irrevocable before the state approval, that is, from the moment it is required or an official process recognition begins, in the case of foundations established by public deed, or from the time of opening of the succession, in the case of foundations established by will. Article 6.º of the framework-law provides for the general rule regarding the foundations' legal personality acquisition, stating that private foundations acquire legal personality upon a state approval (*reconhecimento*) which is individual and within the competence of the prime minister.

The foundation law in Portugal distinguishes nevertheless between the formation deed, either *inter vivos* or *mortis causa*, which is a formalized expression of the founder's intention to create a new legal entity, and the statutes which determine the rights, duties, and internal organization of the foundation. Only the formation deed is mandatory to be submitted by the founder, with the statutes possibly being submitted by the testamentary trustees, the appointed members of the foundation's bodies, or, in any case, the state authority, which has residual competency in this regard.

In strictly legal terms, foundations represent a dual challenge: firstly, because being a phenomenon of private autonomy, they are in the always difficult intersection between private and public law, whether as a result of its purposes, normally of general interest,[24] or whether because of the form of acquisition of their legal

[24] The majority of contemporary legal systems only recognizes the designated public interest or general interest ("public benefit") foundations, where in Portugal, as stated above, the Civil Code

personality, by state approval; and, secondly, for their special location in the theory of legal persons, to the extent that, typologically, unlike the associations or corporations, they have no members, not being owned by someone, even indirectly.[25]

Foundations thus correspond to a mechanism of personification legally available to private persons, specifically designed for the administration of an endowment tied to a purpose, which someone, an individual or an entity, decides to incorporate but in relation to which, for all legal purposes, remains a third party. The characteristic features of the legal type are thus, apart from the purpose, necessarily of social interest, an endowment, a management structure, and the personification, in the sense that only by the formation of a new legal entity,[26] as an autonomous center for imputation of jural relations, endowed with assets for the pursuit of a social purpose, the interests underlying the normative typological hypothesis will be safeguarded.

The establishment of a foundation, which necessarily entails a sufficient asset allocation for the purpose of pursuing a social interest (Article 186, 1 CC), becomes irrevocable from the moment it is required the recognition of the legal personality or an officious process of recognition by the competent authority begins.

12.3.5 Essential Elements

In Portugal, legal scholars usually identify four elements informing the substrate of a foundation (Ferrer Correia 1982, 483): an endowment (*patrimonial element*), a

---

adopts a more open concept of "social interest." There are, however, legal systems that admit foundations of private interest, since lawful, as the German (paragraphs 80 and 81 of the BGB). In Portugal is yet to be held the debate on the admissibility of the foundations of private interest, including family foundations, although it should be made clear at the outset that the uncertainty of the beneficiaries does not necessarily mean social interest (and vice versa) and that the nature of the nonprofit foundations just means a ban on the distribution of profits, not being forbidden the pursuit of economic activities by foundations, provided that these are instrumental for the main mission. For an introduction to the thematic, see Badenes Gasset (1986, 62 and following), Kronke (1988, 56 and following), or De Giorgi (1973, 27 and following).

[25] Serrano Chamorro (2002, 112) states that the specific difference between the foundation and associations, for example, is that their goals may be fulfilled regardless of the person of the founder, what ultimately justifies the legal personality. To this regard, Lopez Lacoiste (1965, 602) talks about a functional ownership or a depersonalization of property which occurs through the foundational structure: regarding the founder, who becomes released of the property by a liberality; regarding the foundation and the board of directors who represent it, because they are mere servants of the foundational goal; and, finally, regarding the beneficiaries, which will eventually be favored but whose indeterminacy do not allow them to claim any individual rights towards the foundation.

[26] Albajedo (1960, 42) draws attention to the need of *personification*, that is, that the foundational incorporation always implies the will (intentional element), not only to create a work, but that this organization becomes an autonomous subject; otherwise, there would not arise as a subject of law but only one organization to an end.

social interest purpose (*teleological element*), a particular form of governance (*organizational element*), and finally, a desire to create a new legal entity (*intentional element*). The Portuguese Civil Code only required explicitly the first two elements, that is, the endowment and the social interest purpose, as indispensable requirements or essential elements for the juristic act that institutes the foundation.

The Portuguese law does not allow therefore the incorporation of a foundation without an endowment, present or future, sufficient to carry out an aim of social interest.[27] This way, the patrimonial and the teleological elements arise as the elements that legally characterize, by definition, a foundation. We could signal here a reflection of the *essentialia negotii* doctrine, that is, the classic division between the essential and accidental elements of juristic acts. While the essential elements contribute to the qualification and would be a condition for the perfection of the internal structure of a juristic act, without which we could not consider it as fully completed, the accidental elements would prove to be merely instrumental or complementary, but not as a necessary condition for the realization of the juristic act.[28]

The same is not true about the organizational element, as there is not any legal provision in the Civil Code regarding the governance of foundations. The applicable norm is therefore the general provision regarding the governance of collective persons, Article 162º, which determines the mandatory existence in the bylaws of a management board of an audit committee, with an uneven number of members of which one should be the president. If the management board is responsible for the day-to-day management of the foundation, according to the Portuguese Court of Auditors, the audit committee is supposed to be an internal control body of the foundation that holds the power to supervise its performance. In general, the powers of the audit committee comprise the examination of the balance sheets and annual accounts of the foundation and the issuance of its opinion. Apart from these two boards, the funder is free to structure the governance of the foundation, an option that constitutes a very liberal approach of the Portuguese law if one considers the importance for foundations of a governance structure with a checks and balances system.

Article 26.º of the framework-law nevertheless introduced an innovation in the legal regime of foundations in Portugal, since it announced a mandatory governance structure for all private foundations, which does not happen in the Civil Code. Thus, in accordance with this article, private foundations shall have the following three compulsory bodies: a board of directors, which is responsible for managing the assets of the foundation, as well as deliberating about proposing amendments to its statutes or modification and termination of the foundation; an

[27] Lopez Lacoiste (1965, 584) states that an act intended to create a foundation without an endowment lacks any sense to the extent that the legal personality, the foundation, is merely instrumental, not substantive in nature, that is, establishes a trustee who will be responsible for certain purposes, but these purposes have no relevance without the proper means to deliver them.

[28] For an historical analysis of the *essentialia negotii* doctrine, in Portugal and abroad, see Pinto Duarte (2000, 79 and following).

executive committee, with day-to-day management functions; and a supervisory board, which is responsible for the oversight of the management and accountancy of the foundation. Beyond this mandatory structure, foundations can still adopt an optional body or committee, adjacent to the compulsory bodies, which consists of a board of trustees or board of founders with the task of ensuring compliance with the statutes of the foundation and with the will of the founder or founders. This organ, although not mandatory, taking into account its mission and composition, is very similar to a company or association's general assembly, this way mitigating the typological differences between foundations and person-based legal persons, a phenomenon that some call "quasi-membership."[29] Finally, this chapter introduces a limitation to the terms of the members of the governance bodies of private foundations, which did not previously existed. Although the initial version submitted by the government to parliament provided for a limitation of 12 years for any term, the final version of the framework-law only provides that the terms of the members cannot be lifetime, except when specifically created by the founder or founders in the formation deed.

If the patrimonial element is essential for the incorporation of the foundation, providing a reason for the state to refuse their recognition, as outlined above, together with the aim of social interest, the teleological element gets preponderant thereafter. This might reinforce the idea that the endowment, although essential, is only instrumental to the realization of the aim of the foundation.[30] That is, we should overcome the notion that a foundation embodies an endowment when, in reality, it is an activity oriented to the pursuit of an aim which the foundation embodies, being the endowment merely an instrument, even if an essential one.[31]

[29] About this, see Hopt et al. (2006, 70). For these authors, one reason for this *blurring* of types can be that of a very liberal law in some countries which allows foundation structures in which the founder or the directors have a position similar to membership of a nonprofit association. In Portugal, it was the law to legally institute these kinds of situations, although not mandatory.

[30] This is the view, for example, of Pedro Pais de Vasconcelos (2005, 142), when he states that "In foundations, the lesser importance of the personal element leads to a greater relative weight of the patrimonial element. This fact has led to the conclusion that in this type of legal entities the patrimonial element is dominant. However, this conclusion does not seem the right one, because the patrimonial element, the mass of goods affected by the founder to the foundation, is nevertheless instrumental in relation to the achievement of the aim." Accordingly, De Oliveira Ascensão (2000, 329), to whom "the endowment itself has no meaning. Although essential, it is instrumental: it only makes sense while enabling the achievement of a purpose." This author argues, however, that the instrumentality that characterizes the endowment does not preclude that it is the structural crucial element which determines the foundational type within the classification of legal persons.

[31] Lopez Lacoiste (1965, 596) points an aspect that seems essential about foundations law, that is, that foundations are not oriented according to ownership or to benefit themselves but according to a mission or function: to allocate private resources to social action, being more about distributive than commutative justice.

12.3.6 Administrative Procedure of State Approval

The new framework-law adds other formalities to the administrative procedure of recognition or state approval of foundations, in what may be considered as a *plus* regarding the provisions of the Civil Code. According to Civil Code, in the act of incorporation, the founder or founders must necessarily, at least, have defined the purpose of the foundation (*teleological element*) and have specified the assets or rights (*patrimonial element*) that will constitute the endowment of the future legal person (Article 186, 1 CC[32]), which must be sufficient for the fulfillment of the assigned purposes. The *teleological element* and the *patrimonial element* are thus legally considered as essential elements of foundations, without which these cannot be recognized or state approved. According to some authors, from the institution act should also result the will to establish a new legal entity, although this intentional element can and must be inferred from the act of institution itself.[33]

Article 22.º of the framework-law sets the necessary steps and requirements for the administrative procedure of recognition or state approval of foundations, as well as for the modification of their statutes and even for its transformation and dissolution, pursuant to and for the effects provided for in paragraph 2 of Article 158. and Articles 188.º, 189º, 190º, and 193º, all of the Civil Code. In relation to the administrative procedure of recognition or state approval of private foundations, this article states that the request must be exclusively submitted online, using the electronic form specifically provided in the Presidency of the Council of Ministers portal and attached with the following elements: (a) identification of the applicant and justification of his/her legitimacy; (b) supporting documents certifying the foundation incorporation as well as the founder or founders' identification and their contribution to the foundation's assets or to its activities financing; (c) document attesting the adequacy or that the initial endowment is sufficient; (d) memorandum describing the foundation's mission and areas of activity; (e) a detailed list of the assets assigned to the foundation as well as donations or long-lasting subsidy agreements, if applicable; (f) oath that there are no doubts or disputes, even potential ones, affecting the initial endowment of the foundation; (g) evaluation of movable property affected to the foundation, by a reputable expert; (h) bank statement of the monetary amount allocated to the foundation (i) certifying authorization when one of the founders is a legal person governed by public law; (j) the statutes and indication of the official publication date;

[32] This article states that "In the institution act the founder must indicate the purpose of the institution and specify the assets that are allocated to the institution."

[33] Cfr. Caetano (1967, 31–32), according to this author "for this act to be complete, it should also express the intention that the fulfillment of the purpose is carried out by an autonomous organization. It is not essential nevertheless that the founder explains this desire, just that the asset allocation is not a burden, or form, of a donation or bequest made to an existing person. If the founder merely expresses the will to dispose the assets for pursuing a permanent purpose, without transmitting them to an existing entity, it is assumed that he/she desires to set up a new entity with legal personality to perform that will."

(k) indication of the delegations' addresses, if applicable; and (l) indication of the appointed members of the foundation's bodies. If the initial endowment includes immovable properties, it shall also be submitted, in addition, the following documents: (a) certified statement of the registration and tax status; (b) certified statement of the renunciation of the preemption rights, if applicable, by the state; and (c) evaluation of the immovable property by a reputable expert. For the application appraisal, the public authority can nevertheless, in the use of its competency, require any other elements it might consider as necessary for the decision (Article 22.º, 6).

The state authority can refuse to grant the legal personality (the recognition) to private foundations based on the following circumstances: lack of any of the elements or the documents that were mandatory; when the purposes are not considered of social interest, namely, because they benefit the founder or his/her family or a restricted universe related with them; the goods are considered insufficient for the purposes of the foundation and when there are no reasonable expectations that this insufficiency will disappear, namely, when the goods are encumbered with burdens that compromise the fulfillment of the statutory aims or do not generate sufficient income to the its fulfillment; statutory noncompliance with the law; existence of any divergence between the will and the declaration in the formation deed or any other documents which are necessary to the formation deed; nullity, revocability, or voidability of the formation deed; and existence of any doubts or disputes, even potential ones, upon the goods that constitute the initial endowment.

As it can be seen, when the process of recognition of a foundation begins, the applicant must meet a set of conditions or requirements, more or less extensive, that if not fulfilled or are not presented will determine at least a request for information from the public authority, under the rules of the administrative procedure, or, at worst, the nonrecognition of the foundation. In relation to the Civil Code, the new framework-law requires more specifications not only about the purposes but also about the financial statements that will constitute the future foundation's asset base.

So, on the one hand, on what concerns the purposes of the institution, beyond the statement of the purposes the foundation intends to continue under the Civil Code, the framework-law also requires a descriptive memorandum with the foundation's areas of activity. Therefore, just a general statement for the purpose or purposes of social interest stated in the act of institution is not enough, but the submission of a plan or an action program within the foundation's purpose or purposes indicated in advance by the founder is also required. This additional requirement is poorly understandable, as the Civil Code determines that a foundation *only* should not be recognized when their purposes are not considered of social interest, being silent about how the foundation will achieve or accomplish these purposes, and could be considered as a mean to constraint the institution of foundations.

On the other hand, on what concerns the endowment, the framework-law requires, beyond the initial indication of the asset allocation to the foundation, as appropriate, the submission of a detailed assets list, an evaluation of the movable property, and, finally, a bank statement proving the amount of money originally allocated to the foundation. This requirement also appears in defiance of what determines the Civil Code, that is, that the recognition of the foundation will only be refused if the assets are not sufficient for attaining the assigned purposes and there are not justified expectations of supplying (No. 2 Article 188.º). This rule has always been interpreted by the Portuguese legal scholars in the sense of an actual or potentially enough endowment to achieve the purposes selected by the founder, which means that recognition should only be refused when the foundation failed to demonstrate the sufficiency of that evidence, which could be actual or potential. It is not mandatory therefore that the sources of income of a foundation shall be beforehand determined. These can include, for example, annual rates for certain dividends from a company that, as such, are not fully quantifiable at the time of the foundation incorporation. What is essential, then, according to the Civil Code, is the existence of *sufficient* assets, present or future, and not an initial endowment or assets.[34] The requirement of the framework-law is, however, in accordance with an administrative practice that has long adopted by the different public authorities that have been responsible for the recognition that is to require an initial minimum endowment of 250,000 euros. The new framework-law provides for the fixation of an initial endowment by an administrative rule (Article 22º, 3), which fixed the 250,000 euros.

Another novelty of the framework-law is to set a deadline for the recognition process, which is absent in the Civil Code. Thus, under Article 22.º, 6, the final decision of recognition should be taken no later than 90 days from the date of the request. Once initiated the process of recognition, the founder, his/her heirs, the executors of the will, or the administrators appointed in the formation deed have the legitimate right the acts of ordinary management relating to the goods or rights of the initial endowment, since these acts are deemed indispensable to the conservation of the mentioned initial endowment. Until the recognition decision, the founder, his/her heirs, the executors of the will, or the administrators appointed in the formation deed are individually and severally liable for the acts performed on behalf of the foundation.

12.3.7 Foundations' Definition

The Portuguese legislator did not present a foundation's definition, merely referring *a contrario* the minimum requirements or elements for their recognition, from

[34] In this sense, Ferrer Correia, De Sà (1989, 334), to whom "The law does not oppose, therefore, the incorporation of foundations without an initial capital, provided that the financing of the planned activities is ensured by other means, i.e. through other resources than the income produced by a capital. (...) Of course, this does not mean that the hypothesis of a foundation without property is conceivable. (...) It is the initial endowment of capital assets that can not be considered as a non-essential element."

which it is possible to extrapolate, if not a definition, at least their features or essential elements.

Thus, while Article 157º of the Civil Code states that "the provisions of this chapter shall apply (...) to the foundations of social interest," Article 188º, on the recognition of the foundations by the public authority, adds: "it will not be recognized a foundation whose purpose is not considered of social interest by the competent authority" and that "it will also be denied recognition, when the assets used in the foundation are insufficient to pursue the assigned purpose and there are no expectations of supplying." According to the transcribed rules, the essential features or elements of foundations are the purpose of social interest and the assets allocated by the founder, which must necessarily be enough to support the former. These characteristics clearly point to a definition of foundation as destination assets for social interest purposes, matching the history of the institute.

It seems feasible, however, even without an explicit provision, to extract a set of features from these characteristics which enable a modern definition of foundation, as follows: *an independent not-for-profit institution incorporated temporarily or permanently to the pursuit of certain purposes of social interest, necessarily endowed with its own assets or with a separate source of income, without members or shareholders and with self-governing bodies.*

The features I mention emerge as more or less consensual, at least in the legal systems of *civil law*. I refer, in particular, the separate legal status (*independent institution*); the permanence, without meaning necessarily perpetuity (*for a limited period or permanently*); the pursuit of nonprofit, without meaning necessarily the indeterminacy of the recipients (*the pursuit of certain purposes of social interest*); the absence of members or owners (*no member or shareholders*); and the existence of a particular form of governance *(with self-governing bodies*).

Foundations are therefore institutions designed to play or perform tasks of general or collective interest, which the state and other nonprofit institutions can also pursuit, joining the designated nonprofit sector. Foundations are entities that stand between the state and the individuals or corporations in the social pyramid to address needs of general interest, translating "one of the most valuable tools for empowering civil society" (Chancerelle de Machete and Sousa Antunes 2004, 6).

The new framework-law, however, for the first time gives a general definition of a foundation as a not-for-profit collective person irrevocably endowed with sufficient assets for the fulfillment of a social interest purpose (Article 3.º, 1). According to the same article (Article 3.º, 2), which also introduced an open list of social interest purposes, these are those which benefit one or more categories of persons other than the founder, his/her relatives, or any other persons with business or friendly relationships. This article therefore, apart from describing the necessary elements that inform the definition of a foundation – a foundation is deemed to have a sufficient endowment to pursue a social interest purpose – specifies which transactions prevent the purpose of a foundation to be considered as of social interest. Strangely, the law does not include in these transactions payments to the members of the governance structure, but one might consider that this is forbidden in the expression *not for profit* which should be interpreted as a *nondistribution constraint.*

The first article of the chapter of the framework-law dedicated to private foundations also gives a definition of private foundation that should be interpreted in conjunction with the more general definition of foundation under Article 3.º. As we recall, according to this article, a foundation is not-for-profit collective person irrevocably endowed with sufficient assets for the fulfillment of a social interest purpose. In accordance with this Article 14º, however, a private foundation is a slightly different institution, no longer endowed with *sufficient assets* which are irrevocably transferred to the fulfillment of a social interest purpose but endowed with *the necessary goods and the economic support* for the pursuit of social interest purposes.

The interpreter shall be questioning therefore why the legislator changed the term *sufficient assets* to *necessary goods and economic support.* One possible explanation may stem from the fact that the Civil Code, in Article 186.º, 1, regarding the formation and the statutes of private foundations, also refer to *goods* – "In the formation deed the founder shall declare the purpose of the foundation and specify the goods that are transferred to the foundation." This repetition of *goods* does not justify however the inclusion of the concept of *economic support,* whose scope and definition are unknown and especially do not justify the replacement of the concept of *sufficient* with the concept of *necessary.* As we know, these two concepts are not equivalent, even in terms of its linguistic meaning: while the first summons a dimension of quantity and adequacy, the second summons a dimension of quality or needfulness. Thus, we admit, by contradiction, that the assets will not always be necessary and sufficient and that the goods can be sufficient but not always necessary. The use of the term *necessary* seems, however, more the result of poor legislative drafting than the result of a conscious and deliberate choice, and we should interpret it as equivalent to the concept of sufficient and hope the legislator corrects this lapse in the future. To this conclusion and interpretation contributes the fact that the concept *sufficient* is used in other provisions, not only in the framework-law but also in the Civil Code: in subparagraph (c) of paragraph 1 of Article 23.º of the framework-law as a basis for refusing to recognize the legal personality of private foundations; similarly, in the Civil Code, the insufficiency of assets is considered a reason for the refusal of the state approval Article 188.º, 3.

The second paragraph of this Article 14.º also reflects a bad legislative technique. According to this number, "Private foundations may pursue any social interest purpose." Now, either in Article 3. of the framework-law, whether the preceding number of the same article, refer explicitly that foundations can only pursue purposes of social interest. Article 3.º even defines what we should consider "social interest" and presents an open list of possible purposes of social interest. When stating that private foundations can pursue any purpose of social interest, the legislator intends to assert that there are purposes of social interest foundations that foundations cannot pursue.

12.3.8 Transparency and Supervision

The new framework-law includes an article as innovative as contradictory which under the label "Safeguard of the foundation institute" (Article 7.º), despite the useful promotion of private supervisory mechanisms contained in its paragraph no. 1, launches an anathema of distrust towards foundations and their founders, even reversing the burden of proof, in the rest of its paragraphs, compromising, one can easily foresee, the incorporation of new foundations. In fact, while paragraph no. 1 of this article states that foundations should approve codes of conduct that (self-)regulate good practices – namely, about the strategic participation of beneficiaries in foundations' activities, transparency of their accounts, conflicts of interest, incompatibilities, and limits to the renewal of their management bodies – , paragraph no. 2 states that it is essential for the state approval of any foundation that the endowment of the foundation assets is not done in detriment or fraud against the creditors of the founder. This is a very reasonable principle, and there are in the Portuguese Civil Code mechanisms that address the issue of creditors' frauds, but in order to guarantee the stated principle, the new law imposes a dramatic burden on the founders, their heirs, or the members of the management board appointed in the incorporation, as we shall see. Indeed, previous to the state approval decision, the founders, their heirs, or the members of the management board appointed in the incorporation deed shall declare on oath, in a separate document, that there are no doubts or disputes, even potential ones, affecting the initial endowment of the foundation (paragraph no. 3). The existence of any doubts or disputes, even potential ones, over the initial endowment of the foundation, may result in criminal liability of the oath's authors and determines the immediate revocation of the state approval. This rule is self-explanatory and, notwithstanding its unfeasible nature, demonstrates an outstanding distrust of foundations from the legislator. In the first place, the notion of disputes and doubts, even potential ones, is very vague and inaccurate and could undermine the incorporation of any foundation in Portugal in the future, as any "potential doubt" raised against the initial endowment of a foundation could determine the refusal of the state approval or the revocation of the previously granted legal personality. On the other hand, if it can be reasonable to expect that the founder is willing to submit an oath regarding his or her personal patrimony, it is not reasonable to expect that their heirs, who are probably willing to do everything to reverse the foundation's incorporation which reduces their inheritance, or the members of the management board appointed in the incorporation deed, who are third parties and lack the knowledge about the contingencies affecting the assets, will be willing to do it. So, in our opinion, this *innovative* article, under the label "Safeguard of the foundation institute," contributes more to the destruction of the foundation institute than to its safeguard.

Article 9.º of the framework-law, under the label "Transparency," imposes the reporting or disclosure of the following information: communication to the Presidency of the Council of Ministers of the composition of the foundation's bodies, 30 days after its appointment, modification, or replacement, as well as the annual accounts and activities reports; submitting the accounts to an external audit, when the foundation's annual income is higher that an amount that is still to be determined; ongoing display in the foundation's website of the incorporation deed, the act of State approval, the act granting the public utility status (when applicable), the identification of the founders, the up-to-date composition of the management and supervisory bodies, the management and accounts reports, and opinions of the supervisory body for the last 3 years; and finally the report of the external audit when mandatory. Private foundations with public utility status shall also have in their websites a description of the initial endowment and the described amount of public funding for the last 3 years. For all private foundations, the annual accounts and activities report shall have sufficient and clear information about the type and global amounts of the attributed grants, the donations and subsidies received, and the assets management. Failure to comply with the provisions of this article blocks the foundation access to any public funding during the year of the failure and while it lasts.

Article 10.º imposes limits on the staff and administrative costs of private foundations with public utility status, applying different regimes for predominately grant-making and operative foundations. For grant-making foundations, that is, foundations that predominately make distributions in cash or payment to their beneficiaries, the limits for staff and administration costs are a tenth of the annual income, of which at least two thirds should be used in the direct pursuit of the foundation's statutory purposes. For the operative foundations, that is, foundations which provide services directly to the community, the limits with staff and administrative costs are fixed in two thirds of the annual income of the foundation. Repeated failure to comply with the limits fixed by this article determines and implies the forfeiture of the public utility status of the foundation.

Article 11.º of the framework-law provides, for private foundations with public utility status and public foundations, for the mandatory and prior authorization by the state authority; otherwise, the transaction should be void, of the sale of assets which were endowed by the founder, and as such specified in the incorporation deed and with special meaning to the foundation purposes.

Article 12.º provides the rules for the transfer of the remaining endowment in case of the foundation's liquidation, allowing the founder to determine, either in the foundation deed or in the statutes, what should be done with the residual endowment. Only in the absence of a founder's explicit determination, the articles provide for the cy-près rule which requires that the assets of the terminated foundation should be transferred to an association or foundation with similar purposes, in the case of the Portuguese law, according to an order of precedence given by the foundation's bodies or the state authority.

One of innovations of the framework-law was to create an advisory board (Article 13.º), within the Presidency of the Council of Ministers, with the following duties: provide opinions on the administrative acts concerning foundations; provide opinions on the results of monitoring actions on foundations; and, finally, take stand, on its own initiative, in any matter within the state authority competency concerning foundations. This advisory board comprised three members proposed by associations representing the foundation sector, appointed by the prime minister, one representative of the Ministry of Finance and one representative of the Ministry of Solidarity and Social Security. The appointed members have a term of 5 years, nonrenewable, and cannot be dismissed.

12.4 Conclusion

Legal scholars and the legislator should challenge the rationale underlying the current legal form which subjects foundations to a legal treatment less favorable than the one which applies to other nonprofit organizations, such as (nonprofit) associations or cooperatives, and even to for-profit entities.[35] In the context of their activities, foundations should be reframed in the attempt to find a new balance between their essentially private nature and the protection of the social interests at stake in their legal configuration.

Since the 1960s, a movement with origins in Germany advocates the need for a reform of the foundations legal framework.[36] At this point, for the first time, the German legal science proposed the possibility of links between foundations and corporations, revealing the potential of the institute to perform a variety of purposes, despite the inevitable resistance from a theoretical point of view. The phenomenon, as described by Zoppini, intended to connect foundations to the production chain, particularly in cases where they arise as possible instruments of economic initiative or of legitimacy of the corporations.[37] It was a radical approach which forced legal scholars to rethink their traditional approach to foundations, that is, that the foundation was a strange figure to the market and that their analysis should focus on the conditions of their incorporation instead of the dynamics of their subsequent activities.[38] That is, legal scholars have always focused their

[35] Predieri (1969, 1117 and foll.) warns to the fact that the foundations' administrative system does not encourage their proliferation, on the contrary, "spesso fa fuggire inorridito il potenziale fondatore, atterrito della lentezza della procedura di riconoscimento, e ancor più dalla prospettiva dei controlli e delle ingerenze amministrative che si leggono o traspaiono dal códice (anche se poi il diavolo è meno bruto di quanto si dipinga), tanto da far nascere i fenomeni, in sostanza patologici, dell'uso di società per azioni, o a responsabilità limitata, a scopo di beneficenza."

[36] About this trend, see Zoppini (1995, 2), who dates its start in the *44. Deutsche Juristen Tag*, of 1962, in which a group of jurists from Hannover raised the followign question: "Soll das Siftungsrecht bundesgesetzlich vereinheitlicht und reformiert werden, gebenfalls mit welchem Grundzügen?" In Spain, also Lopez Lacoiste (1965, 567) reported this new pulse of foundations that survived centuries of hostile legislation and now have a renewed energy, when confronted with the old bodies of dead hand, performing a social function in an organized manner, with an effective model comparing with other institutions and demonstrating that property is not just to have but also to give.

[37] About the links between foundations and corporations, see Valero Agundez (1969).

[38] Zoppini (2005, 371) notes in this regard that there is now an "*outsourcing*" of legal forms for enterprises and can be considered as a "*fact counted*" the typological compatibility between foundations and economic activities.

attention on the fact that foundations are perpetual allocations of endowments which otherwise would be circulating in the economy, neglecting the use of that endowments and the social and economic impact of foundations' activities (Zoppini 1995, 3). This economic and social dimension of the foundation sector is finally being recognized, outside of the legislative reflection itself, and everywhere are popping up studies on the importance of the so-called third sector[39] but also about the foundation sector.[40]

In legal terms, we should emphasize the idea that foundations represent a private law mechanism of personification which private persons, physic or legal, might use in order to fulfill certain specific functions which otherwise would not be attained. We should therefore always keep in mind the answer to the simple the question: "why does someone decide to create a foundation and not a corporation, an association or a cooperative?" The answer shall cross the unique features of foundations: self-governing structures, mission-based, public benefit-oriented, stable, and long-term-focused organizations, and financially independent, with the necessary limitation of liability and a ban on the distribution of any profits.[41]

When addressing a particular legal institution, legal scholars, without prejudice of a careful scientific analysis, should always critically incorporate in their research the specific economic and social context of the object of their study, otherwise facing the risk of extemporaneous appreciations or of compromising their mission. It seems logical therefore that if we conclude that the ideological and paternalistic model of the relationship between state and foundations is exhausted, this might impose a systematic reclassification of the institution or even its typological reconstruction. In the specific case of foundations, it should be taken into consideration, inter alia, if foundations should benefit or not, and why, from a more favored legal treatment as the one which is currently granted to nonprofit associations or cooperatives, for instance, in which their private dimension prevails in the specific legislative solutions.

The aims of social interest that foundations shall legally foster if, on one hand, give these organizations a particular legitimacy in the social spectrum and, on the other hand, imply a specific responsibility to achieve those same goals or objectives. From the privileged legal status of foundations, when declared of public

---

[39] See The Portuguese nonprofit sector in comparative perspective, form 2005, which corresponds to the Portuguese Chapter of the Johns Hopkins Comparative Nonprofit Sector Project, from the Center of Civil Society Studies at the Institute for Policy Studies: http://www.ccss.jhu.edu/pdfs/CNP/CNP_Portugal_Nat_Rpt.pdf

[40] O Feasibility Study on a European Foundation Statute [*ec.europa.eu/internal_market/.../eufoundation/feasibilitystudy_en.pdf*], commissioned by the European Commission, for example, reveals impressive numbers, though estimates on the foundation sector in the EU: 110,000 foundations, collective assets of approximately one trillion euros, annual expenditures of 153 billion euros, a million full-time employees, and two and a half million volunteers.

[41] Badenes Gasset (1986, 8) to this regard states that a foundation is characterized "by the predetermination of the purpose by one individual, and by how the person who has defined the purpose, due the limited duration of human life, cannot address it attend in perpetuity and therefore wants and requests others to continue her/his work fulfilling that purpose."

utility, including the taxation benefits, derives therefore for foundations and their governance structure obligations of accountability and transparency which should not be alienated. In their condition of pure private entities, foundations should not be burden however with unnecessary constraints from state supervision, without prejudice of the syndication of their activities by the courts. Foundations should proactively promote private mechanisms of self-regulation which guarantee the sufficient and suitable conditions for the management of their assets according to high ethical standards and a diligent performance of their activities. The adoption of a governance model that respects the possible separation between the deliberative and executive functions and the adoption of codes of conduct emerge as conditions to ensure the integrity of these institutions.

In addition to a primary legitimacy, based on the private autonomy and the individual freedom of asset disposal, and a teleological legitimacy, which relates to the public benefit aims pursued by foundations, we should envisage therefore a more organic or functional legitimacy. This functional legitimacy can only be ensured by measures that preemptively guarantee the effective governance, transparency, and accountability of foundations, for example, organizational procedures for planning and evaluation that will enable all stakeholders to verify that there is a good use of resources against the performance of the organization.

The primary legitimacy must be therefore continuously updated by a teleological legitimacy, which is embodied in the relevance of their activities, and an organic or functional legitimacy, which materializes in the best practices on what concerns foundations' governance and accountability in order to maximize their social impact. For foundations is not enough to say that they are engaged in public interest activities. This participation should be guided by a permanent quest for a more effective relationship between resources invested and results achieved. The boards of foundations are thus responsible for the ongoing adaptation of the social mandate they were given by the founders and the social needs that affect the environment where they operate.

Any future legislation reform in Portugal should acknowledge the exclusive features of foundations as well as their unique contribution to a more democratic, inclusive, and participatory society.

Bibliography

Albadejo, M. 1960. La persona jurídica. *Revista de Derecho Notarial*, Abril-Junio, p. 42.

Alli Turrillas, J. -C. 2010. Fundaciones y Derecho Administrativoı, Marcial Pons, p. 46/47.

Amado Gomes, C. 1999. Nótula sobre o regime jurídico das fundações particulares de solidariedade social. *Revista da Faculdade de Direito da Universidade de Lisboa*. p. 171/172.

Badenes Gasset, R. 1986. *Las fundaciones de derecho privado*, I, 3rd ed. Barcelona, Librebia Bosch.

Blanch Nougués, J.M. 2007. *Régimen jurídico de las fundaciones en Derecho Romano*. Madrid: Dykinson.

Blanco de Morais, C. 1995. *Da relevância do direito público no regime jurídico das fundações privadas. Estudos em memória do Professor Castro Mendes*. Lisboa, Coimbra Editora.
Caetano, M. 1962. *Das Fundações – Subsídios para a interpretação e reforma da legislação portuguesa*. Lisboa: Ática.
Caetano, M. 1967. *As pessoas colectivas no novo Código Civil*. Lisboa, p. 28
Campos Franco, R. 2005. Defining the nonprofit sector: Portugal. The Johns Hopkins Comparative Nonprofit Sector Project, Working Paper Number 43, September 2005.
Chancerelle de Machete, R., and H. Sousa Antunes. 2004. *Direito das Fundações – Propostas de Reforma*. Lisboa: Fundação Luso-Americana.
David, A. 1959. La vie des fondations. Revue trimestrielle de droit civil, p. 665
De Giorgi, M.V. 1973. Fondazione di famiglia, Rivista di diritto civile, II.
De Oliveira Ascensąą, J. 2000. *Direito Civil – Teorial Geral, Vol. I, Introdução, As pessoas, Os bens*, 2nd ed., 328. Almedina.
Ferrer Correia, A. 1982. Le regime juridique des fondations privees, cultureles et scientifiques – Droit portugais. In *Estudos Vários de Direito*. Coimbra.
Ferrer Correia, A., and A. De Sà. 1989. Algumas Notas sobre Fundações. RDE.
Freeman, D.F. 1991. *The hand book on private foundations*. Santa Ana, Foundation Center.
Hopt, K.J., W.R. Walz, T. von Hippel, and V. Then (eds.). 2006. *The European Foundation, a new legal approach*. Gütersloh: Verlag Bertelsmann Stiftung.
Imbert, J. 1988. Aperçu historique sur les fondations en droit français. In *Le fondazioni, tradizione e modernità*, ed. G. Alpa. Padova: CEDAM.
Kronke, H. 1988. *Stiftungstypus und Unternehmensträgerstiftung*. Tübingen: J.C.B. Mohr.
Lopes, L. 2009. *As Instituições Particulares de Solidariedade Social*. Coimbra: Almedina.
Lopez Jacoiste, J.J. 1965. La fundación y su estructura a la luz de sus nuevas funcione. *Revista de Derecho Privado*, Julio-Agosto, p. 570.
Pais de Vasconcelos, P. 2005. *Teoria General do Direito Civil*, 3rd ed., Almedina.
Pinto Duarte, R. 2000. *Tipicidade e Atipicidade dos Contratos*. Coimbra: Almedina, p. 79
Pomey, M. 1980. *Traité des Fondations d'Utilité Publique*. Paris: PUF.
Predieri, A. 1969. Sull'ammodernamento della disciplina delle fondazioni ie istituzioni culturali di diritto privato. *Rivista trimestrale di Diritto e Procedura Civile* (3), p.1117.
Rescigno, P. 1989. La fondazione: Prospettive e linee di riforma. In *Le fondazione in Italia e all'Estero*, ed. P. Rescigno. Padova: CEDAM.
Schlüter, A., V. Then, and P. Walkenhorst. 2001. *Foundations in Europe, society, management and law*. Gütersloh: Verlag Bertelsmann Stiftung.
Serrano Chamorro, M.E. 2002. Las fundaciones: dotación y patrimonio, p. 77.
Sousa Ribeiro, J. 2001. *As fundações no Código Civil: Regime actual e projecto de reforma, Lusíada Revista de Ciência e Cultura, Série de Direito*, n.os 1 e 2, 71.
Themudo, N.S. 2003. *Roles and visions of foundations in Portugal*. London School of Economics.
Valero Agundez, U. 1969. *La fundación como forma de empresa*. Valladolid: Secretariado de Publicaciones.
Zoppini, A. 1995. *Le fondazioni, Dalla tipicità alle tipologie*. Napoli: Jovene.
Zoppini, A. 2005. Problemi e prospettive per una riforma delle associazioni e delle fondazioni di diritto privato. *Rivista de Diritto Civile, Anno LI, n.º3 Maggio-Giugno*.

Chapter 13
Foundations Law in Spain

Isabel Peñalosa-Esteban

13.1 Spanish Foundations Law

13.1.1 Foundations and Spanish Constitution: Right to Establish a Foundation

Analysis of the Spanish Foundations Law needs to start from the basis of one of its unique characteristics, the recognition of the right to establish a foundation under Article 34 of the Constitution of 1978, which states: "The right to set up foundations for purposes of general interest is recognized in accordance with the Law". That which is established for the right of association (Article 24 of the Spanish Constitution) applies to the right of foundation in that "associations which pursue ends or use means classified as criminal offences are illegal" and, with regard to their dissolution, "associations may only be dissolved or have their activities suspended by virtue of a justified court order". The right to establish a foundation is covered under the rights in Section II, *Rights and Duties of Citizens*, of Chapter II, *Rights and Liberties*, of title I, *On Fundamental Rights and Duties*. Like all the rights and liberties in Chapter II, it is binding for the public bodies and the conditions for exercising the right must be developed by Law, although, unlike the right of association, this shall not take the form of Organic Law. As this right is covered under those in Section II, it is protected by appeal on the grounds of unconstitutionality, which falls within the jurisdiction of the Constitutional Court. Unlike the right of association, the protection of which may be sought by any citizen, it cannot be subject to an appeal for *amparo* before the aforementioned Constitutional Court.

There are historical reasons behind the recognition of the right of foundation under the Constitution in 1978, due to the disentailment process which started at the end of the eighteenth century and essentially took place throughout the nineteenth

I. Peñalosa-Esteban (✉)
Spanish Association of Foundations, C/Rafael Calvo, 18, 4º B, Madrid 28010, Spain
e-mail: ipenalosa@fundaciones.org

C. Prele (ed.), *Developments in Foundation Law in Europe*, Ius Gentium: Comparative Perspectives on Law and Justice 39, DOI 10.1007/978-94-017-9069-7_13,

century in Spain (García de Enterría 1992, 124). Various disentailment processes were used by the liberals in an attempt to eliminate the so-called mortmain and entails, which had been in force up to then, to enable some amortised assets (taken from the free market), and in the possession of certain civil and ecclesiastic institutions, to be transferred. It should be noted that nineteenth-century disentailment legislation did not use the term foundation in the purely formal, civil sense of *universitas bonorum* as opposed to *universitas personae,* but as a synonym for a charitable institution. These sorts of charitable institutions were forbidden at the beginning of the nineteenth century yet were allowed later on, as the serious consequences of their prohibition were noticed. They were allowed, but only with major restrictions. Therefore recognition in the Spanish Constitution of the right of foundation has to be understood within this historical context and in the light of nineteenth-century legislation, which has been in force in part until very recently and which resulted in the disappearance of several institutions of this type with irreparable consequences.[1] Furthermore, as several authors point out, Article 34 of the Constitution prohibits or limits the State, defined constitutionally as a *social* and democratic State governed by the rule of Law, having a monopoly over securing the general interest, ensuring that private initiative may intervene in achieving that general interest (García-Andrade 2005, 28–29).

13.1.2 Distribution of Powers Between the State and the Autonomous Regions

In order to discuss and analyse the legal framework of the Foundations Law, mention must be made, albeit brief, of the system for the distribution of powers between the State and the Autonomous Regions as defined by the Spanish Constitution of 1978. Two types of powers need to be distinguished from the perspective of the Foundations Law. On the one hand, the administrative and supervisory powers – *Protectorate* – attributed to the Autonomous Regions and State Government, respectively, for foundations in their respective areas of competence. And on the other hand, the legislative powers attributed to the different regional parliaments and the State parliament or legislator with regard to legislation on foundations.

All the Autonomous Regions, apart from the autonomous cities of Ceuta and Melilla, have been given supervisory and monitoring powers over foundations, that is, over regional foundations, those which undertake activities *principally* within the territorial area of that autonomous region. These powers are exercised through the corresponding autonomous Protectorates, administrative bodies responsible for said functions in each Autonomous Region. The allocation of these powers does not

[1] García-Andrade (2001) makes a thorough analysis of the desentailment process and the use of the term foundation in a material, not a formal, sense.

remove that of the State, which exercises Protectorate or supervisory functions over foundations at State level, whose activities are undertaken *principally in more than one Autonomous Region*.

The various issues that are affected by the Foundations Law need to be outlined with regard to the legislative powers governing the foundational institutions. On the one hand, as the *right of foundation serving a purpose of general interest* is a right which is recognised under the Constitution; it falls to the State legislator – the Spanish Parliament – to regulate the basic conditions for exercising this right using a State law. Article 149.1.1ª of the Constitution, which attributes exclusive power to the State over the "regulation of the basic conditions guaranteeing the equality of all Spaniards in the exercise of their rights and in the fulfilment of their constitutional duties". Such provisions, affecting aspects such as, amongst others, the definition itself of foundation; the obligation for foundations to pursue purposes of general interest, or to acquire an independent legal personality, an address; and the regulation of foreign foundations, apply to any foundation, whether at State or regional level, and therefore are binding to the legislators of the autonomous regions.

On the other hand, some of the areas affecting the legal system governing foundations involve commercial and procedural legislation – liability action taken against trustees, precautionary suspension by a judge – and the state legislator is solely responsible for its regulation (Article 149.1.6ª of the constitution). Finally, some issues which affect the Foundations Law constitute civil legislation – the procedures for setting up the foundation, the content of its Statutes, endowment, trustee duties and other aspects – and its regulation falls to the State regulator, although without prejudice to the preferential application of some Autonomous Regions who have their own special Law or Law relative to the *fuero* and therefore have regulations which govern certain civil institutions, in which case such regulations shall have precedence over State legislation.

The remaining areas may be subject to regulation by the legislators of the autonomous regions. For the same reason, any other precepts of the state law on foundations which do not affect the areas reserved for the State shall apply only to state foundations, as defined above. Section 13.1.3 below shows that not all the Spanish Autonomous Regions have exercised their legislative powers in the area of foundations; in these communities State legislation applies to regional foundations.

In tax terms, the Spanish Constitution reserves power over *general finances and the state debt*, exclusively to the State (Article 149.1.14ª). Only the Autonomous Regions with their own *foral* regimes – the Basque Country and Navarre – have tax powers and therefore have regulated the tax systems for foundations and non-profit bodies and sponsorship.[2]

[2] The remaining Autonomous Regions only have the power to grant certain tax benefits which apply to donations made by natural persons.

13.1.3 Legal Framework: Critical Analysis

Act 30/1994, of 24 November, on "Foundations and Tax Incentives for Private Participation in Activities of General Interest" *(Ley 30/1994, de 24 de noviembre, de Fundaciones e Incentivos Fiscales a la Participación Privada en Actividades de Interés General)* provided legislative development of the right of foundation which is recognised under the Constitution. This Act regulated the substantive and procedural regime for foundations and the tax system, not only for foundations but also other non-profit bodies, such as associations serving the public interest. At the same time it established the tax incentives which apply to sponsorship. Some Autonomous Regions had passed their own laws on foundations after the promulgation of the Constitution and prior to the State Act of 1994; however, they had done so within the area of their respective powers. Given that certain areas could not and cannot be regulated by the Autonomous Regions, the Act of 1994 constituted a milestone in Spanish foundation Law.

The new law served to put an end to the fragmentary, piecemeal system in place until then and ultimately provided legal security for setting up and operating foundations. The explanatory notes to the Act explain that the updating of legislation on foundations was determined by the constitutional recognition of the right of foundation but was also *due to the importance acquired by the aforementioned right of foundation*. The effect that the Act of 1994 had on the pace at which foundations were created in Spain is vouched for by the aforementioned data, bearing in mind that 65.3 % of the foundations currently registered were created after that date.

Nonetheless, the practical application of the Act immediately brought to light some of its shortcomings and loopholes. On the one hand it was a law which still gave little autonomy to foundations, as it established an ex ante authorisation system for numerous acts of disposition of patrimony. It also granted the supervisory authorities, the Protectorate, a great many discretionary powers, enabling them to judge not only the legality of certain acts but also their expediency. In terms of tax, the Act of 1994 established a catalogue of non-profit bodies based on their legal form as long as they also fulfilled a series of objective requirements and vouched for these before the tax Administration. It declared some, but not all, of the income gained by these bodies exempt, setting a reduced rate for the rest. It also established the regime for sponsorship incentives for donations and contributions to these non-profit bodies made by individuals and companies. Thus, the foundation sector started to contemplate the need to amend this Act, a process which commenced in 2001 and which culminated in the passing of a new Act, Act 50/2002, of 26 December on Foundations (*Ley 50/2002, de 26 de diciembre, de Fundaciones*) at the end of 2002. This time, a different legislative technique was used and the tax regime for non-profit bodies and sponsorship incentives was regulated in a different Act, which was processed and approved at the same time as the Foundations Act: Act 49/2002, of 23 December, on the Tax Regime for non-profit Bodies and Tax

Incentives for Sponsorship (*Ley 49/2002, de 23 de diciembre, de Régimen Fiscal de las Entidades sin Fines Lucrativos y de los Incentivos Fiscales al Mecenazgo*).

The Foundations Act of 2002, currently in force, was really a partial amendment of the previous Act, and one of its objectives was to respond to some of the demands of the foundation sector to combat some of the inflexibility of the previous legislation: simplifying administrative procedures, reducing the control procedures of the supervisory authority and reforming the organisation and operational structure for governing and representing the foundation. This Act certainly did eliminate some of the prior authorisation assumptions laid down in the previous legislation, but some were preserved. Furthermore, some obligations remain rigid, such as devoting a percentage of the income gained by the foundation to fulfilling purposes. And, from the foundation sector's point of view, the procedures have hardly been simplified.

As regards the tax system, Act 49/2002, also currently in force, maintains the same system as its predecessor, setting out a range of entities which, from a subjective point of view, may have recourse to a special or more beneficial tax system and laying out the set of requirements which, from an objective point of view, they need to fulfil. Unlike the previous Act, the tax benefits apply automatically and do not have to be requested exemptions, although their implementation needs to be vouched for year by year, by presenting a report to the tax Administration. This Act constitutes progress in terms of the corporate taxation of non-profit bodies, as almost all their income is declared exempt. However it leaves sponsorship incentives virtually unaltered.

Over the years, some Autonomous Regions have passed different foundation laws or have amended existing ones, within the scope of their respective powers. In this process, the passing of the State laws of 1994 and 2002 constituted a significant boost for the Autonomous Communities to legislate or make amendments in this area, although a few of them have barely made any changes from State legislation and therefore cannot be considered very innovative.

At present, in addition to the State laws, Act 50/2002, of 26 December, on Foundations (*Ley 50/2002, de 26 de diciembre, de Fundaciones)* and Act 49/2002, of 23 December, on the Tax Regime for non-profit Bodies and Tax Incentives for Sponsorship (*Ley 49/2002, de 23 de diciembre, de Régimen Fiscal de las Entidades sin Fines Lucrativos y de los Incentivos Fiscales al Mecenazgo)*, the following laws are in force in the Autonomous Communities mentioned: Act 10/2005, of 31 May, on Foundations in the Autonomous Community of Andalusia (*Ley 10/2005, de 31 de mayo, de Fundaciones de la Comunidad Autónoma de Andalucía*); Act 2/1998, of 6 April, on Foundations in the Canary Islands (*Ley 2/1998, de 6 de abril, de Fundaciones Canarias*); Act 13/2002, of 15 July, on Foundations in Castilla y León (*Ley 13/2002 de 15 de julio, de Fundaciones de Castilla y León*); Act 4/2008, of 24 April, of the Third Book of the Civil Code of Catalonia, relating to Legal Persons (*Ley 4/2008 de 24 de abril, del Libro Tercero del Código Civil de Cataluña, relativo a las Personas Jurídicas*); Act 12/2006, of 1 December, on Foundations of Galician Interest (*Ley 12/2006, de 1 de diciembre, de fundaciones de interés gallego*); Act 1/2007, of 12 February, on Foundations in the Autonomous Region of La Rioja (*Ley 1/2007, de 12 de febrero, de Fundaciones de la Comunidad Autónoma de La Rioja*); Act 1/1998, of 2 March, on Foundations in the Community of Madrid (*Ley 1/1998, de 2 de marzo, de Fundaciones de la Comunidad de Madrid*); Foral Act 10/1996, of 2 July, regulating the tax regime of foundations and sponsorship activities (*Ley Foral 10/1996, de 2 de julio, reguladora del ré gimen tributario de las fundaciones y de las actividades de patrocinio*); Act of the Basque Parliament 12/1994, of 17 July 1994, on Foundations (*Ley del Parlamento Vasco 12/1994, de 17 de junio de 1994, de Fundaciones*); and Act 8/1998, of 9 December, on Foundations in the Valencian Community (*Ley 8/1998, de 9 de diciembre, de Fundaciones de la Comunidad Valenciana*).

Spanish legislation on foundations establishes one legal system and one system of obligations for all foundations, without distinguishing between the different types of foundation and therefore irrespective of their means of funding, funders, trustees or initial or subsequent patrimony. Thus, from a legal perspective, differences cannot be established between operating foundations, patrimonial foundations, and company foundations; however, we define them.[3] Nevertheless, whenever there is debate about the need to amend current legislation and how it needs to be directed, time and again the same issue arises – the validity of the same regulation for an institution, such as a foundation, which is becoming increasingly less monolithic. Opinion on the positive or negative effects of current legislation differs depending on the type of foundation in question. Although the sector has always defended uniform regulation, it should be highlighted that, paradoxically, legislation on foundations, still applied to operating foundations and patrimonial foundations alike, is more perverse and flawed for the latter than in the case of operating foundations. Areas which have already been flagged up such as the obligation to devote income and revenue to fulfilling the foundation's purposes, as shown in a recent study (Petitbò Juan y Hernández Marcos 2009), occasionally make it difficult to preserve the real value of the foundation's patrimony. Warnings of the possible harmful effects of this on patrimonial foundations had already been given as the Act of 1994 was in process and again in 2002, but these have come to light clearly in the current economic climate, with low rates of patrimony profitability and growing inflation. Also, a failure to adequately safeguard the founder's will, in the light of the almost absolute powers of the Committee of Trustees, who can modify some of the issues essential to the foundation and considerably deviate from the will of the foundation, is occasionally another area of uncertainty for patrimonial foundations. Amendment of some of the points of the Statute can be forbidden by the founder, but results in the operation of the organisation are becoming very rigid. Finally the authorisation system, relating mainly to acts of

[3] However, there are other types of bodies, which go under the name *Foundation*, which the Foundations Act itself excludes from its scope of application and which are different bodies to private-Law foundations: some public-Law entities referred to as public-health foundations or National Heritage Foundations. Religious foundations, including the canonical foundations of the Catholic Church, are also governed by their own specific legislation.

disposition of patrimony, do apply to grant making foundations mainly than to operational foundations.

13.1.4 Definition of Foundation

Act 50/2002, of 26 December, on Foundations defines these bodies as "organisations constituted as non-profit organisations whose patrimony is allocated permanently to the fulfilment of general interest purposes, according to the wishes of their founders". The Act of 1994 already contained this definition, and it should be noted that it abandoned the traditional definition of foundations as *patrimonies* intended for general interest purposes. It gives predominance to the organisational element of these entities and considers them *organisations*. In this way it is acknowledged that while foundations are patrimony-based entities, at the same time, as organisations, they are able to generate and provide their own resources towards the fulfilment of the purposes of the foundation. Therefore from a conceptual point of view, we outline the key features of a foundation as follows: (1) organisation, (2) a not-for-profit philosophy, (3) the will of the founder, (4) patrimony and (5) general interest purposes.

We refer here to two of these features: the patrimonial element and general interest purposes, as the essential features of foundations as non-profit organisations.

13.1.5 Endowment

A foundation's patrimony is made up of all the goods, rights and obligations subject to the financial valuation of that which is owned by the foundation. Within the patrimony, considered a whole, two different patrimony masses need to be considered, on the basis of their different legal jurisdiction: the goods and rights which form part of the endowment and the others acquired by the foundation following its constitution, whether or not they affect the endowment. In turn, the foundation's endowment, in accordance with Article 12 of the Act, shall comprise the goods and rights which made up the initial endowment and also by all others which, during the existence of the foundation, have been contributed as such by the founder or by third parties, or which are permanently allocated by the Committee of Trustees for the foundation's purposes.

An endowment *appropriate and sufficient* for fulfilling the purposes of the foundation is an essential condition for its constitution. The Act of 1994 did not include any presumption of a sufficient amount or indicate any minimum endowment for a foundation, leaving this at the complete discretion of the public Administration to classify the foundation in order to determine the amount. Nevertheless, in practice, 6,000 € paid in full was accepted for the constitution of a foundation. However, Act of 2002 established the adequacy and sufficiency of a foundation's endowment, a monetary or other types of good or right, at 30,000 €. Thus, administrative discretionality was reduced, establishing a presumption *juris tantum*, but introducing a potential limitation of the right of foundation.

Amongst the arguments against establishing a minimum limit considered excessive was precisely the argument that the evolution made by the foundation from *patrimony* to *organisation* should be considered.[4] In defence of those who upheld the need to set an initial minimum endowment which required a sufficient financial commitment on the part of the founders, it should be pointed out that many of the foundations were set up with an initial outlay of at least 25 % of the minimum endowment required, with the commitment that the remainder would be provided within a period not exceeding 5 years – a possibility covered under the Act – it proved very difficult to obtain the remaining capital from the founders once this period had elapsed. In the report issued by the Council of State (1636/2002) on the draft bill, the advisory body indicated that establishing a minimum amount to set up a valid foundation was not a requirement "which prevented the constitution of Foundations with financial endowments of less than this amount, but only a presumption juris tantum that the endowment is sufficient when it totals 50,000 euros" – the amount which was initially required in the bill – "This presumption does not release each case from an evaluation of the adequacy and sufficiency of the endowment for the foundation's purposes, it only obliges those Foundations whose endowments are below 50,000 euros to present a first action programme and a financial study to demonstrate their viability using only said resources". It added "The required amount is not excessive for establishing the aforementioned obligation. The intervention of the Protectorate with regard to the sufficiency of the endowment is covered under article 36.2 of the current Act and is consonant with the purpose of said institution which is, as the Constitutional Court Ruling 49/1988 of 22 March states, "to ensure the fulfilment of the purposes of the Foundation and the proper administration of its assets", therefore there should be no objection to their being conferred the aforementioned duty".

In practice, in those cases where the initial endowment amounts to 30,000 €, the Protectorates do not require any other evaluation. However Protectorates very infrequently allow the constitution of a foundation with a lower initial endowment, despite the provision of the Act. In short, it can be very difficult to demonstrate viability by means of a financial feasibility study and the foundation's first action programme, with less than 30,000 € – or even with that amount – particularly in cases where the endowment is not monetary, and especially because it has to be taken into account that the Act sets a specific regime for acts of disposition of the

[4] Following the Act of 2002, the Catalan legislation regulating foundations which set the initial endowment at 60,000 was amended. This rule was amended to place it in line with State legislation.

goods and rights which make up the foundation's endowment, which is contradictory to the provisions of the Act with regard to the initial endowment.

Article 21.1 of the Act establishes "the disposal, for payment or otherwise, and the transfer of goods and rights which form part of the endowment, or which are directly linked to the fulfilment of the purposes of the foundation, require the prior authorisation of the Protectorate, which shall be granted if there is duly proven just cause". Amongst other conditions, the allocation of the moneys received from the disposal must be specified in the procedure for requesting authorisation and for valuing the goods and rights which are to be disposed of. Neither the Act nor the Regulations indicate which cases are considered to have a duly proven cause, and therefore it appears that the Administration has a wide margin in which to grant or refuse authorisation. Furthermore, this is the area which raises most concerns (Article 16.a) of the Regulation on Foundations under the Act, defining the goods and rights which make up a foundation's endowment, stating that "In the case of the disposal or transfer of an endowment's goods and rights, any goods and rights which substitute them shall be preserved within the endowment and it shall incorporate any capital gains which may have accrued". It seems that it can be concluded from this provision, the legality of which is in doubt, that despite the fact that the Committee of Trustees must indicate the allocation of the sum obtained for the goods and rights of the endowment, this allocation must be used for the acquisition of other goods and rights which might be of a different nature – securities, movable and immovable property, etc. – yet they would become the foundation's endowment and thus not viable for allocation to foundation expenditure. Thus, if the endowment may not be used, the foundation would have to cover their expenses, even for the first year, with the return from the endowment; therefore, in practice an endowment lower than 30,000 € would not be sufficient and neither would an endowment which reached that sum.

It is also true that the disposal of a *monetary* endowment is not really an alienation, and therefore it could be argued that the disposal of the endowment, whether initial or subsequent, does not require the authorisation of the Protectorate. However, to conclude the chapter on a foundation's patrimony, the Regulation states "When a foundation sees a serious reduction in their own funds over two consecutive financial years putting at risk the fulfilment of their purposes, the Protectorate may demand that the Committee of Trustees take the appropriate measures to correct the situation". Bearing in mind that, amongst other resources, the foundation's own funds are those of the foundation's endowment, the foundation which spends this endowment would find themselves in such a situation, and this would oblige their Committee of Trustees to replace the spent endowment.

To conclude, although the definition itself of a foundation has evolved, with some practical problems as we shall see, along with the other requirements, it requires a minimum patrimony, in the form of its endowment. A minimum initial amount is set for this and its value must be maintained and increased.

13.1.6 *General Interest Purposes and Beneficiaries of Foundations*

Foundations must pursue purposes of general interest. The Act on Foundations contains a very large list of these, although it is not a closed or numerus clausus list, and therefore many other purposes are possible.[5] This is an undefined legal concept and as such there is some ambiguity as to how they are regulated. However, as García de Enterría states (1996, 72) "the legal concept of public interest or general interest is used in the Constitution, and in all Acts, with an unequivocal intention to limit, which is really very broad (the difference between movable and immovable assets is also broad, and nobody would dare to discuss their scope, although in this case these are a couple of concepts which have been determined) but it is effective. The general interest or the public interest are clear guides used by the settlor to organise institutions or public action". Just as it falls to the supervisory authorities to assess the sufficiency of a foundation's endowment, one of their main missions is to judge the *appropriateness* of its purposes. It falls to the courts to settle any disputes.

The general interest of its purposes is one of the essential requirements for a foundation to be considered a foundation, but this requirement is not limited to the purposes themselves, as intrinsic to them are the beneficiaries. The Act rules that foundations, in addition to pursuing general interest purposes, must benefit generic groups of individuals (Article 3.2), expressly excluding the possibility of setting up foundations with the main purpose of benefiting the founder or the trustees, their spouses or persons with whom there is a similar relationship, relatives up to the fourth degree or separate legal persons who do not pursue general interest purposes (Article 3.3.). The Act does not define what should be understood by the generic concept of beneficiaries. Reference is confined to two particular assumptions. It states that generic groups of people are considered to be the workers of one or various companies; thus, the constitution of labour foundations is allowed, and the assumption of Article 3.3 excludes foundations whose sole or main purpose is the conservation and restoration of assets of Spanish historical heritage. Therefore, the conservation of an asset of cultural interest which an individual or a family – not the foundation – owns or has usufruct over may constitute the purpose of a foundation.

Beyond the doctrinal standpoints which can be taken on the concept of *general interest*, it is worthwhile highlighting some administrative doctrine which has been generated around this concept in the area of tax. Pursuing the general interest is a

[5] Article 3 of the 2002 Foundations Act states: "Foundations will have to pursue general interest purposes such as, defence of human rights, support for victims of terrorism and violent acts, social assistance and social inclusion, civic, educational, cultural, scientific, sports, sanitary, labour, institutional strengthening, development cooperation, volunteering, promotion of social action, environmental protection, promotion of the social economy, attention to people at risk of exclusion for physical, social or cultural reasons, promotion of constitutional values and defence of democratic principles and tolerance, development of the information society, scientific investigation and technological development".

requirement under Act 49/2002 in order for non-profit bodies, including foundations, to receive special or more beneficial taxation treatment. However, although this requirement is stated in tax law in identical terms as those used in the Foundations Act, the Tax Administration in various rulings consider that meeting this requirement demands that the foundation itself should *directly* pursue general interest purposes; they do not consider this requirement fulfilled by allocating income to other foundations. In short, under this interpretation, donor foundations ("grant making foundations") who give help to other entities, finance projects for others and in general do not undertake the activities themselves towards fulfilling their purposes would be excluded from special taxation treatment, it being considered that they are failing to meet general interest purposes in the sense established under tax law. It has to be stressed that this tax law is identical in its wording to the Foundations Act.

This doctrine, which is a clear departure from the literal interpretation of the law and deviates from the will of the legislator, is significant not only in the area of taxation, in considering the most beneficial tax regime to apply to a foundation, but also in the substantive area, for two reasons which are relevant here. The first is because it has been allowed, albeit reservedly by some of the Protectorate's rulings, to deny the registration of a foundation whose purpose is to fund the activity of other non-profit bodies. The second, and perhaps most important, is because it calls into question the ability of the supervisory authorities – the Protectorate – to determine what the general interest is and how it affects other areas of the legal system. As we mentioned, Article 34 of the Constitution covers the right of foundation "for general interest purposes", and it is general interest which justifies public intervention in some aspects of a foundation's life, allocating these supervisory or control functions, by law, to the Protectorate. The Protectorate is in charge not only of monitoring the proper exercise of the right of Foundation and the legality of setting up and operating a foundation, but it also has the more specific function of evaluating the appropriateness of its purpose. It does not appear to be due process that the evaluation made by the administrative body competent to make such an evaluation should be called into question in the area of taxation.[6]

[6] We can also refer to some historical or legislative backgrounds which may refute this theory in the case of foundations. The Act of 1994 and its successor the Foundations Act of 2002 improve on historical regulation and combine the different types of foundations and how they are legally regulated under one concept. Thus foundations are defined as "organisations set up as not-for-profit which, according to the wishes of their founders, permanently allocate their patrimony to the fulfilment of general interest purposes". In addition to establishing a modern concept of a foundation, current legislation improves on the distinction under repealed Decree 2.930/1972, of 21 July, approving the Regulations for Private Cultural Foundations and Analogous Bodies of the Administrative Services in charge of the Protectorate over these foundations, which differentiated the regime for the so-called funding foundations, those awarding grants and subsidies, from promotion foundations, those which had their own programme of activities, or service foundations. Thus the definition itself of foundation under current legislation combines the two elements where there has been constant tension – patrimony and organisation.

As Falcón y Tella (2005) points out on the subject of the dispute in the area of taxation with unit trust companies, "beyond the wording of the applicable regulation, the impossibility of the Tax Agency pronouncing a judgement over areas which are the competence of other bodies" – in this case the National Securities Market Commission – "and especially the impossibility that the pronouncement of the (Tax) Agency should contradict that of the competent administrative body, originates from the very essence of the Rule of Law conceived as a technique for allocating specific powers without which the Administration cannot act (positive Bindung), unlike individuals who may do anything which is not contrary to the legal system (negative Bindung)". He continues "... the decision-making powers that are generally granted the Administration but not the Tax Authorities, so that the civil servants of the latter may determine (solely for tax purposes) the taxable event, but they may on no account make a decision which contradicts any maintained by the competent administrative body in the area in question".[7] We believe that these same arguments serve to put into question the criterion adopted by the Tax Administration in relation to the definition of the general interest pursued by foundations.

13.1.7 General Interest and Economic Activity: The Non-profit Aim

One of the questions which traditionally crops up regarding the definition of foundations is how compatible their being not for profit is with their undertaking financial or business activities, either directly or indirectly. Despite the clarity of the Foundations Act on this matter in Spain, there is constant tension around the subject, and concerns are continually being raised on the general interest and economic activity by legal practitioners, be they the Administration (supervisory bodies or Tax Agency), the courts or even auditors.[8]

Article 23 of the Foundations Act establishes that foundations "may undertake financial activities the aim of which relates to, is complementary or incident to the foundation's purpose, subject to the laws regulating fair competition". The Act also specifies, "they may take part in any financial activities through holdings in companies, in accordance with that which is set out in the following sections". The following sections provide that "foundations may have a holding in corporations in which they are not personally liable for the corporate debt. If this is a majority holding they should report this circumstance to the Protectorate". As a result of the evolution of the foundation sector, any likening of foundations to the

[7] Cazorla Prieto and Blázquez Lidoy refer to this problem (2011, 16 y 17).

[8] An analysis of the evolution can be found in the work entitled *La actividad económica de las fundaciones: tensiones legislativas e interés general* (The financial activity of foundations: legislative tensions and general interest) (Pérez Escolar 2008).

idea of charity and cost-free services has now been completely ruled out. The data shows that the reality of the situation is quite different, given that 56.7 % of the 1,432 foundations consulted, number the provision of services and the sale of assets amongst their sources of funding.

For some, obtaining a payment for undertaking such activities distorts the condition of non-profit. For others, it is the appeal to standards for fair competition and foundations obtaining tax benefits which give rise to opposing arguments. Although the debate has lost some intensity in the foundation sector in its strictest sense, probably due to the clarity of the Act, we should not ignore some of the arguments put forward from other areas in relation to other non-profit bodies like associations, particularly those serving the public interest. In our opinion there is a mixture of different issues in all of these arguments, such as making a profit and its distribution or the definition of the general interest purpose.

In the area of intellectual property, the issue has been raised about reproductive rights collective management organisations. These organisations, in accordance with the Intellectual Property Act (Legislative Royal Decree 1/1996, of 12 April), "may not be profit making", which means that they have to be set up with the legal status of an association. *In their 2009 report on the collective management of intellectual property rights,* the National Competition Commission (CNC) expressed their concerns about the non-profit nature of these organisations; they considered "that these are legal persons genetically predisposed by Law to undertake a typical business activity such as the commercial management of rights of a financial nature". The report concludes on this point, stating that there are no reasons for management organisations to take the form of non-profit bodies, as it reduces the possibility of other financial operators entering the market; therefore, this sector should not be closed to this sort of organisation. In their argument the CNC refers to the Services Directive and their transposition law in Spain, as they require these sorts of restrictions to satisfy the criteria of non-discrimination, necessity and proportionality. Furthermore, the report states: "Likewise, there are sectors of activity other than intellectual property where achieving certain general interest objectives is important, but where the operators are not obliged to set up as non-profit bodies. Otherwise, there is no legal concept of non profit, and it is more than questionable whether the non profit aim implies that it is not possible to distribute profits in the form of dividends between members or shareholders".

Although we agree with the conclusion reached by the CNC, we cannot share the arguments, as it is not the undertaking of a typical business activity, and no more, which distorts the non-profit aim, but the distribution of any profits, not only in the form of dividends but in any other direct or indirect form. The Intellectual Property Act contradicts itself by demanding that these bodies should be non-profit and at the same time requiring that their statutes should include, amongst other things, "the rules governing the systems for the share of proceeds". From our point of view, it is the necessary sharing of proceeds between members, a legitimate and natural function of these entities which calls into question their being assessed as non-profit. Moreover, as they are not associations which serve the public interest, they are not obliged to open up their activities to any potential beneficiaries, and in their statutes they can restrict their activities exclusively to their associates. As we shall see, the area's general interest purposes, by definition general and *open*, cannot be disassociated from the potential beneficiaries.[9]

The non-profit aim has to be viewed in relation to the prohibition of the distribution of profits and therefore to how any patrimony and income influence the fulfilment of the foundation's purpose. As required by Article 27 at least 70 % of income gained must be allocated to the fulfilment of purposes within 5 years (the year the income has gained plus four) and the remainder may be used to increase the foundation's endowment. But this also has to be linked to the concept of general interest with the understanding that intrinsic to this is that the beneficiaries are generic groups of people and that it is not restricted to a specific group such as the organisation's own associates. For those who want to obtain public interest status, the Associations Act states: "their activity should not be restricted exclusively to benefiting their associates and should be open to any other possible beneficiary satisfying the conditions and characters required by the nature of their own purposes". It is a different issue if these bodies, foundations or associations directly undertake financial activities, as long as these are in relation to the foundation's purpose.

There has also been mention of how compatible the non-profit aim and the general interest are with performing financial or business activities with regard to the declaration or revocation of public interest status from associations. Unlike foundations which, having been constituted as such, must pursue general interest purposes, benefit generic groups of people and not distribute any income even if they are dissolved, such requirements are only required of associations that hold the declaration of public interest status. While all foundations are accountable to their corresponding administrative body, associations are only accountable if they hold the above recognition. Otherwise, they are only accountable to their members.

Recently and as Blázquez Lidoy (2011) explains, the Ministry of Interior, the body with the power to declare an association to be of public interest, has revoked this declaration, under the preliminary report of the Ministry of Economy and Finance, from those bodies which undertake financial activities on the markets "arguing that business ventures in markets where there is competition cannot be in the general interest, it must be private. And if this body were to enjoy the tax benefits of Act 49/2002 this might undermine competition with commercial companies. Consequently, they cannot enjoy public interest status or tax benefits".[10] As the author points out, this is a very specific argument, raised about an organisation, but it may have a very general dimension and, we add, not only apply to associations but, by extension, to foundations. This would mean that any public interest association might not be able to retain their public interest status because they have undertaken activities on the markets in competition with others.

[9] Supreme Court Ruling of 4.4.2003.

[10] The literal transcription of the ruling and the arguments used are included in the aforementioned article by Blázquez Lidoy.

From our point of view, there are two arguments which need to be addressed. The first is, in essence, the assumed incompatibility between the general interest and engaging in business activities on the markets. As we have mentioned in reference to such arguments, the fact that non-profit bodies pursue general interest purposes does not equate to cost-free services or the absence of a profit making aim – and we add – it does not imply that they should not be funded by market resources but rather that they should not distribute any profit directly or indirectly to their associates or members. In the case of foundations, the possibility of their engaging in financial activities to fulfil their purposes or even outside the foundation's purposes, as long as such activities do not exceed a certain percentage of the entity's total income and revenue, is also expressly covered in tax law for non-profit entities (Article 3.3. of Act 49/2002, of 23 December).

To address the second argument – any non-profit body which receives tax benefits and undertakes financial activity where there is competition with other companies might infringe laws on the protection of competition – we can refer to recent Supreme Court case law. For these purposes the ruling of 20 July 2009 is very relevant. The court rules on two levels with their ruling on a dispute brought under the previous Act of 1994. The first refers to the status of non-profit bodies from a tax and, a substantive point of view, of those who carry out a commercial activity. The Court, opposing the arguments of the State Lawyer, rejects such arguments:

> In the first place, because a glance at reality shows us that there is practically no sector of activities aimed at meeting general interest needs which nowadays is not the object of profit-oriented companies. The maximalist theory of the defender of the Administration would, for example, exclude a company running a centre for people with physical or mental disabilities from tax benefits merely because it operated in a market which included profit-oriented organisations. Another example: profits are sought in the area of cultural services as well; therefore, a general interest association offering such services would find itself excluded from the regime desired by the legislator. We can continue to repeat examples ad infinitum. The position of the Administration would render title II of the Act irrelevant, making it completely redundant; this result demonstrates the irrationality of this position.
>
> Secondly, an in-depth analysis of the process of Act 30/1994, which we summarised in the previous consideration with regard to this appeal, shows us that, as we have already mentioned, with the provision of Article 24.2 the legislator wanted to prevent structures of cultural interest, whose line of business is primarily run for profit, being included under the legal personification of a foundation or association, on the pretext of serving one of the purposes covered under articles 2.1 and 42.1 (1). Therefore the aforementioned Article 42.2 excludes them when "the principle activity is the undertaking of commercial activities" but not if this type of occupation is a tool for meeting the goals for which they were created. Thus, as we have also seen, Act 30/1994 allows foundations to take part directly or indirectly in commercial or industrial operations and allows them to enjoy the privileged tax regime which applies to entities which allocate at least 70 percent of their net revenue and income obtained "from any concept" to the purposes of the foundation or association [(article 42.1.b)], a concept which includes the proceeds from the aforementioned industrial and commercial activities.
>
> Finally, the interpretation we uphold is confirmed by the current Act 49/2002, of 23 December, on the tax system for non-profit bodies and tax incentives for sponsorship (BOE of 24 December), the successor to title II of Act 30/1994 (sole repeal provision), which stipulates that the activity undertaken by the organisations to which it applies should

> not consist of financial operations "outside their statutory aim or purpose", it being considered that the requirement has been met when "the net business turnover for the financial year from all non-exempt financial activities outside their statutory aim or purpose does not exceed 40 % of the total revenue of the organisation". As can be seen, the mere fact that financial criteria have been used in order to fulfil a foundation's purposes does not exclude a non-profit organisation from the scope of the Act.

Having explained this, the Court moves on to the second level, dealing with the argument put forward by the State Lawyer, in his attempt to refuse the exemption of corporate tax given that "The activity for which the tax benefit is being requested is undertaken in the market in a system of free competition, in such a way that, if their request is granted, this would be discriminatory to competitors, and they would gain an anti-competitive advantage". In this regard the Court states that from the point of view of the law, and in order for a financial activity undertaken by a non-profit body to be considered exempt, it is essential that the activity be linked to the purposes of the entity: "As a general rule the entity's objective and the financial activity it undertakes are not required to be the same, but should be in concert with its purposes. Only when that aim, that activity and those purposes co-exist can exemption be granted. In other words, for those seeking dispensation, the objectives of the entity concerned must be embedded in those of its financial activity (rulings of 19 December, 2007, FJ 4º, 26 December, 2007, FJ 2º, and 19 February, 2008, FJ 2º). And, in this context, the legislator offers some interpretative guidelines on the combination they require for the exoneration to operate. Firstly the activity which produces a return must be directed at fulfilling the general interest purposes of this class of structure; secondly it must not generate any "unfair competition"; and, finally, it should be allocated to a generic group of people".

With regard to the second question, the Court states:

> ...the debate centres on what should be understood, from the effects of Act 30/1994, by "unfair competition". The notion could be upheld strictly, as covered under Act 3/1991, of 10 January (BOE (Official State Journal) of 11 January), i.e. limited to anti-competitive behaviour against the requirements of good faith (Article 5, in relation to the 1st), or more broadly, as under Act 16/1989, of 17 July (BOE of 18 July), covering any action which is liable to impede, restrict or distort competition (Article 1), currently covered in Act 15/2007, of 3 July (BOE of 4 July).
>
> In the Court's view Act 30/1994 applies in the latter sense, because it would be difficult to find the volitional component required under article 5 and the articles which follow it of Act 3/1991 on the distortion of competition arising out of the recognition of a tax benefit regulated by law. Therefore, we understand that the 1994 legislator wanted to refuse dispensation for the proceeds from the financial activities of non-profit entities connected with their corporate or specific purpose, whose exemption from corporation tax might distort the rules of free competition. This understanding is corroborated if we refer to Act 49/2002, currently in force on the subject, which, more stringently demands, for the exemption to be viable, that activities outside the statutory purpose should not infringe the rules on the protection of competition with regard to companies which share the same activity (Article 3.3). This broad and flexible criterion is the one we have applied in the five previous rulings that we have referred to throughout this pronouncement.

As Blázquez Lidoy (2011, 45) states, for the Tax Administration to merely allege that acknowledging the exemption would generate unfair competition is not sufficient in order to deny a dispensation, since, as has been repeatedly stated on other occasions, not all discrimination is unfair competition, it is essential that reasons are given, describing the market that would be affected, its operation and the position of the beneficiary.

Continuing this line of argument, the Court eventually rejects exempting the foundation without entering into the latter analysis, since it considers that the financial activities for which it would be intended do not coincide with the foundation's purpose and are not aimed at the foundation's own beneficiaries: "No great effort is required to acknowledge that this accumulation of financial activities, which are not the specific objective of the foundation's purpose do not coincide with that purpose in the sense desired by the legislator in Article 48.2 of Act 30/1994, since, in addition to occupying a much vaster area than that of that purpose, they would cause, if the dispensation were to be awarded, distortion to the system of free competition, giving an unjustified advantage to the "Real Fundación" in financial activities which do not constitute its particular objective. In the terms of our previous rulings, it is not enough for the turnover for which the benefit is being requested to affect the field of town-planning and construction but rather it needs to show its effects in terms which basically coincide with the "being", "objective" and "purpose" of the foundation, because as we have already stated, it is essential that the quest for general interest which article 42.1 (a) alludes to in Act 30/1994, is inexorably embedded in the financial activity for which exemption is sought".

13.1.8 Other Current Issues Related to Economic Activities

Foundations have been experiencing a boom in the area of research, innovation and development, not only in Spain but in other neighbouring countries. Many foundations with these purposes have been set up by individuals and companies and by public, national and regional Administration. The data gathered by INAEF and Eurostat (1999–2000) included in the report *Giving more for research in Europe: The role of foundations and the non-profit sector in boosting R&D investment* – September 2005 – drawn up by a group of experts at the initiative of the European Commission. For Spain, the report highlights two major phenomena. The first is public-private collaboration in research via public initiative foundations, as a vehicle for channelling public resources devoted to research combined with private resources. The second are the university foundations, highlighting their role in technology transfer, human resources management for research projects and the provision of resources for scientific and technical personnel in these projects. The suitability of foundations as instruments to channel and target small donations for research projects which otherwise would remain dispersed is also recognised. The report concludes that despite the recognition of the role of foundations in the area of research in our country, their resources and impact in this area need to be further developed.

In 2011 a new Science, Technology and Innovation Act (Act 14/2011 of 1 June) (*Ley de la Ciencia, la Tecnología y la Innovación (Ley 14/2011, de 1 de junio)*) was passed in Spain which recognises the current Article 33.1, (b) as a way of promoting investigation into research, innovation and development activities and stimulating cooperation between companies and the use of "legal possibilities for cooperation such as economic interest groupings and temporary joint ventures in which collaborators share investment, implementation of projects and/or the application of the results of the research". In addition, research foundations are recognised under the aforementioned rule as a part of the Spanish science and technology system. However this recognition is paradoxical, if we look at the current substantive regulation of the current Right to Foundation.

As mentioned, the current Act, like the various regional laws, has recognised foundations as operators like any other, permitting company foundations and foundations with companies alike. As we stated, according to the Foundations Act, these may engage in financial activities, the objective of which relates to is complementary or incident to their foundation purposes. Similarly, the Act recognises the possibility that foundations may have holdings in limited liability corporate entities. However, given that members of Economic Interest Groupings are personally and severally liable for its debts, although in a subsidiary way to the group, and members of Temporary Joint Ventures are joint and severally liable to third parties for the acts and operations for the common good, it is considered doubtful whether foundations could collaborate with other entities using these legal possibilities. In practice, although the use by some foundations of Temporary Joint Venture has been allowed in very specific cases and with some limitations, in general this possibility has been rejected, particularly by foundations set up by National State Administration.

As an argument in favour of foundations taking part in this form of collaboration, these possibilities have been considered to constitute yet another scenario in which foundations may directly conduct business activities and as such are expressly permitted under the Foundations Act. However, there would certainly have to be an amendment to the Foundations Act for such a possibility to be clearly allowed, to inject more dynamism into foundations, particularly in the area of research but also in the area of public contracting, and enable them to collaborate with other national, European or international entities, using these legal possibilities, as long as the activities of such entities related to and were carried out in compliance of the foundation's purpose.

13.1.9 The Non-profit Aim and the Dissolution of Foundations

If one of the characteristic features of the non-profit aim is the reinvestment of any profits obtained through the activity of the foundation and the allocation of patrimony towards achieving such purposes, the Foundations Act requires that such allocation should not be distorted even in the case of the entity being dissolved. The goods and rights resulting from liquidation shall be allocated to foundations or non-profit private entities which pursue general interest purposes and whose assets are allocated, even by dissolution, towards achieving those ends or to public entities, not foundation based, which pursue general interest purposes. This precept is also covered in all regional laws on foundations except the Law of the Autonomous Region of Galicia and the Law on Foundations of the Community of Madrid.

Indeed, Article 27 of Act 1/1998, of 2 March, on Foundations of the Community of Madrid states that the goods and rights resulting from the liquidation of an extinct foundation shall be "allocated as foreseen by the founder". Only in a case where the founder has not anticipated this allocation shall this be decided, in the first instance, by the Committee of Trustees, if they have been acknowledged this power by the founder. Otherwise, it shall be up to the supervising authorities to carry out this task. And only in this latter case does the Act require that such assets be allocated to foundations, private non-profit entities or public entities which pursue general interest purposes, which principally undertake their activities in the Community of Madrid, and whose assets, even by dissolution, are allocated to fulfilling such purposes. Under this wording, therefore, unlike state law, the allocation of the foundation's patrimony in the event of its dissolution to other entities which are not necessarily non-profit and also its reversion to the founder regardless of its legal nature would be permitted.[11]

No sooner had the Act been published, senators from the *Grupo Parlamentario Socialista* (Socialist Parliamentary Group) lodged an appeal of unconstitutionality against this and other precepts, as they considered that this release contravenes the Constitution for two reasons: firstly, because the definition of the allocation of assets constitutes a basic condition of the exercise of the right of foundation, which the regional legislator must respect in compliance with Article 149.1.1 of the Spanish Constitution, and secondly, because it violates the institute warranty covered by our Constitution, as new civil bodies are included under the concept of foundation, which already exist in other legislations, such as trusts, where profit is allowed at the time the foundation is dissolved. Thus, they considered that "Under the Foundations Act of the Community of Madrid there are genuine foundations which are altruistic and non-profit-making coexisting alongside "false foundations" which violate the allocation of patrimony to the common good and enable the enrichment of the recipient of the liquidated assets of the foundation".

Years later in the ruling of 21 December, 2005, the Constitutional Court made their judgement and deemed that the aforementioned article of the Foundations Act of the Community of Madrid complied with the rules set in the Constitution, in the terms of Court Consideration Nº 7, as they consider that the perpetual allocation of

[11] The reversion of assets to the founder is a controversial issue in several legal systems and also in the Spanish Foundations Law. See, amongst others, Caffarena Laporta (2009, 29–58).

goods or rights to the service of the general interest cannot be concluded as forming part of the recognisable image of the institution which is preserved in Article 34 of the Spanish Constitution. The legal interest protected by Article 34 of the Spanish Constitution demands that the assets and rights provided to the foundation should serve the "general interest" as long as the foundation is in existence, but it does not prescribe their permanent allocation after the foundation has been dissolved. The considerations add that "in addition, it should not be forgotten that under our legal system the dissolution of a foundation – not regulated as such under the contested Act – substantially escapes the will of the founder, expressed outside the act of foundation, or the body governing the institution, which helps to prevent its sense being adulterated . . . Therefore, if in specific cases serious deviation should arise in the application of the Act, in a way that liquidation produces a profit for the founder or (for the physical or legal persons nominated by the founder) which is incompatible with the general interest that should govern the foundation, the State of Law has sufficient instruments to exercise the appropriate controls. . .". And it concludes, and this is important, that "the description of foundations as non-profit organisations would not be compatible with potential reversion clauses which extended to goods or rights other than those endowed by the founder itself to the foundation".[12]

In conclusion, the Constitutional Court considers that the allocation of a foundation's assets to the general interest is not perpetual, but they are allocated for as long as the foundation exists, making reversion of the goods and rights to the founder acceptable constitutionally, as long as the assets were provided by the founder. This latter issue is not without its practical problems at the time of dissolution, which include any improvements which might have been made to such goods and rights and determining the criteria to be used to value transferred goods and rights. In any case, foundations anticipating reversion of their assets to the founder, if not a different non-profit entity or a public not foundation-based entity, would not be able to benefit from the special tax regime.

13.2 Governance: Regulation and Self-Regulation

There must be a body responsible for governing and representing every foundation which is called the Committee of Trustees, a collegiate body which must be formed by at least three trustees. Both physical and legal persons may be trustees. The Committee of Trustees may delegate their powers to one or more of their members, for which they may set up an internal executive commission or committee, except the powers to approve accounts and the action plan, modification, merger and dissolution powers or any actions which require the authorisation of the supervisory authorities.

[12] Moreno Cea (2010, 600–609) makes an analysis of the constitutional conflict of the Foundations Act of the Community of Madrid and of this ruling.

As we have already mentioned elsewhere (Peñalosa and Sanjurjo 2010), regulation under the Foundations Act of the operating standards of the Committee of Trustees, both in the nomination and replacement of trustees and the way agreements are adopted, is deliberately sparse, as this is one of the areas which should clearly reflect the autonomy of the will of the founder and in setting the purposes of the foundation. Therefore, as established in Article 11.1 (e) of the Act, mention has to be made in the Statutes of the composition of the Committee of Trustees, the rules for nominating and replacing its members, the reasons for its cessation, its remit and the way agreements are considered and adopted.

The *Reglamento de Fundaciones de Competencia Estatal* (Regulation on Foundations under the Competence of the State) approved in 2005 contains, as an innovation, a new complete chapter devoted to governing a foundation, highlighting, of course, that the rules covered in it will apply in the absence of regulation contained in the Statutes. But without prejudice to the regulation in the Statutes, the fact is that the rules contained in this chapter not only fill frequent statutory gaps, they also make up the body or set of practices, decisions and criteria often contained in foundation statutes and on occasion applied to excess by the Protectorates.

However in addition, foundations are and must be included in the self-regulatory phenomenon of the corporate governance of other legal persons and are increasingly voluntarily adopting their own codes of conduct, codes of ethics or good governance as complementary rules to their statutes or as rules to develop them. Sometimes these development rules are purely internal or combine other types of regulation. In addition to regulating how their funds are allocated or the relationship with their donors, or particular guidelines to follow with suppliers, they frequently contain rules on the operation of the governing body. In the absence of hard law, self-regulation takes on a special meaning. However, despite the fact that hard law is sparse in all matters to do with the operation of the Committee of Trustees, these codes and regulations do have to take into account the *statutory reserve*, and therefore they have to fulfil a real function in developing the Statutes in relation to reserved matters, which is not always easy.

There are increasingly more foundations in Spain that have their own codes of good governance, and there are ever more initiatives to promote their adoption by these entities. The Spanish Association of Foundations (*Asociación Española de Fundaciones*) (www.fundaciones.org) provided a guide or set of guidelines to help foundations draw up these codes: *Buen Gobierno y Buenas Prácticas de Gestión. Criterios para su desarrollo por las fundaciones* (Criteria for foundations in the development of good governance and good management practices).[13] This guide not only covers aspects concerning the governance of foundations but also other practices in their management, referring to elements such as transparency and communication, monitoring and financial supervision or the foundation

[13] Another initiative in this area is that promoted by Instituto de Consejeros y Administradores (ICA) that has published a *Guide on Good Governance for Public Benefit Associations and Foundations*, 2013.

relationships with donors and volunteers. As stated in the document preceding these criteria, "As organisations, foundations have been adopting management methods and procedures, seeking better efficiency and efficacy in the use of their resources for performing their activities, in an ever more professional way. As entities which serve the public interest, the legislator has established a supervision system, under which they must regularly submit information to the Protectorate. Nonetheless, it is appropriate that foundations take a step forward both in their management and their transparency".

The foundation sector makes few criticisms of current legislation in relation to the regulation of the Committee of Trustees. Only the provisions referring to trustees offering their services without payment and their signing contracts with the foundation pose a few problems. Given the unpaid nature of the post of trustee, this being another of the features of a foundation as a non-profit entity, if the trustees wish to establish a contractual relationship with the Foundation, be it civil, commercial or even deriving from a work relationship, they must request prior authorisation from the supervisory authority. In practice this poses a few problems, as the Administration may take up to 3 months to respond, when, for example, it might be a matter of hiring a trustee to give a conference to the foundation.

13.3 Transparency, Accountability and Legal Reports

The Foundations Act obliges all foundations regardless of their size, activities or means of funding to submit their accounts annually to the Protectorate – supervisory authorities – on which they depend. Once they have been submitted, the Protectorate formally examines and revises the accounts and the audit report (in the event that they are legally obliged to perform audits or they have done so voluntarily). Once it has been checked that the documents correctly adjust to current legislation, the Protectorate proceeds to file them with the foundations' register. This remains without prejudice to the physical checks which they may carry out as part of their duties within 4 years of submission. The Protectorate shall report any foundations who have failed to present their accounts or rectify any errors of which they have been advised by the Tax Administration.

The Accounting Plan for Non-profit Entities (*Plan de Contabilidad para las Entidades sin Fines Lucrativos*) (RD 776/1998) was passed in Spain in 1998, adapting general accounting rules to the sector. In 2008 the new General Accounting Plan came into effect in Spain, passed in order to adapt accounting to the new International Accounting Standards, which made it necessary to amend the Commercial Code. The effect of the new accounting rules was the partial derogation of the accounting scheme for the non-profit sector. From that moment on and by the resolution of the *Instituto de Contabilidad y Auditoría de Cuentas* (Institute of Accounting and Account Auditing), non-profit entities had to adapt their accounting to the new plan approved for commercial entities, applying their sectoral adaptation to that not covered in the general rules. This gave rise to a temporary situation in which both the supervisory bodies and the foundations had to adapt their obligations to submit their accounts to new legislation in which there were major deficiencies and uncertainties for these entities, and this diverted resources from both the entities and the Administration as they had to devote more time and resources towards meeting their obligations. The *Instituto de Contabilidad y Auditoría de Cuentas* approved some new balance sheet and income statement models for non-profit entities following the new commercial models, but they did not approve a new report model. The new Accounting Plan for Non-profit Entities was finally approved in 2013.

The progressive incorporation of non-profit entities into the different financial activity sectors has led some schools of thought to consider that their accounting obligations and accountability for them should be no different to those of commercial entities. But others hold the belief that given the non-commercial nature of non-profit entities, certain operations regulated under their legislation do not have an appropriate and correct accounting response. These sorts of considerations arose, once again, in the process of drafting the new sectoral adaptation. According to Rúa (2010, 222), despite these considerations, "The problem lies at the source, i.e., when the legislator on foundations decided rightly to enforce accountability, they made the mistake of taking the accounting model of commercial entities and applying it to entities of a different nature. This meant that as the accounting information of the business model was considered "insufficient", substantive legislation on foundations tried to add to the information that they had to submit using specific terminology which does not fit current accounting legislation, which further complicated the situation". The fact is that the accounting information of non-profit entities should serve not only to provide financial information on them but to assess the fulfilment of their purposes, an objective not met by commercial legislation. That is why, sometimes rather mistakenly, other relevant information is added referring to the activities of the foundation, the beneficiaries served or the effective fulfilment of the foundation's purposes. In short, as Rúa (2010, 222) also points out, it is possible that the progressive increase in information obligations has not served to increase the transparency of the information on these entities "but is an accumulation of information, which is occasionally disjointed, very complicated in the way it is prepared and not very useful to its users".

At the same time, the debate on transparency goes beyond the purely legal and refers to the accountability obligations covered under the Foundations Act. The information filed in the Foundations Register is accessible to the public, but as consequence of their mission, foundations and non-profit entities "must convey information to society on their purposes and activities and be accountable to their donors and beneficiaries, on how they manage their resources. Equally, citizens must be informed because they contribute towards their funding, sometimes directly, by contributions, and sometimes indirectly, as foundations enjoy tax benefits and occasionally receive State subsidies. Despite the system of obligations already set out by Law, the self-regulatory phenomenon which we referred to in the previous section on the governance of a foundation is progressively extending to the foundation sector, as a way of promoting transparency and the uptake of best practices.[14] Also the website – www.fundaciones.es – built up by the Spanish Associations of Foundations collects information from all foundations, through the information collected from the sector and supervisory authorities.

13.4 The Savings Banks, Origin, Legal Nature and the Current Process of Transformation: *Special Nature Foundations and Banking Foundations*

The process of restructuring the Savings Banks began in Spain in 2009. These are bodies which are deeply rooted in our country, although they started later here than their European counterparts. Savings banks are defined as foundation-based, non--profit, credit institutions with a social and charitable function; they do not depend on another physical or legal person and are dedicated to attracting, administering and investing the savings placed in their trust. The Constitutional Court, in their ruling of 22 March 1988, highlighted the different nature of savings banks compared to foundations and other credit institutions, irrespective of a description, which due to their structure as legal persons and the largely credit-based nature of their activity might be more appropriate for them. Savings banks are obliged by law to develop programmes of a social, charitable, welfare or cultural nature to protect and help grass-roots needs, to which they must devote all surpluses which do not have to be applied to reserves by legal mandate or allocated to voluntary reserves.

The transformation process of savings banks began in 2009, undertaken much later than the Italian process. It was imposed due to the structural limitations associated with the nature of Savings Banks (*Cajas*), but was accelerated due to the current financial crisis. This process started with the passing of Royal Decree Act 9/2009, of 26 June, and was the start of a major process of integration between various savings banks, changing the map of this sector in Spain. A short while afterwards Royal Decree Act 11/2010, of 9 July, was passed, which opened up the possibility for Savings Banks to undertake their activity via a bank and thus gain access to capital markets. Royal Decree Act 2/2011, of 18 February, launched the third phase of the restructuring process of the Savings Banks.

[14] The *Compromiso Empresarial* foundation: www.fundacioncompromisoempresarial.com has some useful guides and reports which might help foundations on this path. It tackles aspects such as the evaluation of results ("from good intentions to impact"), the definition of mission, and it has even performed research studies on the transparency of Spanish foundations analysing the information they convey via their websites: Martín Cavanna, Construir confianza 2010. *Impulsando la transparencia en la Web de las fundaciones españolas* (Building confidence 2010. Driving transparency on the websites of Spanish foundations).

For many years the *Lealtad* foundation, www.fundacionlealtad.org, has been studying the transparency and best practice of NGOs which volunteer to be the subject of analysis, in order to provide information to potential donors.

Article 5 of Royal Decree Act 11/2010, on government bodies and other aspects of the legal system for savings banks, introduced the possibility of savings banks to engage in their financial activity indirectly. According to this rule savings banks have three options: (a) to remain as savings banks, (b) to become foundations which have at least 50 % of the bank's shares or (c) to remain as credit entities but transfer all their financial assets to a bank, controlling a minimum of 50 % of the capital.

Article 6 of this Royal Decree regulates on so-called special nature foundations, foundations which may be created in three cases, voluntarily by giving up the authorisation to act as a credit institution or in other provisions for withdrawal of authorisation. As mentioned, they must as a consequence lose 50 % of their rights to vote in the bank created for the purpose of transferring their financial assets. They must also become special nature foundations, in the event of the savings bank's intervention in cases provided for in the Act on Discipline and Intervention of Credit Institutions. Savings banks which form part of the so-called SIPS (Institutional Protection Systems), a mechanism for the protection of credit institutions which some savings banks have subscribed to, representing a contractual agreement between various credit institutions whereby they establish a mutual solvency and liquidity commitment, may also agree to become special nature foundations, under the voluntary or compulsory assumptions.

Special nature foundations shall be created by transferring all the patrimony attached to their financial activity to another credit institution in return for shares in that institution. In accordance with the rule, the foundation shall centre their activity to devoting and developing their social and charitable work, for which they may undertake the management of the share portfolio. The foundation must allocate the product of their funds, shares and investments which make up their patrimony to their social and charitable purpose. Subsidiarily, they may undertake activity to promote financial education. The agreement to become a special nature foundation is subject to meeting the requirements for setting up a foundation and means the Savings bank transforms into a special nature foundation. The separation of financial activity, in turn, shall be governed by Act 3/2009 of 3 April, on structural modifications to business corporations.

This legislation has been overcome by Act 26/2013 of 27 December, on Savings Banks and Banking Foundations. According to this regulation, are considered as banking foundations those that hold almost 10 % of the shares of a bank, or have the right to designate a member of the board in the bank, regardless of their origin. Special nature foundations will be transformed into "ordinary" foundations or banking foundations, depending on the shares that they hold, if they do, but other savings banks still existing, under certain conditions, are also obliged to be transformed into banking foundations or ordinary foundations. Moreover, private foundations that fulfil these requirements – more than 10 % of the capital of a bank or right to designate an administrator – have also to be transformed, which could represent, in some opinions, an infringement of the right of Foundations, as far as the new banking foundations are a new figure created by legal imperative while ordinary foundations are private institutions. The banking foundations have a special regulation in the Act 26/2013, which states a different supervisory system and some requirements on good governance practices. Act 50/2002 of Foundations is applied subsidiarily.

13.5 Tax Law

The objective of this section is not an in-depth analysis of the tax regime for foundations in Spain or of the problems which arise from a legal or administrative point of view with the application of current regulations. Some problems have already been noted, when they cannot be disassociated from the substantive rules on foundations. However, we do make a broad-brush reflection of the reforms needed to the Spanish foundation sector.

The requirements for access to the special tax system are some of the most critical issues in the current regime. Act 49/2002, defining these requirements, of course, started with those covered under substantive rules, adapting one system to the other. However, there are a great many issues to do with the substantive system which were not taken into consideration and which could currently even be considered to be contrary to the tax system. Furthermore, some of these tax requirements are also substantive in areas which might be undergoing development by the Autonomous Regions, for example, in the area of the allocation of income and revenue. In addition, tax requirements are naturally a subject for interpretation by the tax Administration, although on an increasingly regional basis separate to the substantive rules, without taking into account that foundations are not entities which are exempt from all control. It should be borne in mind that being covered under the special tax system means being considered an entity which benefits from sponsorship, meaning that incentives do not apply unless requirements are fulfilled.

Some improvements to the taxation of some financial activities are also necessary, as not all those undertaken by foundations are included in the list of activities which are exempt. Some technical improvements are also needed to in the area of local taxation. As outlined, Act 49/2002 provides for the automatic application of exemptions subject to the fulfilment of certain conditions. However, in practice, many of the exemptions in local taxation have really become exemptions upon request. Certain amendments to the Local Taxation Act (*Ley de Haciendas Locales*) are also necessary to adapt some of the exemptions which it provides for any taxable person, to foundations.

VAT is a critical issue in the taxation of foundations, a tax for which foundations are considered end consumers and the structure of which is difficult to adapt to the nature of these entities, decreasing the resources that they allocate for general interest purposes or increasing the price of their services to the end user. The possibility needs to be examined of national refund systems, already in use in other countries, although this is not an optimal solution. At the same time the initiatives underway at a European level need to be looked at for an overall analysis of how VAT operates, focussing on the situation of non-profit entities which, as acknowledged, were not taken into account when the Sixth Directive was drawn up, or to study VAT and how it applies to public entities in relation to exemptions of a social nature.

Another issue raised in our country with regard to VAT – although not in relation to the tax itself – refers to the consideration of this tax in public procurement procedures, when tenderers who are exempt and tenderers who are not exempt from VAT are bidding. Foundations are exempt from VAT in rendering certain services of a social, sports or cultural nature; therefore, their bid does not include this tax, compared to corporate entities who present their bids including VAT. This is not necessarily an advantage for foundations, as not charging the Administration VAT in this case; they cannot deduct the VAT charged. Companies that charge VAT can however deduct the VAT charged and make it neutral. On the issue of how to determine the most financially beneficial bid when tenderers who are exempt and those who are not exempt are bidding, the *Junta Consultiva de Contratación Administrativa del MEH* (Consultancy Board for Administrative Contracting of the Ministry for Economic Affairs and Finances) concluded that VAT should be excluded. However should the Administration, following this criteria, award the contract to a corporate entity whose bid did not include VAT, they would pay the tax charged to them equally without being able to deduct it, as the Administration has a VAT system which is similar to that of non-profit entities. After many proposals from the sector, the additional provision of the Sustainable Economy Act established that the government would draw up a report within 3 months analysing the possibility, within the framework of community legislation, of including VAT in the price of public contracting procedures, when tenderers who are exempt from the tax are bidding, in particular entities from the third sector, bearing in mind the principle of awarding services to the bid which is financially most advantageous for the public administration and the other principles which should govern public contracting. This is a relevant issue not only for the entities but also for the Administration in the current climate of reducing public spending and outsourcing certain services. It is therefore necessary to push for this report to be drawn up, as it would have repercussions for all Administrations.

However the sponsorship system definitely requires improvement. The Act of 2002 did not imply progress in terms of tax incentives for sponsorship, falling far short of incentives provided in other countries. This improvement would help to encourage the participation of citizens and companies in engaging in general interest activities in the different fields in which foundations operate. The aim of awarding tax benefits to those who collaborate with non-profit entities by donations or contributions with no consideration of any type is to promote the general interest activities they undertake and the participation of civil society in these activities. Improved applicable deduction percentages, currently at 25 % for physical persons and 35 % for legal persons, would clearly result in the increased collaboration of individuals and companies, as has been demonstrated in France, where the increase in deduction percentages to 60 % and 66 % on Corporation Tax and Personal Income Tax has resulted in a clear increase in collaboration. Far from considering sponsorship incentives a waste of public resources, it should be acknowledged that the cost of donations goes towards serving the general interest activities undertaken by the private non-profit sector, activities which otherwise would have to be covered by the public sector or they would not be served and would no longer contribute towards social welfare. In some cases the contribution of donors, and therefore their effort, is greater than that of the Public Treasury, as for some the deduction rate is lower than that of taxation. In other cases the deduction is not an effort for the Public Treasury finances as the donations exceed the amounts which can be deducted and therefore incentives are limited.

The deduction percentages which apply to donors and the deduction limits need to be increased, and some of the concepts included in the current Act need to be improved, including collaborative business agreements for general interest activities, sponsorship in kind or priority sponsorship. Priority sponsorship activities, set every year in the General State Budget, beyond any general deductions, are a way of promoting certain general interest activities, which may include cultural activities. However, in recent years the priority activities covered under General State Budgets principally refer to programmes which have been developed either by public entities or private entities but with public funding, therefore not contributing towards the promotion of private initiative in activities of general interest. These activities also need to be given stability as, because they are set annually, some programmes are not receiving continuity or financial support. Furthermore, it would be desirable for the sector to play a part in defining them.

Bibliography

Blázquez Lidoy, A. 2011. Asociaciones que realizan explotaciones económicas: ¿Pueden ser de utilidad pública y gozar de beneficios fiscales?. *Revista de Contabilidad y Tributación. CEF* (340): 39–50.

Caffarena Laporta, J. 2009. Las Fundaciones: fines de interés general, beneficiarios y cláusulas de reversión. *Anuario de Derecho de Fundaciones*: 29–51.

Cazorla, Prieto., and A. Blázquez Lidoy. 2011. Requisitos de acceso al régimen fiscal especial. In *Fundaciones. Problemas actuales y reforma legal*, Cazorla Prieto and others, 16–31. Siero: Fundación María Cristina Masaveu Peterson.

Falcón Tella, R. 2005. Las SIMCAV y el abuso de las facultades de autotutela de la Hacienda Pública. *Quincena Fiscal* 15.

Galindo Martín, M.A., J.J. Rubio Guerrero, y S. Sosvilla Rivero. 2012. *El Sector Fundacional en España. Atributos Fundamentales (2008–2009),* Asociación Española de Fundaciones –INAEF.

García-Andrade Gómez, J. 2001. Algunas acotaciones al concepto formal de fundación en la Constitución Española. *Revista Española de Administración Pública* 155: 107–145.

García-Andrade Gómez, J. 2005. Objeto y alcance de la Ley de Fundaciones. Concepto de Fundación. In *Comentarios a las Leyes de Fundaciones y de Mecenazgo,* Muñoz Machado, S., M. Cruz Amorós, y R. Lorenzo García de, Iustel, 12–62.

García de Enterría, E. 1992. Constitución, Fundaciones y Sociedad civil. In *Las Fundaciones y la Sociedad Civil*, dirs., de Lorenzo García, R., y M. de Cabra de Luna. Madrid: Civitas.

García de Enterría, E. 1996. Una nota sobre el interés general como concepto jurídico indeterminado. *Revista Española de Derecho Administrativo* 89.

Moreno Cea, F. 2010. El Derecho de Fundaciones de Madrid. In *Tratado de Fundaciones*, dirs., de Lorenzo, R., J. L. Piñar, T. Sanjurjo, Thomson-Reuters 587–611.

Peñalosa Esteban, I., y T. Sanjurjo González. 2010. Órgano de gobierno y relación con los poderes públicos. In *Tratado de Fundaciones,* dirs., de Lorenzo R., J.L. Piñar, T. Sanjurjo, Thomson-Reuters 195–250.

Pérez Escolar, M. 2008. *La actividad económica de las fundaciones, Tensiones legislativas e Interés General*. Madrid: Thomson Civitas.

Petitbó Juan, A., y Marcos., Hernández. 2009. La gestión de los recursos económicos de las fundaciones. Anuario de Derecho de Fundaciones, Iustel. Asociación Española de Fundaciones, 59–93.

Rey García, M., y L.I. Álvarez González. 2011. El sector fundacional español. Datos básicos, INAEF.

Rúa Alonso de Corrales, E. 2010. Las cuentas anuales y otros documentos obligatorios de información de las fundaciones. *Anuario de Derecho de Fundaciones*: 221–255.

Chapter 14
Foundation Law in Switzerland: Overview and Current Developments in Civil and Tax Law

Dominique Jakob and Goran Studen

14.1 Permitted Legal Forms for Nonprofit Activities Under Swiss Law

14.1.1 Legal Forms for Nonprofit Organisations in Switzerland

As opposed to the law of obligations where the parties, in principle, are free to enter into a broad range of arrangements and contracts (so-called freedom of contract/ private autonomy), the Swiss corporate law provides only for a limited number of licit forms (so-called compulsory form), the contents of which are restricted (so-called fixed form).

The parties may choose between ten legal entities specified by federal statutory law: a simple partnership [*einfache Gesellschaft*] (art. 530 et seqq.) *BG betreffend die Ergänzung des Schweizerischen Zivilgesetzbuches (Fünfter Teil: Obligationenrecht)* (OR, Federal Act of 30 March 1911 on the Amendment of the Swiss Civil Code (Part Five: The Code of Obligations), SR 220), a general partnership [*Kollektivgesellschaft*] (art. 552 et seqq. OR), a limited partnership [*Kommanditgesellschaft*] (art. 594 et seqq. OR), a company limited by shares [*Aktiengesellschaft*] (art. 620 et seqq. OR), a partnership limited by shares [*Kommandit-Aktiengesellschaft*] (art. 764 et seqq. OR), a limited liability company [*Gesellschaft mit*

D. Jakob (✉)
Center for Foundation Law, University of Zurich, Treichlerstrasse 10, CH-8032 Zurich, Switzerland

University of Zurich, Zurich, Switzerland
e-mail: dominique.jakob@rwi.uzh.ch; http://www.rwi.uzh.ch/jakob; http://www.zentrum-stiftungsrecht.uzh.ch

G. Studen
University of Zurich, Freiestrasse 15, CH-8032 Zurich, Switzerland
e-mail: goran.studen@rwi.uzh.ch; http://www.studenlegalservices.com

C. Prele (ed.), *Developments in Foundation Law in Europe*, Ius Gentium: Comparative Perspectives on Law and Justice 39, DOI 10.1007/978-94-017-9069-7_14,

beschränkter Haftung] (art. 772 et seqq. OR), a cooperative [*Genossenschaft*] (art. 828 et seqq. OR), an association [*Verein*] (art. 60 et seqq. *Schweizersiches Zivilgesetzbuch)* (ZGB = Swiss Civil Code of 10 December 1907, SR 210) and, as a recent development, the investment company with variable capital [*Investmentgesellschaft mit variablem Kapital*] (art. 36 *BG über die kollektiven Kapitalanlagen)* (KAG = Swiss Federal Act of 23 June 2006 on Collective Investment Schemes, SR 951.31) as well as the limited partnership for collective capital investments [*Kommanditgesellschaft für kollektive Kapitalanlagen*] (art. 7 KAG).

Outside the scope of corporate law, foundations are of great significance in the Swiss nonprofit sector. Foundations under the Swiss law are institutional in nature without members or owners and characterised by assets dedicated to serve a specific purpose (Jakob 2006, 49).

14.1.2 Embodiment Pursuant to the Civil Law and Tax Status

In contrast to other legal systems, the Swiss law strictly separates an organisation's form under the civil law and its tax status. The legal form (e.g. association or foundation) is based purely on the criteria laid down in civil law. Hence, an entity does not qualify for example, a as foundation based merely on nonprofit activities it carries out or its compliance with certain (tax) criteria. Its legal status as a foundation depends rather on the compliance with the formation requirements applicable to foundations (art. 80 et seqq. ZGB). The tax law is relevant on a different level: it determines whether or not a selected legal form is a nonprofit entity which can be granted nonprofit status for tax purposes thereby being eligible for tax privileges.

The choice of the specific legal form for a nonprofit organisation is based on numerous reasons. The association [*Verein*], the foundation [*Stiftung*] and the cooperative [*Genossenschaft*] are typically legal forms selected to carry out nonprofit activities. The company limited by shares [*Aktiengesellschaft*] and the limited liability company [*Gesellschaft mit beschränkter Haftung*] with a nonprofit purpose are other possible legal forms.

A formal exemption from Direct Federal and State Taxes is generally possible irrespective of the legal form of the entity or corporate body in question (art. 56 lit. g) *BG über die direkte Bundessteuer* (DBG = Swiss Federal Act of 14 December 1990 on the Direct Federal Tax, SR 642.11).[1] However, certain legal forms are better suited than others for the pursuit of tax-exempt purposes.

[1] For tax aspects, see below.

14.2 Legal Framework for Foundations

Due to its favourable legal and fiscal conditions Switzerland is often referred to as a "paradise" for foundations and founders. The total number of foundations in Switzerland cannot be quantified exactly since family and ecclesiastical foundations are currently not required to be registered in the commercial register. In addition, the quantity of dependent foundations [*unselbständige Stiftungen*] is unknown due to the fact that these forms of foundations are neither obliged nor eligible to be registered in the commercial register. As regards the 17,431 foundations that had been registered as of 1 January 2014, it has to be differentiated between nonprofit foundations and for-profit entities. Excluding employee benefits schemes established in the form of foundations (see below), some 12,900 *conventional* or *ordinary* entities remain that are structured as genuine nonprofit foundations (Eckhardt et al. 2014, 4).

As regards the positioning of the Swiss foundation sector within the broader European perspective, the motion of State Council Werner Luginbühl from 20th March 2009 with its explicit aim of "raising the attractiveness of the Swiss Foundation Landscape" deserves particular attention. Against the background of recently implemented additional tax privileges in other countries (for instance, Germany), the motion argued in support of a modification of general fiscal conditions in Switzerland in line with its neighbouring countries (Jakob 2009, 47). However, the Swiss Federal Council discussed the motion in 2013.

14.2.1 Legal Basis and Types of Foundations

General

The provisions regarding foundations set forth in the ZGB (art. 80-89a ZGB) are based on the "conventional/ordinary" foundation which, by being entered into the commercial register, achieves the right of personality, is supervised by the state and not subject to any elaborate special laws. In addition to ordinary foundation there are special forms of foundations, including ecclesiastical foundations (art. 87 ZGB), employee benefits schemes established in the form of foundations (art. 89a ZGB, art. 331, 331a-f, 361, 362, 673, 674 para. 3 OR) and asset foundations (art. 53g-k BVG), all of which are subject to certain specific regulations. The employee benefits schemes foundations ("pension funds") offer social security to employees of private employers. They are of great practical significance for the financial security of employees and an addition to the basic state insurances for retirement (AHV) and disability (IV). The asset foundations also play an important role in the field of social security as they serve the collective investment and management of employer security company funds. Despite its important practical function and relevance, the asset foundation was not codified until the recent structural amendment of the *BG über die berufliche Alters-, Hinterlassenen und Invalidenvorsorge* (BVG = Swiss Federal Act of 25 June 1982 on Occupational Old-age, Survivors' and Invalidity Insurance, SR 831.40).[2]

Family Foundations

The family foundation (art. 335 ZGB) deserves special attention: it is a foundation serving private purposes and neither required to be registered in the commercial register nor subjected to state supervision. Pursuant to art. 335 para. 1 ZGB, this type of foundation may only be established to defray the costs of upbringing, to endow or support family members or for similar purposes. Under Swiss law, a family foundation must not be established for purposes of mere financial alimony or – a fortiori – for luxury. This restriction is based on the statutory prohibition of the establishment of entailed family estates [*Familienfideikommisse*] pursuant to art. 335 para. 2 ZGB. The Swiss Federal Court has held, however, that art. 335 para. 2 ZGB is not to be considered a mandatory provision of Swiss law within the meaning of art. 18 IPRG (*loi d'application immediate*) as regards foreign family foundations, thus removing a long-lasting legal uncertainty. As a consequence, foreign legal entities are admissible in Switzerland even if they are in conflict with art. 335 para. 2 ZGB (Jakob et al. 2010, 860; Jakob 2008b, 539).

Corporate Foundations

Furthermore, company-affiliated or corporate foundations [*unternehmensverbundene Stiftungen, Unternehmensstiftungen*] which are neither regulated nor mentioned in the Swiss foundation law are a very common feature in practice. Corporate foundations exist in two forms: directly supporting foundations and holding foundations. *Directly supporting foundations* [*Direktträgerstiftungen*] have a long-lasting tradition in Switzerland as entities providing social services by means of operating hospitals, schools, care centres, foster homes, etc. In addition to this type of corporate foundations, holding foundations have emerged over the past few decades. The latter are foundations holding a significant share in a corporation which operates a commercial business. The legitimacy of corporate foundations has long been controversial insofar as they pursue an economic purpose (Riemer 2001, 517). This controversy has been settled by a landmark decision in 2001 when the Federal Court argued in support of the legitimacy of corporate foundations pursuing an economic purpose (Jakob 2006).[3]

---

[2] BBl 2010, 2017 et seqq.

[3] BGE 127 II 337 et seqq.

Dependent Foundations and Trusts

A general distinction has to be made between independent foundations with own legal personality and so-called dependent foundations [*unselbständige Stiftungen*]. A dependent foundation is not a legal person, but comprises special funds transferred by the founder and permanently linked to a specific purpose (Jakob 2012, 10–11, 2006, 81). The special funds are usually based on a free endowment (donation, legacy/heritage, bequest) and can be held in trust or administered subject to certain provisions laid down by the parties involved. Dependent foundations are currently gaining momentum in Switzerland in the context of so-called umbrella foundations [*Dachstiftungen*] (Studen 2011).

No matter how the dependent foundation is structured (i.e. either as a *trust model* or a *donation on condition*), its main characteristics are separate earmarked assets for a special purpose linked to a third person. In this regard, the Swiss private law does not provide any specific norms. Therefore, the relevant substantive law (law of donation, inheritance law) has to be consulted to answer any existing questions of law. Some authors call for an analogous application of the provisions on (independent) foundations as defined in the Civil Code (ZGB) in case of remaining gaps in the relevant law (Riemer 2001, 511), whereas others argue in favour of a more nuanced approach (Studen 2011, 109).

Trusts as the Anglo-Saxon variety of dependent foundations are often used as devices for estate and tax planning, asset protection as well as charitable purposes.[4] As is the case in most of the civil law countries in continental Europe, the Swiss legislator has not yet implemented the instrument of the trust into national law. However, the Hague Convention of the Law Applicable to Trusts and on their Recognition of 1 July 1985 became effective in Switzerland on 1 July 2007. As a consequence, trusts established in other jurisdictions are recognised under Swiss law as a foreign legal form sui generis (Jakob and Picht 2010, 856; Jakob and Gauthey Ladner 2008, 453–458).

Public Law Foundations

Finally, public law foundations have to be mentioned. This particular form of foundation is subject to federal and cantonal public law, pursuant to art. 59 para. 1 ZGB. In most cases the establishment of public law foundations is based on individual legislative acts (Hürlimann-kanp and Schmid 2010, 277).

---

[4] For a general comparison of charitable trusts and foundations in Switzerland, see Edgar H. Paltzer and Patrick Schmutz, "Switzerland: are charitable trusts an alternative to charitable foundations?", Trusts & Trustees (2008), 357–368.

14.2.2 *Definition of the Foundation*

General

The Swiss law does not provide for a definition of the notion of foundation in art. 80 et seqq. ZGB. According to art. 80 ZGB, a foundation is established by the endowment of assets for a particular purpose. Based on this a foundation can be described as an independent pool of assets provided with legal personality dedicated to a particular purpose (Hausheer and Aebi-Müller 2008, 346). The term foundation under Swiss law therefore includes the following characteristics (Jakob 2006, 38): the intention to establish a foundation, a purpose, assets and an organisation (which can also be appointed following the establishment).

Within the system of legal persons under the Swiss private law the foundation is considered an institution (art. 52 ZGB); hence, it is the only non-corporate legal person under the Swiss nonprofit law.

Purpose

The founder is generally free to determine the purpose of the foundation (so-called freedom to establish a foundation) (Jakob 2012). However, general limits laid down in law must be observed in the process of the formulation of the purpose. In particular, the selected purpose must neither violate the compulsory law nor fundamental moral values (Grüninger 2010). A foundation may have a public benefit, a solely private or even a mixed purpose [*gemischte Zwecksetzung*], but cannot be of a self-serving nature (no *foundation for the founder* or a *self-purpose foundation*). Foundations serving political purposes are allowed within the general restrictions.

Assets

The law does not stipulate requirements as regards the nature of the dedicated assets. As a consequence, the founder can provide the foundation with a plethora of assets-including real estate, cash, intellectual property, securities, claims against third parties or even claims against the founder personally.[5] A preceding factual transfer from the founder to the foundation is not required since the existence of a commitment under the law of obligations to transfer the assets is considered sufficient.

The founder is also free in determining the scope of the assets. However, the foundation has to be provided with sufficient assets to fulfil its intended purpose (so-called means-ends relation [*Zweck-Mittel-Relation*]). According to the practice adopted by the Federal Foundation Supervisory Authority, the initial capital must

[5] BGE 99 II 261 et seqq.

be at least CHF 50,000 which, strictly speaking, contradicts the freedom of the founder. If the foundation has been established initially with a smaller capital amount, the founder has to provide evidence indicating the receipt of additional sufficient funds after the formation. If the foundation's assets prove to be insufficient in relation to its purpose, art. 83d para. 2 ZGB applies analogously, thus enabling the supervisory authority to transfer those assets to another foundation pursuing the same or a similar purpose.

Organisation

The foundation's governing bodies as well as the type and method of administration are specified by the foundation deed or charter (art. 83 para. 1 ZGB). The founder may provide further details, instructions or rules regarding the organisation by means of written regulations; this procedure may facilitate certain alterations or modifications of the organisational structure if deemed necessary.[6] In any case, a foundation requires a supreme body which ensures the foundation's legal capacity and which is responsible for its management and representation.

According to art. 55 ZGB, the foundation acquires rights and obligations by the concluding transactions of its governing body which may consist of one or several natural or legal persons. The governing body is often referred to as a foundation council [*Stiftungsrat*], foundation board of directors [*Stiftungsvorstand*], foundation commission [*Stiftungskommission*] or board of trustees of the foundation [*Stiftungskuratorium*] (Hausheer and Aebi-Müller 2008, 353).

Art. 83a ZGB provides for a general accounting obligation. Pursuant to art. 83b ZGB, foundations are also obliged to appoint external auditors.

Other organs are optional and often exist as controlling bodies or internal advisory boards. Furthermore, the management of the foundation may be subdivided, for instance, by the installation of a committee accompanying the executive board.[7]

Subsequent organisational modifications are permitted by way of an exception pursuant to art. 85 ZGB where such a step is urgently required in order to preserve the foundation's assets or safeguard the pursuit of its purpose.

14.2.3 Formation

Foundations acquire legal personality upon their entry in the commercial register (art. 52 para. 1 and art. 81 para. 2 ZGB, art. 94 HRegV; so-called registry or normative system). Apart from its effect of publicity, the entry in the commercial

[6] BGE 76 I 77.

[7] BGE 120 II 137 et seqq., 141.

register also has a constitutive effect.[8] Prior to the entry, the foundation may obtain the legal position of an unborn child [*Nasciturus*] (art. 31 para. 2 ZGB). Public law, family and ecclesiastical foundations are currently not required to be entered in the commercial register to obtain legal personality (art. 52 para. 2 ZGB). In these cases, a voluntary entry has solely declaratory effect.

The actual endowment transaction [*Stiftungsgeschäft*] – the act of dedicating assets – is a unilateral legal transaction not requiring acknowledgement. The desired legal effect is achieved by the mere declaration of intent expressed by the founder. The foundation deed requires the following information (Hausheer and Aebi-Müller 2008, 349): the intention to establish an independent foundation, the identification of the assets to be dedicated as well as the description and formulation of the foundation's purpose.

As for the rest, the founder is free to set up, structure and organise the foundation virtually at his or her own discretion. It is admissible to establish a foundation in a legal transaction inter vivos (art. 81 para. 1 ZGB) or by testamentary disposition (art. 81 para. 1 in conjunction with art. 493 para. 1 ZGB). Ever since the revision of the law on foundations of 8 October 2004,[9] the founder is also permitted – contrary to a previous view expressed by the Swiss Federal Court[10] – to establish a foundation by way of a contract of inheritance.

14.2.4 Supervision

Foundations, as the only legal entity under Swiss private law, are generally subject to supervision by a state authority (art. 84 para. 1 ZGB). The existence of a state supervision is the reverse side of the fact that foundations, as opposed to other legal entities, do not have owners or members and therefore as such lack the *natural* internal control mechanism.

The main objective of the supervision is to monitor the foundation in order to ensure that it carries out its activities in accordance with its purpose and the will of the founder. Therefore, the supervisory authority has to make sure that the foundation's organs do not act illegally or immorally or take any decisions and conclude transactions in breach of the foundation deed or the written regulations. In this context, the supervisory authority is entitled to give appropriate binding instructions to the foundation's bodies and to sanction any committed misconduct.[11] The legal relationship between the foundation and the supervisory authority is subject to public law as the latter is exercising public authority (Hürlimann-kanp and Schmid 2010, 283). Article 84 para. 1 ZGB deals with issues of competence and stipulates

[8] BGE 120 II 137, 141.

[9] AS 2005, 4545.

[10] BGE 96 II 273.

[11] BGE 108 II 497, 499.

that foundations are supervised by the state authority to which they are assigned (Confederation, Canton or Commune). In this regard, the foundation's purpose and the local sphere of its activities are essential: the competence lies with the state community that would be responsible for the activity in question in the hypothetical case of non-existence of the foundation.[12]

If the foundation's purpose and activities are of significance throughout Switzerland, the Confederation is the competent supervisory authority. On this federal level, nonprofit foundations are supervised by the General Secretariat of the Federal Department of Home Affairs (art. 3 para. 2 lit. a *Organisationsverordnung für das Eidgenössische Departement des Innern (OV-EDI = Organisational Ordinance for the Federal Department of Home Affairs)*).

Pursuant to art. 84 para. 1bis ZGB, the Cantons may subject foundations at communal level to supervision at cantonal level. The internal cantonal competence of the supervisory authorities is regulated by the cantonal introductory laws to the ZGB. For instance, pursuant to Section 34 para. 1 number 2 EG ZGB of the canton Zurich, the municipal council is responsible for the supervision of foundations which by virtue of their nature or purpose belong to the municipality of Zurich. Corresponding provisions apply to the supervision exercised by the district and cantonal councils within their respective area of regional competence (Section 37 and Section 44 para. 2 number 12 EG ZGB of the canton Zurich). The cantonal supervisory authorities have been reorganised as a consequence of the structural amendment of the BVG (Jakob et al. 2011, 47).

Judicature and doctrine draw a distinction between preventive (pre-emptive) and repressive (restoring) supervisory measures. Preventive supervisory measures are, inter alia, guidelines and requirements in respect of the investment of assets as well as obligations on the governing body to report annually and to submit foundation regulations, including any modifications thereto. The repressive means are intended to remedy the consequences of mistakes made by the foundation organs. Potential repressive measures include, inter alia, reminders, warnings, reprimands, revocations of decisions made by the foundation's organs, substitute measures, fines, criminal complaints and in serious cases even the removal of the foundation's board members. The competence to dismiss board members is mandatory and cannot be excluded by way of a contrary will of the founder.[13] However, as regards discretionary decisions of the foundation organs, the supervisory authority is limited to review only their legality; as a result, questions of usefulness or expedience of board decisions are excluded from scrutiny. Furthermore, the supervisory authority must always apply the principle of proportionality when implementing supervisory measures.[14]

Art. 83d ZGB provides for a special provision if the foundation's system of organisation proves inadequate, if the foundation lacks one of the prescribed

[12] BGE 120 II 374.

[13] Judgement of the Swiss Federal Court of 19 January 2009, case 5A_274/2008.

[14] Hans Michael Riemer, *Personenrecht des ZGB* (Bern: Stämpfli Verlag, 2002), 272.

governing bodies or if one such body is not lawfully constituted. In these cases, the supervisory authority must take the necessary measures which may include in particular: setting a time limit within which the foundation must restore the legally required situation, appointing the body which is lacking or appointing an administrator at the foundation's cost. According to case law, the board of trustees may only be dismissed as a last resort and merely if the behaviour in question constitutes a breach of law or if it does not comply with the foundation's regulatory framework or its purpose. In addition, the use of the foundation's assets for its intended purposes must be affected or at risk and other less severe measures must prove to be less promising. It is not necessary, however, to establish culpable conduct of the board.[15]

Finally, the supervisory authority may change the organisational structure of the foundation (art. 85 ZGB) or modify its purpose in order to promote the founder's actual will and his intentions (art. 86 ZGB).

14.2.5 Change of Purpose and Organisational Modifications

A foundation does not have a will of its own in the legal sense. Instead, it is the first and foremost task of the foundation's governing body to administer the will of the founder as stipulated in the foundation deed. It goes without saying, however, that even the most diligent founder is not able to anticipate all future events: facts and circumstances which were considered to be essential at the time of the establishment of the foundation may have changed or the organisational structure may become outdated and obsolete over time.

Therefore, pursuant to art. 85 ZGB modifications of a foundation's organisation are permitted as an exception provided that the reorganisation is urgently required in order to preserve the foundation's assets or to safeguard the pursuit of its purpose. In addition, the supervisory authority may amend the objects (purposes) of the foundation according to art. 86 ZGB if they have altered in significance or effect to such an extent that the foundation has plainly become estranged from the founder's intentions. In both cases, the competence for the implementation of the relevant modifications lies with a special federal or cantonal authority (as set forth in art. 85 and art. 86 para. 1 ZGB). Whereas changes of the foundation's organisation are possible only at the request of the supervisory authority with the board merely being heard, modifications of the foundation's purpose can be requested both by the supervisory authority and since January 2006 also by the governing board of the foundation.[16]

---

[15] BGE 105 II 321, 326.

[16] Dominique Jakob "Das neue Stiftungsrecht der Schweiz", *Recht der Internationalen Wirtschaft* (2005): 675.

Since this revision of the foundation law, a simplified procedure exists for minor or insignificant changes of the foundation's purpose as well as minor organisational modifications (art. 86b ZGB). Finally, art. 86a ZGB was introduced: the founder himself may request a change of the foundation's purpose provided (i) that the foundation deed reserves the right to change the purpose and (ii) that at least 10 years have elapsed since the foundation was established or since the last alteration requested by the founder. If the foundation pursues a public or charitable purpose (and therefore benefits from tax exemption), the altered purpose must likewise be public or charitable. The right to change the foundation's purpose is neither transferable nor heritable and, in case of a legal entity as founder, expires at the latest 20 years after the establishment of the foundation. The implementation of art. 86a ZGB was both politically and dogmatically controversial because, strictly speaking, it contravenes the underlying separation principle as regards the founder and the foundation [*Trennungsprinzip*] – traditionally one of the pillars of the Swiss foundation law.[17]

14.2.6 Dissolution and Merger of Foundations

A foundation is bound by the will of the founder, and therefore, as opposed to corporations, it cannot dissolve itself. The dissolution of a foundation under Swiss law requires specific circumstances.

The competent federal or cantonal authority may dissolve a foundation on application or of its own accord if the foundation's purpose has become unattainable and cannot be maintained by modifying the foundation deed or if its purpose has become unlawful or immoral (art. 88 para. 1 ZGB). Any interested party may file an application or bring an action for the dissolution of the foundation (art. 89 ZGB).

The law on foundations does not provide a special provision for the distribution of assets and the liquidation procedure, thus the general provisions laid down in art. 57 and 58 ZGB apply, the latter of which refers to the provisions governing cooperatives and companies limited by shares (art. 913 OR; art. 736 et seqq. OR).

In 2003, foundations have been provided with the possibility to merge and to transfer assets pursuant to art. 78–87 *BG über Fusion, Spaltung, Umwandlung und Vermögensübertragung* (FusG = Swiss Federal Act of 3 October 2003 on Merger, De-merger, Conversion and Transfer of Assets, SR 221.301). However, foundations are still neither allowed to demerge nor to change their legal form by way of transformation. A merger is permitted only if it is objectively justified and, in particular, if it is aimed at preserving and achieving the foundation's objectives

[17] For details, see Dominique Jakob, in Dominique Jakob and Andrea Büchler (ed.), Commentary Civil Code, art. 86a ZGB. Dominique Jakob, "Das Stiftungsrecht der Schweiz im Europa des dritten Jahrtausends", *Schweizerische Juristen-Zeitung* (2008a: 536).

(art. 78 para. 2 FusG). The merger agreement is concluded between the supreme governing bodies of the foundations involved and is subject to the approval of the competent supervisory authority (art. 79 para. 1 and art. 83 FusG). The merger must not alienate the purpose of the foundation and, where applicable, has to comply with the requirements regarding a change of purpose set forth in art. 86 ZGB (art. 78 para. 2 FusG).

In addition to a merger, foundations may transfer all or part of their assets and liabilities to other legal entities (art. 86 and 87 FusG), with the aforementioned provision of art. 78 para. 2 FusG applying accordingly.

14.3 Duty to Audit

14.3.1 General

The regulations on auditing and auditors are essentially covered by the legal provisions governing companies limited by shares and the new Federal Act of 16 December 2005 on the Admission and Oversight of Auditors (Audit Oversight Act, AOA). The AOA implements an admission procedure for all natural persons and agencies providing auditing services. The auditing supervisory authority examines whether the applicant complies with the statutory requirements (art. 2 lit. a and art. 3 et seqq. AOA).

The substantive auditing provisions are set forth in the section of the Code of Obligations regarding companies limited by shares. These regulations apply equally to other legal entities that are subject to auditing.

14.3.2 Foundation

Accounting

The audit is closely connected to the obligation to keep accounts. The governing body of the foundation has to keep business records in accordance with the regulations pertaining to commercial accounting as set forth in the Code of Obligations (art. 83a para. 1 ZGB). If the foundation conducts a commercial operation in pursuit of its purpose, the provisions of the Code of Obligations on accounting and the presentation of annual financial statements apply mutatis mutandis (art. 83a para. 2 ZGB). This provision can be justified by the increased interest of the foundation's beneficiaries, creditors and donors in respect of the use of funds in case of a commercial business activity.[18]

[18] Dominique Jakob, *Verein – Stiftung – Trust: Entwicklungen 2007* (Bern: Stämpfli Verlag, 2008b, 62).

As far as the accounting is concerned, the regulations as set forth in art. 958 et seqq. OR apply. Art. 83a ZGB in conjunction with art. 957 para. 2 OR provides that foundations which are not required to appoint an auditor only have to keep records about their income, expenses and assets – an alleviation especially for smaller foundations.[19]

Audit

Art. 83b ZGB stipulates the general obligation to appoint auditors. The obligation to conduct audits is subject to exceptions: family and ecclesiastical foundations are generally excluded (art. 87 para. 1bis ZGB). Secondly, the supervisory authority may exempt a foundation from the duty to appoint external auditors pursuant to art. 83b para. 2 ZGB in conjunction with the according bylaw (so-called opting-out) if the foundation has minor assets (total assets of less than CHF 200,000 in two consecutive business years) and if it does not publicly call for donations. However, the waiver of the obligation to conduct audits does not exempt the foundation from its general obligation to give account to the supervisory authority. Exempt foundations may – voluntarily – conduct an audit in three different ways: in a limited version, as an ordinary (full) audit as well as an audit which does not strictly follow statutory regulations (so-called opting-in, art. 83b para. 4 ZGB).

As regards the substantive law, art. 83b para. 3 ZGB refers to the provisions of the Code of Obligations on external auditors for public limited companies. As a consequence, a foundation is subject to an ordinary audit if it exceeds two of the following parameters in two consecutive business years: total assets of CHF 20 million, revenue of CHF 40 million and an annual average of 250 full-time employees (art. 727 para. 1 No. 2 and 727b para. 2 OR in conjunction with art. 83b para. 3 ZGB). If these limits are not exceeded, the foundation is subject to a limited audit of its annual financial statements (art. 727a and 727c OR in connection with art. 83b para. 3 ZGB). Therefore, foundations are at least subject to a limited audit.

A specific feature of the Swiss foundation law is the ability of the supervisory authority to demand an ordinary audit from foundations which in fact are subject to a limited audit if this is considered necessary to reliably assess both the financial and profit situation of the foundation in question (art. 83b para. 4 ZGB). Finally, according to art. 83c ZGB, the auditors must provide the supervisory authority with a copy of the audit report and all important communications with the foundation.

---

[19] Message Regarding the Amendment of the Code of Obligations; BBl 2008, 1589, 1738 et seqq.

14.4 Liability

The main difference between communities under law (such as the partnership) and corporations is that in the latter case only the legal entity is liable for its debts. Likewise, a foundation with its institutional nature is liable for its obligations essentially with all of its assets.

14.4.1 Liability Under the Law on Foundations

Liability of Foundations

As has already been pointed out, the Swiss foundation is a legal entity acting through its governing body. The governing body binds the legal entity vis-à-vis third parties by concluding transactions as well as by their other actions (art. 55 para. 1 and 2 ZGB). The foundation is liable to third parties with its assets for any obligations resulting from the actions of its governing body.

Liability of the Board Members

Swiss foundation law does not provide a specific basis for the liability of the foundation's organs. The appointed board members are thus liable according to the general provisions. The organs may be liable internally (as regards the liability to the foundation) both in contract and tort (art. 41 et seqq. OR) while externally (as regards the liability to beneficiaries and third parties) only in tort (art. 55 para. 3 ZGB in conjunction with art. 41 et seqq. OR).

In case of a person who regularly acts on behalf of the foundation without being officially appointed as the foundation's organ (so-called factual organ [*faktisches Organ*]), the individual may be internally (in view of the foundation) liable both as an agent without authority (art. 419 et seqq. OR) and under the law of tort (art. 41 et seqq. OR). Externally (as regards the liability to beneficiaries and third parties) the factual organ is only liable in tort (art. 55 para. 3 ZGB in connection with art. 41 et seqq. OR).

Internal Relationship

In general, a board member is appointed by contract (the so-called organ agreement [*Organträgervertrag*]). This agreement sui generis is mainly based on the provisions on employment law and agency contracts. The board member is liable if actual losses or damages occurred as a result of his breach of contract; furthermore, liability requires fault on the tortfeasor's part and a sufficient causal link between the infringement and the damage. The relevant standard of care is defined in art. 321e para. 2 OR. This is the case even if it is assumed that agency contract law applies in general because art. 391 para. 1 OR refers to the provisions on employment law (Lanter 2001).

Art. 419 and 420 OR constitute the basis for the internal liability of the factual organ. The general principles of liability in contract apply equally to factual organs, and, as a result, the same standard of care is applicable to both the factual organ and an appointed board member.

External Relationship

Externally, the foundation is liable with all its assets to third parties. Additionally, the acting board members may personally be liable for their wrongful acts (art. 55 para. 3 ZGB) (Huguenin 2010).

As regards the external relationship, the question arises whether or not the beneficiaries may raise a claim directly against the board members, for example in case of a culpably caused decrease in the foundation's assets diminishing or eliminating the beneficiaries' entitlements to benefits. In Switzerland, the beneficiaries do not have the right of action to the benefit of the foundation in the meaning of an *actio pro fundatione*. In addition, beneficiaries do not have claims under the foundation law against board members because the contract between the individual board member and the foundation has no third-party effect. The foundation law in Switzerland lacks a provision extending the contractual relationship between the organs and the foundation to third parties; furthermore, the special provisions on companies limited by shares and cooperatives are not applied analogously. A contract for the benefit of a third party is, in theory, possible but has no significance in practice (Jakob 2006, 259). As a consequence, there is no contractual liability of the board members towards beneficiaries. As far as a non-contractual liability is concerned, it has to be differentiated between direct and indirect damages. The beneficiary may assert a claim pursuant to art. 55 para. 3 ZGB in conjunction with art. 41 OR only in case of direct damages or losses (Jakob 2006, 260).

14.4.2 Excursus: Failure to Comply with the Obligation to Pay Social Contributions

Additional legal provisions may provide the basis for the organs' liability in special circumstances. For example, the personal and joint liability as regards outstanding social insurance contributions is based on the general legal liability of employers pursuant to art. 52 *BG über die Alters- und Hinterlassenenversicherung* (AHVG = Swiss Federal Act of 20 December 1946 on Old-age and Surviving Dependants Insurance, SR 831.10).

14.5 Tax Aspects

14.5.1 General Information on the Swiss Tax System

In Switzerland, the Confederation on the one hand and the Cantons and Municipalities on the other hand levy taxes on the income of natural persons and the profit of legal entities. Furthermore, on a cantonal and municipal level, natural persons are subject to property taxation, whereas legal persons have to pay capital taxes.

The tax law governing nonprofit organisations is laid down in the *BG über die direkte Bundessteuer* (DBG = Swiss Federal Act of 14 December 1990 on the Direct Federal Tax, SR 642.11) as well as the Federal Act on the Harmonization of Direct Taxes of Cantons and Communities *BG über die Harmonisierung der direkten Steuern der Kantone und Gemeinden* (StHG = Swiss Federal Act of 14 December 1990 on the Harmonization of Direct Taxes of Cantons and Communities, SR 642.14). However, those regulations are sparse and require further interpretation. Therefore, the Swiss Federal Tax Administration released the circular letter no. 12 of 8 July 1994 on the tax exemption of legal persons that pursue public, charitable or educational and cultural purposes and regarding the tax deductibility of donations. This circular letter essentially lays down the long-standing practice adopted by the Swiss Federal Court with regard to the tax exemption of nonprofit legal persons under the law of direct federal taxes. However, the circular letter is non-binding for the tax authorities (Koller 2007, 443).

In addition, most Cantons levy an inheritance and gift tax, although federal law does not impose an obligation for the introduction of such taxes. Several Cantons that originally imposed these taxes have abolished them over the past few years in order to strengthen their competitive position.

Furthermore, the Confederation has the exclusive competence to impose a value-added tax *BG über die Mehrwertsteuer* (MWSTG = Federal Act of 12 June 2009 on Value Added Tax, SR 641.20), a withholding tax (VStG) as well as stamp duties on transactions and certain securities (StG).

By and large, the practice is of substantial importance in the field of nonprofit tax law. This is a result of the fact that the tax privileges for nonprofit organisations as well as the law governing donations and contributions provide only for a rudimentary regulatory framework (Koller 2007, 444).

14.5.2 Status of a Tax-Privileged Organisation

General

With regard to direct taxes, the same principles apply to both direct tax advantages of organisations and indirect tax advantages of donors by means of tax deductibility. Donations to a tax-exempt nonprofit organisation may – up to a certain extent – be deducted from the donor's income or profit tax provided that the nonprofit organisation has its registered office in Switzerland. On the other hand, nonprofit organisations with registered offices outside Switzerland benefit from direct tax advantages in the form of exemptions from the tax on profit and the cantonal taxes on capital. Thus, the legal situation of foreign foundations carrying out activities in Switzerland corresponds to the legal practice adopted in the STAUFFER case.[20] The ECJ ruled that the exclusion of foreign legal entities from tax privileges for nonprofit organisations under German tax law and, as a consequence, the differential treatment of resident and non-resident charitable foundations constitutes a breach of the free movement of capital as set forth in art. 63 of the Treaty on the Functioning of the European Union. This problem does not arise, however, in the context of indirect taxes (e.g. value-added tax, inheritance and gift tax) (Koller 2007, 447).

Requirements for a Tax Exemption of Legal Persons

Pursuant to art. 56 lit. g DBG, legal persons which pursue public or charitable purposes are exempt from taxes on profits that are exclusively and irrevocably dedicated to such purposes. The same applies accordingly to cantonal taxes on profits and capital (art. 23 para. 1 lit. f StHG).

Nonprofit Purpose

Direct Taxes

Both the Federal Act on the Direct Federal Tax (DBG) and the Federal Act on the Harmonization of Direct Taxes of Cantons and Communities (StHG) use the undefined legal concept of *public benefit* [*Gemeinnützigkeit*] in their respective formulation of the requirements for tax exemptions. The relevant provisions (art. 56 lit. g DBG and art. 23 para. 1 lit. f StHG) correspond to a large extent. The difference is merely that the provisions of the StHG cover both the exemption from taxes on profits as well as capital since the Cantons, contrary to the Confederation, impose capital taxes on legal persons.

The Federal Tax Administration defines the term *public benefit* in its circular no. 12 of the year 1994 in greater detail. The circular letter stipulates two cumulative requirements that must be met in order to qualify for tax advantages. On the one hand, the activities of the organisation in question must be in the general public interest; additionally, the activities must be of an *altruistic* or *selfless* [*uneigennützig*] character.

---

[20] Judgement of the ECJ of 14 September 2006, case C-386/04.

The relevant public opinion is decisive in answering the question whether or not an activity is in the general public interest. The common good may be promoted by activities in charitable, humanitarian, health-promoting, ecological, educational, scientific and cultural areas.[21] The circular letter no. 12 expressly mentions as examples social care, art and science, education, the promotion of human rights, the protection of the environment, homeland and animals, as well as development aid. The public benefit is determined by the overall opinion and view of the society.[22] Furthermore, the circular letter no. 12 requires the class of beneficiaries to be open; as a consequence, distributions must not be restricted, for instance, to members of a certain family, association or profession.[23]

An activity is considered to be of a selfless nature if it is neither linked to the economic and personal interest of the legal person nor its members and/or affiliated persons.[24] According to the case law of the Swiss Federal Court, a nonprofit organisation and its employees have to make sacrifices for the sake of the greater public good.[25] This must be reflected in the remuneration of the governing body of the nonprofit organisation. The members of the governing body are generally supposed to carry out their activities on a voluntary basis and can be reimbursed only for their expenses. Board members can be remunerated, however, for extraordinarily performed tasks outside the conventional scope of the governing body.[26] As a general rule, an activity is not seen as being selfless or altruistic if the organisation is carrying out commercial activities-unless such activity is subordinate to a nonprofit purpose. The business activity may only have an auxiliary function and as such must not be the sole economic basis of the legal person.[27] In the case of equity investments, the nonprofit purpose of the organisation must have priority over the preservation of the company; this requires the organisation to be financially supported by substantial funding from its company as well as the actual use of those funds for nonprofit activities (Koller 2007, 453–454).

The general public interest is by no means limited to purely domestic activities. Therefore, a legal person that is not active in Switzerland, but in another country or throughout the world, may also be exempted from Swiss taxes provided that its activities correspond – from a Swiss perspective – with the general public interest. The actual realisation of such purposes must be evidenced with appropriate documentation, such as annual reports or annual financial statements. The requirements on the verification are stricter if the purposes and objectives of the organisation are

[21] Circular letter number 12, no. II. 3. (a).

[22] BGE 114 Ib 277, 279.

[23] Circular letter number 12, no. II. 3. (a); cf. judgement of the Swiss Federal Court of 2 February 2009, case 25_592/2008.

[24] BGE 114 Ib 277.

[25] BGE 113 Ib 7, 9 et seqq.

[26] Cf. practice instructions of 18 January 2008 of the association of Swiss Tax Authorities (SSK), 39 et seqq.

[27] BGE in ASA vol. 19, 328 et seqq.

pursued abroad compared to a purely domestic activity.[28] Legal entities with registered offices abroad are equally exempted from Swiss taxes if they, in principle, are subject to taxes in Switzerland because of a sufficient connecting factor, for instance, as a property owner in Switzerland (Koller 2007, 455).[29]

Value-Added Tax

The revised value-added tax law (MWSTG) entered into force on 1 January 2010. As was the case under the previous statutory provisions, nonprofit organisations with annual revenues up to a figure of CHF 150,000 are generally exempted from tax liability (art. 10 para. 2 lit. c MWSTG). In addition, certain revenues of nonprofit organisations are exempted from the value-added tax (art. 21 no. 12, no. 13, no. 17 and no. 27 MWSTG). As for the definition of nonprofit organisations, art. 3 lit. j MWSTG refers to art. 56 lit. g. DBG and therefore requires the exclusive and irrevocable pursuit of public and nonprofit purposes. According to art. 18 para. 2 lit. a and lit. d MWSTG, donations and subventions are not regarded as a compensation and are thereby excluded from the scope of the value-added tax. Under the new value-added tax law, the receipt of donations – in contrast to the receipt of subventions – does not give rise to a pro rata pre-tax deduction (art. 33 MWSTG). Finally, pursuant to art. 37 para. 5 MWSTG associations and foundations are able to make use of the flat-rate tax method (Jakob 2009, 506; Jakob et al. 2009, 9 seqq.).

Inheritance and Gift Taxes

The Cantons have the exclusive competence to regulate and levy inheritance and gift taxes. Donations made to nonprofit organisations are often exempted from those taxes. Due to their cantonal character, the different tax laws lack a uniform definition of the requirements for a tax exemption based on public benefit.

Immovable Property Gains Tax

The exclusive competence to introduce and regulate immovable property gains taxes lies equally with the Cantons. However, the federal provision of art. 23 para. 4 StHG stipulates the obligation to impose immovable property gains taxes on legal entities which are otherwise exempt from taxes. As a result, a foundation which exclusively pursues nonprofit purposes and therefore has the status of a tax-exempt organisation is nevertheless obliged to pay immovable property gains taxes in case of a sale of its real estate at a profit.

[28] Circular letter number 12, no. II. 3. (a). For details on the administrative requirements in practice, see Harold Grüninger, "Stiftungsstandort Schweiz – für Europa attraktiv?", *Stiftung & Sponsoring* (2008a), 28.

[29] Practice instructions of 18 January 2008 of the association of Swiss Tax Authorities (SSK), 17 et seqq.

Public Purpose

In addition to the tax exemption based on nonprofit purposes, both the DBG and the StHG provide for a tax exemption for legal entities that pursue public purposes. According to circular letter no. 12, the notion of public purposes covers only a limited scope of activities which – in contrast to nonprofit purposes – have to be closely related to public tasks and which do not require any sacrifices from the organisation or its employees (Koller 2007, 454–455).[30]

The term "public purpose" is interpreted restrictively. For instance, even though the existence of political parties is vital for the functioning of a democratic society, a party itself does not pursue a public purpose; it rather canalizes, focuses and represents the interests of its members. Thus, a political party is not considered as an organisation eligible to receive the tax-exempt status under Swiss law (Scherrer and Greter 2007, 33).[31]

Legal Entity

General

In principle, legal entities are subject to taxation (art. 49 lit. a and b DBG). This applies on the basis of personal affiliation if the legal entity's registered office or its actual administration is located in Switzerland resp. in a Canton (art. 20 para. 1 StHG, art. 50 DBG). The registered office (so-called principal fiscal domicile) is the place determined as such in the articles of incorporation or an equivalent decision by the competent body. The legal person is fully taxable at its principal fiscal domicile with a view to any income and property which is not subject to taxation in another fiscal domicile due to a special statutory regulation or a bilateral tax treaty (Scherrer and Greter 2007).

The exemption from such tax liability is set forth in art. 56 DBG. Art. 56 lit. g DBG requires the nonprofit activities to be carried out by a legal person. Natural persons may not demand tax exemption for assets reserved for nonprofit purposes even in case of guarantees providing that the assets in question will not be used for any other purposes at a later date (Koller 2007, 445). Legal persons who dedicate only a portion of their funds exclusively and irrevocably for nonprofit or public purposes may be eligible for a partial tax exemption provided that their tax-exempt activity is an essential activity and that their accounting provides for a clear separation of the tax-exempt funds from other assets and income.[32]

[30] Circular number 12, no. II. 4.

[31] Circular number 12, no. II. 4.

[32] Circular letter number 12, no. II. 5.; so-called segment accounting [*Spartenrechnung*].

Some specific regulations exist for the different legal entities. In theory, any legal person may qualify for a nonprofit status, but some legal entities raise issues due to the relevant provisions under the civil law.

Foundation

Foundations as well must "*pursue public or nonprofit purposes*" (art. 56 lit. g sentence 1 DGB) in order to benefit from tax privileges. For this reason family foundations – contrary to ecclesiastical foundations (art. 56 lit. h DBG, art. 23 para. 1 lit. g StHG) and employee benefits schemes foundations (art. 56 lit. e DBG, art. 23 para. 1 lit. d StHG) – are not exempt from taxes (although a partial tax exemption is possible in the case of a mixed/combined purpose). A corporate foundation is considered nonprofit provided that the interest in maintaining the company serves a nonprofit purpose and if the foundation does not carry out management activities (art. 56 lit. g sentence 2 and 3 DBG, art. 23 para. 1 lit. f sentence 2 and 3 StHG).

The Swiss foundation law does not explicitly stipulate a non-distribution constraint. However, this restriction for tax-exempt foundations is a result of the notion of public benefit. Additionally, the practice regarding the compensation of leading organs can be seen as a Swiss manifestation of the non-distribution constraint.

Excursus: Pursuit of Educational and Cultural Purposes

Apart from public and nonprofit purposes, the pursuit of educational and cultural purposes qualifies for exemption from taxes (art. 23 para. 1 lit. g StHG; art. 56 lit. h DBG). The pursuit of educational and cultural purposes does not require the activities in question to be selfless and altruistic (Scherrer and Greter 2007, 38 et seqq.).

The notion of "educational and cultural purposes" lacks a legal definition, but it is derived from the constitutional freedom of religion and conscience set forth in art. 15 para. 1 *Bundesverfassung der Schweizerischen Eidgenossenschaft* (BV = Federal Constitution of the Swiss Confederation of 18 April 1999, SR 101). The judicature of the Swiss Federal Court regarding the definition of this concept is rather casuistic.[33] According to the circular letter,[34] a legal entity is considered to pursue educational and cultural purposes that are eligible for tax privileges if it maintains and promotes a common belief – irrespective of the confession or religion in question – by means of lessons and through church services throughout Switzerland.

---

[33] BGE 107 Ia 126, 130.

[34] Circular letter number 12, no. III. 2.

14.5.3 *Taxation of Organisations Eligible for Tax Privileges*

General

Nonprofit organisations are basically exempt from profit taxes on the federal level and from profit and capital taxes on the cantonal level provided that the relevant requirements are met. As a result, income dedicated to nonprofit purposes (e.g. donations) is not subject to taxes. This may lead to problems of demarcation.

Questions of Demarcation

As regards foundations, it is particularly questionable how to treat the income which originates from asset management (a) as well as special purpose and commercial business activities (b).

Asset Management

Nonprofit organisations do not have to pay profit taxes on capital interest, dividend income, etc. On the other hand, income from capital shares in companies is only exempted from taxes if the organisation's interest in maintaining and preserving the company serves a nonprofit purpose.[35]

Special Purpose Business and Commercial Business

A special purpose business is an entity that carries out economic activities which are indispensable for the realisation of the organisation's purpose (e.g. an approved school operates a training workshop). In this case, the profits made from special purpose businesses are exempted from taxes. Supporting businesses that are clearly subordinate to the nonprofit purpose are permitted (e.g. kiosk at a museum). In principal, the same applies to other commercial businesses: profit-making activities do not change the nonprofit character of an organisation as long as they are subordinate to the overall organisational activities (Koller 2007, 464 seqq.).

14.5.4 *Excursus: Stamp Duty Law*

In practice, the Stamp Duty Law is primarily important for cooperatives. A so-called emission duty is imposed on the preservation or increase of the nominal

---

[35] Circular letter number 12, no. II. 3. (c).

value (against payment or cost-free) of ownership rights in the form of shares in a cooperative, stocks, contributions in limited liability companies, etc. (art. 5 para. 1 lit. a StG).

14.5.5 Taxation of the Founder and the Donor

Deductions for Voluntary Contributions

Voluntary Contributions (Donations)

Donations within the meaning of tax law are voluntary contributions of money or other assets to legal entities with their registered office in Switzerland which are exempt from taxes based on their public or nonprofit purposes (art. 56 lit. g DBG) (art. 33a DBG, art. 9 para. 2 lit. i StHG). Endowments and additional funding are also included.

Natural Persons

The income tax law allows natural persons certain socio-politically motivated deductions (e.g. donations, alimony and support payments under the family law), a complete list of which is provided by the law (art. 9 para. 2 StHG, art. 33 DBG). Article 33a DBG, which is in force since 1 January 2006, also includes the above-mentioned voluntary contributions. Monetary contributions as well as contributions in kind from CHF 100.00 or more per fiscal year made by natural persons are deductible from their income, whereas the maximum deductible amount is 20 % of the taxable income decreased by certain expenditures (art. 26–33 DBG resp. art. 33a DBG).

However, membership fees paid to associations are not included in the list and are therefore considered nondeductible living expenses in terms of art. 34 lit. a DBG. Since an association is entitled to receive membership fees as defined in the articles of association, their payment is not considered a voluntary contribution under civil law which would be deductible according to art. 9 para. 2 lit. i StHG and/or art. 33a DBG – even if it is an association that is exempted from taxes due to its benefit to the public or its pursuit of a public purpose (Scherrer and Greter 2007, 89).[36]

The Cantons specify independently the maximum deduction allowed under the cantonal and municipal tax laws (art. 9 para. 2 lit. i and art. 25 para. 1 lit. c StHG).

[36] Circular letter number 12, no. IV. 1. (a).

Legal Persons

With reference to legal persons, the federal tax law provides that voluntary contributions of money and other assets to nonprofit legal entities with their registered office in Switzerland are deductible from the taxable net profit as business expenses in the amount of up to 20 % of the net profit (art. 59 para. 1 lit. c DGB). The contributions may not be deducted when determining the net profit.[37]

Special Topics

Differentiation Between Donation and Sponsorship

Contrary to donations, sponsorship contributions serve advertising purposes. They are intended to maintain a company's public reputation in contradistinction to the commercially oriented business activities.[38] Therefore, sponsorship contributions are not tax deductible according to art. 33a DBG. In some cases, the demarcation between deductible donations and nondeductible sponsorship contributions proves to be difficult. It is worth looking at the value-added tax law which differentiates between donations and sponsorship contributions as follows:

The value-added tax is payable on the tax payers' revenues resulting from the supply of goods and services within Switzerland unless such revenues are explicitly exempted from the value-added tax (art. 18 in connection with art. 21 MWSTG). Therefore, the so-called exchange of services relationship is at the core of the taxable object. A characteristic is the internal economic connection. The service is provided quid pro quo (Boschung and Reding 2006, 783). As a result, it is considered a sponsorship contribution within the meaning of the value-added tax law if the recipient receives services in return,[39] while a donation is the provision of money or noncash benefits without receiving any reward in return. Donations are so-called non-revenues which are not subject to the value-added tax.[40]

In the past, the differentiation between nonprofit donations and taxable sponsorship contributions was made pursuant to art. 33 aMWSTG (in force from 1 January 2006 to 31 December 2009). According to this provision, nonprofit organisations did not perform a service in return if they mentioned the name of the contributor once or repeatedly in a neutral form or if they used the logo or the firm's trade name in publications (art. 33 aMWSTG). On the other hand, advertising performances such as adverts in magazines, posters and clothes as well as loudspeaker announcements mentioning the firm or individual referring to its or his business or

---

[37] Circular letter number 12, no. IV. 1. (b).

[38] BGE 115 Ib 111, 118.

[39] BGE 126 II 443, 459.

[40] German Boschung and Roland Reding, "MWST und neues Stiftungsrecht", *Der Schweizer Treuhänder* (2006): 783.

professional activity were qualified as a service in return (Koller 2007, 468; Jakob 2005, 676). Under the new law, art. 18 para. 2 lit. d MWSTG stipulates explicitly that donations are not considered as a remuneration due to the lack of service in return and therefore are excluded from the scope of the MWSTG. Art. 3 lit. i MWSTG defines the term donation as a voluntary contribution without the expectation of a service in return. This also applies to contributions which are mentioned in a publication (once or repeatedly) in a neutral form, even if the firm's trade name or logo is used. The above-mentioned differentiation between nonprofit donations and taxable sponsorship contributions still exists under the new law.[41]

Deductibility of Donations Made Abroad

The law clearly provides that the receiving organisation must have its registered office in Switzerland (art. 33a and art. 59 para. 1 lit. c DBG; art. 9 para. 2 lit. i and art. 25 para. 1 lit. c StHG). Donations made to organisations with their registered office abroad are not deductible from direct taxes. The same applies in practice – despite the contrary view of the legal doctrine (Luuk et al. 2009, 499) – to donations made to Swiss business premises of foreign nonprofit organisations.[42]

This regulation's compliance with European law is – unlike the tax benefits applicable to nonprofit organisations which do not require an organisation's registered office to be located in Switzerland – questionable in the light of the judgements of the ECJ in the cases of STAUFFER[43] and PERSCHE.[44] However, there is no direct impact for Switzerland as it is not a member of the EU.[45]

14.5.6 Procedure

A nonprofit organisation may request a general tax exemption order from the competent tax authority outside the regular taxation procedure (Koller 2007, 473). The tax authority may review the issued order at any time.

It is, therefore, the duty and responsibility of the tax authorities to check whether or not an organisation (still) meets the material conditions necessary for a tax exemption. Foundations are subject to additional supervision by the administrative

[41] For details, see the informational letter MWST-Info 05 "Subventionen und Spenden" of the EStV from January 2010.

[42] See the practice instructions of 18 January 2008 of the association of Swiss Tax Authorities (SSK), 18.

[43] Judgement of the ECJ of 14 September 2006, case C-386/04.

[44] Judgement of the ECJ of 27 January 2009, case C-318/07.

[45] As regards the development of European nonprofit law and the currently debated draft of a supranational "European Foundation", see Dominique Jakob and Goran Studen, "Die European Foundation – Phantom oder Zukunft des europäischen Stiftungsrechts?" (2010): 61–107.

unit (Confederation, Cantons, Municipality) which they have the closest ties with according to their nature and purpose (art. 84 para 1 ZGB). However, the competent supervisory authority is not responsible for tax matters and thus cannot make any decision about a possible tax exemption of a foundation based on its nonprofit status; as a consequence, the supervisory authorities do not check whether the foundation in question and its activities fulfil all the necessary tax requirements for granting an exemption.

14.6 Corporate Governance and Nonprofit Organisations

14.6.1 General

In practice, associations and foundations are the main legal entities for the pursuit of non-commercial (ideal) purposes in Switzerland. In contrast to the regulations regarding for-profit entities under the Code of Obligations (in particular, the company limited by shares), the statutory provisions on associations and foundations in the Civil Code (art. 60–89 ZGB) are – intentionally – broad due to their concept of providing legal instruments for the pursuit of ideal and thus non-commercial purposes. With the exception of accounting and audit, the parties involved (association members, founders) are given wide room for manoeuvre (Riemer 2006, 513) which corresponds with the autonomy of associations and the freedom of the founder.

However, since a couple of years the sector increasingly faces the trend to apply corporate governance principles to nonprofit organisations (foundation or nonprofit governance). This has led to joint projects of relevant (umbrella) organisations in order to create codes providing certain conduct guidelines.

14.6.2 Developments

The above-mentioned development is reflected in the Swiss foundation practice which considers implementing corporate governance rules in the sense of foundation governance (Jakob 2006, 528 et seqq.; Sprecher 2010). Considerable results have already been achieved as regards the codification of conduct guidelines: The Swiss Foundation Code of the Association of Swiss Foundations, published on 25 October 2005, is specifically designed for foundations and includes recommendations and guidance. Furthermore, the Swiss NPO Code of the Conference of Presidents of Large Humanitarian and Relief Organisations dated 31 March 2006 is generally applicable to all nonprofit organisations and introduces the principle comply or explain.

Despite early scepticism in literature (Riemer 2006, 513), these regulations – which are based largely on voluntary implementation and participation – are gaining significance in practice and certainly promote both transparency and good governance in the nonprofit sector (Jakob 2008b, 119).

Additional points that can be subsumed under the term corporate governance include:

Measures in the event of over-indebtedness and insolvency: The reform act of 8 October 2004 already enshrined the principle of creditor protection in the Swiss foundation law (art. 84a ZGB). Where there are grounds for concern that the foundation is over-indebted or will no longer be able to meet its obligations in the longer term, its governing body must draw up an interim balance sheet at liquidation values and submit it to the external auditors. If the foundation has no external auditors, the governing body must submit the interim balance sheet to the supervisory authority which will take the appropriate and necessary measures.

Costs of management and administration: Foundations have to – either directly or indirectly – use all of its funds to fulfil their purposes. A foundation may lose its nonprofit status if it utilises less than 50 % of its funds for the tax-privileged purpose. Although it is quite difficult to compare different foundations in regard to their respective ratios of total expenses and management costs, it may be – as a rule of thumb – assumed that management costs below 10 % of the total expenses are considered low and as such do not cause problems; costs of 10–20 % are generally considered appropriate (Lang and Schnieper 2007, 143 et seqq.).

Bibliography

Boschung, G., and R. Reding. 2006. MWST und neues Stiftungsrecht. *Der Schweizer Treuhänder* 10: 783–789.

Christen, C. 2005. Ein Überblick: Rechtsformen von Nonprofit-Organisationen. *Verbands-Management* 2: 50–61.

Eckhardt, B., D. Jakob, and G. von Schnwsbein. 2014. Der Schweizes Stiftungsreport.

Grüninger, H. 2008a. Stiftungsstandort Schweiz – für Europa attraktiv?. *Stiftung & Sponsoring* 4: 26–27.

Grüninger, H. 2008b. Aktuelles aus dem Stiftungs- und Gemeinnützigkeitsbereich – neue Stiftungen, Literatur, Entscheide. *Successio* 1: 55–63.

Grüninger, H. 2010. art. 80–89bis, 335 and 349–359 ZGB. In *Basel commentary, civil code I: art. 1–456 ZGB*, 4th ed, ed. Honsell Heinrich, Nedim Peter Vogt, and Thomas Geiser. Basel/Geneva/Munich: Helbing Lichtenhahn Verlag.

Grüninger, H. 2013. Aktuelles aus dem Stiftungs- und Gemeinnützigkeitsbereich. *successio*: 116–127.

Hausheer, H., and R.E. Aebi-Müller. 2008. *Das Personenrecht des Schweizerischen Zivilgesetzbuches*, 3rd edn. Bern: Stämpfli.

Huguenin, C. 2010. art. 27, 52–59 ZGB. In *Basel Commentary, Civil Code I: art. 1–456 ZGB*, eds. Heinrich Honsell, Nedim Peter Vogt, Thomas Geiser, 4th edn. Basel/Geneva/Munich: Helbing & Lichtenhahn.

Hürlimann-Kaup, B., and J. Schmid. 2010. *Einleitungsastikel des ZGB und Personenrecht*. Zurich: Schulthess.

Jakob, D. 2005. Das neue Stiftungsrecht der Schweiz. *Recht der Internationalen Wirtschaft – RIW* 9: 669–678.
Jakob, D. 2006. *Schutz der Stiftung*. Tübingen: Mow Siebeck.
Jakob, D. 2008a. Das Stiftungsrecht der Schweiz im Europa des dritten Jahrtausends. *Schweizerische Juristen-Zeitung* 104(22): 533–542.
Jakob, D. 2008b. *Verein – Stiftung – Trust: Entwicklungen 2007*. Bern: Stämpfli.
Jakob, D. 2009. Entwicklungen im Vereins – und Stiftungsrecht. *Schweizerische Juristen-Zeitung* 105(21): 505–508.
Jakob, D. 2012. Vor Art. 80–89a Z6B. In *Commentary civil code*, ed. Jakob, D., and A. Büchler. Basel: Helbing & Lichtenhahn.
Jakob, D., and D. Gauthey Ladner. 2008. Die Implementierung des Haager Trust Übereinkommens in der Schweiz. Praxis des Internationalen Privat- und Verfahrensrechts – *IPRax*, 453–458.
Jakob, D., and P. Picht. 2010. Der trust in der Schweizer Nachlassplanung und Vermögensgestaltung. *Aktuelle Juristische Praxis – AJP* 7: 855–886.
Jakob, D., and G. Studen. 2010. Die European Foundation – Phantom oder Zukunft des europäischen Stiftungsrechts? *Zeitschrift für das gesamte Handelsrecht und Wirtschaftsrecht – ZHR* 174: 61–107.
Jakob, D., L. Schweizer, and G. Studen. 2009. *Verein – Stiftung – Trust: Entwicklungen 2008*. Bern: Stämpfli.
Jakob, D., L. Schweizer, and G. Studen. 2010. *Verein – Stiftung – Trust: Entwicklungen 2009*. Bern: Stämpfli.
Jakob, D., K. Messmer, P. Picht, and G. Studen. 2011. *Verein – Stiftung – Trust: Entwicklungen 2010*. Bern: Stämpfli.
Koller, T. 2007. Gemeinnützigkeits- und Spendenrecht in der Schweiz. In *Spenden- und Gemeinnützigkeitsrecht in Europa*, ed. R.W. Walz, L. von Auer, and T. von Hippel. Tübingen: Mow Siebeck.
Lang, N., and P. Schnieper. 2007. *Professionelles Management von Stiftungen*. Basel: Helbing & Lichtenhahn.
Lanter, M. 2001. Stiftungen und Verantwortlichkeit (Haftung). In *Die Stiftung in der juristischen und wirtschaftlichen Praxis*, ed. H.M. Riemer. Zurich: Schulthess.
Luuk, J.O., S. Oesterhelt, and M. Winzap. 2009. EuGH Report 2/09. Steuer Revue, 497–510.
Paltzer, E.H., and P. Schmutz. 2008. Switzerland: Are charitable trusts an alternative to charitable foundations? *Trusts & Trustees* 14(5): 357–368.
Riemer, H.M. 2001. Stiftungen im schweizerischen Recht. In *Stiftungsrecht in Europa*, ed. Hopt K. J., and D. Reuter. Cologne: Carl Heymann
Riemer, H.M. 2002. *Personenrecht des ZGB*, 2nd ed. Bern: Stämpfli.
Riemer, H.M. 2006. Corporate Governance-Richtlinien für Vereine und Stiftungen aus juristischer Sicht. *Schweizerische Juristen-Zeitung* 102: 513–516.
Scherrer, U., and M. Greter. 2007. *Der Verein in der Praxis – Organisation und Steuern*. Zurich: Schulthess.
Sprecher, T. 2010. Was ist und was leistet Foundation Governance?. *Jusletter*. v. 27. 04. 2010. 1–30.
Studen, G. 2011. *Die Dachstiftung*. Zürich/Basel: Helbing & Lichtenhahn.

About the Authors

Dr. Oonagh B. Breen is a Senior Lecturer at the Sutherland School of Law, University College Dublin. A graduate of UCD and Yale Law School and a qualified barrister, her teaching and research focuses on matters relating to comparative charity law and policy. She has published extensively in the fields of charity regulation and reform both nationally and internationally. Oonagh is a member of the European Law Institute's Working Group on the Statement on the European Foundation Statute and previously served as an Advisory Group member to this project.

Isabelle Combes began her career in 1985 with Bureau Francis Lefebvre before joining White and Case (Paris office) as a lawyer specialized in tax and property right issues. Since 2005, she is the legal manager of the Fondation de France, and is a member of the European Foundation centre's Legal Committee.

Zoltán Csehi, Prof. Dr., is a Hungarian citizen and Professor of Private and Commercial Law. He did his Habilitation and Ph.D. at the ELTE University Budapest; LL.M. (legum magister) at the University of Heidelberg; Dr. jur., Budapest; and M.A. (art history), Budapest. Positions held by him include: Chair of the Private and Commercial Law Department, Faculty of Law, Pázmány Péter Catholic University, Budapest; Member of the Drafting Committee of the new Civil Code of Hungary, 2010–2012; and Research Professor of Humboldt-Foundation, Germany, University Cologne, Institut für internationales und ausländisches Privatrecht, 2006. His membership in professional bodies include: President of the Hungarian-German's Lawyers Society, as of 2012; Secretary, Private Law Committee of the Hungarian Academy of Sciences, as of 2012; and Member of the Budapest Bar. His publications in legal sciences include: 5 books, more than 20 publications in foreign language and more than 70 publications in Hungarian.

Alison Dunn is a Senior Lecturer in Law at Newcastle University, UK. Her research specialises in the field of charity law and the regulation of civil society, focusing in particular upon the legal responses to political participation and policy

C. Prele (ed.), *Developments in Foundation Law in Europe*, Ius Gentium: Comparative Perspectives on Law and Justice 39, DOI 10.1007/978-94-017-9069-7,

formation. She has published widely in this field; see http://www.ncl.ac.uk/nuls/staff/profile/alison.dunn#tab_publications. The research for her chapter was completed with the aid of an award from the Arts and Humanities Research Council.

Rui Hermenegildo Gonçalves is Legal Counsel of the Calouste Gulbenkian Foundation and Deputy Director of the Office of the President of the same institution, in Lisbon. He has a Law degree from the Law Faculty of the University of Coimbra and he is currently finishing his Ph.D. in Law at New University of Lisbon. He has published several articles about foundations and the non-profit sector in Portugal. He is a photographer and a music collector.

Dominique Jakob, Prof. Dr., M.I.L. (Lund), joined the law faculty of the University of Zurich as a Professor for Private Law in 2007. In 2008 he established the "Center for Foundation Law" (www.zentrum-stiftungsrecht.uzh.ch) at the University of Zurich. Professor Jakob's main fields of research are international estate planning and wealth management (including trusts) as well as national, comparative, European and international foundation law (with a focus on Swiss, Liechtenstein and German relations). He is author of numerous publications in Switzerland and abroad, member of the advisory boards of various institutions and acts as counsel to governments, financial institutions, companies, foundations, associations and private clients.

C. Helen C. Overes is Associate Professor of Company Law at the Faculty of Law of the Vrije Universiteit in Amsterdam. Her research focuses on law on associations, foundations and charity organisations.

Isabel Peñalosa Esteban, Ph.D. in Law, is Director of Institutional Relations and Legal Affairs of the Spanish Association of Foundations.

Since 2003 she is active in the Spanish Association of Foundations, and earlier in Spanish Confederation of Foundations, since 2001. She is a regular speaker at courses and seminars on legal and fiscal regime of foundations and third sector organizations. She is also author of several articles and papers on individual and collaborative publications.

Chiara Prele, Dr., is an expert in foundation law and non-profit law in Italy. She works both as an independent counsel of some Italian foundations (among them foundations of banking origin) and appointed to the management of cultural foundations. She is author of books, numerous publications and articles in professional journals, mostly about foundations and other third sector entities. In 2007 she published "La fondazione. Evoluzione giuridica di un istituto alla ribalta" (Edizioni Fondazione Giovanni Agnelli, Torino, 261 pages), the most comprehensive and updated compendium on Italian foundation law. She lectures at courses and seminars, in Italy and overseas. She is also a style coach.

Kateřina Ronovská, Dr. Iur., Ph.D., graduated from the Faculty of Law, Masaryk University in Brno, the Czech Republic, where she is currently employed as an Associate Professor in the Department of Civil Law. She is involved in the systematic study of law on foundation and association in the European context, involved in international projects in the field of comparative law, the author of numerous publications and articles in professional journals. She is a member of the Expert Group of the Committee for the Application of New Civil Law Legislation in the Czech Republic.

Francesco A. Schurr is a Professor of Law and Head of the Chair for Company, Foundation and Trust Law (www.uni.li/gesellschaftsrecht) at the Institute for Financial Services, as well as Program Director of the Master of Laws (LL.M.) in Company, Foundation, and Trust Law (www.uni.li/llm-gesellschaftsrecht) at the University of Liechtenstein. Francesco is the Academic Director of the Liechtenstein Annual Convention on Foundation Law (www.uni.li/stiftungsrechtstag) as well as the Liechtenstein Annual Convention on Trust Law (www.uni.li/trustlaw) at the University of Liechtenstein. Previously Francesco was Professor for Private Law and Comparative Law at the Law School of the University of Innsbruck/Austria and Deputy Director of the Department of Italian Law. Francesco has published numerous articles and books on Consumer Protection Law, Law of Foundations, Trust Law, Contracts and European Private Law.

Goran Studen, Dr. LL.M. (Cambridge), is a Senior Research Assistant for Civil Law and Civil Procedure Law at the University of Zurich, a Lecturer at the University of Liechtenstein and an Attorney-at-law in Zurich. Dr. Studen, who has specialized in estates, corporate and individual wealth planning as well as philanthropy, advises Swiss based and international clients including institutions and authorities. He has authored numerous publications in Switzerland and abroad and is co-founder of the Swiss initiative "Association of Young Foundation Experts".

Tymen J. van der Ploeg (1947) studied Law at Leyden University, The Netherlands. He worked from November 1972 until his retirement in August 2012 at the Faculty of Law of the VU-University at Amsterdam, since 1992 as Full Professor in Civil Law, especially law on legal persons and partnerships. He taught company law, law on associations and foundations and on religious communities and published – and still publishes – about these topics, also from a comparative perspective, as well as about the relation of NGOs with government.

Ralitsa Velichkova, born in 1973, is Executive Director of Bulgarian Center for Not-for Profit Law (BCNL) – the leading resource center for NGOs in Bulgaria. She is specialized in providing legal assistance and building capacity of NPOs with a particular focus on legal and tax issues, including public benefit status, public reporting and transparency, cross-sectoral partnerships, government funding, self-regulation and codes of conduct, philanthropy and volunteering. Specific areas of research interest are the links between public policy issues and the NPO-related legislation and the practical effects of the legislation upon the development of viable and accountable non-profit sector. From June 2005 to June 2007 Ms. Velichkova worked as a legal advisor with the USAID Judicial Strengthening Initiative in Bulgaria. Ms. Velichkova is an attorney-at-law specialized in the field of commercial, administrative law and litigation.

Birgit Weitemeyer holds the Chair of Tax Law and is Director of the Institute for Foundation Law and the Law of Non-Profit Organizations at the Bucerius Law School in Hamburg. She completed her legal studies and doctorate in Kiel in 1996. Afterwards, she worked as a research assistant at the University of Kiel and occupied a Chair at the Helmut-Schmidt-University in Hamburg. In 2003 she completed her post-doctoral studies at the University of Kiel receiving the venia legendi. From 2004 to 2007 she occupied a Chair at the Technical University of Dresden. She is editor of many important magazines and member of many important legal associations.

Johannes Zollner has been Professor for Austrian and International Corporate and Commercial Law at the University of Graz since April 2013. Between 2011 and 2013 he was Professor for Private Law at the University of Klagenfurt. His research activities have concentrated on corporate law, capital market law the foundation law.

The manufacturer's authorised representative in the EU is Springer Nature Customer Service Centre GmbH, Europaplatz 3, 69115 Heidelberg, Germany. If you have any concerns regarding our products, please contact ProductSafety@springernature.com

Printed and bound by CPI Group (UK) Ltd, Croydon, CR0 4YY
22/09/2026
02220945-0012